The Harrowsmith
Salad Garden

A Complete Guide to Growing and Dressing
Fresh Vegetables and Greens

Turid Forsyth and Merilyn Simonds Mohr · Camden House

CAMDEN
•HOUSE•
✦✦✦✦✦✦
PUBLISHING

© Copyright 1992 by Turid Forsyth and
Merilyn Simonds Mohr

CANADIAN CATALOGUING IN PUBLICATION DATA

Forsyth, Turid
    The Harrowsmith salad garden

Includes index.
ISBN 0-921820-41-0

1. Vegetable gardening.   2. Salad greens.
3. Salad vegetables.   4. Salads.   I. Mohr, Merilyn.
II. Title.

SB321.F67 1992   635   C92-093447-1

Trade distribution by
Firefly Books
250 Sparks Avenue
Willowdale, Ontario
Canada M2H 2S4

Printed and bound in Canada by
D.W. Friesen & Sons Ltd.
Altona, Manitoba, for
Camden House Publishing
(a division of Telemedia Publishing Inc.)
7 Queen Victoria Road
Camden East, Ontario
K0K 1J0

Design by
Linda J. Menyes

Photographs by Turid Forsyth

Contents page photograph by David Bell

Front cover photograph by Ernie Sparks

Colour separations by
Hadwen Graphics
Ottawa, Ontario

Printed on acid-free paper

For Luise

Acknowledgements

Our thanks to David Bell for his scientific interest and hours of digging, seeding, weeding and eating; to Marg Phelan, Lois and Raleigh Robertson and the people of the Queen's University Biological Station for evaluating the overflow of our garden; to Pandora De Green for reading the manuscript with a chef's eye; to Janette Haase and Rob Arthur for sharing their garden with us; to Jennifer Bennett for being on call; to our families and friends, who selflessly sat through salad tastings; and to our editor Tracy C. Read for bringing the book to final fruition. Also thanks to the following people at Camden House: art director Linda J. Menyes; assistant editor Catherine DeLury; editorial coordinator Susan Dickinson; editorial assistant Jane Good; and associates Lois Casselman, Charlotte DuChene, Laura Elston, Christine Kulyk, Kathryn MacDonald, Mary Patton and Johanna Troyer.

Contents

Salad Days

Gardens and Gastronomy

Introduction

My approach to Turid's garden never varies, no matter how hard I try. Once a week for the past year and sporadically for three years before that, I put Kingston at my back and headed north on the old stagecoach route, Lake Ontario receding behind me as I sped toward the rising shoulders of the Canadian Shield. When the villages fell away, I turned right onto a ribbon of road that wound eastward between tree-lined lakes; past the open field of nesting boxes, a suburb for bluebirds set up by Queen's University biology students; around the bend and up the hill, where a tree stands sentinel, holding a granite boulder high in a crook of branches. I passed these landmarks and more, waiting for the telltale dip in the road that signalled Turid's lane. I always missed it and miss it still each time I pass. I catch her deep blue mailbox out of the corner of my eye, slam on the brakes, back up the hill and swing into the twin ruts that lead deep into the woods. Bushes scrape the sides of the car, then I see the sweep of the roof, and I am there.

Turid's is the epitome of the northern garden: its land wrested from the woods, its soil nurtured with muck wheelbarrowed from the swamp and watered daily from an artificial pond, its produce fattening deer and mice in the fall. Her garden defies an unforgiving climate and a recalcitrant geography. It is audacious, demanding— and breathtakingly beautiful.

Turid is an artist—a painter and a photographer —so it is not surprising that her garden transcends practical necessity. It is satisfying to eat the fruits of one's labour, of course, but Turid finds as much joy in the play of light through an orach leaf, the round, aquatic succulence of a golden purslane or the resonance of red nasturtiums against jade globe basil. The artistic empathy she brings to her garden design seems to please even the plants, for they thrive under her care.

For 10 years, I weathered rabbits and year-round frosts in northern Ontario, growing all the food for the family table. Although I learned to outwit the cutworm and to ripen tomatoes despite June blizzards, it never occurred to me to turn my vegetable

8

Turid's May garden displays a departure from traditional row planting.

patch into a garden that would rival a flowerbed in beauty. But ignoring the decorative and concentrating only on the delectable is not tolerated at the table, where culinary tradition demands that food look as good as it tastes. Turid brings that philosophy to the garden and introduced me to the aesthetic pleasures of growing what we eat.

Turid conceived this book as a continuum between garden and table. Gardening books abound, as do cookbooks, but nowhere is there a book that takes a gardener from seed to salad bowl, explaining not only how to grow a lettuce but when to pick it for maximum nutrition and flavour, how to care for it in the kitchen and how to serve it.

She brings to the project her magnificent garden, her years of botanical interest and her expertise in growing vegetable varieties appropriate for salads and for northern climates. Although my own garden is now reduced to a narrow strip on a city lot, I contribute my skills in the kitchen and at the writing desk. While Turid experimented with new cultivars, I juggled oils and vinegars to produce delicious ways of serving them. We spent our Sunday afternoons tasting—nibbling variety after variety of carrots to find the one with the best flavour and texture for eating raw; smacking our lips over a row of cucumber salads, one with a little more dill and a little less salt, one with yogurt instead of sour cream. We hosted tasting parties where our friends were enjoined to sample half a dozen variations on a beet salad or four

kinds of homemade mustard. Our tongues often tired, but our enthusiasm never waned. For us, this is gardening and gastronomy at its best: eating a salad that is organically grown, handpicked at its peak and dressed with one's own heady combination of herbs and vinegars.

Eating fresh, uncooked food is now fashionable, but it is not new. Ancient Babylonians, Persians, Egyptians, Chinese, Greeks and Romans all ate salads. The oldest surviving cookbook, written in the first century A.D. by the Roman epicure Apicius, contains recipes for salads. The word itself comes from *sal*, Latin for salt, and derives from the Roman habit of dipping chicory leaves in salt before eating them, much the way we eat radishes today. The addition of vinegar was originally intended to aid digestion. Only recently have scientists discovered that the acid also halts the loss of vitamin C from cut vegetables.

After the fall of Rome, raw vegetables fell out of favour. Everything was cooked. And almost everything was ascribed some medicinal value, physical or psychological. Lettuce remained as popular among monks as it had been among debauched Romans, but instead of piquing lust, the cooked leaves were pressed to the forehead to cure headache.

It wasn't until this century that fresh food again returned to the table, partly because of improved transportation and storage and partly because we recognize the health value of fibre, trace minerals

and vitamins. After 2,000 years, we have come full circle, back to the Roman and Greek predilection for rawness, though one hopes the cycle does not return us to their practice of eating still-quivering mice dipped in honey and larks' tongues freshly plucked from gaping beaks.

A recent survey established the top five taste trends in the United States: salads, seafood, chicken, fresh vegetables, fruit. The same trends appear in Canada. Between 1970 and 1988, consumption of fresh vegetables increased from 83 to 125 pounds per person per year, while the consumption of canned vegetables dropped by a third. Beans and peas have declined in popularity, but mushrooms have tripled, and broccoli has jumped from half a pound to 5 ½ pounds per person per year.

People are obviously eating more fresh food—and presumably more salads. Vegetables contain more vitamins when raw than when cooked, and if dressed lightly, they are lower in fat than are many prepared foods. But salads are not always healthy. In the *Dialogues* of Gregory the Great (549 A.D.), there is a story of a greedy nun who came across a large and succulent lettuce in a monastery garden. Not bothering to say grace or bless the plant, she took a big bite, swallowing a small devil who was lolling on one of the leaves. The nun fell into a fit, and an exorcist was summoned. When the devil reappeared in her mouth, he complained bitterly to the exorcist: "Why blame me? What have I done? I was sitting on this leaf, and she came along and swallowed me up."

This lesson on greed, haste, ingratitude and hygiene should serve as a modern parable to those who buy their salad vegetables in the supermarket. For a time, lettuce in stores and at salad bars was sprayed with sulphites to keep the greens from turning brown. Now, sucrose and fatty acids have been approved by the American government for sprinkling on fruits and vegetables. The coating contains sugar and beef fat and slows ripening and wilting. Irradiation is on the way as a means of preserving freshness. Hydroponic lettuces are sometimes sprayed with gases that activate chlorophyll production, creating that insistent green. Any vegetable that has a high water content will also soak up chemical pesticides and fertilizers. As Ogden Nash quipped, "It's a wise child that knows its fodder." And unless a vegetable is certified organically grown, the best way to know what is in the salads we eat is to grow them ourselves.

The other disadvantage of buying salad fixings is the narrow range of choices offered by most supermarkets. Until recently, 'Iceberg' was the sta-

Fava beans in front, mustard at the back and edible flowers along the edge are ready for July harvest.

ple lettuce. Now romaine and endive are usually available, and red leaf lettuces are creeping onto the shelves, but there are dozens and dozens of delicious greens that you can only obtain by growing them: mâche, arugula, mustard greens, purslane, baby head lettuces, 'Sugar Loaf' chicories. Sometimes the produce is for sale but at an exorbitant price. Two dollars buys one radicchio or two packages of seed, from which I can grow enough for a banquet. And mine will be fresh, unlike the poor radicchio limp from its transcontinental travels. The trip from garden to table must be short to be healthful, especially for delicate foods like tomatoes and leafy greens that must be eaten within two days for full nutritive value. In terms of economy, quality and availability of exotic species, nothing can compare with homegrown salads.

We chose the vegetables for this book by their quality when served fresh. Some cultivars are bred for uniformity or long storage. What we looked for was flavour, texture and visual appeal when eaten raw or only lightly steamed. With each

vegetable, we give some background, both botanical and mythological, then describe how to grow it, how to harvest it and how to prepare it for the salad bowl. Along the way, we offer dozens of recipes and preparation tips.

The book begins with lettuce, the salad-bowl staple. At the end of the first chapter, we introduce mesclun, a European approach to salad greens that is as easy as it is visually appealing. The second chapter describes the greens other than lettuce, some familiar, like spinach, but many unfamiliar to Canadian gardens. Chapter Three describes how to grow and use essential salad herbs. This is followed by "solo salads," three chapters devoted to garden vegetables that make salads on their own—asparagus, beans, potatoes. Chapter Four describes salad vegetables that prefer cool conditions; Chapter Five is reserved for those which thrive in midsummer; and Chapter Six brings together salad vegetables that mature and sweeten without light, like finochio and chicory. Finally, Chapter Seven explains how to make a perfect vinaigrette and dress

a salad with edible flowers and garnishes. (Each chapter includes references to the seed catalogues from which the cultivar mentioned can be ordered. They are found in parentheses after the variety names; on page 153, you will find a key to these seed catalogues. Plants' Latin names are also given so that you will know exactly what you are getting.)

We encourage you to start the book at the back, however. In "Practical Matters," you will find our techniques for preparing the soil and growing vegetables from seed to harvest, all garnered from firsthand experience. In each plant description, we discuss only those ways in which that plant's care varies from standard practice.

One of the most appealing aspects of salad gardening is the variety it offers. The number of vegetable cultivars is almost unlimited, with new breeds appearing every year. And in the kitchen, what constitutes "salad" is limited only by your imagination. Between these covers, we offer the classics and the iconoclasts. The rest is up to you.

11

Noble Beginnings

Boston to Romaine

Chapter One

The ribald 16th-century French storyteller Rabelais told a tall tale of six pilgrims who one day sought shelter in a lettuce patch. That evening, the giant Gargantua developed a hankering for lettuce salad. He tramped into the garden where the lettuce heads grew as tall as plum trees and carried off handfuls of greens to wash in the local fountain. The pilgrims, inadvertently plucked with the leaves, swam for their lives in the swirling water. Then Gargantua scooped up the lettuce—and the pilgrims—and shaking them vigorously, dumped the lot into an oak cask huge enough to hold 300 hogsheads. He doused the leaves (and the pilgrims) with salt, vinegar and oil and began to eat, downing the salad, pilgrims and all, with a huge draft of red Burgundy.

Not much has changed in the 450 years since Rabelais wrote *Gargantua and Pantagruel*: the lettuce heads may be a little smaller and pilgrims in somewhat short supply, but a salad composed simply of lettuce and dressed with a vinaigrette still satisfies mightily, as it has for almost 3,000 years.

Lettuce is first mentioned in a list of plants grow-ing in the famous gardens at Babylon in 800 B.C. The ancestor of all the varieties of lettuce now grown is *Lactuca serriola*, a biennial of the Compositae family that has grown wild in Asia, Eurasia and the Mediterranean since ancient times. The leaves of the original lettuce formed neither a rosette nor a head but sprouted from a tall, thick stalk: it looked much like a huge, bolted Bibb. The Greeks called it asparagus—a term they used indiscriminately for any green with a phallic growth habit.

The Romans developed the plant into the compact, headed shapes we know today. The Romans loved lettuce. Pliny the Elder listed nine cultivars, including a white, a purple and a red variety and one which had stalks so tall, broad and strong that they were woven into trellises and garden gates. The emperor Diocletian even abdicated the throne to cultivate the leafy green. When his successor tried to convince him to return to politics, he replied, "If you saw what beautiful lettuces I am raising, you would not urge me to take up that burden again."

"Lettuce" derives from the French *laitue,* which,

An alternate planting of 'Slow Bolt' and 'Red Sails' looseleaf lettuce creates a colourful garden bed.

like the Latin *lactuca,* means "milky." Much of the lore surrounding this innocent-looking vegetable is sexual, related, as is its name, to the creamy juice in the stalk. On one hand, lettuce has always been considered an aphrodisiac. In Egypt, the temple to Min, god of procreation, was surrounded by gardens of lettuce fed to Min's sacred white bull to increase its sexual potency. In Roman mythology, Jupiter's cupbearer, Hebe, was purportedly the child of Juno's coupling with a wild lettuce.

At the same time, lettuce carried a reputation as a sexual suppressant. Pythagoras suggested his disciples eat lettuce to curb their erotic desires. In the Middle Ages, women were advised not to plant too much lettuce lest it hamper their ability to conceive, and young men shunned it at the table, calling it "the enemy of pleasure and the poison of love." A poultice of lettuce leaves "bound to the cods" was prescribed to "restraineth immoderate lust."

Perhaps the inhibiting effects of lettuce were partly due to its ability to induce sleep. Lettuce wafers, made by drying the juice from the leaves, were once prescribed as a narcotic for insomniacs, the wounded and those about to undergo surgery. Even as late as the last century, home-remedy books prescribed a decoction of one lettuce head simmered in a pint of water for 20 minutes, the liquid to be drunk at bedtime for a peaceful, uninterrupted sleep. Folk medicine was not far wrong: scientists have discovered triterpenoid alcohols—sleep-inducers —in the latex sap of lettuce, and now a drug, *Lactucarium germanillium,* or lettuce opium, is produced from the sap of *Lactuca sativa* and prescribed for persistent involuntary erections.

Its sexual side effects notwithstanding, lettuce is the most popular salad vegetable in North America today. Each person on the continent consumes an average of 25 pounds of the greens every year. Commercial growers harvest about three billion heads annually to supply our craving. Lettuce is consistently the fastest-moving item in the grocery store, whether the heads sell for $2 in January or 49¢ in July. No wonder those in the food trade have nicknamed lettuce "green gold."

Most of the lettuce sold in North American stores is of the 'Iceberg' type, one of the least inspiring forms of *Lactuca* ever devised. "A pallid package of rigidity," wrote Ogden Nash, "a globe of frozen insipidity." It is pervasive not because it is especially delicious or healthful but because it is tough, able to survive the journey from market garden to grocery store relatively unscathed. Researchers are now working on ways to flatten its bottom so that it will sit more securely on the shelf.

'Iceberg's' stranglehold on the North American salad bowl is loosening as consumers discover that there is more to lettuce than watery crunch. Romaines, curly leaf lettuces and Bostons are making inroads, but novice gardeners will be surprised at the multitude of cultivars they can grow. A hundred years ago, an American seed house offered 114 distinct kinds of lettuce; today's gardeners have more than 800 varieties to choose from: red, green, speckled, curly, smooth, succulent, silky, spring, summer or fall, as big as a basketball or as small as a fist.

Growing your own lettuce gives you access to varieties that would make Diocletian swoon, but it also gives you healthier greens. 'Iceberg' is at the bottom of the nutrition scale: it doesn't have enough vitamin content to be worth recording. None of the lettuces are as nutritious as salad greens such as spinach and watercress—they are, after all, 90 to 95 percent water. But the deep green lettuces contain vitamin C and vitamin A in the form of carotene, both of which have antioxidant properties that are believed to inhibit cancer. In a review on the prevention of stomach cancer, the National Academy of Sciences Committee on Diet, Nutrition and Cancer concluded that ''protective factors may include consumption of milk, raw green or yellow vegetables, especially lettuce, and other foods containing vitamin C.'' You get these benefits with almost no calories, little salt and lots of fibre to scrub the digestive system; a pound of romaine has the same fibre as six slices of whole wheat bread, with only one-sixth the calories.

Even if you are addicted to 'Iceberg,' there are good reasons to grow it rather than buy it. It is cheaper, of course. A package of seed costing $1.75 contains about 900 seeds, which works out to about one-tenth of a cent per head. But more important, commercially grown lettuce is likely contaminated with chemicals, some of them having toxic effects. Because lettuce absorbs so much water, it may also absorb the pesticides and microscopic bacteria dissolved in that water. Recently, hepatitis A outbreaks in Kentucky and Georgia were traced to lettuce most likely infected by pickers who live in squalid migrant camps thousands of miles away in Mexico, Texas and California. If for no other reason than this, a strong case can be made for growing your own lettuce under conditions you trust.

The hundreds of varieties of lettuce fall into five main categories. *Lactuca sativa* (var. *angustana,* or asparagus lettuce) has a fat central stalk that marks it as the closest descendant of ancestral lettuce. A variety known as celtuce, or stem lettuce (*L. sativa* var. *asparagina*), is popular in China, where it is used more like celery than lettuce. Rarely grown in North American gardens, it is nevertheless an excellent cutting lettuce.

Most lettuce grown on this continent, however, comes from one of the following three groups. Lettuces that form distinct heads are *Lactuca sativa* var. *capitata,* a category that subdivides into crispheads, such as 'Iceberg,' which produce a compact, hard, tight ball of leaves that stays together when cut, and butterheads (sometimes called looseheads) such as Bibb and Boston, whose delicate leaves form

a softer, more open head, reminiscent of a blowsy carnation. The most recent addition to the lettuce family is *L. sativa* var. *longifolia*, more commonly known as romaine, or cos, which produces an elongated, tulip-shaped head of crisp leaves that tuck firmly around one another. Finally, there are the looseleaf, or nonheading, lettuces (*L. sativa* var. *crispa),* which form open rosettes of distinct leaves.

Lettuce is known for its genetic diversity: in any given sowing, some seeds will not conform to type—crispheads that don't head up, for instance. Plant scientists take advantage of this and are now experimenting with lettuces that straddle varietal boundaries: for example, 'Crisp as Ice,' an intermediate between a butterhead and a crisphead, and 'Wallop,' an intermediate between a crisphead and a romaine. The most common, however, are intermediates between romaine and butterhead. 'Winter Density' grows upright enough to be called a romaine but is much crisper than a butterhead. The intermediates are among the most interesting varieties to try.

These categories differentiate on the basis of growth habit: tight heads, loose heads, tall heads, no heads. Within each category, there are lettuces of every colour and texture imaginable, but there are also varieties bred specifically for different growing conditions.

Most lettuce grows best in spring and fall, when the weather is cool and the soil damp. Cool, sunny weather produces not only the most delicate flavour but also the most colourful leaves, particularly in the red and speckled varieties. The prolonged heat of summer makes most lettuce bolt, but scientists are now developing heat-resistant varieties that can stand the Dog Days of summer.

Even at the best of times, however, the lettuce harvest is relatively short, with only a week between peak condition and running to seed. As a result, many gardeners have a glut of lettuce for a few weeks in late spring and early summer, then none for the rest of the season. By carefully selecting her seed, sowing weekly and adjusting her growing technique to the season, Turid harvests lettuce from early May to late October, enjoying fresh greens even in high summer, when most lettuce gardens are studded with flowering stalks.

The chart on pages 28-29 groups Turid's favourite lettuce varieties as early, midseason and late. They are at their prime in 45 to 90 growing days, depending on the variety—looseleafs need only a month and a half, but crispheads take up to three months to form a tight head. From the start, get into the habit of making a small sowing once a

week. Continued from early March to late August, this weekly ritual will provide you with fresh lettuce salads for six months of the year.

Early lettuces are sown between early March and late May for harvest in June and July. They like cool growing conditions but must be protected from frost during the first part of their lives. They are usually sown indoors. Midseason lettuce is sown between June 1 and July 1 for harvest in July and August. The weather outdoors is often cool enough that they can be sown directly in the garden, although they have to be protected from the high-summer heat. Late lettuce is sown between early July and late August for harvest in August and September, until frost. These lettuces cannot stand summer heat and must be germinated in a cool, shady place. With frost protection, the late-lettuce season can extend until the snow falls. A few varieties do well in all growing seasons.

Only in winter is Turid's garden lettuce-poor. In most parts of Canada, it is simply too difficult to carry over the fragile greens from October to May. It can be done, of course: sowing seeds in August, mulching the young plants heavily, removing the protection the following spring when the danger of frost is past. But this is a lot of work and unreliable, given fluctuating temperatures and the ravenous winter appetites of deer and mice. Turid finds that if she starts seeds very early indoors and transplants them to a cold frame, she has fresh lettuce at exactly the same time as if she had overwintered lettuce plants from the autumn before. And the spring-sown crop is far more likely to produce a healthy harvest of greens.

To get a head start on the lettuce season, plant seed indoors very early, around the middle of February, then transplant to a cold frame to mature by mid-April or early May. Forcing lettuce is a type bred especially for this purpose. The seed is very expensive—in one catalogue, forcing varieties cost $2.25 for one-eighth of a gram, compared with $1.75 per gram for most other lettuce seed—but it is still much cheaper than buying heads at the supermarket. The National Gardening Association recommends the widely available 'Grand Rapids' as a forcing lettuce, and The Cook's Garden, a seed house specializing in lettuce, offers several others, including 'Akcel,' a French forcing variety, and 'Delta,' a British butterhead developed for ultraearly harvest.

Whether you sow a forcing variety in mid-February or wait until March to begin traditional early lettuces, the method of starting the first crop of seedlings is the same. In fact, Turid starts most of her lettuce indoors: this gives her more control over the well-being of the young seedlings during the first few weeks of life. Once they are strong and growing, they have a better chance of surviving and thriving in the garden. Although bolting is usually associated with hot weather, a German scientist recently discovered that lettuce tends to bolt early if exposed to temperatures below 50 degrees F during the three-week period after sowing. Throughout the spring, therefore, at least until overnight temperatures stay above 50 degrees, early lettuce is best started indoors and moved outside no sooner than three weeks after sowing.

Turid generally starts most of her early lettuce around April 1, except for the crispheads, which grow so slowly that she starts them three weeks earlier. Use the method described on page 143. Although you can sow lettuce in flats, Turid prefers large propagating trays, 11 by 21 inches, employing the row insert usually recommended for leeks and onions. The insert looks like a hot-air register and is available with 10 troughs running the length or 20 troughs running the width, each an inch wide, an inch deep and perforated with drainage holes.

Fill the insert (or flats) with sterile planting mix. If using garden soil sterilized with boiling water, wait several hours before planting, since lettuce germinates best at cool temperatures. Sow a different variety of lettuce in each strip of soil, or sow one cultivar successively during the next six to eight weeks. Label each strip with the cultivar and the sowing date.

Pour the fine seed onto white paper, and using tweezers, place the seed at the rate of three per inch in a depression pressed into the soil. Cover lightly with peat—lettuce seeds need light to germinate—mist well, and keep at 68 to 70 degrees F. The seeds sprout in 4 to 10 days. Move the seedlings to a cool, bright location, or set them under lights.

When the seedlings have their second set of leaves, thin to an inch or so apart and fertilize. About a month after sowing, when the seedlings are approximately 1½ inches tall, start hardening them off, preferably in a cold frame. "I always wait for a day when it's warm enough that I feel comfortable sitting outside in a lawn chair," says Turid.

While the lettuce seedlings harden off, prepare the garden beds. Because lettuces are not deep feeders, the bed need not be deeply dug, although the topsoil should be rich, with plenty of nitrogen to produce crisp, sweet leaves. It is a good idea to work lots of organic matter—leaf mould, compost or a cover crop like buckwheat—into the top 6 to 8 inches of soil. The organic matter acts like a sponge, holding water near the roots. In crop rotations, plant lettuce where deep-feeding brassicas grew the year before; the lettuces take advantage of nutrients left near the surface. Later in the spring, plant lettuce in beds used for short-lived crops like spinach or corn salad. It is so decorative that it works beautifully as an edging for flowerbeds and borders. Because lettuce thrives in either full sun or dappled shade, plant it on the east side of tall vegetables such as pole beans and corn, but leave enough space for air circulation to prevent disease.

On an overcast day when the last frost date is past and the seedlings are sufficiently hardened off, transplant the early lettuce to the garden. Check the seed envelope for specific instructions, but in general, plant looseleaf seedlings 4 inches apart, romaine 6 to 8 inches apart and the butterheads and crispheads a foot apart. Dig the holes for all the transplants at once so that when the seedlings are lifted from the tray, their roots will not be exposed to air and sun any longer than necessary.

Turid offsets every other row, planting the whole bed in a diamond pattern. If she is planting a bed of mixed lettuce, she starts at the back with romaine, the tallest, then heading lettuce and finally looseleaf lettuce at the front. Garden for your eye as well as your mouth: use your imagination to create bands of red and green varieties, zigzag patterns of frilly, smooth, speckled and ruby-edged, May-green and jade-green leaves.

Dig the holes about 2 inches deep, and water until they are very moist. With a sharp tool, loosen the edges of one strip of soil in the propagating tray. Lift out about half the strip, then carefully tear off the individual seedlings and drop one into each watered hole. Make sure they don't sit much deeper in the hole than they did in the tray. Pat the soil around the stem, and give it a watering of transplant fertilizer. Shelter the seedlings, removing the boughs or lattices after a week. Mulch the soil with well-rotted compost, hay or straw to keep it cool and moist. About three weeks after transplanting, fertilize the lettuce with fish emulsion, applied as a spray, or manure tea fed directly to the soil after prying back the mulch. Lettuce has to grow fast to be sweet.

The key to good lettuce throughout its growing life—full, large heads of succulent, deep green leaves—is water. Common lettuce complaints, such as bitterness, bolting and disease, are linked to slow growth, which is usually caused by insufficient moisture. Because lettuce is a shallow-rooted plant with big leaves, it has little drought resistance. Water daily, preferably in the morning to reduce evaporation losses; watering late in the day may leave foliage damp overnight, encouraging disease and soft, mushy hearts. At least once a week, soak the lettuce bed deeply. The soil should never be soggy or dry.

Toward the middle of May, when the seedlings started indoors are filling out and the first salads are within sight, we begin seeding early lettuce directly in the garden, continuing the habit of sowing a row every week. (Be sure the temperature in your garden is consistently above 50 degrees F.) There are two methods of direct seeding. In the first, draw half-inch-deep furrows 8 to 12 inches apart across the raised bed. Soak the trenches with water, and plant the seeds three per inch. Cover with a quarter-inch of soil, somewhat deeper than you would indoors, so that the seeds don't dry out. Mist daily to keep the ground moist. Three weeks later, thin to the correct distance for the variety, eating the tiny seedlings or transplanting them to other parts of the garden.

The other method of direct seeding is to broadcast the seed over the garden bed. It is essential in this case for the soil to be weed-free: once the lettuce seeds sprout, it is often difficult to distinguish noxious invaders from edible plants. Before broadcasting, spread a sheet of plastic over the prepared bed and let the sun burn off any weeds that have sprouted. Remove the plastic after a week, and give the raked, weed-free bed a good watering just before sowing. Toss the lettuce seed in a large container with two or three spadefuls of fine soil. Scoop it out by the handful, and sprinkle loosely over the bed. Scatter a thin layer of fine soil over the top, then a layer of peat to hold the moisture in. With the back of a rake, press down lightly over the whole bed, and give it a thorough misting. The peat must be kept moist until the seeds sprout.

Instead of broadcasting one variety over a whole bed, try strip planting. Divide the bed into bands 6 to 8 inches wide; diagonal bands are attractive and make good use of space. Broadcast different lettuce varieties successively in each band, creating strips of red and green, tall and short, round leaves and spiky. The seeds sprout in 3 to 10 days, depending on the weather. Keep the bed moist during the first two weeks, then when the seedlings are about 1½ inches tall, thin them according to the seed-packet information, giving them adequate growing room in all directions. Transplant or eat the thinnings. Broadcasting and strip planting are especially effective with looseleaf varieties.

Sowings of early lettuce continue until about

'Winter Density': a butterhead-romaine cross for all seasons.

June 1, when heat-resistant summer varieties take over. You can sow these directly in the garden, or for more control, use propagating trays as described above, but instead of starting the seeds indoors, place the trays outdoors close to the house under a lean-to trellis. With the seedlings isolated for the first three weeks in this outdoor "nursery," you can give the tender plants precisely the right level of sun and moisture, watch for pests and diseases and generally pay them more attention than if they were planted in the main salad garden. If you choose instead to seed directly, plant the lettuce to the east of tall, slow-maturing vegetables such as Brussels sprouts or asparagus so that the tender greens have afternoon shade as the summer heats up.

Around July 1, Turid puts away the midseason lettuce seed and gets out the late lettuce varieties. Late lettuce is planted throughout July until late August. Choose varieties for later plantings carefully so that the lettuce matures before the first frost. Sow seed for the late lettuce in propagating trays, germinating them outdoors in the same sheltered conditions. Transplanting and care are the same, except that as the days grow cooler and the autumn rains come, watering is not as necessary. Too much dampness in fall (and spring) may lead to downy mildew and grey mould. As long as the soil is unfrozen, the lettuce will continue to grow. One eastern Ontario gardening friend uses a floating row cover to extend the harvest in the fall, doubling the

thickness when temperatures fall below freezing. In 1991, he was still harvesting lettuce the first week of December.

As the season draws to a close, instead of transplanting the seedlings into the salad garden, plant them in a container close to the kitchen door. On the east side of her house, Turid built a wooden box a foot wide, a foot deep and about eight feet long and filled it with good soil that she replenishes after each lettuce harvest is over. When a frost threatens, she throws a tarp over it; in high summer, she shades it with a lattice. Using a method that is convenient, controlled and contained, she gathers three harvests—early, midseason and late—just a few steps from the dining-room table.

There are three ways of harvesting lettuce. Throughout the season, you can harvest by picking the larger outer leaves while the centre of the lettuce keeps growing. When the lettuces are mature, the heads full and the rosettes plump, you can cut off the entire head close to the ground.

But lettuce is also harvested by using scissors to shear the leaves close to the ground when they are only a few inches high, allowing them to resprout for a second and third harvest—a technique called cut-and-come-again. Not only does this bring the tenderest leaves to the table, but seedling leaves have up to twice the vitamin content of mature lettuce.

Cutting lettuce is popular in Europe, where it is labelled *Schnittsalat* in Germany, *à couper* in

France and *de taglio* in Italy. On this continent, lettuce is rarely labelled cut-and-come-again, but you can experiment by leaving a clump of seedlings to snip off when they are a few inches tall, allowing the rest to mature in the traditional way. Many varieties lack the vigour to resprout well, but looseleaf lettuces are generally well suited to this harvesting technique. A couple of crispheads and romaines have also been developed for vigorous regrowth, and The Cook's Garden even offers an intermediate type called 'Matchless.' The Cook's Garden seed catalogue is one of the few that have separate listings for cutting lettuce, but others are sure to follow suit, as this is a burgeoning area of salad-garden interest.

During the growing season, cutting lettuce demands slightly different care. Sow the seed by broadcasting thickly at the rate of a teaspoonful for every three square feet of soil. Prepare the bed carefully to remove all weeds: cutting lettuces are neither thinned nor cultivated, so weeds that grow between the seedlings will be harvested with the lettuce leaves. If the weed is lamb's quarters, it won't do you any harm, but nightshade may make you sick. The best defence is learning to identify common local weeds.

Broadcast or strip plant the cutting lettuce as described above, but do not thin. The cut-and-come-again bed requires no hoeing or weeding, but since the plants are fast-growing and shallow-rooted, you have to keep a very close watch on moisture levels. Water the bed especially well during germination and the first two weeks after the seedlings sprout. Thereafter, water once or twice a day. After about four weeks, harvest the cutting lettuce by shearing a strip of plants back to 2 inches. Progressively harvest the entire bed this way.

By the time the last strip is sheared, the first plants have already sprouted new growth. Add some fish-emulsion fertilizer, then wait a week or two before beginning the next harvest. Some gardeners continue the cycle, cutting back the lettuce three or four times, but in our experience, these harvests are poor and often bitter. Instead, dig up the bed after the second harvest, revive the soil with a generous dressing of well-rotted manure, and replant it with another lettuce or a salad vegetable appropriate to the evolving season.

Whether you harvest tiny 2-inch leaves or 10-inch butterheads, lettuce does not last long once it is picked. Severed from its roots, the plant begins to lose more water than it is taking in, the hydrostatic pressure in the cells falls, and the leaves become limp. 'Iceberg' lettuce has tough cell walls that do not easily collapse, so leaves stay crisp for up to three weeks. Romaine also holds its water well, but butterheads and looseleafs wilt quickly.

Lettuce is at its plumpest and sweetest in the morning. Researchers at the U.S. Department of Agriculture discovered that lettuce picked at 7 a.m. contained 70 to 260 percent more glucose and 20 to 120 percent more fructose than that picked at 2 p.m. So do your harvesting early in the day.

As soon as lettuce is picked, wash the leaves well. Remove the core of head lettuces—both crispheads and butterheads—before washing them. There is a trick to this that works cleanly every time. Hold the head gently but firmly in both hands, and bring it down smartly on the counter, hitting exactly on the centre of the core. Turn the head over, grasp the core between your fingers, twist lightly, and pull it out. Then hold the head upside down under a gentle stream of running water, separating the leaves. Crispheads are so tightly folded that they do not get dirty inside. Simply turn them right side up, and let them drain in a colander. Butterheads, especially Bibb varieties, are dirt traps, however, as is any looseleaf lettuce with deeply frilled leaves. These cannot be washed properly under the tap. Instead, fill a sink with barely lukewarm water, and slosh the heads up and down; the leaves wilt slightly, releasing the dirt in the folds. Recrisp the leaves by plunging them into cold water.

Dry lettuce leaves thoroughly before making a salad. The traditional method is to swing the leaves in a wire basket. Or use a spinner, one of the few plastic kitchen gadgets worth having. (You can also wrap the leaves lightly in a clean towel and pat them dry.) Tear the washed leaves into pieces, spin them, and place the whole spinner in the refrigerator until the rest of the salad ingredients and the dressing are ready. If you are in a big hurry and want supercrisp lettuce, you can put the leaves in the freezer for a few minutes. (This, incidentally, is for cooks who like to live on the edge: if the water in the cells freezes, the membranes puncture, producing lettuce as crisp as steamed spinach.)

To store lettuce for more than an hour or two, wrap the spun leaves in a damp paper towel and place in a plastic bag or tightly covered container in the refrigerator. It lasts this way for a few days. All is not lost if lettuce loses its crispness, however: it can still be used in a "wilted" salad or in soup.

Greek philosopher Aristoxenus watered his lettuces with vinaigrette the evening before he harvested them. This seems an unlikely way to dress a salad, but it may be preferable to the standard procedure in North American kitchens, which con-

sists of dumping a waterfall of dressing over innocent leaves. The practice so appalled Ogden Nash that he wrote in a limerick, "Is this dressing upon my lettuce / Or is it a melting popsicle?"

Never pour any kind of dressing over lettuce leaves. Instead, mix the oil and vinegar and herbs in the bottom of the salad bowl, macerate together with a wooden spoon, and allow the dressing to sit until the salad course is needed. Just before serving, whisk the dressing to an emulsion, add the washed and dried lettuce leaves (allow about one-third to one-half cup (75 mL-125 mL) of dressing and 8 cups (2 L) of loosely packed leaves for a salad for four) and toss gently until each is coated *thinly*. There should be just enough dressing to moisten the leaves but not drown them. Serve immediately. Dressed lettuce soon grows limp: the osmotic pressure of the vinegar or lemon juice and oil destroys the cell walls' ability to retain water.

The tossing of the salad can become a mealtime ritual, a fitting end to the cycle that began with picking up the tweezers to place the seed in the narrow strips of soil. I like to do it right at the table, where, if the salad is served at the end of the meal as a palate cleanser before the wine and cheese, it becomes a moment of quiet drama. In France, the youngest daughter of marriageable age used to toss the salad with her hands, in deference to the fertility legends attached to lettuce.

Lettuce is so common a component of salad that the two words have become almost interchangeable in the North American lexicon. Indeed, it is hard to think of a salad without at least a garnish of lettuce leaves. It seems that is nothing new. Two centuries after Rabelais wrote *Gargantua*, John Evelyn wrote a book on salads called *Acetaria: A Discourse of Sallets* in which he extolled the reign of lettuce over the salad bowl. " 'Tis not for nothing that our Garden-Lovers and Brothers of the Sallet have been so exceedingly Industrious to cultivate this Noble Plant and multiply its Species, for . . . lettuce ever was and still continues the principal foundation of the universal tribe of Sallets." To which we can only add, *bon appétit*.

High-Summer Salad Dressing

Summer to us means tomatoes. Instead of chopping them in a typical once-through-the-garden salad of lettuce, tomato and onion, dry them and make this dressing, delicious tossed with a bowlful of crisp lettuce leaves. You can buy *pumate*, the sun-dried tomatoes of Italy, or make them yourself (see page 105).

2	cloves garlic	2
	Pinch of coarse salt	
½ cup	drained, chopped sun-dried tomatoes	125 mL
⅓ cup	pitted Mediterranean black olives	75 mL
⅓ cup	roasted red pepper (see page 100) or pimento, drained	75 mL
⅓ cup	red-wine vinegar	75 mL
2 Tbsp.	balsamic vinegar	30 mL
¾ cup	olive oil	175 mL

Mash garlic and salt to a purée. Add tomatoes, olives and red pepper, and mash to a grainy purée. (A food processor is an asset but not essential.) Blend in the vinegars, then add the oil in a steady stream, beating to form a soupy dressing. Chill until ready to use, but bring to room temperature half an hour before serving.

Makes enough for three large salads.

Heading Lettuce
Lactuca sativa var. *capitata*

The choice for North American gardeners until recently was between the crunchy crispheads and the fragile butterheads. Increasingly, European Batavian lettuces combine the best of both types.

CRISPHEAD

The crisphead's tightly wadded ball of pale green leaves epitomized by the ubiquitous supermarket 'Iceberg' was bred for uniformity and durability: it survives mechanical handling without bruising, it can be transported long distances without wilting, and it has a shelf life of up to three weeks, characteristics that endear this lettuce to food merchants. Crispheads fell out of fashion with salad gourmets, abandoned for the more flavourful and succulent butterhead and looseleaf varieties, but the Batavian crispheads from Europe are doing much to restore the reputation of this lettuce type.

Crisphead lettuce has its place. It is the crunchiest green and the longest-lasting, qualities appreciated in the kitchen. A leaf sits on a sandwich from breakfast till lunch without going limp; a slice supports heavy chicken salad without sagging; slender shreds remain crisp even on hot tacos. Only crispheads combine crackling crunch with airy lightness— the garden equivalent of meringues.

Crispheads were the first heading lettuces offered by seed houses; the butterheads came later. By the late 19th century, when W. Atlee Burpee developed 'Iceberg,' a preference for heading lettuce over looseleaf varieties was well established. The 1888 Burpee catalogue lists 23 *capitata* varieties, 3 romaine and only 1 looseleaf lettuce. By comparison, The Cook's Garden 1991 catalogue lists 14 looseleaf, 6 romaine, 7 crispheads and 20 butterheads.

The familiar 'Iceberg' has a solid, pale, fully blanched heart and few outer leaves. Many other cultivars are now available, among them the popular 'Great Lakes' developed for agribusiness. 'Iceberg' types with beautiful wine-red leaves include 'Rosy' (CG). 'Minilake' from Stokes (ST) reportedly matures a week before most others. A crisphead to watch for is a new miniature 'Iceberg' with which genetic engineers at the U.S. Department of Agriculture station in Salinas, California, are experimenting. The tiny heads, expected in supermarkets by 1993, have the same taste and texture as traditional 'Icebergs,' but because the cells are denser, the nutritional content may prove to be higher.

For home salad gardeners, however, we recommend the European Batavian lettuces. More heat-resistant than 'Iceberg' types, the Batavian lettuces grow in much more open, looser heads, green to the heart, yet they retain the shine and crunch typical of crispheads. They look like a cross between a Bibb and an 'Iceberg.' The Batavians offer a much wider variety of leaf size and shape, from the puckered and frilly 'Rouge Grenobloise' (SH) to the toothed leaves of the early Batavian 'La Brilliante' (CG) and the deeply notched 'Reine des Glaces' (CG). Only a few catalogues, however, identify the cultivars as Batavian. If a crisphead is described as open, dark green or red, with interesting leaf shape, it is likely Batavian.

Several Batavian varieties, such as 'Red Grenoble' (CG) and 'Cocarde' (CG), an oak-leaf crisphead with bronze tips, can be harvested as cut-and-come-again lettuce, though the head must be sacrificed for the supercrisp baby greens. 'Green Ice' (CG) has shiny, dark green, fringed, savoyed leaves and can be harvested as a cutting lettuce in spring, leaving a few plants to head up later in the season. The same is true of 'Red Grenoble,' which has glistening wine-red leaves. In Turid's garden, 'Rouge Grenobloise' never does form a head but has become a favourite crisp cutting variety.

Among the common lettuces, crispheads are the most demanding to grow. To produce firm heads, they need a constant supply of water and better soil than most greens. Although generally slower to bolt than butterheads, the tight balls take longer to mature and must be planted very early to produce heads before hot weather sets in. Even then, a sud-

Mixed looseleaf varieties combine to make a spring salad.

den heat wave can send the flower stalk bursting forth. Therefore, confine crispheads to early and late sowings, and choose varieties that are both heat-resistant and slow to bolt. Check days to maturity carefully—crispheads require a longer growing season than any other lettuce, some as long as 98 days. (Growing the Batavian crispheads as cutting lettuces bypasses these problems and provides a harvest in less than two months.)

Start early crispheads about three weeks before other lettuce. Plan the sowing date so that the heads mature before the brunt of the hot weather hits. For late crispheads, work backward from the expected first frost date. Crisphead seeds sprout well in midsummer: the seeds germinate at soil temperatures of up to 85 degrees F, while the butterheads germinate poorly above 77 degrees, a condition known as high-temperature dormancy. Nevertheless, crisphead seedlings do not like to be too hot. Transplant them in the lee of an asparagus hedge or taller vegetables such as brassicas, or shade them with a lattice laid on blocks over the bed. Turid once tried transplanting fall crispheads under a tepee of pole beans, but there was so much shade and so little air circulation that they rotted.

Transplant crispheads 12 to 16 inches apart —they have the largest spread of all the lettuces. If you are transplanting in August for late crispheads, ease the transition with good shade cover and plenty of moisture and organic matter. Without rich soil, lots of elbowroom and water, the

plant will not form a heart. The most important of these three, however, is water. Once a week, give the bed a deep soaking, an inch or two of water. Mulch around the heads to hold the moisture in the soil. If you don't mulch, water more often, at least every second day. Never sprinkle crispheads from above; water becomes trapped in the head. Instead, lay the hose on the ground, or aim the water at the base of the plant. Fluctuations in moisture contribute to bitterness, bolting and tip-burn, an unsightly edging of brown around the leaves. Remove any diseased leaves that form, but do not harvest outside leaves for salads during the season; wait for the head to mature.

Harvest the head before it is fully formed, when there is still some give to it and it is green to the core, with some of the benefits of leaf lettuce yet most of the crunch of its kind. The best heads are light for their size, indicating looseness and crispness. If you wait until the head is as tight as a cabbage, it will likely be bitter or, at least, tough and flavourless and low in nutrition.

Cut off the head at soil level, and remove the outer leaves; toss them and the dug-up roots on the compost pile. Be sure to harvest all crispheads, even those not quite fully formed, before the hard frosts in the fall. Turid's romaine and butterhead survived a few below-zero nights nicely, but the crisphead froze beyond redemption, even though it was a variety called 'Frostproof,' which, according to the catalogue, "withstands brief

A stuffed crisphead salad with yogurt cheese.

salads, where its silvery shine and characteristic crunch are welcome. Slice crispheads into wedges, and use as a vehicle for creamy, chunky dressings of the Thousand Island type. The firmest crispheads can even be stuffed. If you slice or shred a crisphead, use a stainless-steel knife and serve immediately: cut edges may darken with metal oxides.

Stuffed 'Iceberg' Salad

Yogurt cheese is a delightfully creamy, healthful substitute for cream cheese. To make it, simply empty a quart (1 L) of plain, natural, fat-free yogurt into a colander or funnel lined with a double layer of cheesecloth or a drip coffee filter. Allow to drain overnight in the refrigerator. Use the drained liquid for scones and the ''cheese'' in the following recipe.

1	small 'Iceberg' lettuce	1
½ cup	yogurt cheese or cream cheese	125 mL
2 Tbsp.	blue cheese	30 mL
2 Tbsp.	grated raw carrot	30 mL
1 Tbsp.	finely chopped green pepper	15 mL
2 Tbsp.	finely chopped raw tomato	30 mL
1 Tbsp.	onion juice or grated raw onion	15 mL
	Salt & pepper to taste	
	Dash of hot-pepper sauce	

With a knife, hollow out the head, leaving a ''wall'' of lettuce about the thickness of the width of your thumb. (Save the scooped-out lettuce for a shredded salad.) Blend remaining ingredients and spoon them into the cavity. Wrap the head in plastic, and set it in the refrigerator until just before serving.

To serve, set the whole crisphead on a plate, cut side down, and garnish around the perimeter with tomatoes and basil or parsley. At the table, slice the 'Iceberg' into wedges and serve.

BUTTERHEAD

While technically and taxonomically in the same family as crispheads, butterheads are altogether different. They also form a head, but instead of stiff, crackling leaves tightly folded into a compact ball, they produce tender greenery that wraps loosely around a soft heart, more like a rosette than a head. Although they are sometimes called looseheads, the term butterheads is more apt: the tender leaves fairly melt in the mouth and are so delicate that

periods of frost.'' The harvest may be extended, however, with floating row covers.

Crispheads seem particularly sensitive to ring spot, a disease that leaves small brown spots on the outside leaves and rusty streaks on the ribs. Prevent it with good ventilation. Aphids and slugs are not as partial to crispheads as they are to butterheads and looseleaf varieties. Mildew and downy mildew, which cause large yellowish patches between the veins of older leaves, may

be a problem in autumn, when conditions turn cool and wet. Avoid overcrowding and overhead watering, and improve the ventilation.

Once they are harvested, crispheads last a week or more in the refrigerator. Remove the core by whacking on the counter, run water into the cavity, drain thoroughly in a colander, and wrap in plastic to store. Although a crisphead does not make a particularly appealing tossed salad on its own, it is excellent sliced thinly and added to mixed green they can be bruised by wind, rain or even picking. Unlike crispheads, they cannot be mechanically harvested, and they do not travel well— witness the exhausted Bostons on the supermarket shelf—but to gardeners, they offer superior flavour, exquisite texture and more healthful salads. Butterheads contain four times more iron, three times more vitamin A and 50 percent more protein and potassium than crispheads.

Butterheads mature three to four weeks sooner than crispheads. Better adapted to growing during short days, they are well suited to northern gardens. Most of the late lettuces come from this group or are crosses between butterheads and romaine. The range of colours—from lemon-green to deep lime and pomegranate-red—makes these edible rosettes particularly decorative in the garden and in containers.

The best-known butterhead lettuces are Bibb and Boston. Bibb is a Kentucky limestone lettuce that was developed by Major John Bibb, an amateur horticulturist. Arguably the first gourmet lettuce, it was dubbed Mr. Bibb's lettuce by Bibb's neighbours, and although never formally christened, a whole subspecies of lettuce now bears his name. Large, floppy outer leaves fold over a heart that is as yellow and smooth on the tongue as butter. The delicate flavour is offset by an unfortunate tendency to bolt in hot weather, although recent strains attempt to correct this.

'Buttercrunch,' my personal favourite and one I wait for with the anticipation of a child at a candy counter, is a Bibb-type lettuce. I like it because the head is so fully formed and crunchy that it can almost be classified as a crisphead, yet it has buttery leaves. More heat-resistant than most Bibbs, it is less tolerant than the Bostons. 'Buttercrunch' produces smallish heads, very deep green for a butterhead, and robust leaves that have more flavour and texture than most lettuce of this type.

Boston lettuce, paler and slower to mature than Bibb, has a richer flavour. Once, when I was recovering from pneumonia, a friend brought me not chicken soup but a salad made from a head of Boston dressed with fresh watercress, yogurt and dill. I would pick up my bed and walk for a salad like that any day. 'White Boston' (BL) was the standard for years, and now many improved strains have evolved from it, including 'Ostinata' (ST), which matures in just eight weeks.

For early and late plantings, Turid recommends 'Red Boston' (ST), a striking red lettuce with leaves that gently fold back to reveal a pale green centre. In the garden, the plants look like enormous burgundy roses, and they deepen to an even richer red during the cool nights of autumn. It is quite frost-hardy yet reasonably heat-resistant, making it a good variety for a long growing season. Sown in early April and thinned to 10 inches apart, the plants produced obvious heads by the end of June, and we were still eating them in July after the 'Buttercrunch' planted on the same date had bolted. Turid sowed another crop in flats in August and transplanted it in September, mulching with pond weeds. We ate the heads until late October, when the hard frosts hit. In late spring, 'Red Boston' has a mild taste with a slight edge to it that some people find bitter; in the fall, the cool weather deepens the colours and sweetens the taste. 'Red Boston' is particularly striking interplanted with the pale May-green 'Canada Boston' (ST). Extremely heat-resistant, it was very slow to bolt and slightly milder and crunchier than the red variety.

European butterheads are considered the finest of all, and they are becoming more available in North America. 'Green Mignonette' (NI, BL) is a crisp, sweet, compact butterhead purportedly well suited to hot climates. We did not have good luck with 'Merveille des Quatre Saisons' (SH, BL), which nevertheless enjoys a good reputation.

'Pirat' is a widely available red butterhead from Switzerland and a good all-season lettuce. Known as Sprenkel lettuce, it has pale green leaves mottled with purplish bronze streaks and a tender heart that blanches under the overlaid leaves to a creamy yellow. Planted 8 inches apart in the planter box, the heads matured in 65 days. Uniform in size and good-tasting, they weathered several frosts, surviving until mid-October. Two other midseason choices are the popular Mantilia strain of 'Kagraner Summer' and 'Hilde,' a giant white Boston (DA).

A century ago, there was an epicurean rage for miniatures, and that food-fad cycle has come around again. In the garden, miniature varieties such as 'Tom Thumb' require spacing of only 6 inches apart, compared with the 9 to 12 inches needed by most butterheads.

Butterheads are not as fast-growing as looseleaf lettuce but fit nicely between leafy types and the crispheads, maturing in 60 to 75 days. Because of their tender leaves, protect seedlings from heavy rain and wind. Space plants generously for good ventilation, and water early in the day to avoid soft hearts susceptible to rot.

Remember the butterhead's tenderness, too, at harvest and in the kitchen: handle it gently, cutting off the whole plant at the base when it is mature. Store it in the refrigerator in a plastic bag for only a day or two. Wash just before use, tearing the leaves from their base and plunging them several times into warm water. (Boston types in particular tend to trap dirt in their creases.) Drain well, then spin briefly. *Never* slice a butterhead: the cut turns black. Tear the leaves into bite-sized pieces, or preferably, leave them whole for guests to cut, providing they aren't gargantuan. Dress very lightly immediately before serving: this lettuce wilts faster than either crisphead or looseleaf types.

Sweet Garlic Dressing

The perfect spring dressing to complement the unadorned butteriness of a Boston or a Bibb and to use up the last of the winter garlic. Although this dressing uses an entire bulb of garlic, it is sweet, mild and relatively low in oil.

1	whole garlic bulb	1
1 Tbsp.	white-wine vinegar	15 mL
1 Tbsp.	extra-virgin olive oil	15 mL
1 Tbsp.	safflower oil	15 mL
¼ tsp.	honey (optional)	1 mL
	Dash of salt (optional)	
	Freshly ground pepper	

Separate and peel the garlic cloves and place in a very small saucepan with enough water to cover. Bring to a boil, then reduce heat and simmer until the garlic is tender, about 15 minutes. Remove garlic cloves, increase heat, and boil the liquid until only two tablespoons (30 mL) remain. Put the cloves in a sieve, pour the hot liquid over them, and mash them through into a small bowl, using the back of a wooden spoon. For a nuttier flavour, roast the garlic, unpeeled, at 325°F for about an hour, until it is easily pierced with a fork. Squeeze out the pulp and blend with two tablespoons (30 mL) of water or chicken stock.

Whisk the vinegar and oil into the garlic, and flavour with honey and salt and pepper. The consistency is quite thick and creamy. We find it needs no salt at all. For a stronger flavour, substitute balsamic vinegar or half-and-half balsamic and white-wine vinegars.

Makes about one-third cup (75 mL), or enough for two heads of Boston lettuce—about 6 servings.

Romaine Lettuce
Lactuca sativa var. *longifolia*

Romaine is the lettuce Gargantua ate laced with pilgrims. According to one source, Rabelais introduced the lettuce to France in 1534, bringing the seeds to Paris from Rome, where the pope grew it in his private gardens. For a while, it was called Paris lettuce, so popular was it among the gourmets of that city, but gardeners called it *le laitue romaine,* Roman lettuce. Romaine did not originate with the Romans, however; they adopted it from a Greek island that gives the lettuce its other name, cos. These Mediterranean roots account for one of romaine's most endearing qualities: it likes the heat. While other greens wilt and bolt in the summer sun, romaine stays crisp, sweet and contained.

Romaine has spoon-shaped leaves with thick, juicy midribs that enfold one another to produce an upright, elongated oval head. It has as much texture as and more flavour than a crisphead, and it is more healthful, containing six times more vitamin A and three times more calcium. The basis of the famous Caesar salad, romaine stands up better to tossing than butterheads, and the leaves have enough crunch and flavour to support thick, pungent dressings. The pale inner leaves are especially tasty, somewhat nutty in flavour.

Romaine takes a little longer to form a mature head than a butterhead lettuce does—about 75 days. In its early stages, this lettuce resembles a tulip, with stiff upright leaves that make excellent "dippers" for salsa and herbed yogurt. (Some say Socrates drank his hemlock from a romaine "spoon.") The head becomes progressively tighter until, at maturity, it resembles pak choi. In a mixed lettuce bed, it adds an unusual vertical element.

Although romaine has the reputation of being more difficult to grow than other lettuce, we find it no more troublesome. Treat it exactly like other heading lettuce, giving it a little less room, since it grows upright in tight cylinders rather than spreading rosettes. Transplant 6 to 8 inches apart. Most varieties form heads quite well, but if the leaves seem loose or if you want a very pale, blanched heart, tie them loosely with twine as they approach maturity. Romaine is generally subject to the same pests and diseases as other lettuce, although the green variety seems especially sensitive to ring spot. Harvesting the outer leaves does not deter the plants from forming heads.

Extremely heat-resistant and slow to bolt, romaine makes an excellent midseason lettuce. Varieties are also available that grow well in cooler conditions. For forcing and for early-spring sowing, Turid recommends 'Parris Island,' a widely available vigorous romaine that produces uniform heads. This is probably the cultivar found at the supermarket. While somewhat less fla-

vourful than other romaines, it is very reliable and grows well in cooler conditions, making it a good choice for autumn harvests too. 'Valmaine' (BL) is another early romaine that Turid likes because of its delicious savoyed leaves.

The best all-season variety, in our opinion, is 'Winter Density,' also easily obtainable. This butterhead-romaine intermediate develops a heavy, dark, compact head about 8 to 10 inches high that looks like a tall 'Buttercrunch,' opening more like a rose than a tulip. It can be grown in spring, summer and fall, but it is especially noted for its frost tolerance. The Cook's Garden also offers 'Craquerelle du Midi,' another intermediate that produces open-hearted romaines, which grow well in hot weather.

The fertile intermarrying of crisp romaine and loose butterheads has produced a dwarf, the very popular 'Little Gem.' Also known as 'Sugar Cos,' it is extremely sweet and mild and is likely the lettuce served when you order "hearts of romaine" from the menu of posh restaurants. Their small size makes the leaves perfect for dips, but their real advantage is rapid growth: they mature in just under 60 days, producing bright green 6-inch heads. Because of its butterhead parentage, 'Little Gem' resprouts quite well and can be harvested as a cutting lettuce, although in general, romaine is not a good cut-and-come-again crop.

Red romaine may prove to be too unusual for some salad bowls, but it is not a new idea: speckled and bronze cos are listed in turn-of-the-century gardening books. 'Rosalita' (JO) has chocolate-brown leaves with a light green centre rib and deep green veins; it is as startling and beautiful as a magnolia. Turid harvested leaves in mid-June from an early-April planting, and in autumn, it survived several hard frosts, giving us delectable Caesars until late October. 'Rouge d'Hiver' (CG) forms a looser head, and while it is a good all-season romaine, the colour intensifies dramatically with the cool evenings of autumn.

There are also miniature red romaines, such as 'Red Leprechaun'(CG). Larger than 'Little Gem,' it produces 8-to-12-inch-tall heads of savoyed burgundy leaves, with hearts that fade from pale pink to cream. 'Rubens Dwarf Romaine' (SH) is a semidwarf with lime-green hearts and leaves the colour of cranberries.

Romaine is as hardy in the kitchen as it is in the garden; it lasts longer than either looseleafs or butterheads. Tear romaine leaves, and separate the midrib on larger leaves. If it is tough, throw it out; otherwise, slice it and add to the salad like celery.

Keep the tiny inner leaves whole. You can prepare an undressed salad a few hours ahead of time without its deteriorating.

Romaine is mentioned in a 19th-century American recipe as an ingredient in Summer Salad, a mixture of romaine, mustard leaves, watercress, radishes and cucumbers, sliced very thinly, tossed with a heavy dressing of oil and vinegar, cream and sieved hard-cooked eggs, then "heaped in a salad bowl on a lump of ice" and garnished with fennel heads and nasturtiums. Romaine is firm enough to withstand such a burden. It can even be cooked as a warm salad. In a tablespoon (15 mL) of olive oil, sauté a cup of thinly sliced radishes, four cups (1 L) of thinly sliced romaine and two tablespoons (30 mL) of fresh dillweed. Toss with salt and pepper, sprinkle with a teaspoon (5 mL) of balsamic vinegar, and serve immediately while still warm. Add thin strips of sun-dried tomatoes for a delicious variation with a truly Roman touch.

The Original Caesar

Contrary to popular myth, Caesar Salad did not get its name from the Roman lettuce in the recipe. It was invented by Alex Cardini Sr., an Italian World War I flying ace who joined his brother Caesar in a restaurant venture in Tijuana, Mexico. First called Aviator's Salad, it was dedicated to the pilots of the nearby San Diego air base, who referred to it as Caesar's Salad—and the name stuck.

10	romaine leaves	10
6	½ -inch slices of French bread	6
¼ cup	olive oil	50 mL
3	cloves garlic	3
6	anchovy fillets	6
1	egg	1
1 Tbsp.	freshly squeezed lime juice	15 mL
1 tsp.	Worcestershire sauce	5 mL
¼ cup	freshly grated Parmesan cheese	50 mL

Wash, spin and refrigerate the romaine. Lay the bread slices on a cookie tray and crisp in a 400-degree-F oven. Brush with a tablespoon (15 mL) or so of the oil, and return to the oven to brown. Crush the garlic and anchovies together, mash in a tablespoon (15 mL) of oil, then spread the mixture on the crisped bread.

Coddle the egg by pouring boiling water over it in a small saucepan and cooking for 1 minute. Break

'Speckles': a delicious early looseleaf.

the egg into a mixing bowl; the white should be opaque and just barely setting. Whisk the egg with the lime juice, Worcestershire and remaining oil until thick. Toss the romaine with the dressing and sprinkle on the Parmesan. Serve with the garlic toasts on the side. Makes a large salad for two.

Few people make the original Cardini Caesar today. More typically, the garlic, anchovies, egg, juice and oil are whisked together and tossed with the romaine, croutons and Parmesan. Lemon is usually substituted for lime juice. For an unusual presentation, dip whole romaine leaves in the dressing and fan them on a plate, sprinkling with Parmesan and croutons before serving. (Because the egg is not fully cooked, this dressing must be used immediately. Do not store leftovers.)

Looseleaf Lettuce
Lactuca sativa var. *crispa*

Looseleaf lettuce is designed for those who cannot wait two months for the first green salad. It doesn't form a head but grows in a profusion of leaves from a central base, maturing in as little as a month. The easiest lettuce to have in the garden, it grows anywhere almost anytime in the growing season. Gardeners with short summers have better luck with fast-growing looseleaf lettuce than with heading types, and looseleaf lacks the delicacy that makes head lettuce persnickety to grow.

There is, it seems, a looseleaf lettuce to suit every taste: curly or frilled, flat or scalloped, shiny or matte, primly compact or relaxed and spreading, red or green, speckled or streaked, with textures from chewy to crisp. The only thing the horticultural scientists can't make looseleaf lettuce do is form a head, but that is its greatest strength. Because the sun penetrates right to the heart of the leaves, it scores highest among the lettuces in nutritional value—it contains three times more calcium and vitamin C and six times more vitamin A than do crispheads.

There are perhaps more varieties of looseleaf lettuce than there are of any other. Most grow in upright clusters of leaves. The so-called Salad Bowl varieties grow in full, spreading bouquets that literally fill a salad bowl. There is a green strain and a dark maroon strain of these big, loose, frilly rosettes; they make a spectacular salad bed or edging when interplanted. The looseleafs are particularly appropriate for children's gardens because, besides being pretty, germination is almost always close to 100 percent and harvest can begin about five weeks after seeding. And finally, it is the looseleaf varieties that shine as cutting lettuce. Many are so vigorous that they happily resprout for several harvests of tender greens.

One of the most reliable looseleafs for early planting is 'Black Seeded Simpson,' a very old, easily obtainable variety that is among the earliest of the looseleafs, maturing in only 40 days. Its juicy, light green leaves are wavy, crisp and flavourful. 'Speckles' (BL) is an excellent early looseleaf that resprouts well as a cutting lettuce. We sowed it in mid-April and harvested from mid-May to mid-June. The leaves are the shape of an earlobe, a light beigy green splattered with rust-red speckles as if someone had shaken a fountain pen over the lettuce bed.

For early and midseason crops, 'Prizehead' from Ontario Seed Growers (OSG) proved prolific, growing loose bundles of fleshy, wide, red-speckled leaves 7 inches tall and 10 inches across. It was slow to bolt and was resistant to the dry, hot spells of July. Similarly, 'Lollo Rossa' (CG) is a frilly, crimson-edged Italian lettuce well suited to the increased heat of midsummer. Both 'Lollo Rossa' and its pale green relative 'Lollo Biondo' are excellent cutting lettuces for all seasons, but the best is a new 'Lollo Rossa' variation called 'Valeria' (CG), a vigorous, fringed cutting lettuce that looks like an auburn Afro in the garden. Among the most unusual red looseleafs is 'Red Deer Tongue' (NI), an heirloom variety with twisting, triangulated leaves that form a cluster similar to an open romaine. Its flavour is excellent, although in Turid's garden, it bolted early.

For a midseason looseleaf, Turid recommends the widely available 'Red Sails,' which matures in 45 days. It is the most heat-resistant looseleaf and grows equally well in the shoulder seasons. This shiny red-bronze looseleaf is easy to grow and is much larger than the commonly recommended 'Ruby.' The familiar 'Green Ice' is technically a Batavian crisphead, but in Turid's garden, it fails to make a head and instead grows as a crunchy, savoyed cut-and-come-again looseleaf that thrives in spring and early summer (see page 17).

Varieties that are good for early crops usually grow well in the fall too. Some looseleaf lettuces, however, thrive in all three seasons. For example, the widely available 'Grand Rapids' can be started early in the greenhouse or planted outside in high summer directly in the planter box. "It is a never-fail lettuce," says Turid. The leaves grow very quickly in a spreading, open rosette, reminiscent of endive. Turid also recommends 'Red Rebosa' (NI), an oak-leaf Salad Bowl lettuce that matures in 50 days. Oak-leaf lettuce, found on many ancient lists of "sallet plants," is uncommonly beautiful, with deeply lobed, delicate leaves that look as if they might have grown on an oak tree; those of 'Red Rebosa' are dark maroon, lightening to chartreuse toward the centre. Although the loose, frilly leaves have a very open growth, if the seedlings are planted about 4 inches apart, the oak-shaped leaves stand up, creating 9-inch-tall bunches. It is very slow to bolt, and although we grew it only in summer, it has the reputation of being winter-hardy.

Not to be outdone by the baby crispheads and butterheads, there are also miniature looseleaf lettuces that mature very early and are particularly

A miniature 'Tom Thumb' butterhead.

appropriate for containers and limited spaces. 'Baby Oak' (JO) is an all-season oak-leaf, much smaller than usual. Miniature looseleaf lettuces are ideal for windowsill plantings or as an edible ground cover sown between annuals in a flowerbed.

The best strategy with looseleaf lettuce is to grow lots of different kinds and make regular plantings every week over the entire season, choosing varieties to suit the weather. Although looseleaf lettuce thrives when sown directly in the garden, Turid still recommends starting most varieties in trays or flats so that you can take better care of them when they are young and fragile. Transplant upright types as close as 4 to 6 inches apart; give spreading types up to a foot of space. Cutting lettuces, of course, are broadcast across the salad bed.

Some spreading varieties may be hard to mulch because the leaves break off when handled. Provide lots of water and side-dress regularly, although they don't need as much fertilizer as heading types. Generally speaking, these plants are healthier than other lettuce, being less prone to rot and mildew, but they still need elbowroom for good ventilation. Watch for aphids during dry spells.

Start gathering outside leaves about three weeks after sowing. You can harvest traditional looseleaf lettuce by picking off the large outer leaves or by cutting off the mature plant an inch above the ground. Harvest the cutting lettuce by shearing the plants when they are only a few inches tall.

Looseleaf lettuce is firmer in texture than but-

terhead and lies somewhere between crispheads and butterheads in terms of perishability: it won't last as long in the refrigerator as an 'Iceberg,' but it will remain appealing, undressed, longer than a Boston or a Bibb. Wash the leaves individually, spin-dry, and store in a plastic bag in the refrigerator. When making a salad, it is best to tear large leaves, although slicing at the last minute won't leave dark stains, as is the case with crispheads.

Of all the lettuces, looseleaf is indispensable to the salad cook. Individually, young leaves cradle a tomato slice or two at the side of a sandwich plate; a potato salad for four nestles inside a large Salad Bowl leaf. Used as garnishes, added by the handful to bowls of mixed greens or composing a salad on their own, looseleaf lettuces are as versatile as they are beautiful. Dress them carefully, preferably in a light vinaigrette that allows the flavour and texture of the leaves to come through.

Arnie's Well-Dressed Greens

Named for a friend who learned to cook in Paris—he earned his room and board by preparing Sunday dinner for a family of ruthlessly discriminating gourmands—this salad dressing is perfect for a simple bowl of mixed garden greens. The recipe is exactly as it was given to me.

Start with a bit of balsamic vinegar in a bowl. Squeeze in the juice of half a lemon. Add a dollop or two of Dijon mustard, somewhere between a half-teaspoon (2 mL) and a teaspoon (5 mL). Press or mash three or four cloves of garlic, and add a few drops of soy sauce. Stir this together, then add the best-quality olive oil in a thin stream, whisking briskly until the mixture thickens. Add the greens to the bowl, and toss lightly just before serving.

MESCLUN: SHEARED DELIGHT

Mesclun. Its name may be unfamiliar and the growing method peculiar to gardeners raised on straight-edged North American principles, but it is undoubtedly one of the most exciting innovations in the salad garden—and in the salad bowl—in this century. In the dialect of Provence, the sunny province of southern France that extends from the Alps to the Mediterranean coast, *salade de mesclun* means a mixed-up mess of wild baby greens. Seeds of herbs, cutting lettuce and leaf vegetables are mixed and broadcast onto the soil, then harvested when the greens are only a few inches high by mowing a wide swath with scissors. The greens are then tossed, premixed, into the salad bowl.

The salad you serve will be a collage of colours and textures: every shade of green from verdigris to chartreuse, deep burgundies, seashell pinks and burnt umbers; delicate ferny sprigs, leaves rippled and frilled and lobed, miniature palm fronds and smooth little scoops. There is nothing remarkable about a mixed salad—chef's salad, after all, with its toss of tomatoes, onions and 'Iceberg,' is a restaurant staple—but this mixed salad consists entirely of leaves, wonderful in their variety, as marvellous to the palate as to the eye. Eating such a salad offers a succession of flavours and textures as each plant is savoured alone, then in combination, a symphony of taste punctuated with brilliant solos. The surprise comes when your guests discover that the salad arrives at the table exactly as it is grown—a tangled profusion of leafy greens.

The idea is still revolutionary on this side of the Atlantic, but it is rooted in European practice, one that derives from harvesting salads in the wild. Turid remembers wandering over the fields west of Würzburg shortly after World War II, gathering wild plants for the table: watercress from streambeds, corn salad (mâche) from pastures, chicory and plantain from roadsides and dandelion greens from backyards and meadows. It didn't seem like gourmet fare then—these were often the only green vegetables they had to eat—but now the delicious variety of these wild greens is being appreciated again, and cultivation techniques have been developed that bring the mixed pleasures of the pasture into the kitchen garden.

In Italy and southern France, market vendors sell huge baskets of tender young greens—mâche, arugula, mustard, cress—that shoppers mix by the handful into bags of mesclun. In Italian, the small greens are *insalatine,* a diminutive of *insalata*, salad. In this country, mesclun can be bought only at gourmet shops in the largest cities, where greengrocers pay gardeners up to $30 a pound for the greens. Outside these centres, only a home garden can provide such a delicacy. And it is a truly individual one, because the mesclun you concoct is as unique as your signature.

Any cut-and-come-again green is appropriate for mesclun. Virtually every mix contains lettuce and often other "cool" mild greens: purslane, mâche, spinach. For those with a sensitive palate, the entire salad can comprise such greens, the variety coming from texture rather than taste. But most people spice the mild greens with "hot" leafy ones—mustard, cress, arugula —in proportions to match their culinary courage. Herbs such as parsley, rocket, coriander, fennel and dill are added for flavour and a few edible blossoms tossed in for colour. The real skill comes in combining plants for flavour, texture and visual appeal—for example, piquant shungiku, crunchy purslane and an oak-leaf lettuce with edges burnished as if by a sunset. Add to this the challenge of choosing varieties that grow at roughly the same rate, in the same season and under the same conditions—after all, they share the same bed —and one can begin to see why mesclun is so exhilarating for the salad gardener.

For those who are just getting started, some seed companies, such as Shepherd's and The Cook's Garden, offer ready-made mesclun mixes, usually identified as mild, piquant or spicy. Saladisi is a new one from Thompson & Morgan (TM). Only rarely do these prepared mixes identify the actual plants, although you might be able to figure it out for yourself once the seedlings are up.

Mixing your own mescluns is not difficult, however. There are traditional combinations, such as Mesclun Niçoise, which mixes tart endives and chicories; Provençal, which concentrates buttery leaf lettuce spiced with nutty arugula, nippy dandelion leaves and chervil; and *misticanza* from northern Italy, which contains five parts lettuce and four parts chicory. We divided our mescluns into early, midseason and late mixes. If you start seeds on a windowsill in March and end with a mesclun under cold frames in November, it is possible to enjoy this delicacy in all its nuances for at least half the year.

When selecting mesclun plants, base the blend on your ideal mixed green salad, choosing proportions as you would in the kitchen. This requires some experience with garden greens. Any of the lettuces mentioned in this chapter or the exotic greens described in the next are appropriate for mescluns, as long as they are cut-and-come-again. Add herbs from Chapter Three, endives from Chapter Four and your leftover onion seed. Read through the plant descriptions and make your choices, or be guided by our favourites, listed below. If, when you taste the mix, you find something you don't like, simply weed it out and continue harvesting the bed; this is sometimes necessary anyway with plants such as arugula, which become progressively more pungent and soon tower above the rest.

To some people, it might seem like a lot of unnecessary trouble to premix a bed of garden greens. After all, why not just go to the garden and harvest 5 to 10 different herbs and greens, each growing in its own plot under conditions ideal to the individual plants? The answer is partly aesthetic: a bed of mesclun is exquisitely beautiful in its profusion, so unlike the monocultural rows typical of the kitchen garden. But it is also practical: because the plants are so tightly packed together, there are virtually no weeds and the soil stays moist and cool, which is the way most greens like it.

Careful bed preparation is essential to ensure that the mesclun is weedless. Wild plants like the protected, moist conditions in the mesclun bed as much as the lettuce and cress; they easily go unnoticed. Meticulously weed the bed when you dig the soil in the fall, and lay dark plastic over it for a week or so in the spring to burn off new shoots before planting. Even so, several common weeds creep into our beds: lamb's quarters, purslane, shepherd's purse, clover, vetch, dandelion, ragweed, sometimes milkweed and deadly nightshade. Clover and lamb's quarters are a welcome addition to the mesclun, but the last two can be poisonous, especially if allowed to mature to the flower and berry stages, respectively. Take the time to learn to identify common local weeds, and be able to distinguish poisonous varieties. Leave nontoxic weeds in the mix if you like, but do it consciously. Provincial ministries of agriculture usually have good pamphlets on local weed species.

Like cutting lettuce, mesclun can be planted by broadcasting or by strip planting individual greens in adjacent bands. Prepare the bed and sow as for cutting lettuce (page 16), mixing the various seeds together in the desired proportions in a bowl. Alternatively, scatter a pinch of each seed individually over the bed. As a rule of thumb, up to a tablespoon of seed thickly sows a square yard of soil, but since seeds vary dramatically in weight and size, from pebblelike spinach to fine-grained arugula, you will have to use your judgement. Sow about 2 square feet per person: a 3-by-3-foot bed produces a week of successive harvests for a family of four.

Strip planting is a good idea if you want greens of various sizes and different growth habits in the same mesclun. In this case, broadcast diagonal bands of seed, one type per band, with the tallest to the north or west, moving progressively toward the shortest. After the strips are planted, randomly poke in the seeds of pungent herbs, onions and plants such as bronze fennel or red orach. You don't want a whole strip of these spicy greens, but highlighted here and there in the bed, they will end up in the salad when you snip across the bands.

Because mesclun grows so fast in such a small area, keep a close eye on moisture levels, watering once or twice a day. Cultivation and thinning are not required; a little weeding may be. After about

MESCLUN MIXES

Early Mesclun

Sow direct mid-April to early May for May and June harvest.

SPICY MIX: Baby pak choi 'Mei Qing Choy' (NI); mustard greens 'Red Giant' (NI); mustard spinach 'Tendergreen' (NI); shungiku (BL); garden cress 'Extra Curled' (DO); arugula (NI); mizuna (NI).

DECORATIVE MIX: Upland cress (DO); radish 'Sparkler' (DA); spinach 'Longstanding Bloomsdale' (DO); chicory 'Crystal Hat' (NI); chervil 'Plain Leaf' (HU); leaf lettuce 'Red Sails' (W), 'Speckles.'

GARNISH: English daisies, primulas, cowslips, apple blossoms, violets.

Midseason Mesclun

Sow direct May through June for midsummer harvest.

HERB MIX: Sweet basil; onion 'White Lisbon'; borage; arugula; lettuce 'Valmaine,' 'Oakleaf,' 'Lollo Rossa,' 'Red Rebosa'; fennel 'Bronze'; beet green 'Erbette.'

GARNISH: Shungiku, Johnny-jump-ups, borage and chive flowers.

Late Mesclun

Sow direct mid-July through August for harvest to early October.

AUTUMN MIX: Mustard 'Green-in-Snow' (NI), 'Osaka Purple Redwood' (RE); mustard spinach 'Mizuna' (NI); garden cress 'Extra Curled' (DO); lettuce 'Little Gem,' 'Winter Density,' 'Rossa di Trento'; 'Rape-Salad' (RE); onions; radish 'Sparkler' (DA); winter chervil (NI); chicory 'Castel Franco di Variegata.'

GARNISH: Garlic chives, nasturtiums, pansies, anise-hyssop, chrysanthemums, fennel flowers, marigolds.

six weeks, start harvesting, using scissors to shear a strip back to less than 2 inches. In strip-planted beds, shear perpendicular to the bands of plants so that the salad contains a little of each green.

When the whole bed is harvested, add some liquid fish-emulsion fertilizer to encourage healthy new growth, and wait a week or two before beginning the second harvest. We found that a bed yielded no more than three harvests, after which you should dig it up, fertilize and start fresh. When the bed is dug, transplant individual plants such as New Zealand spinach, basil, chervil and orach to other parts of the garden, where they can mature beyond mesclun size.

Turid grows mesclun throughout the season from early spring to late fall, starting it indoors under lights in March, in boxes in the lee of the house during the Dog Days of summer and under glass when the weather becomes cool. Throughout the season, wherever there is an opening in the garden, she sows some mesclun. As long as a batch is sown every 10 days or so, the dinner table is continuously supplied with a wild salad that tastes reminiscent of the south of France.

Early Mescluns

Early mescluns are composed of cool-season greens and can be grown in fall as successfully as in spring. Choose a protected site that has a southern exposure and is relatively immune to late frosts. Spread dark plastic over the soil to warm it up. Instead of waiting to seed directly in the garden, you can start a mixture in a cold frame or on a windowsill in a box 2 feet square and 4 inches deep. In the second week of April, Turid broadcasts the first early mix outdoors on a prepared bed 3 feet by 4 feet; 10 days later, tiny seedlings are up, and six weeks later, we are enjoying our first mesclun salads. The time from sowing to harvest progressively shortens to about a month as the nights become warm and the temperatures stabilize.

Spinach is good in a spring mix, as are the endives, mustards, baby pak choi, chervil, garden cress, rape and any looseleaf lettuce that prefers cool conditions, such as 'Black Seeded Simpson' and 'Green Ice.' Italian mixes usually include radishes for green tops and spicy red roots that, when pulled, aerate the soil for the second growth. Our earliest mix contains roughly equal amounts of endive, chervil, arugula, 'Crystal Hat' chicory, 'Red Sails' looseleaf lettuce and garden cress. This is a striking mesclun, with frilly maroon lettuce leaves weaving through an emerald and May-green carpet of rocket and endive, spiked here and there with fernlike cress and chervil. The mix is refreshing and a little pungent because of the bitter chicory and endive. The arugula grows much faster than the rest and quickly becomes unpleasantly sharp; it is best to pull it out before the second harvest. Another good spring mix consists of equal parts red orach, mustard spinach, upland cress, dill, miner's lettuce and mizuna. The miner's lettuce grows in the shade of the mizuna, which is thinned out after the first cutting.

Midseason Mescluns

Because many greens prefer cool conditions, plant midseason mescluns in shady locations. Turid sets a growing box, 2 feet by 3 feet by 6 inches deep, on the east side of the house to protect the greens from the hot midafternoon sun. This makes it handy to check for pests and dryness. You can also sow the mesclun in the garden under a floating row cover, under lattices supported on blocks or between rows of tall vegetables.

If the mesclun bed is fully exposed, protect it with boughs as soon as the seed is planted, filtering the sunlight until the seedlings are up and established. After the first midseason harvest, water well, fertilize with fish emulsion, and stick boughs in the bed again to shade the plants during their second growth. Leave the cover on for about a week until the plants are reestablished.

For midseason mescluns, look for varieties that claim to be particularly heat-resistant. Romaine, bronze fennel, some endives and summer looseleaf lettuce, such as 'Red Sails' and 'Oakleaf,' seem to do well. Avoid plants with a tendency to turn bitter in the heat. One of our favourite summer mescluns combines onion, coriander, arugula, basil, beet greens, 'Speckles' and 'Oakleaf' lettuce and 'Rossa di Verona' chicory. We spot-plant bronze fennel, which eventually pokes above the mat of greens like stray feathers on a duck's back.

During the hot days of summer, water the mesclun bed at least twice a day, in early morning and evening; never let it go dry. After the seeds have sprouted, fertilize with fish emulsion. Properly cared for, a midseason mesclun grows very quickly. The mesclun Turid sowed on June 12 was ready for a first harvest on July 9.

Late Mescluns

Since late mescluns are sown during the heat of summer, it is a good idea to choose a bed close

Unthinned mesclun greens grow like a meadow.

slivered hazelnuts. It is a salad guaranteed to stimulate the palate and the dinner-table conversation.

Spiced Bitters Dressing

This is an excellent dressing for mesclun, especially a summer or fall mesclun, when the greens may be a little bitter.

2 tsp.	crushed allspice berries	10 mL
¼ tsp.	salt	1 mL
½ tsp.	black pepper	2 mL
1 tsp.	sugar	5 mL
½ tsp.	Dijon mustard	2 mL
½ cup	peanut oil	125 mL
3 tsp.	angostura bitters	15 mL
2 Tbsp.	red-wine vinegar	30 mL

Whisk together the first six ingredients. Add the bitters and vinegar, and continue whisking until the mixture emulsifies. Keep cool until serving. Whisk again and toss with a mesclun of spicy greens. As a variation, substitute four teaspoons (20 mL) of chopped fresh herbs for the allspice.

Provençal Vinaigrette

Salade de mesclun originated around Nice, where the leaves, grown in the monastery gardens of the Franciscan friars at Cimiez in the hills north of the city, were once presented in special baskets by children to their favourite adults. In the traditional mix, dandelion, arugula, purslane and chervil made up the small leaves, while the bulk of the salad comprised red Treviso chicory, white bitter chicory, oak-leaf lettuce and romaine. The classic dressing of Provence is a fruity olive oil, but the distinctive yet subtle flavour of nut oils complements mild mescluns perfectly.

¼ cup	walnut oil	50 mL
¼ cup	extra-virgin olive oil	50 mL
¼ cup	white-wine vinegar	50 mL
1 Tbsp.	freshly squeezed lemon juice	15 mL
½ tsp.	sugar	2 mL
1 tsp.	finely grated lemon rind (optional)	5 mL
	Salt & pepper to taste	

Whisk the ingredients until emulsified. Toss with a mesclun of mild greens, and garnish with toasted walnut halves. If desired, substitute almonds and almond oil or hazelnuts and hazelnut oil.

to the house, where you can keep an eye on it. At first, it will need some shelter from the sun, but it will appreciate the warmth later on. Turid covers the bed with a bamboo curtain, which she rolls back as the sun's intensity wanes.

Starting on July 25, she begins to sow the cool-weather greens for the late mesclun: corn salad, looseleaf lettuce, endives, chicories, upland cress, chervil, parsley and tall herbs such as borage and arugula, which protect the lower-growing plants. We were still cutting this mix in mid-September, and certain plants, such as mâche, continued to produce until October.

In early August, she plants a very cold-hardy mesclun composed mainly of endive, chicory, 'Green-in-Snow' mustard and onions. In the early fall, this mix tends to be a little bitter, but it can be sweetened by putting a box over the entire bed for a few days to blanch the greens.

Because mesclun plants grow so close together, they are usually very clean and therefore require little preparation in the kitchen. Harvest the salad early in the day as you would lettuce. Swish the leaves in a basin of cool water to wash them, spin-dry, and put the spinner in the refrigerator until you are ready for the salad. (If the mix gets too tangy toward the end of the harvest, add a few handfuls of lettuce leaves to dilute the piquant greens.) Pick a variety of colourful blossoms—calendula, violets, pansies, borage, dianthus, nasturtiums, chives—wash them carefully, and store separately.

Prepare a simple vinaigrette, using light vinegar or lemon for a mild mix and a more robust vinegar, such as cider or balsamic, for bitter greens. To be true to this salad's French origins, use a pure olive oil, Dijon mustard and a tarragon or white-wine vinegar of the highest quality. Immediately before serving, toss the greens lightly in the vinaigrette—about half a cup (125 mL) for eight cups (2 L) of greens—and mound in individual salad bowls or on a garnish leaf such as malva in summer or ornamental kale in autumn. Sprinkle with edible blossoms (pages 132-33) or, for variety, toasted walnuts or

Some Salad-Garden Favourites

*E = Early: sow early March to late May for June/July harvest.
MS = Midseason: sow early June to early July for July/August harvest.
L = Late: sow early July to mid-August for August/September harvest.
**See page 153 for key to seed catalogues.
†From sowing to harvest in Turid's garden.

Lettuce	Season*	Cultivar	Catalogue**	Days to Maturity†	Description
Crisphead Lettuce (75 + days, seed to harvest)	MS	'Frostproof' or 'Latehead'	DO	90	Firm, medium head, dark green with pale heart
	E, MS	'Frosty'	ST	98	Deep green 6-inch head, stands some heat and light frost
	E	'Great Lakes'	W	85	Large, fringed, tight head
	E, MS	'Green Ice'	CG	60	Fringed, savoyed, deep green, crisp rosette, excellent
	E, MS	'Rosy'	CG	90	Slow-bolting, red, small head
	E, MS, L	'Rouge Grenobloise'	SH	55	Burgundy, Batavian type
Butterhead Lettuce (60-75 days, seed to harvest)	E, MS, L	'Buttercrunch'	W	75	Robust, deep green 9-inch head
	E, L	'Canada Boston'	ST	68	May-green, crunchy, 12-inch head
	MS	'Hilde'	DA, PG	60	Loose 8-inch head, thin leaves, light green, tender
	MS	'Kagraner Summer'	W	60	Compact 8-inch head
	E, L	'Mescher'	PG	70	Deep green, sweet 8-inch head, firm leaves edged with red
	E, MS, L	'Pirat'	W	65	Loose 10-inch head, May-green with copper tint, light-frost-hardy, wilts quickly when picked
	E, L	'Red Boston'	ST	68	Red outside, pale green centre, sweet 10-inch head
	MS	'Summer Baby Bibb'	SH	57	Tender 5-inch head, miniature, sturdy, fast-growing
	E, MS, L	'Tom Thumb'	W	60	Loose 6-inch head, light green, sweet, miniature

Lettuce	Season*	Cultivar	Catalogue**	Days to Maturity†	Description
Romaine Lettuce (75 + days, seed to harvest)	E, MS, L	'Little Gem'	CG, SH	60	Miniature butterhead-romaine cross, 6 inches tall
	E, L	'Parris Island'	W	75	Sweet, bright green, 12 inches tall
	E, L	'Rosalita'	W	75	Deep purple head, yellow heart, crunchy, nutty, 10 inches tall
	E, MS, L	'Winter Density'	W	60	Butterhead-romaine cross, 8 inches tall, lush green, superior
Looseleaf Lettuce (45-60 days, seed to harvest)	E, MS, L	'Australian Yellow'	BL	60	Mild, light green, bigger and better than 'Black Seeded Simpson'
	E	'Black Seeded Simpson'	W	40	Forcing and cutting lettuce, light green, large mature rosette
	E, L	'Dunsel'	DA	50	Large cabbagelike leaves, prone to bolt
	E, MS, L	'Grand Rapids'	W	45	Light green, vigorous
	MS, L	'Prizehead'	BL	60	Red tinted soft green, lush
	E, L	'Red Deer Tongue'	NI	60	Triangular leaves, intermediate romaine, highly recommended
	MS, L	'Red Rebosa'	NI	50	Red cutting oak-leaf Salad Bowl type, winter-hardy, slow-bolting
	E, MS, L	'Red Sails'	W	45	Deep bronze, outstanding, tender, heat-resistant
	E, MS, L	'Royal Oak Leaf'	CG	50	Large open rosettes, deep green, lush
	E, L	'Speckles'	BL	45	Thin, lobed, red-speckled leaves, low-growing, good for windowsills
	E, MS, L	'Valeria'	CG	45	Red cutting lettuce, 'Lollo Rossa' type, good for windowsills

Exotic Greens

Arugula to Watercress

Chapter Two

Salad today is practically synonymous with lettuce, so rarely does the contemporary cook include other greens. Yet in the 16th and 17th centuries, salads contained 20 or 30 ingredients and often a dozen greens. Mâche, dandelion, watercress, miner's lettuce, mustard greens, arugula, spinach, purslane— the names may be unfamiliar, but these greens have a long history in the salad bowl too. We call them exotic not because they are foreign—many are domesticated cousins of plants that grow in Canadian meadows and forests—but because they are rare in northern gardens and North American salad bowls.

Exotic greens have a wider, subtler range of textures, flavours and colours than lettuce. Often, they offer more nutrition per bite. Like lettuce, they are high in fibre and low in fat and calories, but dark greens such as spinach and watercress are high in beta carotene, the substance in plants that converts to usable vitamin A in the human body. Researchers at the Harvard Medical School recently found direct evidence that beta carotene, an antioxidant, slows the progression of athero-

sclerosis, possibly by inhibiting the formation of low-density lipoprotein (LDL) cholesterol. Greens are also high in another antioxidant, vitamin C. Both vitamins may act as cancer preventives: in studies around the world, people with the lowest cancer rates eat an abundance of dark green (and dark orange) vegetables. And some greens, like mustard, belong to the family of cabbages, which seem to have an extra edge as cancer antidotes.

Not only are they more healthful than lettuce, but greens grow over a wider range of garden conditions. Although midseason cultivars have been developed, lettuce is happier in the cool weather of spring and fall, while many greens thrive in heat and willingly take over the salad bowl in July. Some, like miner's lettuce, grow well in the shade; others, like New Zealand spinach, tolerate dry, sandy soil. Even if your soil and climate do not produce good lettuce, you are bound to find greens in this chapter that will give you lush salads.

Many greens are at home in a mesclun bed, resprouting for second and third harvests when

30

sheared as a cut-and-come-again. When adding them to the mesclun mix, take into account their particular growing habits and flavour. Corn salad lags far behind arugula, spinach is limited to spring and fall, mustard spinach quickly grows pungent, and upland cress likes partial shade. Some are better broadcast in a bed of their own, sheared like a mesclun and added to the salad bowl after the fact.

Like 16th-century gardeners, we have divided our herbs and greens into "hot" and "cool" seeds. The grouping has nothing to do with growing season but refers entirely to taste. In combining greens for a mesclun or even for a mixed leafy salad, sweetness must be balanced with piquancy, crisp succulence with buttery smoothness. As John Evelyn wrote in his classic *Discourse of Sallets,* published in 1699, "All should fall into their place like the notes in music, in which there should be nothing harsh or grating."

COOL GREENS

Corn Salad
Valerianella locusta

One of Turid's earliest memories is of trudging rubber-booted behind her father through stubble fields, looking for the fist-sized green rosettes that sprouted where the sheep had grazed. Around the patches of salad greens lay dark little sheep berries steaming in the cool spring air.

That story goes a long way toward explaining the name of this delicious salad plant, which neither tastes nor looks at all like corn. Known by more than a dozen names, the most common—corn salad, field salad, sheep salad and lamb's lettuce— all derive from the preference of this wild green for newly tilled, richly manured fields. The Italian name *douceur* refers to its remarkable sweetness, and the French name *mâche* stems from the word for fodder, suggesting the eagerness with which pastured animals seek out this delicacy.

Corn salad has a peripatetic history, popping in and out of salad bowls over 300 years. In the 17th century, it was a popular winter green in England, but it gradually fell out of favour until, by the 19th century, it was dismissed as a weed. William Cobbett, a vigorous proponent of the cottage garden, wrote, "This is a little, insignificant annual plant that some persons use in salads, though it can hardly be of any real use where lettuce seed is to be had."

Some gardeners still hold it in low esteem: one recent book sniffs, "Corn salad will never win any

Mâche salad with red onion, dressed with cider vinegar and yogurt.

prizes in a gourmet contest." But our experience is closer to that of French connoisseurs, who prize the succulent rosettes and have developed salads exclusively devoted to mâche. It is quite easy to grow, self-seeds if allowed to flower, stays sweet for months after the lettuces are bitter and is bright and crisp long after other greens have succumbed to frost. In fact, a little frost actually improves the flavour. With care, mâche can be overwintered. In France, the leaves are eaten during Lent, being the only fresh green to survive the February chill.

Corn salad was a staple in the walled herb gardens of European monasteries, where it sometimes went under the names milkgrass, cornell salad and potherb. Although abundant in iron, there does not seem to be any medicinal lore attached to the greens, other than John Evelyn's contention that "corn-sallet is loos'ning and refreshing."

Corn salad is very pretty and low-growing, with dark green, firm-textured, slightly spoon-shaped leaves that form an open rosette 4 to 6 inches across and 3 inches high. Individual plants look like lit-

tle hunter-green pom-poms, although the leaves stand more erect when competing with other greens in a densely sown mesclun. Indeed, it is leaf shape rather than flavour that seems to intrigue plant scientists: we tried several of the 10 or more varieties offered by seed companies, and while all tasted similar, they differed in appearance.

The very hardy 'Coquille de Louviers' (RE) has cupped leaves that hold dressing well; 'D'Etampes' (CG) sports prominent veins in its leaves; 'Piedmont' (CG) is a heat-resistant variety with long, pale leaves almost like miniature flour scoops; 'Verte à Coeur Plein' (RE) has round, smooth, intensely green leaves that bunch together in a very full heart; 'Blonde Shell' (NI), with its small but substantial shell-like leaves and silvery undersides, was Turid's favourite, especially for mescluns. 'Vit' (JO) was the most reliable; with all the others, germination was slow and erratic. There are also baby mâche such as the 2-inch-wide 'Elan' (CG). Although we have not yet seen it, we expect that North Americans will soon be able to buy seed for Italian corn salad (*Valerianella eriocarpa*), a North African plant which reportedly thrives in hot weather and whose 5-inch, slightly hairy leaves are even milder in flavour than *Valerianella locusta*.

If you allow an individual plant to mature, it sends up a central stem about 8 inches tall topped with delicate basketlike blooms in pale forget-me-not blue. Harvest some for mesclun salads, for they are as delicious as the leaves. After flowering, the rosette on the ground fades, losing its freshness, although it doesn't become bitter. Gather the corn salad seeds for next year, or allow the plant to self-seed—corn salad is a welcome volunteer in our gardens. In their early stages, the seedlings are quite distinctive and are not likely to be pulled as weeds.

Corn salad is a two-season crop, growing best in the cool weather of spring and fall. For a very early harvest, sow corn salad indoors. On March 1, we started some in 4-inch-deep flats, sowing the seeds an inch apart and setting the box on a bright windowsill; they need light but not heat to germinate and sprout in about 11 days. On April 1, we moved the box to the cold frame, and within three weeks, the little rosettes were ready to harvest like a mesclun or to transplant into the garden.

Corn salad seedlings are very frost-hardy. As soon as the ground is workable—about the time you plant peas—sow seeds directly in the salad garden. We plant our first corn salad outdoors around April 1. Plant the seeds a quarter-inch deep, one per inch, in rows a foot apart, or broadcast them in their own bed.

Although corn salad is a delicious addition to mescluns, the plant grows too slowly and sits too low to the ground to be broadcast with a mesclun mix. It is quickly overwhelmed by the looseleaf lettuces and fast-growing greens such as arugula and mustard spinach. We recommend broadcasting mâche in a strip near the mesclun patch and plucking the rosettes or individual leaves to toss into the salad bowl with the mesclun.

Corn salad prefers a very rich, well-manured soil and seems to do well intercropped with onions in a deep bed. Keep it well watered; it needs lots of moisture. Corn salad is especially slow-growing in early spring: planted early in April, the seeds took three weeks to sprout, and it was two months before the first good harvest. Rural gardeners should keep a close eye on seedlings: rabbits, groundhogs and mice prefer this green above all others, so it must be protected where necessary.

Gradually thin the plants to stand 4 inches apart. Within 45 to 60 days, depending on the cultivar, corn salad matures to rosettes 4 to 6 inches in di-

ameter. Harvest these by cutting close to the ground to keep the heads together, or gather one or two large leaves from the outside of each plant to encourage new growth for a prolonged harvest.

The planting on April 1 gave us corn salad until the plants sent up flower stalks in early July. In the heat of summer, growth becomes less vigorous, and the plants bolt. The leaves don't become bitter, but neither are they as sweet and succulent as in the cool seasons.

At the end of July, we planted corn salad for a second harvest. To protect the young seedlings from the midsummer sun, we seeded in boxes on the east side of the house, where they were shaded during the hottest part of the day. If sowing directly in the garden, protect with lattices or boughs, or plant in the lee of taller vegetables. Corn salad thrives at that time of year. Seeds needed only 11 days to sprout. By early September, after two months without the delicate greens, we once again had corn salad thinnings for the kitchen. In mid-October, after several hard frosts had killed off the lettuce, the corn salad was in its prime.

Some varieties are winter-hardy and provide an early harvest the following spring if plants become established before winter. Sow the corn salad a month before the first frost date, mulch heavily, and in April, remove the mulch so that the plants start growing again. We dutifully protected the rosettes with hay, fantasizing about the early-spring salads the catalogues promised. They did not, however, warn us about the deer. The animals pawed away our mulch and chewed all the corn salad to the ground. Next year, we will put a cold frame around the bed before we mulch. Even so, in this northern climate, we suspect that an equally early crop can be had with less effort and more assured success by starting seeds indoors in planter boxes and moving them to the cold frame.

In the kitchen, the low-growing, densely packed corn salad rosettes require thorough washing. Remove the outer ring of yellowish leaves, separate the inner leaves carefully, and swish in a sink of warm water to loosen all the sand particles. Handle carefully: leaves are easily bruised. Serve smaller rosettes on their own. Alone, corn salad has a subtle, nutty flavour that is best brought out with simply a little walnut oil and salt and coarsely ground pepper. The rosettes remain crisp and don't collapse like other looseleaf lettuces if they stand in vinegar for a while. Add rosettes or leaves in a fairly high proportion to mesclun salads, where they ameliorate the nip of arugula and mustard greens. Garnish salad plates with small whole rosettes.

In his *Dictionary of Cuisine*, Alexandre Dumas said that corn salad, which he deemed a herb, should be "eaten with beets, celery, white chicory and endive." Indeed, the classic French way of serving mâche is *Salade Lorette*, a mix of young leaves, thinly sliced, cold cooked beets and a julienned stalk of celery, dressed with a garlicky vinaigrette of lemon juice and olive oil.

Jekyll and Hyde Salad

Mediaeval chefs believed that hot greens should always be balanced by cool, the spicy leaves which stimulate the passions tempered with the leaves of soothing plants. In this salad, cool mâche and hot arugula are perfectly matched. The blue and yellow edible flowers are equally complementary.

	Equal parts mâche & young arugula leaves	
	Borage flowers & calendula petals	
1	egg yolk	1
3 Tbsp.	freshly squeezed lemon juice	45 mL
1 Tbsp.	dry white wine	15 mL
1	small green onion, chopped very fine	1
1 tsp.	Dijon mustard	5 mL
½ cup	olive oil	125 mL
¼ tsp.	salt	1 mL
	Freshly ground pepper	

Wash and spin or pat dry the leaves, and put them in the refrigerator to crisp. Whisk the egg yolk, adding the lemon juice and wine gradually. Whisk in the onion and mustard. Add the olive oil, whisking to an emulsion. Season with salt and pepper.

Makes enough dressing for 12 cups (3 L) of greens—a large salad bowl heaping full. (Because of the raw egg yolk, use the dressing immediately, and do not keep any leftovers.)

Miner's Lettuce
Montia perfoliata

Rarely mentioned in gardening books, miner's lettuce is one of the few salad greens native to this continent. Thought to have originated in Cuba, it is sometimes called Cuban spinach. In California, it was dubbed miner's lettuce because it was often the only green available to those who panned for gold in the arid West Coast hills. Lettuce and spinach both give the wrong impression of this dainty little plant, however: it is neither lush nor leafy, yet it is succulent enough for the salad bowl.

Miner's lettuce is a low-growing, hardy annual that has a unique look among salad plants. The first leaves are lance-shaped at the end of long, slender leaf stalks. In Germany, these are harvested as a seedling greenhouse crop, and the plant is cut back before true leaves develop. The second leaves have even longer petioles that rise to about 6 inches from a common base. Balanced at the tip of each stalk is a ''collar'' comprising two opposite leaves fused together so that they wrap around the flowering stalk like a green tissue around the bouquet of dainty white flowers which bloom inside. The leaves, although not prolific, are thick and tender, typical of the related purslanes and portulacas that survive so well in dry regions.

Miner's lettuce grows wild from British Columbia to Mexico and east to North Dakota. Seeds are not widely available, although a few seed houses, such as The Cook's Garden and Redwood City, carry them. You may find them listed as 'Claytonia.'

Sow the seeds in spring as soon as the soil is workable. In a shady bed prepared as for cutting lettuces, broadcast the small seeds, cover lightly, rake in, and press down the soil with the back of the rake. Water well. We prefer to broadcast miner's lettuce as part of a mesclun mix, where it benefits from the protection and moist soil that come with having so many close neighbours.

Seeds sprout within 11 days. You can thin broadcast plants to stand 6 inches apart, but we leave them to grow thickly into a ''meadow'' for shearing. Begin harvesting about five weeks after sowing, picking a few leaves from each plant or cutting the whole plant to within an inch of the ground with scissors. After shearing, we water the bed well and fertilize it so that it resprouts. Properly cared for, miner's lettuce yields two or three cuttings as a cut-and-come-again crop, never becoming bitter.

Flowering does not hamper the harvest at all. Plants broadcast on April 15 began to flower in early June, but we continued to add miner's lettuce to our salads until early July. This salad green grows best as a spring and fall crop, but you can sow it in succession throughout the growing season if the garden bed lies in partial shade. By midsummer, however, the leaves of our early-spring crop become leathery, and we turn to other greens until the fall crop is ready.

Wash miner's lettuce very gently, and pat the delicate plant dry before using. The leafy cups of flowers are very attractive mixed with darker greens, although they add little flavour. The na-

tives of the Pacific Coast reportedly found the wild variety so bland that they seasoned the leaves by piling them over ants' nests. The disturbed insects sprayed the greens with formic acid, giving them a little more bite. Lacking ants' nests, mix miner's lettuce with watercress, red mustard or other spicy greens.

Although we eat this dainty green most often as part of a mesclun salad, we occasionally indulge in a spring salad composed entirely of miner's lettuce, complete with white flowers and dressed with a delicate yogurt vinaigrette (page 139).

Purslane
Portulaca oleracea

Purslane, said 19th-century radical William Cobbett, is ''a mischievous weed that Frenchmen and pigs eat when they can get nothing else.'' Then, lead us to the Parisians and the swine, for purslane is a delight, a thick, juicy, leafy green as delectable and as eagerly awaited as 'Sugar Snap' peas.

Purslane is a native of eastern India, where it is eaten raw, boiled or pickled—the seeds can even be ground for bread—but the plant now also grows wild throughout the temperate world. It is gathered and eaten everywhere except North America, where most gardeners regard the invasive little spreader with loathing: they would no sooner introduce it to the garden than they would burdock. The prejudice is deeply rooted. Samuel de Champlain, one familiar with its delights, was bewildered by the attitude of natives on the coast of Maine to purslane, ''which grows in large quantities among the Indian corn and of which they take no more account than weeds.''

Such prejudice is self-defeating, however, for cultivated purslane differs markedly from its undomesticated cousin. The wild plant is low-growing, spreading like frost on a windowpane, its ruby-red stems studded with small, round, green leaves that are almost as meaty as lima beans. Cultivated purslane grows upright in low bushes, producing large, pale, greenish yellow leaves with silvery undersides. The plant looks almost aquatic. Perhaps this is where it gets its common name, Indian cress, a name less likely to dissuade gardeners from growing this wonderful salad plant.

Cultivated purslane exists in both a green and a golden form, although we have grown only the latter—'Goldgelber' from The Cook's Garden. The green variety apparently grows taller, with thinner leaves; the golden has thick leaves the size of quarters. It is considered somewhat less hardy than

the green and is not really golden but a very pale yellow-green, its delicate colour the result of a thicker epidermis rather than weaker colouring. Purslane's flavour is bland, with a slight acidity, like snow peas infused with lemon. (The cultivated variety lacks the bite of wild purslane.)

Not surprisingly, considering its succulence and its acidity, purslane is 90 percent water and very high in vitamin C—a cup of leaves contains more than an equivalent amount of orange juice. It is also relatively high in riboflavin, vitamin A and iron. John Evelyn does not exaggerate when he describes purslane as ''being eminently moist and cooling, quickens Appetite, asswages Thirst, and is very profitable for hot and Bilious tempers, as well as Sanguine, and generally entertain'd in all our *Sallets*, mingled with the hotter herbs.''

Heat- and drought-resistant, purslane thrives in the hottest garden situation. When corn salad and miner's lettuce are past their prime, purslane takes over, bringing continued mildness to the salad bowl. Only a cold, wet summer transforms it into a miserable, slug-infested plant.

Do not succession-sow this green. Plant it once in late spring for a continuous summer harvest. The seed is tiny and should be broadcast, but it grows too slowly to compete well as part of a mesclun. Instead, broadcast purslane in a bed of its own, and shear it as a cut-and-come-again to add to the mesclun salad. Because it is so decorative, it is an ideal edible ground cover to forestall erosion at the edge of raised beds.

Since purslane likes the sun, sow it in a bright, south-facing bed, on light, well-drained soil. In cold weather, purslane seedlings damp off easily, so don't plant it too early. Wait until the soil is warm and the weather is settled, or start seeds indoors in late spring, harvesting the purslane as a cut-and-come-again right in the box or transplanting the seedlings to the garden after the cool nights have passed. The seedlings can be spot-planted throughout a mesclun that has developed some bald patches. You can also sow in cold frames or under cloches, uncovering the plants after the weather warms.

Purslane can be picked within a month after planting, but it typically needs about 60 days to mature. Turid sows her purslane outdoors around May 20, thickly broadcasting the seed in a bed and covering it very lightly with soil. A week later, tiny sprouts appear. Two weeks after sowing, she thins the plants to 2 inches apart and fertilizes the bed lightly with fish emulsion or manure tea. The purslane begins to branch out. At the end of June, when the plant is about 4 inches

Nasturtium leaves and purslane rosettes with decorative scarlet runner flowers.

little round leaves spreading horizontally look like ballerinas with twirling skirts.''

Pick the purslane only as needed, since it deteriorates rapidly. Pick tender green rosettes, using both the leaves and the stems, which resemble bean sprouts in texture. Purslane is a wonderful complement to green salads, but it can also become a salad on its own. Either way, it adds a distinctive crunch and pale green colour to a meal. We like it tossed with dark green spinach or corn salad leaves dressed with a creamy mustard-yogurt dressing. Fruit goes especially well with its lemony taste. Try this *salade composée*, a mixed salad composed of several disparate elements, creatively combined on individual serving plates. Lightly brush each plate with walnut oil, and arrange purslane with nectarine sections over the top. Sprinkle with a teaspoon (5 mL) of walnut oil and 10 hazelnuts thinly sliced and blended with four ground coriander seeds.

Baqli

Purslane has a fine international standing—Mexican cooks call it *verdolaga*; the Chinese, who know it as *carti-choy*, use it in stir-fry dishes; to the French, it is *pourpier*—but only in Middle Eastern cookbooks are you likely to find recipes for purslane salads. This is a variation of the Lebanese *Slatat al-Farfhin*, which calls for wild purslane gathered first thing in the morning.

4 cups	loosely packed purslane	1 L
1	small onion, chopped	1
1	tomato and/or cucumber, peeled & diced (optional)	1
1	clove garlic	1
	Pinch of coarse salt	
¼ cup	freshly squeezed lemon juice	50 mL
¼ cup	olive oil	50 mL

Wash and drain the purslane. Add onion and tomato or cucumber, if desired. Mash garlic clove in salt, whisk in lemon juice, then oil. Add dressing to salad, then toss lightly. The simple lemon vinaigrette complements the purslane perfectly. It may be too sour for some tastes. If so, reduce the lemon juice, or replace half of the juice with mild vinegar and stir in a little honey.

SPINACH GREENS

Once called the "prince of vegetables," spinach has suffered a reversal of reputation over the past few

tall and the individual leaves are an inch in diameter, she takes the first harvest, shearing the purslane down to an inch or two, from which it re-sprouts in even bushier growth. At the same time, she thins the plants to stand 4 inches apart.

Purslane is remarkably healthy and pest-free, although gardeners with heavy soil and cool, wet summers may experience some problems with slugs. Plants that are too close together or too wet may also develop smoulder, a fungal disease.

By mid-August, after two or three harvests, the plant becomes determined to build buds. Turid digs up most of the bed but leaves some plants to set flowers, nondescript little yellow buds that, like other portulacas, open only in the sun. Once the little flowers appear, purslane loses its fresh flavour and toughens.

"I love this plant in my garden and in my salad," says Turid. "The taste is unlike anything else, and the way it grows is so beautiful and unique. The

Malabar spinach, mixed greens and a tangy sprig of mountain spinach, with Chez Piggy's Poppy Seed Dressing.

hundred years. Even the cartoon character Popeye has not restored it to a place of honour at the dinner table. Spinach might have sent Popeye's biceps popping, but the slimy goo gushing from the can did little to improve the vegetable's image.

The problem, in our view, lies not with the plant but with the chef; if spinach is cooked, it should be steamed only in its own dew. Spinach is at its best as a salad plant, and only those who eat tender, young, fresh-picked leaves can know what a succulent, flavourful green spinach can be.

True spinach (*Spinacia oleracea*) is something of a finicky garden guest. Unless its particular soil and climate needs are met precisely, it bolts, grows bitter or fails to germinate altogether. As a result, a number of spinach lookalikes are cultivated in gardens around the world. Orach, New Zealand spinach, malabar spinach and spinach beet are all eaten like spinach but improve on the original by being easy to cultivate, perennial or particularly heat-resistant. Plucked when young and tender, the leaves of any of these plants make a nutritious,

beautiful, tasty addition to a mixed green salad.

Spinach itself grows well only in the cool spring and fall growing seasons. In high summer, when it goes to seed, heat-loving orach and New Zealand spinach replace it. Gardeners with sandy soil have better luck with New Zealand spinach, and those with limited space appreciate the climbing malabar spinach. But malabar cannot be grown in a mesclun, and orach is too slow to keep up with other greens; spinach beet is as good as or better than true spinach when sown in the mesclun bed.

Spinach
Spinacia oleracea

Spinach is a member of the goosefoot family, Chenopodiaceae, which includes the common garden weed lamb's quarters. Although it is native to Persia, one of the earliest references to spinach is in a list of gifts sent to the Chinese by the King of Nepal in 647 A.D. Apparently, the Moors introduced it to the West by way of Spain. For a long

time, it was known in Europe as *olus Hispanicum*, the Spanish vegetable.

Arab physicians used spinach in their pharmacopoeia, but it was also a common food. The 16th-century herbalist John Gerard cultivated it in his famous garden in Holborn, England, noting in his *Herbal* that spinach was a medicinal potherb "used in sallades when it is young and tender."

Indeed, as a food, spinach is good medicine. Its extremely high concentration of carotenoids, including beta carotene, mark it as a promising antidote to cancer. Italian scientists believe spinach is a powerful block to the formation of carcinogenic nitrosamine, and Japanese research shows that it significantly lowers blood-cholesterol levels in test animals. Aside from its high vitamin A content, spinach is a good source of iron, potassium, thiamine, riboflavin and vitamin C. It has almost as much water as lettuce but three times the protein. Unfortunately, it is also extremely high in sodium—126 milligrams per cup.

There are two types of spinach, identified by

the texture of the seed. Rough-seeded, or prickly, spinach (also called winter spinach) is most commonly grown in North America, but the smooth-seeded, or round-leafed, spinach is more common in Europe and is considered by many to be superior, because it grows in thicker, more compact tufts. Seed for both types is now available in North America, although catalogues rarely indicate which is which. If you buy from specialty seed houses, the Latin name *Spinacia oleracea* var. *inermis* indicates that the variety is smooth-seeded. For example, the widely available 'Bloomsdale Long Standing' and 'America' (DO) are smooth-seeded. 'Munsterlander' and 'Sohsho,' both from Redwood City (RE), are rough-seeded.

Spinach is a fast-growing annual whose first grasslike sprouts are swiftly followed by a rosette of broad, arrow-shaped leaves that may be savoyed or smooth, according to the variety. We sow ours outside the first week of April; the seedlings are up in about two weeks. The plant matures in six weeks and, depending on conditions and cultivar, soon sends up a tall spike of tiny flowers. By mid-June, the plants are in bud, on their way out of the garden. Limit spinach, therefore, to the spring and fall growing seasons, planting it from early April to mid-May and again from late July to late August. It is hardly worth bothering about during the Dog Days of summer, when it bolts almost as soon as it is up.

Spinach needs cool weather, relatively short days, plenty of moisture and adequate elbowroom. It grows best in sun or partial shade, in a bed with rich, moist soil, where it can develop quickly and yield a good crop of leaves before going to seed. Prepare the bed by digging in manure deeply. Spinach likes a pH of 6.5 to 6.7; it won't thrive if the soil is below 6.5, yet over 6.7, a manganese deficiency may develop. If your soil is light and sandy, grow New Zealand spinach instead.

Spinach seedlings are very hardy. If beds are prepared and mulched in the fall, seed can be sown as early as six weeks before the last spring frost. Pull back the mulch, warm the soil with clear plastic for a few days, then sow the seeds thinly, dropping them about an inch apart over a small bed or in shallow furrows 15 to 20 inches apart, covering them with half an inch of soil. When the seedlings are an inch tall, thin them to stand 4 inches apart, adding the thinnings to salads. Succession-sow spinach every two weeks until early June.

As the weather warms, sow spinach between tall crops such as brassicas or in the lee of an asparagus hedge or under lattices: partial shade helps forestall bolting and bitterness. (Spinach

and beans are said to be good companion crops.) It is a good idea to mulch around the plants to retain moisture and keep the soil cool.

Forget spinach in July, but by mid-August, start sowing again as the weather cools. Spinach sown in early September and protected under heavy straw or fern mulch winters over to the following spring, treating gardeners to fresh greens a few weeks after the mulch is removed.

Spinach also does well broadcast densely in its own bed or mixed in a mesclun. The profusion of plants keeps the soil cool and moist, essential for good spinach. Spinach hates to be crowded, but thinning young plants to 2 inches apart produces a low meadow of cutting spinach.

Harvest spinach greens when there are five or six leaves on the plant, six to eight weeks after sowing, depending on the climate. Don't twist off the leaves: break or cut them cleanly, plucking the outside growth while they are still young and tender to encourage continual harvests. In summer, you can harvest up to half the leaves of a plant without harming it. If you cut the whole plant close to the ground, it resprouts readily for a second harvest.

Spinach is prone to downy mildew and blight, so select disease-resistant strains like 'Melody,' and keep an eye out for yellowing or curling leaves. Spinach leaf miner, aphids and nematodes can be a problem but more often affect fall crops.

For those without adequate supplies of compost or manure, garden writer Gertrude Franck recommends using spinach as instant compost. She sows an early crop, cuts the leaves to rot where they fall and allows the roots to disintegrate underground. When the spinach is completely rotted, she cultivates and plants her garden seeds.

Like all low-growing greens, spinach must be washed carefully. The old custom of washing spinach in seven waters is extreme, but two or three baths is a good idea, especially for savoyed leaves. Fill a sink with warm water, swish the leaves around, drain, pat dry and store in a perforated plastic bag in the refrigerator for a day or two only.

Because spinach tastes somewhat "earthy" and has fairly stout, fleshy leaves, it can stand strong-flavoured dressings and even ones that are served hot. My family's favourite whole-meal salad is a bowl of spinach topped with sliced mushrooms, green onions and thin strips of red peppers, tossed with a hot dressing made by sautéing a quarter of a pound (125 g) of bacon until crisp and mixing it with a quarter of a cup (50 mL) of reserved fat, a third of a cup (75 mL) each of cider vinegar and water or beef broth and a pinch each of cel-

ery salt and sugar. Serve immediately, sprinkled generously with grated cheese.

During some parts of the season, there will be more spinach in the garden than even a spinach fanatic can consume. Luckily, spinach is one of the few garden greens that freeze well. Pick large leaves, blanch a few at a time just till they wilt (about 2 minutes), squeeze them dry, and freeze them, either whole or chopped, in plastic bags. They can be used later to make an excellent Middle Eastern cooked spinach salad, *Borani Esfanaj*. Thaw a pound (500 g) of spinach and drain it. In a tablespoon (15 mL) of olive oil, sauté an onion lightly, toss with the spinach, then chill. Strain two cups (500 mL) of yogurt through cheesecloth an hour, then mix in two cloves of crushed garlic, a quarter of a cup (50 mL) of walnuts and freshly ground pepper to taste. Chill the yogurt mixture, and just before serving, mix the yogurt and spinach together, garnish with mint leaves and serve as a salad appetizer with pita triangles.

Chez Piggy's Poppy Seed Dressing

Raw spinach salad is virtually unknown in Germany. Turid was first introduced to the green leaves tossed with white mushrooms in a slightly sweet vinaigrette. This is how it is served at our favourite local restaurant, where the chefs generously share their recipes.

¾ cup	canola oil	175 mL
¼ cup	cider vinegar	50 mL
2 Tbsp.	lemon juice	30 mL
2 tsp.	sugar	10 mL
2 Tbsp.	honey	30 mL
2 Tbsp.	each sesame seeds, poppy seeds & chopped scallions Salt & freshly ground pepper to taste	30 mL

Whisk oil, vinegar and lemon juice together. Add the sweeteners and continue to whisk. Add seeds, scallions and salt and pepper. This is especially good drizzled over spinach garnished with mushrooms and slivered red peppers. Crumble feta cheese on top for a whole-meal salad.

Mountain Spinach, Orach
Atriplex hortensis

This ancient annual is thought by some to be the oldest cultivated plant. The Greeks and Romans

A mesclun mix: mustard spinach, tendergreen, mizuna, miner's lettuce, upland cress and orach.

ate it boiled, and it has been popular in England from the early 16th century. It has long since naturalized along North American seacoasts, where it is sometimes called saltbush because of its preference for brackish waters. For years, orach has been cultivated and eaten under the common names French spinach and mountain spinach, yet it has failed to make a hit here with salad fanciers. Few seed houses offer it, and those that do often list it with the herbs.

That is not entirely surprising. Orach is beautiful, tender and mild when very young, but the leaves quickly become tough and strong-tasting. It is worth growing because it is so heat- and drought-resistant and it adds a hearty, colourful touch to a salad, but plant it only as a midseason cut-and-come-again.

There are three varieties of orach: white or yellow (the type usually grown in France), green and red, a highly ornamental variety. (The Cook's Garden sells all three.) All are erect, branching annuals that grow up to 6 feet tall if allowed to mature. The

leaves are like wavy-edged lances sitting at the end of long petioles. The young leaves are pearly grey with a silvery sheen not unlike lamb's quarters. The texture is chewy and slightly mucilaginous with a grassy, milky flavour. 'Red Orach' (BL, NI) is especially attractive, both in the garden and on the table. The square stem, red striped with pale green, tastes like Swiss chard.

For salads, grow orach in rich, moist, slightly alkaline soil. Start early indoors, or sow directly in the garden late in the spring when the soil is warm. Orach is too slow-growing to be part of a mesclun mix. Instead, broadcast orach seed in strips or beds, covering with half an inch of soil. The plants sprout in about 10 days, although erratically in our gardens. Thin gradually to about 2 or 3 inches apart, and after six weeks, when the plants are a few inches tall, harvest by shearing as you would a mesclun bed. To use as a salad green, harvest orach before it is 6 inches tall.

Give orach about 2 feet of growing room in all directions. Harvest young leaves as long as they

are sweet and tender, but remember to pinch out the main stem to encourage bushiness and remove flower heads to promote leaf growth. Once the weather becomes hot and dry, the plant quickly runs to seed and the leaves become unpalatable. But because red orach is so decorative—backlit by the sun, it glows with the colours of a sunset— let one or two plants mature in the salad garden.

Culpeper wrote, "It is a herb so innocent that it may be eaten in the leaf salad," and indeed, it has not only a pleasant flavour but an intense red colour that adds a brilliant highlight to the mesclun salads of early summer. It is generally too textured to be eaten on its own, but it combines beautifully with mâche. Add some blue violets or pink dianthus for colour. Serve with a nut oil/lemon juice vinaigrette.

New Zealand Spinach
Tetragonia tetragonioides

New Zealand spinach has the distinction of being the only potherb that Europeans derived from "down under." Sir Joseph Banks, the botanist on Cook's 1770 voyage to New Zealand, discovered the green plant growing at the edge of forests in sandy, brushy land. Cook's crew ate it daily, staving off scurvy; Banks took seeds back to England, planting them in Kew Gardens. For years, this spinach was grown in England as a houseplant, but eventually, it moved outdoors, where gardeners discovered that it tasted good and didn't bolt in the heat of summer like conventional spinach. It was cultivated commercially in southern France as a hot-weather spinach substitute but otherwise did not invade market gardens. As a result, the type grown today is virtually the same as the wild spinach that Cook's crew harvested more than two centuries ago.

A semihardy annual, New Zealand spinach has fleshy, slightly savoyed leaves about a third the size of those of spinach, in a subdued dusky green rather than the typical deep, vibrant hue. This spinach grows slowly, spreading to 3 or 4 feet in width and only a foot in height. It has a mild flavour but a tougher texture than true spinach. Nutritionally, it contains somewhat less iron than spinach but a similar quantity of vitamins and minerals. While not widely available, seed is sold by Nichols, Johnny's, Blüm and Stokes.

Grow New Zealand spinach as a midseason crop: it can't take the cold but doesn't object to heat. As long as there is enough moisture, it provides a harvest of mild-tasting greens all summer. Prepare a bed in full sun or dappled shade. Sow the seed in May after the last frost, at the same time you plant early corn. As my neighbour used to say, the soil should be warm to the touch of a bare bum. The seed is a hard, nutlike fruit that germinates very slowly. Scarify or soak it overnight before sowing. For a salad ground cover, sow the seed thinly 2 inches apart in a bed or in rows 1 to 2 feet apart. Thin the seedlings to 12 inches. To get a head start, we planted ours indoors on April 21 and transplanted the seedlings to the garden in mid-June, setting the plants along the edge of the raised beds as erosion control.

About eight weeks after sowing, harvest the first leaves, pinching a few young stems from the base of each plant. Discard the stalks and use only the leaves. Pruning the young plant back like this encourages new growth. A single sowing lasts throughout the summer if you shear it periodically in cut-and-come-again fashion. Remember to give it a generous soaking of water now and again, and watch for root aphids.

When grown quickly and harvested young, New Zealand spinach is refreshing. But because of its leathery texture, it is best used as a stimulating minor ingredient in a mixed green salad or steamed for a cooked spinach salad (see page 37).

Malabar Spinach
Basella spp

A native of the East Indies, this slow-growing plant produces spinachlike leaves on long, creeping stems 4 to 6 feet long. Trained up a fence or trellis, the plant yields a prolific, delicious spinach harvest in very limited space. There are both green (*Basella alba*) and red (*B. rubra*) varieties of malabar spinach, often mixed together in the seed packages, since except for colour, the plants are identical.

According to the 1885 edition of *The Vegetable Garden*, there was apparently another species, *B. cordifolia*, which was introduced to France from China in 1839. Called 'Very Broad-leaved Chinese Malabar Nightshade,' it was proclaimed superior to the other two, because its leaves were both larger and more abundant. Unfortunately, the seed does not seem to be available now. Even regular malabar is relatively hard to find. We grow 'Malabar Climbing Spinach' from Nichols; only a few other seed houses offer it, such as Park, Redwood City and Blüm.

Though in fact a biennial, malabar spinach is cultivated in the north as an annual. Because it is so slow-growing, you should start seeds indoors in peat pots six to eight weeks before the last frost. The seeds are very tough, so they must be soaked or scarified before planting. When thinning to the sturdiest plant per pot, be sure to note the colour of the stem and keep a few plants of each type. Transplant the hardened-off seedlings into the salad garden after all chance of frost has passed, setting them a foot apart in a bed with afternoon shade.

Planted on March 26, our malabar spinach was only 4 inches tall when we transplanted it into the garden at the end of May, but when the weather eventually warmed, it began to grow much more enthusiastically, reaching 3 feet by late August. The plant yields throughout the summer with little help except occasional waterings and doses of fertilizer. It is very frost-tender, easily destroyed by the first below-freezing night.

In Canadian gardens, malabar spinach is unlikely to reach the impressive 6-foot height promised by California-based catalogues, but it has nevertheless become our favourite midsummer spinach substitute. Some of the leaves are as big as an outstretched hand, very fleshy, with a mild flavour and a texture somewhat like that of purslane. Beautiful mixed with light-coloured greens, it is equally attractive served on its own.

Malabar Spinach Salad

Since the Malabar coast lies at the southwestern tip of India, it seems appropriate to include an Indian salad. This recipe gets its distinctive flavour from asafetida, a dried gum resin available in Indian stores.

3 cups	chopped spinach	750 mL
3 Tbsp.	coarsely grated unsweetened coconut, preferably fresh	45 mL
3 Tbsp.	chopped roasted peanuts	45 mL
½ tsp.	cumin seed	2 mL
	Pinch asafetida	
1 Tbsp.	soy oil	15 mL
1½ tsp.	lemon juice	7 mL
¼ tsp.	each salt & sugar	1 mL

Combine spinach, coconut and peanuts in a salad bowl. Heat cumin in oil until the seeds change colour. Add asafetida, then remove from heat. Whisk in the remaining ingredients, cool, whisk again, and pour over the salad.

Perpetual Spinach
Beta vulgaris (Cicla Group)

Sometimes called sea spinach because it grows profusely near the ocean, this hardy biennial is a type of chard whose large, dark, fleshy leaves are eaten raw in salads. Chard and beetroot are the results of two extremes of selection from the same species, *Beta vulgaris*. "Leaf beet," or perpetual spinach, is a primitive form between the two. The young leaves of chard, beet and perpetual spinach are all delicious raw in salads, but 'Perpetual Spinach' (CG) has been developed specifically for this purpose. Its leaves are somewhat coarser in flavour and texture than spinach, but it produces an abundant, virtually trouble-free crop that can be harvested over a longer period than can spinach: this so-called spinach beet seldom runs to seed until its life cycle is completed late the following spring.

In the fall, prepare a bed liberally dressed with manure or compost. In midspring, sow the seed thinly half an inch deep in rows 15 inches apart. Thin the seedlings to a foot apart, and when they are growing strongly, fertilize. Keep the soil continuously moist. Harvest the greens by picking the outside leaves of the plants before they become too large. Frequent small harvests encourage an ongoing crop all summer. If the plant is allowed to mature, however, the leaves become coarse. Even when the leaves are young, the flavour is stronger than that of true spinach.

Perpetual spinach is perhaps best grown as a cut-and-come-again. All three forms of *Beta vulgaris* —chard, beet and perpetual spinach—sprout so easily from direct seeding that they are perfect in mescluns from early May on. It is certainly our first choice spinach for a midseason mesclun; 'Erbette' (CG) puts on fast, vigorous growth throughout the hottest part of the growing season. As well as mixing perpetual spinach into the mesclun, we broadcast seeds in strips in early May, thinning them to 2 inches apart and mowing them like a meadow for June salads. One sowing provided endless harvests. Sow again in late July for an autumn harvest of fresh young greens.

Wash and spin-dry the leaves, adding whole young leaves, chiffonaded older leaves and thinly sliced stems to mixed green salads.

HOT GREENS

Arugula
Eruca sativa

I once overheard a curious conversation in a little Toronto café, one of those places where the staff wears Birkenstocks and exotic menu items are offered without translation or explanation.

"Do you like arugula?" a woman asked, lifting a forkful of leafy green salad to her mouth.

"Never been there," her companion replied suavely, "but I was in Martinique last winter, and it was awesome."

Like corn salad, arugula is an old-fashioned semihardy annual that is making a comeback, one of a handful of garden greens that have been "discovered" by California gourmets. And rightly so. Its limited appearance in seed catalogues, we suspect, is not owing to the shortcomings of the plant but rather to inadequate advice on how best to grow and harvest it. Cultivated incorrectly, arugula tastes as rank as the vilest weed, but given water and picked at its prime, it is indispensable in the spring and autumn salad bowl.

Native to the Mediterranean and western Asia, arugula represents yet another branch of the mustard family Cruciferae. Its name, which admittedly sounds like a Caribbean island, is derived from the Italian *ruca* or *rucula*. The peppery green is also sometimes known as Italian cress, partly because of its taste but also because, in

Mixed greens with yellow pear tomatoes.

physical appearance, it closely resembles garden cress. For centuries, however, arugula has come to the table as rocket, pronounced not like a spaceship but like its French name, *roquette*. Rocket may not be as romantic or exotic a name as arugula, but it is evocative of both the taste and the growth habit of this salad plant: it shoots up fast, provides a burst of scrumptious greens, then, before you know it, is over. Its flavour has a similar trajectory, moving quickly past sweet and spicy to unbearably hot. Its name alone should remind you to taste this little green before you add it to a salad.

Rocket has been grown in North America for 350 years: it was on a list of seeds bought from Robert Hill, grocer, by John Winthrop Jr. in 1631. But it has long been cultivated and gathered wild in Europe, where it was much prized—and denounced —for its association with pleasure. Virgil, a Roman who wrote his poem *The Salad* during Christ's lifetime, refers to rocket greens as "foul provocatives of lust." In 1578, Dodoens' *A Niewe Herball* takes the same line: "The use thereof stirreth up bodily pleasure, especially of the seed." One of the so-called hot seeds, "it must never be eaten alone, but alwaies with lettuce or purcelaine." By the early 19th century, according to the 1807 *Botanist's Dictionary*, arugula was "little known, having been long rejected on account of its strong ungrateful smell," although one suspects its fall from grace had something to do with its reputation for arousing passion.

John Evelyn, writing during the less prudish 17th

century, includes arugula in his list of essential salad ingredients. It adds a unique touch to the salad garden and the salad bowl. One seed catalogue describes its taste as having "the same punch as green onions but without their aftertaste." To us, the taste seems spicy, nutty, more like horseradish mixed with hazelnuts. Quite apart from its wonderful flavour, however, arugula is rich in vitamin C and minerals, giving a plain lettuce salad a healthy boost.

Arugula is one of the least picky plants in the garden. Essentially a cool-weather plant, it grows well in early spring and late fall, but if given light afternoon shade, it also produces during midsummer. It grows in almost any soil and germinates even during the coldest, wettest spring, bursting out of the ground within five days of sowing. Broadcast the seed in deeply spaded soil as soon as the ground is workable, or plant arugula as you would corn salad, a quarter-inch deep in rows a foot apart. Thin the seedlings to 4 or 5 inches apart. Keep them well watered, since dryness intensifies the spiciness. Within four weeks, when the plants are a couple of inches high, they can be harvested. John Evelyn declared 300 years ago that the young leaves immediately following the seedling stage are the best for the salad bowl, and we agree.

Arugula grows close to the ground as a rosette of deeply lobed leaves, bluish green offset by a very distinct white middle vein. If thinned, each rosette spreads to about 10 inches, but thickly broadcast, the leaves reach up. These first leaves can be harvested as a cut-and-come-again crop, but don't let them grow higher than 6 inches. Some gardeners report up to five harvests from a single patch, but the most we ever get is three. After that, the leaves taste unpleasantly bitter.

Rigorously cutting back the plant will slow it down—as will a little shade—but eventually, arugula sends up a branching central flower stalk 3 feet tall, studded with deep green leaves even more pungent than the rosette. About two months after seeding, the plant sets little four-petalled flowers, white with pronounced purple veins. The leaves of the plant are then too hot to be used as anything but a herb. The blossoms and light green buds, however, are delicately spicy. The seedpods, when they appear, are reminiscent of mustard: long, slender and smooth, with a nutty flavour. After the leaves are unusable, we gather unripe seedpods to add nutty flavour and crunch to late-spring salads.

Seeds from the first crop can also be used for subsequent sowings, which continue until late August. Arugula proved quite frost-hardy, surviving in the garden after several hard frosts. It can per-

Arugula underplanted with mild-tasting purslane.

haps be overwintered if protected, although the deer prevented us from verifying the claim.

Arugula often self-seeds, and Turid always welcomes the volunteers that escape from the bed. Together with borage, lovage, dill and chives, arugula is one of the five herbs Turid adds to her daily salads, wherever she lives. "This little white crucifer blossom is so nice in an annual border. The plant is lofty and blooms at the same time as corn poppies. Mature plants last until after the frost. We have always

grown it—in Arizona, Costa Rica and Canada."

Arugula is one of the five ingredients in the traditional Mesclun Niçoise, which also includes curly endive, cutting chicory, dandelion and broad-leaf cress. Arugula is so fast-growing and undemanding that we add it to all our mesclun mixes, albeit in small proportions because of its spicy taste. In early-spring mixes, five parts arugula to five parts of any other greens is not overpowering, but such a mix is unthinkable later in the summer, when

arugula's flavour is more intense. If it becomes too aggressive, pull it out and continue to harvest the remaining greens.

Arugula may take some getting used to. Those who like it unflinchingly use it solo. Italian restaurants often serve it alone with a strong garlicky vinaigrette. In the spring, try tossing three cups (750 mL) of arugula with a teaspoon (5 mL) of shallots, a cup (250 mL) of berries and a vinaigrette of 1 ½ tablespoons (22 mL) of balsamic

41

vinegar and a tablespoon (15 mL) of olive oil. In the fall, it goes well with rich-flavoured tomatoes and a balsamic vinaigrette or the sun-dried tomato dressing on page 105. In the summer, you can add a chopped leaf or two of arugula to the salad bowl as a substitute for watercress.

Bakoola

Moroccans make a salad with arugula gathered wild from the fields and cooked. In this adaptation, the greens are raw, but the original intent—matching hot greens with a hot sauce—remains intact. A mortar and pestle is traditional, but a food processor speeds the dressing to the table.

4 cups	arugula	1 L
1	small, dried red chile	1
½ tsp.	salt	2 mL
5	small cloves garlic	5
½ cup	chopped coriander	125 mL
½ cup	chopped parsley	125 mL
5 Tbsp.	extra-virgin olive oil	75 mL
1 tsp.	paprika	5 mL
1 tsp.	ground cumin	5 mL
	Juice of two limes	

Wash and spin-dry the arugula. Crisp in the refrigerator. Pound the chile and salt with the garlic using a large mortar and pestle. Add the coriander and parsley, and pound to a paste. Heat a tablespoon (15 mL) of oil, and cook the paprika and cumin briefly to bring out the flavour. Add the herb paste and lime juice, cover and cook for 5 minutes. Whisk in remaining oil. Cool and toss with the arugula, adding only enough to blend well with the greens.

THE CRESSES

The cresses belong to a group of plants known as the wild potherbs, keeping company with purslane, sorrel, lamb's quarters, field mustard, chicory, dandelion and Canadian thistle, or wild cardoon. Cresses are among the oldest salad plants known, cultivated in the Far East and the Near East and moving westward to the Mediterranean, where the little low-growing greens were considered a brain stimulant. In ancient Greece, a mother would likely be heard scolding a sluggish child, "Eat cress!"—an admonishment that seems more practical than "Perk up!" The Greeks regarded cress as a cure for insanity, and it was always served at banquets as an antidote to drunkenness. Although it was collected from the wild for centuries, it had become a staple in monastery gardens by the Middle Ages, its high vitamin and mineral content prized for medicinal purposes. John Gerard, however, described it as a "sallade herbe" to be eaten with tarragon and rocket. Eating a cress salad puts you in good company: its first menu appearance is in the 14th century when Taillevent, chef to Charles VI of France, served it between the fourth and fifth courses "alone, to refresh the mouth."

It is often uncertain which cress is being described in archival records, since there are hundreds of varieties of the nippy green. The cresses most commonly cultivated and eaten in salads are all members of the mustard family: garden cress (*Lepidium sativum*), a quick-growing, hardy, upright annual; upland cress (*Barbarea verna*), a hardy biennial; and watercress (*Nasturtium officinale*), a spreading perennial that prefers to bathe its roots in clear-flowing streams.

The cresses share the sharp, pungent taste and a preference for cool conditions typical of the mustards. Watercress and upland cress are virtually interchangeable in flavour, so for those without a handy stream, upland cress is a viable alternative. Garden cress is slightly hotter but does extremely well as a cut-and-come-again plant and is therefore ideal in a mesclun. All the cresses become unbearably spicy and go to seed quickly in hot weather, but for cooks who cannot tolerate onions or who are trying to cut down on salt, cress adds the requisite bite to a salad.

Garden Cress
Lepidium sativum

Garden cress, also known as peppergrass, or pepper cress, is native to Persia but is now naturalized around the world as a weed. The garden cresses are such a large group that they can be subdivided again into four basic types: common cress, curled cress, broadleaf cress and golden cress. Common cress has slightly serrated leaves, curled cress has deeply serrated leaves much like chervil—it makes the prettiest garnish—and broadleaf cress has leaves 1 inch wide and 2 inches long. Despite their dissimilar appearance, they taste the same and share the same preferences in growing conditions.

Garden cress is a bright green plant that is so fast-growing, it reaches the salad bowl within a month of sowing, just ahead of arugula. It is best sown and harvested as a cut-and-come-again green and is therefore perfect in very small proportions in a low-growing mesclun mix. In general, garden cress likes light, cool, moist soil, becoming hot and going to seed when the weather is too warm or the soil too dry. Because it is ground-hugging and shade-tolerant, garden cress grows well between other crops; it will be particularly happy when intercropped with carrots and radishes. Left to its own devices, it becomes a lofty annual that is decorative when planted with corn poppies and flowering arugula.

Sow successive crops of garden cress directly in the salad garden as long as the soil is workable, from the end of March to September. Broadcast the seed with a mesclun mix, sow it in strips, or plant the seed a quarter-inch deep, two to an inch, in rows 6 inches apart. Pluck some of the first seedlings whole, thinning the plants to at least an inch apart. When plants are 2 inches tall, harvest by snipping the greens close to the soil. Young seedlings can be cut back four or five times before going to seed, although they become tougher and more peppery as the weather warms.

The growth habits of cress change with the seasons. Seeds planted in a bed with good southern exposure take as many as 11 days to germinate in mid-April but only 24 hours in early August. For summer plantings, we shade the soil with a trellis for the first week until the seedlings are established, then harvest often before the leaves manage to become too spicy. Even then, it matures quickly; by September, it sends up a 2-foot, branching centre stalk with tiny white flowers and seedpods. Allow the pods to develop, and use the dried seeds as a pepper substitute.

In 1869, Alexandre Dumas wrote in his *Dictionary of Cuisine* that garden cress was "the healthiest of the *fines herbes*. It is rarely found on the markets of large cities, since it begins to wilt as soon as it is picked, and in cultivation, it goes to seed too quickly. Children and old maids amuse themselves by growing this decorative cress on dampened cotton."

While it is true that cress seeds sprout on moistened fabric, the flavour is better when the seeds are sprouted in soil—as they can be very easily—for a peppery midwinter salad that doesn't cost a fortune. For an indoor harvest, simply sow the seed thickly in a flat of sterilized soil or peat. Instead of topping the seed with soil, cover the flat with a sheet of glass to retain moisture. When the seeds germinate, remove the glass and moisten the soil with cool water. Cut the seedlings for salad when they are 2 or 3 inches tall. The British traditionally sprout mustard (*Sinapis alba*) the same way and make an appetizing winter salad—often called a "small salad"—of two parts cress, one part mustard and a bit of chopped apple dressed with a vinaigrette and a few rose or nasturtium petals.

Cress and Witloof Salad

Because cress grows well in the shade, there was a theory among Puritans that the dainty green was the work of the devil and "no consumer of its leaves would profit with good health lest it was mingled with foodstuffs harvested in pure sunlight." This recipe flouts such superstitions, combining garden cress grown indoors on a windowsill with witloof, a chicory grown entirely in the dark (see page 121).

¾ cup	plain low-fat yogurt	175 mL
2 Tbsp.	cider vinegar	30 mL
2 Tbsp.	finely chopped garden cress	30 mL
½ tsp.	Dijon mustard	2 mL
½ tsp.	sugar	2 mL
1 tsp.	fresh tarragon or ½ tsp. (2 mL) dried	5 mL
1	clove garlic, mashed Witloof	1

Whisk together the dressing ingredients and allow to sit for half an hour so that the flavours blend. Wash and dry the witloof, and cut in half lengthwise. Pull apart each half into three sections, and arrange them decoratively on individual plates. Drizzle with watercress dressing, and garnish with watercress sprigs.

Upland Cress
Barbarea verna

Young upland cress looks more like arugula than garden cress or watercress. It is a fairly coarse plant that grows in dark green tufts or rosettes about 12 to 16 inches across. Each leaf stem is 6 to 8 inches long, lined with small, clasping round leaflets and ending in a large round terminal lobe.

Upland cress is often called winter cress, because even without mulch, it overwinters in temperate areas. Its Latin name stems from the fact that this is practically the only edible green still growing brightly on December 4, Saint Barbara's Day. Saint Barbara is the protector of miners and others working the quarries, and according to lore, their wounds were healed by laying on leaves of St. Barbara's cress. The spicy little plant is also called Belle Isle cress, American cress, land cress and scurvy grass, which alludes to its high concentration of vitamin C. There is a closely related species, *Barbarea vulgaris*, also referred to as winter cress, but this is actually the wild cousin, a noxious weed that looks like arugula with yellow flowers. It is often found in new meadows and recently cultivated land. In its native form, it looks like a wild mustard, but close to the ground are the small basal leaves familiar to gardeners.

A hardy biennial, upland cress grows best in rich, moist soil. It tolerates considerable dampness and some shade, so it is the perfect plant to occupy a north-facing niche or to intercrop with tall brassicas. We planted it along the edge of a stone wall, and together with the sedum, it looked like a rock-garden plant.

Upland cress can be grown throughout the season, but it does best in spring and fall. For a constant supply, sow in rows about 10 inches apart every three weeks from April to August: scatter the small seeds, and cover with a layer of fine soil. Germination takes one to three weeks. When the plants are big enough to handle, thin to 6 inches apart. The seedlings grow slowly as the weather warms.

Although seed catalogues estimate that the plant matures in about 50 days, it can be in the salad bowl much sooner. Harvest the outer leaves first, but as the plants age, use the growth from the centre. When harvested early, the leaves taste mild—a whole salad can be made with young upland cress, but with the heat of summer, it quickly passes its prime and becomes very sharp. Use mature leaves discreetly as a salad herb.

In early August, sow upland cress for harvesting until the snow flies and again the following spring. Young seedlings grow extremely well in the cool nights of autumn. Harvest their leaves as you would looseleaf lettuce before thinning the plants as usual. Mulch them before snowfall. As soon as the snow melts, the makings for the first spring salad will appear. By mid-May, the biennial sends up a 1 ½ -foot-tall branching flower stalk covered with bright yellow four-petalled blooms.

Because it tastes so similar, upland cress is a good watercress substitute for those who don't have a stream. The seeds are not as commonly found as garden cress and watercress but are currently offered by Dominion, Richters, J.L. Hudson, Nichols and Redwood City. Look for upland cress under the listings for herbs.

Watercress
Nasturtium officinale

Watercress has the distinction of being the only salad plant to grace a coat of arms. While hunting one hot summer's day, it is said, Louis IX of France grew thirsty. Because no water was at hand, he was presented with a bunch of watercress to chew. Refreshed, the king vowed to honour the plant and the place it grew. Since then, the coat of arms of the city of Vernon bears the fleur-de-lis, the royal symbol, and three bunches of watercress.

Watercress remains nearly identical to its wild ancestor. Native to Europe, it has naturalized extensively on this continent. It is not only very hardy—and thus available in cool climates long after other greens are over—but it is also a veritable sponge of vitamins and minerals. Watercress is high in vitamin C, contains three times as much vitamin E as lettuce and is rich in A, B_1 and B_2. It has almost triple the calcium of spinach and is a valuable source of copper, iron and magnesium.

The botanical name for watercress, *Nasturtium*, is Latin for nostril torment, a fair description of the pungency of this plant. Its leaves are round, more succulent and darker green than those of the other cresses. A perennial aquatic plant, it has branching, creeping stems that turn up at the tips and root freely at the nodes; a bouquet sprouts readily in a small container of water.

Watercress grows best alongside a freshwater pool or quiet-flowing stream; it likes wet feet. Although it may grow submerged for a short time during spring runoff, it will not tolerate raging torrents or waters that dry up in summer. Watercress needs very clean running water for a constant cool bath and dappled sunlight rather than total shade.

When Turid first moved to her country place 10 years ago, she started watercress seedlings in two six-packs. They did not thrive, and she transplanted a mere handful of leggy plants to the banks of the stream. During the first growing season, only four developed into cushions of watercress, about a foot in diameter. But some branches must have torn loose, because the next year, there were dozens of plants growing downstream. Within six years, watercress carpeted the banks for over a mile. "We are lucky," she says. "We can slip on our rubber boots, descend into the brook and pull up plants by the bucketful."

Although the seed is available from many seed houses, watercress is not, strictly speaking, a garden plant. If you have the right aquatic conditions —a clear flowing stream about 50 degrees F, preferably one that meanders through limestone and between shady trees—then by all means grow it, but have the water tested to make sure it is not polluted. Start seeds indoors, sowing them on top of moist, sterile soil to which a little ground limestone has been added. Keep the soil constantly moist. When the plants are well rooted, transplant to larger pots sitting on a tray of pebbles filled with water, or move them directly to a sunny, clear brookside.

Instead of seeding, you can buy a fresh bunch of watercress at the grocery store and cut the stems in pieces, each with a joint at the top. Stick them in damp soil; in a few days, roots will start to grow. Transplant outdoors when the cuttings show a few new leaves. Be sure the roots have good contact with the stream bank, and build a small stick fence around them so that they don't wash away if the stream swells.

In the absence of a stream or pond, grow watercress in a large plastic tub filled with potting soil and placed inside another filled with fresh clean water. For convenience, set it near an outdoor water tap: the seeds won't germinate and the plants won't grow unless the soil is wet.

Whether started from seed or cuttings, grown in a stream or a bucket, watercress matures in just under two months. Harvest the leaves as peppery salad greens until small white flowers, much like those of sweet alyssum, appear. With established beds, check the plants early in the spring; flowering starts around the beginning of June.

In July, the plants are a foot tall, bearing half-inch-long, candlelike seedpods. By early August, the old plants have died back to reveal a new mat of young plants crowding together around the old stems and branches. Some of the new plants dislodge and float downstream to take root elsewhere along the bank. Around the end of August, the second harvest begins, continuing until the first hard frosts. Collect watercress by shearing off the top 4 inches or, when the plants are growing rapidly in the early spring, by pulling up whole plants. Cut the roots off right in the stream; some may take hold and start new plants.

Whether harvested from the wild or from your own streambed, always wash watercress very well before using it. (If collected wild from unknown waters, it might be wise to add halazone tablets to purify the water and soak the greens for half an hour before rinsing them.) Watercress stores well in the refrigerator. Stand the plants in a glass of water, and they'll last a week. Unlike parsley, watercress does not freeze well, so use it during the growing season and sprout garden cress indoors to add flavour to winter salads.

Early in the season, watercress is mild enough to serve alone with a simple oil and lemon juice vinaigrette. After June, however, use it discreetly as a herb. Try adding a third of a cup (75 mL) of

lightly packed watercress leaves to the egg-mustard stage of mayonnaise (see page 139). Whir until smooth before adding the oil. This nippy dip is especially delicious with tender asparagus tips. In the fall, the French serve *Salade Cressonière*, made with equal parts watercress and potatoes, freshly cooked and barely cooled, tossed with a vinaigrette and sprinkled with a garnish of chervil, parsley and finely chopped hard-cooked egg.

Multi-Cress Salad

Although cresses are usually used as potherbs to spice up a bland lettuce salad, you can make a spicy salad with more than one type of cress and enjoy the subtle nuances of the three varieties.

1 cup	upland cress	250 mL
1 cup	watercress	250 mL
1 cup	spinach leaves	250 mL
1	small butterhead lettuce	1
	Handful of garden cress	

Toss together the washed and crisped cresses, spinach and lettuce, torn into pieces. Add several sprigs of curled garden cress. Dress with a lemon vinaigrette and a generous grinding of black pepper.

MUSTARD GREENS

Mustards are rarely grown in kitchen gardens on this side of the Atlantic. The familiar yellow blooms stud field after field in the Western provinces, where mustard is grown commercially for seed and oil, but at home, it usually stands in the flowerbed, if it is grown at all. This is a shame, because not only does mustard produce quantities of granular seed to grind into a spicy condiment (see page 129), but the young leaves also make delectable salads. Cut close to the ground shortly after they sprout, mustard greens have a crisp texture and a piquant taste that should make them as commonplace as spinach in salad bowls.

Mustards are hardy annuals of the family Cruciferae, a clan of 2,000 species that includes the similarly peppery cress, radish and horseradish. The three most common species are the seed mustards: black mustard (*Brassica nigra*); white mustard (*B. alba*), sown with cress for the traditional British sprout salad; and Indian, or brown, mustard (*B. juncea*).

All mustards can be sown as cut-and-come-again plants. *Brassica juncea*—often referred to as leaf mustard—includes var. *crispifolia*, also known as

southern curled, a common mustard in the American South and thought to have been brought from Africa with the slaves. Mizuna (*B. juncea* var. *japonica*) is a newcomer to North America that is destined to become popular for both its unusual shape and its extreme mildness.

Another category of brassicas—*Brassica rapa* —has the same growing habits and distinctive, nippy mustard taste to its leaves. Large enough to be subdivided into several groups, it includes mustard spinach (Perviridis Group) and Chinese mustard, or pak choi (Chinensis Group). Finally, lumped in with the cut-and-come-again mustards is salad rape (*B. napus*), which is not technically a mustard but which plays a similar role in the garden and in the kitchen.

Not only do mustard greens taste good, but they have a lower percentage of water than lettuce (89 percent, compared with 95 for butterhead), and they are second only to spinach in terms of protein. They are very high in vitamins A and C—one cup contains as much as an orange —and have twice as much calcium as spinach, as well as substantial amounts of iron, phosphorus and B vitamins, all with only 35 calories per cup. Little wonder that old-timers prescribed a mess of mustard greens as a spring tonic.

Mustard greens are so called because of their peppery taste. When considered for a mesclun, mustard should be thought of in the same way as cress: a little goes quite a long way. Despite its Asian origins, mustard is a hardy, cool-weather crop, not a midsummer green: as the daytime temperatures rise, so does the piquancy of the leaves.

In general, leaf mustards are quick to mature, needing only 40 to 60 days to grow from seedlings to seed producers. They germinate quickly and within a month are ready for a cut-and-come-again harvest. Therefore, they are best sown *in situ*. They can be succession-planted, but because they thrive with multiple cuttings and are hardy enough to survive light frosts, two sowings are sufficient: one in early April as soon as the soil can be worked and another in early August for a late-fall harvest.

In crop rotations, plant mustard after peas and beans. It prefers a light, sandy loam with a pH of 6 to 7.5 but prospers almost anywhere and even tolerates mildly alkaline conditions. It likes full sun and is a heavy feeder; to give it lots of nitrogen for a quick start, dig in plenty of manure, and side-dress with well-rotted manure or compost every two weeks or so. And pay special attention to moisture: don't let this garden guest become dry. Water regularly, and you will be rewarded with mild, crisp

'Red Giant' leaf mustard, foreground, and baby pak choi, 'Mei Qing Choy.'

range of varieties developed for colour, vigour and leaf shape—broad and flat, richly curled, savoyed and feathery. The names are usually evocative: 'Green Wave' (JO) has foot-long savoyed leaves; 'Southern Giant Curled' (BL, PA) is exceptionally long-lasting; 'Green in Snow' (BL, NI, ST), the best known of the Chinese mustards, is extremely vigorous and hardy, suitable for sowing in late summer or autumn for a later fall/winter crop. 'Miike Purple' (CG) is true to its name, with huge leaves accented with purple veins. It is more peppery than most, so use sparingly. 'Osaka Purple' (CG, JO, BL) has dark purple leaves with bright white veins, an outstanding addition to the mesclun mix. The most common red mustard is the widely available 'Red Giant,' with larger leaves than 'Osaka' and a flavour like Dijon. Since they all have similar growing habits, choose them according to how their leaf shape and colour complement the mesclun bed and the salad bowl.

Sow and harvest as described above, being judicious with proportions—they are the truly peppery of the mustard greens.

Sherry Mustard Greens

Robust greens such as mustards, watercress, arugula or even escarole and chicory (page 81) deserve an equally hearty dressing. This vinaigrette draws its flavour from Spanish sherry vinegar, aged in wooden barrels like balsamic vinegar until the flavour is rich and mellow, the perfect companion to exotic, sharp-flavoured greens.

⅓ cup	oil, half extra-virgin olive & half walnut	75 mL
2 Tbsp.	sherry wine vinegar	30 mL
1 Tbsp.	minced shallot	15 mL
1	small clove garlic, minced	1
¼ tsp.	freshly ground black pepper	1 mL

Whisk the ingredients together until emulsified. Toss with fresh washed and dried greens.

Mizuna
Brassica juncea var. *japonica*

This mustard has no common English name, but it is so widely grown in Japan that the Chinese call it Japanese greens. The seed houses that offer it (SH, CG, NI, BL) list it both ways. By whatever name, mizuna is a leafy mustard

greens. The penalty for neglect is a scalded tongue.

Broadcast mustard as part of a mesclun or alone in beds. Or sow three to five seeds per inch, half an inch deep, in rows 12 inches apart. A 10-foot row of mustard easily produces enough greens for a family of four. It is most tender and delicious at 4 to 6 inches high, when it can be harvested by shearing. Don't wait too long, since most are prone to bolting. Mustard is vulnerable to the same pests as other brassicas (see pages 148-49), notably the cabbage butterfly and the flea beetle.

At the time of the first harvest, you will see how close the mustard plants are growing: already the stems are thick. Thin them a bit to aerate the soil and to give the plants some elbowroom for their second growth spurt. Shear the broadcast beds again before the plants are 6 inches tall, check the spacing, fertilize, and continue as before.

When the greens become too bitter for the salad bowl, convert the bed to a mustard hedge by thinning the plants to a foot apart and letting them mature. (You can do the same with mustard planted in a mesclun, pulling up all but the mustard plants when the mesclun harvest is over.)

Mustard grows 2 to 6 feet tall, depending on the variety. Sown in early April, mustard spinach, for instance, is waist-high and flowering brilliantly by mid-June, with shoots of piquant yellow blossoms that are delectably edible. Both the flowers and unripe seedpods add a zesty crunch to a salad, the mature seeds of some varieties can be ground into mustard, and the bushy, mature plants of all the mustards are irresistibly beautiful as a decorative salad-garden border. Cold-hardy yet relatively heat-resistant, these plants are tailor-made for Canadian conditions. For both Turid and me, a garden without a hedge of mustard is unthinkable.

Leaf Mustard
Brassica juncea

Thought to have developed in India, this large-leafed, pungent mustard is the most common species grown in North America. There is a wide

Malabar spinach, radicchio, pale green looseleaf lettuce, nasturtium leaves and a shungiku flower create a memorable salad.

green that lends itself well to mescluns. It is milder than almost all the other mustard greens and the most decorative, with glossy, bright green fernlike leaves that have strong white middle veins. Because it withstands heat, cold and some frost, Turid uses it throughout the growing season as a decorative edging plant, even though, like all the mustards, it is good for salads only when it is very young.

Turid adds mizuna to her early mesclun, broadcasting it directly in the salad garden around April 15. Three weeks later, the leaves are 3 inches tall and ready to harvest. Mizuna is peppery and crunchy with a flavour like sorrel. The mesclun resprouts for a second harvest in early June, but already the mizuna is almost too hot to eat. Although some sources promise up to five harvests, we let it go rather than try for a third. When we clean out the mesclun bed, we allow a few individual plants to mature into rosettes 6 to 8 inches high and a foot or so across. In early August, we sow it again and eat the fresh

feathery leaves long after frosts have killed the lettuces and tender greens.

Tendergreen, or Mustard Spinach
Brassica rapa (Perviridis Group)

Its large smooth leaves have earned it the spinach name, but 'Tendergreen' (PA, NI, BL) tastes nothing like that mild, meaty family. It has the savoury nip characteristic of the mustards, but in terms of piquancy, it is among the mildest of them all and can stand the longest in the garden without becoming unbearably hot. It is also one of the most popular mustard greens in North America, not only because of flavour but because it tolerates both frost and hot weather and is very slow to bolt, outlasting even the most long-standing spinach.

Except for the obvious white veins, the dark green leaves of tendergreen look quite like spinach and are unlikely to elicit comment from unexperimental diners. When the plants are very young, use the smaller leaves whole in mesclun salads.

We used tendergreen in a couple of mesclun mixes, and its light green leaves contrasted beautifully with the deeper greens of cress and mâche, but when it was 4 inches high, it was already quite pungent. Because it is very fast-growing, it should be used with greens of similar habit, such as mizuna, purple leaf mustard, baby pak choi and rape. With slower-growing greens like upland cress, miner's lettuce and looseleaf lettuces, tendergreen provides some shade in the first harvest but should be pulled out for later harvests when it becomes hot and gangly.

Chinese Mustard, or Pak Choi
Brassica rapa (Chinensis Group)

This plant is a perfect example of the perversity that comes into play in the naming of plants. Pak choi, or bok choy (same plant, different spelling), is the Cantonese name for what is commonly known as Chinese mustard, since it is, in fact, a mustard originating in China. It is closely related

46

to *Brassica juncea* and grows much like the other mustards, which is why we include it here. It does, however, have a different look, more like green Swiss chard, with thick, white, swollen stalks and midribs that support bright green, spoon-shaped leaves, often ruffled and curling. 'Chinese Pak Choi' and 'Shanghai Pak Choi' are both suitable for salads, but the hardiest is 'Japanese White Celery Mustard,' all from Nichols. Our favourite is the widely available baby pak choi 'Mei Qing Choi,' which grows into a 7-inch, tulip-shaped plant when not cut for early greens.

In general, one drawback to the Oriental mustards is their sensitivity to day length: as the sunlight increases, they quickly go to seed. Although researchers are beginning to develop non-sensitive cultivars, it is best to limit plantings of pak choi to the spring and fall seasons. Sudden hot spells, dryness or transplanting cause bolting, so give mature plants the care they need.

Pak choi is a fast-growing, robust plant. Broadcast as part of a mesclun, it can be sheared five or six weeks after sowing and should produce a second cut-and-come-again harvest. To obtain individual mature plants, sow the seed directly outdoors as soon as the spring frosts pass, setting the seed half an inch deep, about three per inch. Seeds germinate within 10 days. Thin the seedlings to stand 2 inches apart, hoe, fertilize, and spray with rotenone against flea beetles, if necessary. After another two weeks, thin to 4 inches apart, using the thinnings in salads.

'Mei Qing Choi' matures in about 45 days to a 7-inch tulip-shaped plant with leaves that are used whole and succulent white stems that are sliced into salads. The leaves add a dash of bright green and a zippy, mustardy taste. The texture is rubbery, more like cabbage than lettuce. By midsummer, the leaves are past their prime, but we continue to chop flower buds and seedpods into our mesclun salads. In early August, we start over again, sowing the fall crop of pak choi, which is even healthier and less insect-prone than the spring crop.

Salad Rape
Brassica napus

Much of the commercially grown mustard—and even the seedlings one buys labelled as mustard or cress—is actually a brassica known as rape. The deeply lobed leaves are a more intense bluish green than those of leaf mustard. A valuable cover crop planted to add humus to exhausted soil, rape is also a reliable mesclun green, heat- and cold-tolerant, with a slightly bitter flavour that tastes more like cabbage than mustard.

Salad rape germinates at very low temperatures and survives dips as low as 50 degrees F, which makes it a good crop for unheated greenhouses and cold frames. It is virtually pest-free. Because it is slow to run to seed, it can be harvested longer than mustard or cress. One gardener reports a spring harvest that extended for four months of cut-and-come-again salads. Left to its own devices, salad rape grows 2 to 3 feet tall, but even then, the leaves still make good salads. We grew 'Rape-Salad' (RE), although 'Hungry Gap' is the best-known variety.

Shungiku
Chrysanthemum coronarium

Known to the Chinese as *tong ho* and sometimes listed in seed catalogues as 'Chop Suey Green,' shungiku is a recent immigrant to North American salad gardens. Like arugula, the cresses and mustards, this daisylike plant is extremely sharp-flavoured, so it must be used sparingly in a mesclun mix. Nevertheless, like a dash of Tabasco in a pot of chili, it adds a piquancy that soon makes plain lettuce salads seem unpalatably bland.

Native to the Mediterranean, shungiku has been so passionately adopted by the Orient that it is now most generally known by its Japanese name. And rightly so. Shungiku is a chrysanthemum, the national flower of Japan. In *Honso Komoku*, a 16th-century Japanese herbal, the chrysanthemum was the chief ingredient in a formula for longevity: a powder made from roots, stems, flowers and shoots, taken three times a day, would, within a year, turn grey hair back to its natural colour; within two years, replace lost teeth with new ones; and within five years, it promised, "an old man of 80 would become like a boy again."

Commonly called garland chrysanthemum, edible chrysanthemum and crown daisy, this stout annual looks much like the other members of the Compositae family, with deeply indented staghorn leaves branching profusely from a strong central stem. Ours grew to about 3 feet in height, a shrub-like bush that was 2 feet wide and studded with bright yellow daisies about 1 ½ inches in diameter. The leaves are not at all succulent; even when young, they are a dry-looking greyish green; the mature plant adds a sombre, dusty tone to the garden. Only the youngest leaves are palatable as a salad green, but more mature leaves can be used as a herb, and the flowers make a beautiful and delicious garnish all summer long.

Many seed companies now offer shungiku (CG, NI, JO, HU), although it may be hard to find the listing: Redwood City places it under Japanese greens, and Stokes lists it with its Chinese vegetables.

Because shungiku needs moist, cool conditions to keep it tender and mild, it is best sown as a salad green in spring and fall. It grows in almost any soil but does best if kept lightly shaded. Because it is fast-growing and reasonably hardy, it is ideal in an early-spring mesclun. The first time we grew shungiku, we harvested the young leaves after six weeks, and they were already too tart for our taste. Therefore, sow it in very small proportions in a fast-growing mesclun that can be harvested in a month, when the plants are only 4 to 6 inches tall. It does not do particularly well as a cut-and-come-again, because the second growth is quite coarse and bitter. After the mesclun is harvested, one plant left to its own devices in a border provides lots of seeds for next year, and if planted early enough, it grows so vigorously that it self-seeds in July for a second harvest of tender greens that same autumn.

Instead of broadcasting shungiku as part of a mesclun mix, sow seed thinly, about half an inch deep, every 2 inches, in rows 18 inches apart. Gradually thin by harvesting seedlings whole when they are 2 to 4 inches high. After six weeks, thin plants to 6 inches apart, and fertilize the bed. Within two months, the plant begins to flower and may eventually grow to 4 feet, at which point it will almost certainly need some support. We found the harvest dates suggested by some seed companies misleading. Instead of 80 days from seed to harvest, salad greens developed in 30 days and flowers bloomed within 60.

The furry green foliage and bright flowers of mature individual shungiku are striking. Cut back to a foot, a row of shungiku makes a pretty, compact border of edible greens. Trim plants so that they resprout. Shungiku flowers right up until frost, providing blooms varying in colour from pale yellow to deep orange.

In the Orient, shungiku is, above all, a potherb, lightly cooked rather than eaten raw, even in a salad. In Craig Claiborne's *The Chinese Cookbook*, there is a recipe consisting entirely of dressed chrysanthemum leaves, lightly steamed for about 3 minutes, then drained, freshened with cold water, squeezed, chopped and dressed with a quarter of a cup (50 mL) of light soy sauce, a tablespoon (15 mL) of dry sherry, two tablespoons (30 mL) of sesame oil and a teaspoon (5 mL) of sugar. The dish is garnished with finely diced bean curd and served cold as an appetizer salad.

Herbal Delights

Basil to Tarragon

Chapter Three

"A salad without herbs," says Turid, "is like beer without hops"—possible but not preferable. The sharp, intense flavour of herbs such as sorrel, basil and thyme stimulates the taste buds, awakening our mouths to the subtleties of gentler greens.

But herbs do more than perk up the palate. In the Middle Ages, they were planted not with the vegetables but in a separate "physic" garden. Hyssop was cleansing; parsley, diuretic; mint, a headache cure. Medicine often slipped into magic. Borage brought contentment; thyme bolstered courage; sage promised eternal life; rosemary gave eternal youth. The claims seem exaggerated, but science has since confirmed that herbs add important vitamins and minerals to the diet. Parsley, for instance, contains more vitamin A than spinach.

Health benefits aside, herbs earn a place in the salad bowl on the strength of good taste alone. Although the name derives from *herba*, the Latin word for grass, herbs are far from bland. Their flavours are pungent, sometimes perfumy, lifting a green salad from the commonplace to the exotic.

Herbs, more than most salad ingredients, have national associations: dill with Germany, tarragon with France, oregano with Italy, rosemary with Greece. A herb also has a distinct culinary character that marries it to certain vegetables, whether by custom or because, for example, basil really is the best complement to tomatoes, savory the ideal partner for beans. The aesthetic role of herbs should not be underestimated either: feathery bronze fennel, deep purple basil or yellow-edged lemon thyme relieves the monotonous monochrome of creamy potato or cucumber salads.

The flavour of herbs ranges from the delicate innocence of chervil to the spicy bite of shiso and the resinous undertone of epazote. The last two may be unfamiliar to Canadians, but they are well known to Japanese and Mexican cooks, respectively. Although a herb garden composed of such standbys as parsley, sage, rosemary and thyme is adequate, seeds are now available that allow a sampling of more unusual culinary additions: sorrel, perilla, salad burnet, fennel, arugula. When Turid

Starlike borage flowers, tricoloured Johnny-jump-ups, purple perilla, celerylike lovage and feathery dill fill this herb basket.

was young, her mother would send her out to the garden for a bouquet of parsley, borage, dill and lovage for the salad. These are still her favourites, but every year, we expand our herbal horizon a little.

Sometimes the borderline between salad green and herb is indistinct, determined solely by how much goes into the bowl: greens by the handful, herbs by the pinch. French sorrel, for instance, is often described as a cut-and-come-again plant, but it can be used as such only in the first weeks of spring. For most of the season, this perennial tastes so strong that a little goes a long way, so we include it as a herb. Arugula, on the other hand, is primarily a cutting green and is therefore described with the exotics, even though, at maturity, it is so hot that it comes to the salad as a herb.

Of the hundreds of herbs in nature, only a handful are common to the salad bowl. They are separated into three categories according to how they are grown: annuals, tender perennials and perennials. Salad herbs can be scattered throughout the garden, planted to complement the vegetable they

flavour, but we always give them a bed of their own—a permanent home for the hardy perennials and a summer place for the more tender herbs.

"When I am in a hurry or on a rainy day, I don't want to have to put on my boots and go wandering out among the cabbages for a sprig of fennel," Turid says. "I want all my herbs close together right outside the kitchen door, where I can snip off a sprig or two of whatever I want, annual or perennial."

For a household of two to four people, a herb garden 20 feet long by 3 feet wide is generous. Turid's follows a pathway up to her country house; mine occupies the tiny yard in front of my city house. The hardy perennials—lovage, sage, French tarragon, winter savory, thyme, chives and garlic chives, French sorrel and salad burnet—are always there, like furniture. Around them grow the tender perennials—oregano, sweet marjoram, mitsuba, rosemary and bay—that are moved outdoors every spring. In the remaining open spaces are the annuals—parsley, chervil, borage, basil, coriander and summer savory—sown fresh every year. Here

and there among the herbs bloom the edible flowers that grace our salads: scented geraniums, Johnny-jump-ups, scarlet nasturtiums, daisies and citrus marigolds. Tall, invasive or prolific herbs get their own private beds. Dill and mustard hedges border the garden. Lovage grows like a gargantuan garden ornament against a house wall.

Since most herbs like full sun, locate the herb bed in the open and design it so that the plants don't shade one another. For instance, plant thyme on the south edge, with basil behind, then fennel, then dill at the back. At maturity, the herbs will be stepped from 6 to 12 to 24 inches and finally to 5 feet. Urban gardeners with shady yards need not be alarmed. Many herbs survive in dappled shade, although their growth may not be as lush. And some actually prefer relief from the summer sun: bay, chervil, parsley, tarragon, chives, lemon balm, mitsuba and perilla.

Herb gardens are often stuck in a rocky back corner of the yard where nothing else survives. This may work for oregano or creeping thyme. But to develop volatile oils, most herbs need soil as fertile and care as diligent as does any vegetable or flower. Prepare the herb bed exactly as you would the other gardens, digging the soil deeply and enriching it with organic matter. This is best done in autumn so that the soil can rest over the winter. While the bed is under snow, draw a garden design that incorporates your favourite annual and perennial herbs, keeping in mind that the little seedlings you buy or grow quickly become bushes.

Most herbs reproduce from seed, but it makes more sense to buy perennials as plants, because a package of seed often costs almost as much as a single seedling and you rarely need more than one. With some perennials, sprouting from seed is not an option: French tarragon doesn't produce viable seed, rosemary is notoriously hard to start that way, and distinctive cultivars of oregano don't come true from seed. Buy individual plants from specialty herb houses; local nurseries and markets now carry a good variety too. Or ask friends or neighbours with herb beds for cuttings or root divisions from their established plants.

Regardless of when they are ordered, perennials usually don't arrive until the end of May, when all danger of frost is past. In the meantime, start the tender annuals indoors: basil, perilla, leaf celery, parsley and chervil. Planted indoors in early April, they will be ready to move to the herb garden just when the perennials arrive.

In early May, a couple of weeks before the last frost, harden off the herbs started from seed, those started from cuttings and the tender perennials overwintered indoors. Prepare the soil by removing weeds and digging in manure or compost if you didn't do so in the fall.

Plant all the annuals and perennials at the same time, toward the end of May. Set the pots around the herb bed according to your plan. Then transplant the seedlings one by one (see "Practical Matters," page 140). After the seedlings are planted, sow the hardier annuals—arugula, borage, coriander, dill, fennel, summer savory—in the spaces between, poking nasturtium seeds along the edge to create an edible flower border.

Some of Turid's herbs receive special treatment. Coriander, which goes to seed quickly, has its own planting box close to the house. She uses a lot of it in the kitchen, shearing off the boxed-in plants like a cut-and-come-again mesclun. Arugula she sows with corn poppies in the ornamental flowerbed. It grows fast and becomes too rangy to be comfortable in the herb bed. "And the lofty white flowers look so well with the poppies," she says.

For gardeners with limited space, almost any herb is happy in a container; a combination of purple basil, perilla, salad burnet and parsley is both decorative and edible. Tender perennials are especially appropriate for containers because they must be moved indoors at the first hint of cold weather.

Some annual herbs—arugula, coriander, borage, chervil, parsley and dill—sprout fast enough that they can be mixed with mescluns, where they benefit from the shade of other greens and the extra attention of the gardener. When the mesclun is finished, dig up the herbs and transplant them to the herb bed. These hardy annuals also tend to reseed themselves year after year, although they may show up where they are not entirely welcome. They can be moved when they are very tiny by carefully lifting a shovelful of the volunteers and transplanting the entire group to a more appropriate place in the herb bed. After 10 days, thin the group to one or two of the healthiest plants.

About a month after planting the salad herb garden, when the annuals have sprouted and the transplants are settled in, mulch the bed, particularly the perennials, with compost or old manure. Watch that none of the plants dry out, and keep them weeded. Most of the new transplants will be ready to harvest by the end of June, the perennials in an established bed even earlier.

By mid-July, many start to pump their energy into flowers, not leaves, so unless you are after the seeds, lengthen the herb harvest by picking off the flowers as they form. Pick your bouquets for winter use then. Don't wait too long: herbs are at their most flavourful when young and tender. In midsummer, cut back established perennials—lovage to a foot, tarragon and lemon balm to a few inches, thyme even closer to the ground. Give them a good soaking and a sidedressing of fertilizer to prepare them for their second growth. Don't touch the first-year perennials; they need all their strength to develop into sturdy plants. From late August to the first frosts, harvest the second growth from the trimmed-back herbs. And remember to collect the seeds from coriander, dill and fennel.

In autumn, watch the weather closely: the first frost kills tender perennials and most annuals. When the nights feel chilly, dig up the tender perennials, preparing a slightly bigger pot every year for each herb. Lift out the plant, trim the foliage and the rootball by a third, and cut out the old woody stems. Limit mature plants to less than 3 feet in height. Otherwise, they will be too cumbersome for this seasonal shuffle. When digging up the tender perennials, pot a few annual herbs for an indoor garden: mint, lemon thyme, parsley and globe basil adapt well to a windowsill that is bright but cool. Be sure the plants and soil are bug-free before bringing them indoors.

The first frost reduces tender herbs such as basil to black mush, but others—salad burnet, parsley, winter savory and arugula—continue

Vegetable/Herb Complements

Classic vegetable-herb complements are listed below. Taste is more personal than definitive, however. To experiment with new combinations, breathe a crushed herb leaf deeply, then the salad and vinaigrette or sauce. Continue sniffing, back and forth, until the two aromas blend. If they seem compatible, add the herb and try the taste test. I have found that a mix good to the nose is rarely unpleasant to the tongue.

Vegetable	Herb Complements
Beans	Savory, dill, oregano
Beets	Bay, savory, thyme, tarragon, chervil
Brassicas	Caraway, dill, savory, tarragon
Carrots	Thyme, dill, rosemary, mint, perilla
Cucumbers	Dill, salad burnet, borage, chervil
Eggplants	Oregano, basil, sage, sweet marjoram
Peas	Mint, rosemary, savory, tarragon, sorrel
Potatoes	Dill, parsley, rosemary, lovage
Squash	Savory, thyme, rosemary
Tomatoes	Basil, oregano, rosemary, coriander, chervil

to stay green and can be harvested even after the snow falls. In many northern gardens, if you hill these up with soil, old manure or straw, the harvest lasts until November and beyond.

Before the ground freezes, clean out the leafy succulent herbs, pulling up the annuals and cutting back the perennials. Improve the soil by digging in well-rotted manure, but there is no need for mulch: the perennials survive the cold without cover. After the herb bed is established, take time every second or third year to remodel it. (This job can wait till spring, but there is often too much else to do then.) Dig up the perennials, divide them, and replant a small piece in either the same place or a new spot, replenishing the hole with manure. Give the extra plants to friends.

In the kitchen, herbs must be washed and dried thoroughly before they are cut to release their essential oils. Spin herbs in the lettuce spinner, or pat dry with a towel; damp herbs turn to mush when they are cut. Mound the clean dried leaves on a cutting board. Hold a chef's knife or sharp cleaver with one hand on the handle and the other near the tip, then rock the knife, heel to tip, over the herbs, lifting only the handle and moving it slowly in a semicircle, cutting back and forth over the leaves until they are finely minced. You can also use a top-handled herb knife that has a curve to match the bottom of a round wooden herb bowl. The exceptions are chives and dill, which can be snipped with sharp scissors.

Fresh herbs are always preferable, but for half the year, Canadian cooks must make do with dried or frozen herbs or the essence of the herb preserved in vinegar or oil (see page 138). Pungent, woody herbs such as oregano, thyme and sweet marjoram dry with little loss in flavour. Cut them just before they bloom, when the leaves carry the most concentrated oil; harvest them early in the day after the dew is off and before the sun strikes the plant. Cull less-than-perfect leaves, and bunch the stems into a bouquet, hanging it upside down in a dry, airy place—a porch or woodshed, not a humid greenhouse. Or pick the leaves off the stems, and spread them on a screen to dry. When the foliage is crisp, pack it into dark bottles or wooden boxes, storing them in a cool, dark cupboard. Light quickly diminishes the potency of a herb. Never store dried herbs in the refrigerator, because warm kitchen air condenses inside the jar and shortens the herbs' life span.

In recipes calling for fresh herbs, use a third to half as much dried herb. A good trick is to chop the dried herb with an equal amount of fresh parsley, which is easy to grow on the windowsill year-round. Parsley seems to pick up the flavour of a dried herb and give it an almost fresh taste.

Some herbs, such as sweet marjoram, become more pungent as they dry; others, such as basil, lose so much essence that they become pale shadows of their fresh summer selves. For these herbs, it is best to find alternative means of preservation. Tarragon, basil and chervil readily impart their flavour to vinegar and oil; parsley, dill and coriander freeze well. Wash the leaves and pat dry, then chop finely. Spread the chopped herb on a tray to freeze quickly, then spoon the frozen leaves into a plastic bag or recycled container. Throughout the winter, scoop it out by the spoonful for dressings.

Frozen or dried, nothing competes with fresh herbs, however, so as soon as the new spring crop is flourishing, dump last year's remains on the compost. Another season has begun.

Chiffonade

Leaves that are too hairy or bitter to be tolerated whole in the salad bowl can be finely slivered to add just a hint of their colour, texture and taste.

Pick large leaves from a pungent herb such as red perilla or a coarse-textured herb such as borage. Wash and dry the leaves, then stack three or four together, and roll them tightly into a bundle.

Hold the bundle firmly at one end, with your fingers curled into the leaves for safety. Square the end by cutting off the tip with a sharp knife, then slice across the roll at one-eighth-inch intervals, producing whisker-thin strips known as chiffonade.

ANNUAL HERBS

Basil
Ocimum basilicum

Basil has one of the most sacred histories of all the herbs. A native of India, basil grows in pots outside Vishnu temples and in Hindu family courtyards, where it is invoked to ensure the birth of children. Egyptians mixed it with myrrh and incense to embalm the dead; Greeks considered it an emblem of mourning and Romans a symbol of love; both uttered curses when sowing basil to ensure its germination. John Keats combined them in his poem *Isabella*, in which the heroine buries the head of her murdered lover in a pot of basil and waters it with her tears. Despite—or perhaps because of—its passionate history, basil deserves a place of prominence in the salad herb garden.

There are more than a dozen basils from which to choose. While not all of them are appropriate for salads, they have in common a characteristic clovelike flavour. There are anise basils, cinnamon basils, lemon basils and camphor basils, mammoth basils and diminutive 'Piccolo' basils, ruffled basils and smooth-leaf basils, May-green and deep purple basils.

'East Indian' from Richters (RI) has velvety, grey-green leaves and a very strong clove flavour. 'Dark Opal' (RE) and 'Purple Ruffles' basil (RI) both have dark purple, strong-flavoured leaves that make them more suitable for the flower border than the salad bowl. 'Lettuce-Leaf' basil (ST) is milder, with large, serrated leaves in bright summery green. 'Spicy Globe' from Park Seed is a little round hedgehog of a plant, about 8 inches in diameter and 5 to 8 inches high. It is a lovely ornamental and an unusual edging plant, especially when it is sown alternately with purple basil. It adapts well to the indoors, but don't bother attempting to grow it for pesto or copious salads—the harvest from the little branches of these diminutive half-inch leaves is relatively small.

The best salad basil, in our estimation, is common 'Sweet Basil.' This widely available cultivar grows about 1½ feet tall and almost as wide, with dark green, fuchsialike leaves. Those who use basil with abandon, as we do, should never be without this prolific, slow-bolting cultivar. Some books recommend 10 plants for a family of four, but to provide a full winter's supply of pesto, you will likely need more.

Basil can be planted *in situ*, but it's a good idea to start a few plants indoors in order to get a healthy jump on the season. Press the seeds into a six-pack of plastic pots, five per pot. Water well, and cover with black plastic. To germinate, the seeds need darkness and a temperature around 70 degrees F. Every day, take the time to shake the condensed moisture off the inside of the plastic, then cover the pots again. Four days later, when the seedlings are up, remove the plastic and move them to a cool windowsill. Thin to two or three plants per pot, harden them off, and then transplant into full sun. You can begin harvesting the outside leaves as soon as the plant is established. With sweet basil, be sure to pinch off the centre stalk so that it bushes out, and remove flower stalks as they form. Basil is extremely frost-sensitive. Harvest the winter supply before the end of August, and watch for chilly nights. Before it gets too cold, bring 'Spicy Globe' indoors. The others are overly leafy and lettucelike for transplanting, but this variety is compact enough for the winter windowsill.

Keep basil by drying or preserving in oil or vinegar.

Pesto

Basil to us is the essential ingredient in *pesto*, although the term technically refers to any sauce made with herbs ground to a pulp with a mortar and pestle. We make it with a food processor and freeze tubs of the mix, spooning it onto vegetables solo or adding it to vinaigrettes and mayonnaise. The tangy sauce goes with just about everything: pasta, potatoes, green beans, tomatoes. If pine nuts are expensive, substitute almonds, but in case of allergies, warn your guests. Toasting the pine nuts or almonds in the oven or in a cast-iron frying pan brings out the flavour.

2 cups	fresh basil leaves	500 mL
¼ cup	fresh parsley (optional)	50 mL
½ cup	Parmesan cheese, freshly grated	125 mL
¼ cup	pine nuts, toasted	50 mL
2	large cloves garlic	2
½ cup	extra-virgin olive oil	125 mL
1 tsp.	salt	5 mL
½ tsp.	freshly ground black pepper, or to taste	2 mL

Put the first five ingredients in the food processor or blender, slicing the garlic into two or three pieces first. Whir until pine nuts and garlic are finely chopped. Add the olive oil slowly while the machine is running. Stir in salt and pepper, adjusting the seasonings to your personal taste. Garlic aficionados may want to add an extra clove or two.

When freezing batches of pesto, purée the basil, parsley and oil, adding the cheese, garlic, pine nuts and seasonings just before serving for a fresher taste.

Borage
Borago officinalis

A hairy herb native to the Mediterranean, borage is especially popular in Germany, where a green butterhead salad without a few chopped borage leaves is almost unthinkable. Pliny called the plant *euphrosinum* because it supposedly makes people happy. The name in Arabic means ''father of sweat.'' But on this continent, it is mainly known as the honey plant, so attractive is it to bees. We, too, like borage's starlike blue flowers; they taste wonderfully sweet and are beautiful in salads.

Borage is a slightly coarse, voluptuous denizen

Common 'Sweet Basil' is the basil of choice for pesto.

of the herb bed. It has a thick stem and big, hairy leaves which, although always mild in flavour, have such a rough texture that they must be chiffonaded when mature. Nibbled alone, the leaves have a dry taste followed by a slightly soapy foam in the mouth, but chopped very finely in a salad, they impart a distinctive, musky cucumber flavour.

In its early stages, borage looks like mullein. If the flower stalk is pinched out, it remains a compact rosette, but you miss the best part of the plant

that way: drooping, sky-blue flowers with finely pointed petals and black stamens thrusting from a creamy red-rimmed cup. The flavour of the blooms is delicate, easily overpowered by spicy or bitter greens, but strewn over a mild mesclun, the sweet honey taste comes through.

There is no point in starting borage indoors; it is difficult to transplant. Instead, starting in May, plant seeds about four per inch in the back of the herb bed, covering with a quarter-inch of fine soil.

File the hard black seeds, or soak them overnight to hasten germination. Within a week, shoots are up. As the seedlings develop, thin the young plants until they are spaced a foot apart. One or two mature plants is usually plenty for salad use. Borage is one of the heaviest feeders in the annual herb bed, so water regularly and mulch the soil; otherwise, the big fleshy leaves wilt during the day. Borage grows about 3 feet tall and may need staking, since it stays in the garden for the entire growing season.

Borage seeds itself readily. Turid rarely plants it in the herb bed, since volunteers inevitably appear. Because borage germinates so rapidly and is especially delicious when small, she adds it to her cut-and-come-again mescluns.

Harvest the smallest leaves to flavour green salads. Add chiffonaded mature leaves to dressings for tomato salads. Enjoy the edible flowers as a finishing touch on mescluns and cucumber salads as long as you can. Borage does not dry or freeze well, but the flowers are a sweet addition to oils. John Gerard heartily recommended the little blue stars ''for the comfort of the heart, for the driving away of sorrow and increasing the joy of the mind.''

Chervil
Anthriscus cerefolium

One of the oldest-known flavouring plants, chervil is a native of Russia and western Asia that travelled via Asia Minor to Europe. The Greeks called it *chairephyllon*, the herb of joy. It certainly makes salad makers happy, because it enhances the flavour of everything it touches.

In France, where it is known as *cerfeuil*, this delicate herb is considered an essential ingredient of two kitchen basics: *bouquet garni* and *fines herbes*. The French use it more liberally than any other nationality. It looks so much like parsley that seed houses and cookbooks often suggest chervil as a substitute for parsley, an act I now consider culinary treason. Chervil's flavour is delicately aniselike, similar to that of fennel but sweeter.

Chervil is so perishable that it seldom appears in produce markets. It has a reputation among gardeners as a ''problem child'' because it is sometimes tricky to start, but we find it easy to grow. And because it self-seeds, you may have to start it only once.

Although chervil is usually seeded outdoors, Turid recommends starting some plants indoors around the middle of March, at the same time as parsley, Hamburg parsley and leaf celery—''All the problem children in the same nursery.'' Because chervil has a taproot and does not transplant

Salsa cruda with fresh coriander is a staple of Mexican cookery.

well, start the seed in 2-inch peat pots, planting five seeds per pot. Allow them about a week in a warm place to germinate, then gradually thin to the best plant. By the middle of May, start hardening them off in a cold frame. Plant outside in a very moist, semishady spot, leaving 6 to 8 inches between plants. Used exclusively as a salad herb, six plants should be enough for a family of four, although soup cooks may want more.

Starting chervil indoors gives the gardener more

control, but we also sow it directly in the herb bed and add it to various early and late mescluns. Broadcast the seeds on the ground, and cover them lightly with soil; they need light to germinate. Thin the seedlings when they are a few inches tall, or let them grow like a mesclun meadow.

Chervil grows into a beautiful little bush, about a foot tall and a foot wide, with fernlike, yellowish green leaves. There are two types of chervil, the biennial parsnip-rooted chervil, which we do not grow, and salad chervil, which is an annual. There are three annual varieties: plain-leaf chervil, with flat, open leaves; curled-leaf chervil, more ornamental and good for garnishing; and winter chervil, a cultivar with a short-day cycle that tolerates both very cold and very hot weather. Ideal for kitchen-windowsill gardens, winter chervil has plain leaves and the same flavour as all the chervils.

Chervil blossoms are tiny white flowers in compound umbels that resemble Queen Anne's lace. Sprigs make a lovely garnish. Keep most of the flower stalks pinched back, however, so that the plant produces a generous leaf harvest. Plain- and curled-leaf chervil may not thrive in hot weather, especially in full sun, but they are quite hardy, so you can enjoy the herb fresh well into October.

Don't bother drying chervil; it loses most of its flavour to the air. Instead, mix batches of *fines herbes* by finely chopping equal parts parsley, chives, chervil and tarragon, and spread on a tray to flash-freeze for half an hour. Store in a plastic container in the freezer, and remove by the teaspoon throughout the winter.

Coriander
Coriandrum sativum

Some people call the seeds of this plant coriander and the leaves Chinese parsley, or cilantro. All three names are correct and refer to the whole plant, the edible leaf as well as the round, yellowish brown seed. The pseudonyms provide a clue, however, to the cuisines that most rely on the herb—Chinese and Mexican cooks would be lost without it.

Coriander derives its name from the Greek word for bedbug, purportedly because of the smell. Never having sniffed the insect, we cannot attest to the association, but the small, round, striped seeds do look a little like beetles. The seeds are remarkably durable: they sprout even five years after harvest and have been found in Bronze Age ruins, making it one of the oldest spices known.

Although Westerners know coriander mainly as a spicy seed, it has long been cultivated as a salad leaf, one that in its early stages closely resembles flat-leaf parsley. It is very rich in vitamin C, which may explain the somewhat citrus flavour. Noted food writer Elizabeth David compares the taste of coriander to that of orange peel mixed with sage, which aptly describes the odd blend of sweetness and dusky pungency characteristic of this herb. Coriander tends to elicit an extreme response from those who eat it: some loathe it, while others cannot get enough.

Turid prefers to grow coriander in its own container, a box 15 by 10 by 4 inches deep, filled with good soil. Depending on the season, the box sits on the windowsill or the steps or is moved around the summer garden. She soaks the seeds overnight, then sows them an inch apart. "Don't thin the plants," says Turid. "Let them grow into a little meadow." To harvest, she simply shears the plants like a mesclun. After the coriander is clipped, she empties the box on the compost, adds fresh soil and starts again, providing the kitchen with a constant supply of fresh young coriander.

Coriander can also be seeded directly into the herb bed on a 2-by-2-foot patch of well-drained soil. It likes full sun but keeps its prized first leaves longer in partial shade. Poke the seeds half an inch deep and an inch apart. Cover with peat to retain moisture, and water frequently until germination.

When coriander comes up, it looks like celery or Italian parsley; later leaves are feathery and fine-grained, like chervil. The plant develops a very strong centre stalk that starts to branch at ground level, growing to a lacy shrub 2 feet wide and up to 2½ feet tall. Clip it back throughout the summer for a prolonged leaf harvest. Richters and Nichols sell 'Chinese Coriander,' a cultivar that the catalogue claims does not bolt into flower as easily as common Indian or seed coriander.

Fluctuating weather conditions hasten maturity, so keep an eye on the coriander. The flowers bloom like miniature Queen Anne's lace at the same time as blue anise-hyssop, yellow mustard and red nasturtium, making a picture that would inspire Monet. The blooms attract bees to the garden, and you can eat the flower buds and young seeds too.

For a seed harvest, cut the branches as soon as the seedpods change from green to ochre. Hang them upside down in a paper bag to dry. The bags will catch the ripening seeds. (It isn't a disaster if the seeds ripen fully on the plant: a volunteer crop will sprout later in the season or early the next spring.) Store jars of seed in a cool, dry, dark place. Use them to sow fresh coriander, add them whole to pickles, or crush them with a mortar and pestle to spice up winter vinaigrettes.

Toss very young, tender leaves whole into salads. When the flavour grows stronger, mince the leaves and toss in small quantities with the greens. The leaves lose a lot of flavour when they are dried. Instead, preserve them in oil or make a chutney and freeze it, adding dabs to flavour vinaigrettes throughout the winter. Chopped in a vinaigrette, coriander is particularly good with beets and tomatoes. It is a staple in Mexican restaurants,

where it's mixed with onions for sprinkling on tacos.

Coriander is an annual, but there is an unrelated herb known as Vietnamese coriander (*Polygonium odoratum*), which is grown as a tender perennial (RI). Buy an individual plant, harden it off outside, then dig it into the garden like rosemary and bay, after all danger of frost has passed. Before cold weather arrives in September, bring it indoors for the winter, giving it good light. Vietnamese coriander looks somewhat like a foot-high willow bush. The taste is hot and sharp, not fresh and light like true coriander, and the leaf is somewhat leathery. But in the winter, it is an acceptable substitute.

Salsa Cruda

Salsa simply means sauce, but here it refers to the raw tomato chutney at the centre of every Mexican table, eaten as a dip for tortilla chips or as a side dish. The key to an authentic salsa is fresh cilantro. Cooks often substitute parsley, but only cilantro lures the flavour of Mexico into a northern kitchen. We suggest adding the jalapeño last, stirring in half a teaspoon at a time until it is hot enough for you.

4	fresh ripe tomatoes	4
1	green pepper	1
1	medium Spanish onion	1
1	large clove garlic, or more to taste	1
1	fresh jalapeño pepper OR	1
1 Tbsp.	canned hot pepper	15 mL
2 Tbsp.	minced fresh coriander leaves	30 mL
1 Tbsp.	extra-virgin olive oil Juice of 1 lime Salt & pepper to taste	15 mL

Seed the tomatoes (page 105) and the green pepper. Chop all the ingredients finely. Mix together, marinating for at least two hours, preferably six. Adjust the seasonings to your taste, adding more garlic and jalapeño if you like a salsa lip-scorching hot. Drain the salsa to serve, but keep it marinating in its liquid in the refrigerator, where it lasts for a day or two without losing quality.

Dill
Anethum graveolens

If coriander bespeaks China and Mexico, then dill says Poland and Germany. All the cold European countries seem addicted to it, yet dill is so little known on the Mediterranean rim of the continent that it is often confused with fennel or anise in French dictionaries. In North America, it has found its niche as a pickle herb and is not particularly well used otherwise. The name apparently derives from the old Norse word *dilla*, meaning dull, which seems an undeservedly harsh judgement.

While milder than its cousin caraway, dill has a slightly anise flavour that perks up salad greens. The plant itself is beautiful, with delicate fernlike foliage and large umbels of bright yellow flowers. I grow it as a hedge between the road and the herb bed, partly because of its looks, partly because I want a generous supply and partly because this plant grows so tall that I want it on the northern edge of the garden, where it won't shade low-growing plants. The seeds are so hardy that once you have a hedge, you will likely have volunteers throughout the garden the next spring. This may be less true of a new variety called 'Dukat Dill' or 'Tetra-Dill' (CG), developed specifically for its lush foliage and delayed flowering.

Dill is an annual herb of the parsley family that grows 3 to 5 feet tall and loves the sun and light, well-drained soil. Prepare a 2-foot-wide hedgerow or an area about 4 by 4 feet, digging in organic matter and some lime for an abundant seed harvest. Rake in the tiny seeds loosely. Sprinkle a layer of fine soil over top, and water well. Sow generously: the thinnings are delicious. Pull them until the remaining plants are 8 to 10 inches apart.

Because dill has a taproot, it does not transplant easily, but when the seedlings are very young, you can move them by the shovelful to another spot, thinning to one plant per group once they have become established.

Harvest the feathery leaves all through the growing season. Self-seeded dill starts to flower in June and continues through August. The yellow umbels attract butterflies and bees, but they are also colourful and delicious in salads. You don't have to clip off the buds as they form: unlike most herbs, dill foliage remains tasty even after the plant flowers, although the plant needs heavy watering to support so much activity. The young seeds are also good to eat, crunchy and typically licorice-flavoured. Allowing the plant to go completely to seed shortens the leaf and flower harvest. Instead, watch the flower heads closely, and just as the seeds start to ripen, snip the umbels and either eat them or spread them in a warm place to dry. When the seeds are ripe, thresh them off the plant, winnow out the chaff, and store them for winter salads

and next year's crop. In the fall, as the hedge fades, you will notice a second harvest sprouting at its base from seeds that have dropped on the soil—one of dill's many bonuses.

Dill seed and dill weed—the slightly derogatory term for the foliage—purportedly render cabbage, cauliflower, cucumber and Jerusalem artichokes more digestible. (They are also reputed to counteract witches' spells.) Snip dill weed finely into green salads, marinades and potato salads, and use fresh sprigs as feathery, edible garnishes. Don't be miserly. In coleslaw, add chopped dill at a rate of one cup (250 mL) per pound (500 g) of shredded cabbage. To a vinaigrette of a quarter-cup (50 mL) of rice vinegar and half a cup (125 mL) of extra-virgin olive oil, add two crushed garlic cloves and two tablespoons (30 mL) of fresh dill. Let it stand for an hour or two, then serve over cucumbers, Jerusalem artichokes or fresh mild greens laced with chopped dill flowers.

For winter use, leaves can be chopped and dried, but they are better frozen and best preserved in oil or vinegar.

Epazote
Chenopodium ambrosioides

This pungent Mexican herb, from the same family as spinach and Good King Henry, is grown most commonly in Yucatàn, but it is not unknown elsewhere. In 18th-century Verona, it was called *allemand*, because Germans favoured an epazote infusion to soothe the nerves and dispel intestinal parasites. It is still referred to as Mexican tea, although in that country, it is eaten rather than drunk.

Epazote grows wild in the Tropics and is naturalized as far north as New York City. There are two types, one with very dark green leaves and another with broader, lighter leaves; we have grown only the former (NI), but both apparently taste the same. This plant grows very tall—at maturity, it reaches 4 feet—with a central pink-and-green-striped stalk. The long, serrated leaves jut out horizontally, and at the axils sprout tiny spinachlike flowers.

This vigorous plant prefers rich soil and full sun. Once it is established, a hard pruning does not seem to do it harm. Start it indoors in peat pots the first week of April, pressing the tiny seeds lightly into the soil. At a temperature of 70 to 80 degrees F, the seeds sprout in 10 days, although the seedlings are so tiny, they are barely visible. Leave small groups unthinned in their pots. After six weeks, they are still only an inch or two tall. Harden off the plants in the cold frame, and transplant the pots to a very

sunny spot, setting them about 8 inches apart. When they are growing well, thin to the strongest one. Two or three plants are plenty for a family. The plant itself is not particularly attractive; it looks a little like stinging nettle. When it is about a foot tall, pinch the leading stem to encourage bushy growth. Harvest leaves until they taste too hot—usually around August 1—then cut the whole plant back. If you like the look of it, leave it in the garden; it is quite frost-hardy and reseeds easily.

Like perilla, epazote has an aromatic, resinous taste that bursts immediately on the tongue but fades quickly, prompting another bite to renew the memory. Throw young leaves into a mixed green salad. It is somewhat like coarse spinach. As the aromatic oils develop, chop the leaves finely, and use smaller quantities. We found this herb especially good in Greek salad, the retsina-like flavour blending perfectly with tomatoes, cucumbers, onions, feta and lemon. Try substituting epazote in any recipe that calls for oregano; it has a similarly resinous taste.

Ensalada Guanajuato

In Mexico, epazote is the herb of choice for beans. The more kinds of beans, the better, say the cooks in the colonial town where this salad originated.

1 cup	each cooked pinto, garbanzo, black, green & wax beans	250 mL
½	green pepper, sliced in strips	½
¼	red onion, sliced thinly	¼
3 Tbsp.	red-wine vinegar	45 mL
6 Tbsp.	extra-virgin olive oil	90 mL
½ tsp.	salt	2 mL
1 Tbsp.	chopped epazote, or to taste	15 mL
1	clove garlic, crushed	1
1	tomato, chopped	1
3 Tbsp.	mayonnaise	45 mL

Mix together all but the last two ingredients, and marinate overnight. Just before serving, add the tomato and the mayonnaise (or substitute yogurt).

Serves 6 to 8.

Fennel
Foeniculum vulgare

For gardeners with a respect for tradition, fennel is indispensable to a complete herb garden. It is one of the five ingredients in Chinese five-spice powder, one of the four mediaeval hot seeds and one of the nine holy herbs of the Anglo-Saxons. Although the use of fennel as a vegetable dominates in Italy, France makes most use of it as a culinary herb. Every part is edible: roots, stems, leaves, flowers and seeds. In Indian restaurants, a little tray of fennel seeds comes with the bill, the equivalent of the North American after-dinner peppermint; even in a salad, a sprig of fennel is like a burst of candy, so sweet and delicate is its mild licorice flavour.

Common fennel looks a lot like bushy dill or an elongated Florence fennel. (Catalogues sometimes refer to herb fennel incorrectly by Florence fennel's Latin name, *Foeniculum vulgare dulce*.) It grows as a perennial in warmer climates, but Canadian gardeners should treat fennel as an annual and grow it like dill, although the season is not long enough for it to reseed itself.

Sow fennel directly as soon as the weather settles. The seeds germinate within two weeks; gradually thin them to 6 inches apart. You can start snipping sprigs for salads within a few weeks.

Fennel seeded in May will flower from August to September, sending up yellow umbels on stems reaching 5 feet in height. The flowers attract butterflies, particularly the swallowtail: watch for the larva, a tiger-striped green, cream and black caterpillar, nibbling on the leaves. Aside from butterflies, fennel is virtually pest-free—and we hardly consider these lovely winged creatures pests.

Bronze fennel (*Foeniculum vulgare nigra*) is a highly decorative cultivar with a metallic golden red patina that deepens to dark bronze as the plant matures. It tastes almost the same as green fennel —perhaps a little stronger—but the coppery foliage adds remarkable colour to the garden and to the salad bowl.

Long considered an appetite stimulant, fennel certainly titillates the taste buds. The foliage is flavourful even when young, falling somewhere between mild dill and tart caraway. An essential ingredient of court bouillon, fennel sprigs are also used to wrap fish for grilling, but they are best in salads. Mince fennel into little threads for green salads, add to carrots and squash, and garnish finochio salads with the tiny yellow flowers. Or blend four teaspoons (20 mL) each of the herb and the bulb with two-thirds of a cup (150 mL) mayonnaise or yogurt, and serve as a dip with cherry tomatoes.

It is possible, of course, to have too much of a good thing. According to Dumas, ''the odour, at first agreeable, becomes disagreeable when fennel

Dill: a herb for the flower garden.

is used too freely, as it is, for example, by the Neapolitans, who put it into everything.''

Parsley
Petroselinum hortense

''Take parsley away from the cook,'' wrote an 18th-century gastronome, ''and you leave him in a situation where it is next to impossible for him to practise his art.'' Parsley is one of the most common herbs in Canadian kitchens and certainly the most ubiquitous in stores. It is not as easy to grow as it is to buy, but with a little care, you can produce enough to lace your salads year-round.

Because of the chlorophyll it contains, parsley is considered a natural breath freshener, a good herb to match with dressings redolent of garlic. It has more vitamin A than spinach has and is an excellent source of vitamin C. One large sprig contributes the recommended daily dose of both, as well as some protein, iron and a lot of potassium. The iron is, unfortunately, largely unavailable to the body because of the presence of oxalic acid, which binds some of the calcium and iron, preventing absorption through the digestive tract.

There are several types of parsley, varying more in appearance than in taste: curled-leafed (var. *crispum*) is the most popular type for salads and for garnishing. Flat-leafed parsley (var. *neapolitanum*) is probably the original form. It has the same distinctive flavour but looks more like dark green

celery. Until the end of the last century, it was called Neapolitan parsley, but now it is more commonly known as Italian parsley. Hamburg, or ''rooted,'' parsley (var. *tuberosum*) provides both a salad herb and an edible root. The plant supplies flat leaves all summer, flavourful but not as rich as Italian parsley, and in the fall, a crop of skinny white roots that look like anorexic albino carrots.

As well as these true varieties, there are the parsley lookalikes: Japanese parsley, or mitsuba, and Chinese parsley, better known as coriander.

Parsley prefers either sun or partial shade. It normally grows to about a foot in height but produces lusher, bigger bushes when given some shade and grown on heavier loam with lots of moisture. Curly varieties are decorative enough for the flowerbed. Turid plants it in the shade of calendula, although she loves it with lobelia in an annual flower border.

Because parsley is so commonly available, gardeners often assume it is easy to grow. But germination is often slow and erratic, and sometimes seed won't sprout at all. This is because parsley is actually a biennial grown as an annual. The seeds need moisture and intense cold to break their dormancy, conditions that would naturally prevail if the plant reseeded itself and the seeds lay in the soil over the winter. The technique used to break parsley's dormancy is called stratification, or cold treatment (see page 143). Seed houses sometimes stratify parsley seed for gardeners; check the package to avoid duplicating the process.

Fill peat pots with soil, and pour on boiling water. While the soil is still warm to the touch, sow the prechilled seeds, five per pot, picking them up with tweezers. Light seems to be beneficial, so cover the seeds only barely with soil. Sprout in a cool room, 60 to 65 degrees F, keeping the soil moist. In a week or so, all the seeds will sprout. After the second leaves appear, thin to one healthy plant per pot. After they are hardened off, transplant about 8 inches apart in a partially shaded spot.

Turid always starts some parsley indoors so that she can control the process. But she also sows seed directly outdoors to make sure she has enough. Indoors is reliable; outdoors, when it works, is prolific. Freeze the seed first (gardeners in a hurry can toss the seed packet into the freezer overnight), pour boiling water over a row or a patch about 2 feet by 4 feet, then sprinkle the seeds over it. Cover thinly with potting soil, and do not let the area dry out while the seeds are germinating. When the plants have their true leaves, thin to 8 inches apart —about eight plants, enough for a family of four.

Since new growth springs from the centre, harvest leaves from the outside of the plant. Continue throughout the season, using what you can and freezing the rest. (This preserves the flavour much better than drying.) Partway through the summer, side-dress with fertilizer. In the fall, transplant a few plants into containers and move them indoors. Parsley is quite hardy and will last into the winter if protected with mulch or in a cold frame. In warmer climates, gardeners can overwinter parsley and, provided they remove the flower stalks as soon as they appear, enjoy a spring harvest before the new sowing is mature.

Parsley has two main virtues: it neutralizes the pungency of onions and garlic, and it enhances the flavours of other herbs without dominating them. We throw sprigs into virtually every kind of salad, from spring greens to fall coleslaw, but the herb is particularly good with potatoes and tomatoes and is indispensable in tabouleh and pesto. It is an essential ingredient in *fines herbes* and in green mayonnaise, made by mixing half a cup (125 mL) of mayonnaise with a tablespoon (15 mL) each of white-wine vinegar, minced parsley and minced fresh herbs such as dill, chives, chervil and tarragon. We agree with Dumas, who wrote, ''Parsley is the obligatory condiment of every sauce.''

Perilla
Perilla frutescens

Sometimes listed in catalogues as shiso, perilla is used extensively in Japanese cooking. On this continent, it is grown mainly as an ornamental for its large, ruffled purple leaves redolent of bitter lemon and chervil. There is also a green variety with cinnamon-scented leaves, which is widely used in Korean cookery. The green-leafed form is milder and preferable for salads; the purple is startlingly beautiful as a garnish, but because the flavour is pungent, it must be used sparingly in dressings. We find both relatively harsh, but perilla may be an acquired taste; the seed packet from Tsang and Ma, an Oriental seed house in California, describes the herb as ''addictive.''

Perilla is one of the most striking herbs in the garden. The red variety has square green stems, like sage and peppermint, supporting leaves that resemble frilled maroon taffeta, with a coppery sheen on top and a more intense purple underneath. The leaves are deeply furled, folding in on themselves like maple leaves in the fall. Spread out, they are up to 5 inches long, voluptuously heart-shaped with deep serrations. It looks a little like 'Purple Ruffles' basil but is much easier to grow and is particularly

The mixed garden: mint, chervil, tarragon, parsley, borage, nasturtiums and scallions.

attractive contrasted with the lighter green of the 'Sweet Basil' and the colourful, friendly heads of the Johnny-jump-ups. The green variety is less impressive, resembling nettle, with the same square green stems and spinach-green leaves that have a bronze-purple cast in the sun.

Appropriate for borders and planter boxes, perilla grows about 1 ½ feet tall and a foot wide. It is an undemanding plant, appearing to enjoy sun, shade and partial shade with equanimity.

Soak the seeds for two hours before planting, then sow them, 10 or more per 2-inch peat pot (the seeds are very tiny), and barely cover with soil. At 70 degrees F, the tiny seedlings are up within two weeks. Germination is erratic, and they grow very slowly. After the seeds sprout, move the pots into the light for about three weeks before hardening off. Don't thin them too soon: it takes quite a while to determine which plants are strongest. Wait until the seedlings are about an inch high, then thin to three per pot. When the weather is reliably warm, transplant the pots into the herb bed, setting them a foot apart. Let them settle for a week, then pinch out the weakest plants, leaving one per group. Perilla tolerates heat but needs regular watering. Pick off the flower stalks to maintain a good leaf harvest.

If for nothing else, red perilla is worth growing as a garnish: no other herb adds such a deep, rich maroon accent to a dish. Chiffonade the leaves, and sprinkle on green salads with yellow flowers. The flavour is best suited, however, to Oriental marinades, where the sesame oil and soy sauce mitigate the herb's bitterness and bring out its flavour. You can also add a little red perilla to herb vinegar to give it a delicate pink colour. For most salad use, however, grow green perilla, which adds a refreshing cinnamon-curry flavour to salads with no bitter, burning aftertaste.

Savory, Summer
Satureja hortensis

Often called the bean herb, savory has a spicy but not overpowering pungency that marries well with many vegetables. Summer savory is an annual, milder than its perennial cousin, winter savory (*Satureja montana*). The summer variety grows very quickly into little foot-high bushes of aromatic, grey-green leaves that beg to be stroked as you pass.

Accommodating itself to hot, dry spots where other plants won't grow, summer savory is a very easy plant in the herb garden. Sow seeds outdoors around May 15, presoaking a patch of soil a foot wide and about 4 feet long at the edge of the herb bed. Generously broadcast the tiny seeds, cover with a fine layer of soil, and firm down with the back of a rake. In soil kept uniformly moist, seeds sprout within 10 days. When seedlings are 2 inches high, thin them to 6 inches apart, using the pungent little thinnings in green salads. Summer savory grows quite fast, the stems thrusting up like broom bristles and supporting each other with their branches. If given good soil and full sun, summer savory grows 1 ½ to 2 feet tall.

Just as the tiny white flowers start to appear, pull up the bushes, shake the soil off the roots, and hang the whole plant to dry. Whether or not you use much savory in cooking, the herb bundles lend a spicy fragrance to the kitchen.

Savory is so perfectly paired with beans that in Germany, it is known as *Bohnenkraut*, the bean herb. Use a teaspoon (5 mL), minced, with two cups (500 mL) of cooked, dried or fresh green beans, a small chopped onion, a sliced stalk of celery and a teaspoon (5 mL) of capers, dressed in a white-wine vinaigrette. Unlike parsley and basil, which become bland as they lose moisture, savory retains its flavour as it dries and is perfect for winter sauces and dressings. It goes well with cabbage, Brussels sprouts, beets, asparagus, artichokes and, of course, beans. A branch boiled with brassicas staves off the unpleasant odour that usually permeates the kitchen.

TENDER PERENNIALS

Marjoram, Sweet
Origanum majorana

Cooks and gardeners often consider oregano and sweet marjoram interchangeable, but there are important differences. The flavour of both may be sweetly resinous, but sweet marjoram is not as hot as its Italian cousin. Oregano is winter-hardy in some parts of Canada, whereas sweet marjoram almost always has to be overwintered indoors or planted anew each spring. Oregano thrives in arid soils, spreading as far as you let it; marjoram needs a more fertile bed and remains a semicompact clump suitable for pots or window boxes. We find the look and flavour of these relatives quite different and grow them both, but garden conditions may force you to choose between them.

Sweet marjoram is a tender perennial that can be sown as an annual in northern gardens. Growing a foot or so tall, it is a good edging for a raised-bed herb garden. A member of the same family as mint and a close relative of thyme, it does not perfume the air as these herbs do. You actually have to crush the leaf to release the fragrance that, according to mythology, is the result of Aphrodite's touch. At one time, it was strewn on floors to sweeten the air as it was bruised underfoot.

Sweet marjoram is best propagated by cuttings taken in October (see rosemary, page 61). Unlike rosemary, however, it also grows well from seeds started indoors in March. Press the tiny seeds into individual peat pots filled with soil; they need darkness and about 75 degrees F to germinate. When the sprouts are up—usually within a week—move the plants to a cool, bright location. Around the first week of May, harden them off, then transplant into the herb garden, setting them about 6 inches apart. Pinch out the centres to make bushy plants that grow about a foot high, with deep purple stems and greyish green leaves. The flowers are inconspicuous, tiny white whorls arranged in clustered spikes. Keep them pinched off to promote foliage. Sweet marjoram is an easy plant to grow, bug-free, un-demanding and needing no mulch or fertilizer. In soil that is overly rich, the plants become too lush, with leaves low in volatile oils.

In the fall, let the plant die. Or for fresh marjoram all winter, dig up the whole plant, trim it back by a quarter, transplant it into a 6-inch pot, and bring it indoors.

Even though it tastes like oregano, sweet marjoram lacks the aromatic intensity so essential to pizza and tomato sauce. Its mildness, nevertheless, is sometimes preferable in raw salads. Even so, use fresh marjoram with discretion, adding it to potato, tomato and eggplant salads. If you don't have savory, marjoram makes a good bean herb. The leaves dry well, becoming quite pungent. Use them also to flavour oils and vinegars.

Mitsuba
Cryptotaenia japonica

Although its common name is Japanese parsley, this is not real parsley. Mitsuba is rather closer to honewort, a wild plant whose common name is wild chervil and whose Latin name is *Cryptotaenia canadensis*. Apparently, early French Canadians were very fond of it in soups.

Mitsuba has long leaf stalks topped with pale green leaves that look like oversized, light green Italian parsley. Its flavour is also parsleylike, with a hint of celery. Like Hamburg parsley, the whole plant can be used: harvest the leaves and stems for salads, and steam the roots like parsnips.

Mitsuba is a perennial, but in northern gardens, it is usually grown as a hardy annual. Sow the seeds outdoors as soon as the ground can be worked, covering them with half an inch of fine soil. This woodland plant prefers a moist, shady corner of the herb bed; if exposed continuously to the sun, the leaves mottle and turn yellow. The seed germinates well and quickly shows a bit of green if the planting site is kept moist.

Within two months, you can start harvesting leaves and pulling up individual plants until the remainder are thinned to about 6 inches. In parts of the Orient, mitsuba grows 4 feet tall, but here, it rarely reaches more than a foot. Later in the summer, the plant sends up parsleylike flower stalks topped with little white umbels. Snip them off to prolong the leaf harvest, or let the plant reseed itself.

In October, transplant a couple of mitsuba into pots of rich earth, and bring them indoors. It makes a better houseplant than parsley, lasting longer because you cut fewer of the large leaves. In the spring, transplant it back to the garden.

Container herbs: purple perilla, round-leafed salad burnet and coarse-leafed epazote.

Use mitsuba much as you would parsley, but a little more sparingly, since it has a stronger taste. Use whole leaves in green salads, or chop and sprinkle on cucumber salads.

Oregano
Origanum spp

Although the name suggests close family ties with sweet marjoram, oregano is a different species.

Many kinds of oregano are offered by seed companies, but the best one for the kitchen is Greek oregano (*Origanum* spp), whose white flowers distinguish it from the others. This is the only variety with the peppery taste and pungent scent worthy of a Greek salad. For those who prefer a milder taste, however, we recommend the yellow-leafed golden oregano.

Oregano is native to the Mediterranean and prefers hot, sunny conditions. Grow it in the stoni-

est, driest, hottest corner of the herb bed; it is especially good in rock gardens. Planted in well-drained soil either as seeds, seedlings or cuttings, it grows into a foot-tall bush with square, woody stalks and velvety leaves. Just before the little grey-white flower heads open, harvest the stems, hanging them upside down in paper bags.

Turid's oregano always winter-kills, even though gardening friends farther north seem to be able to keep theirs from year to year. The difference ap-

60

pears to be snow cover. If there is heavy snowfall or if you cover the plant with evergreen boughs, it may survive outdoors. To be on the safe side, treat it like a tender perennial and bring it indoors for the winter. Dig it up, prune it back, and repot it, transplanting it back outside in the spring together with the bay and rosemary.

Originally prescribed to restore the appetite of people with unsettled stomachs, oregano today has a place in salads. Its flavour, however, is quite sharp and aromatic, so much so that Turid has all but abandoned it in favour of the milder marjoram. Nevertheless, for those who appreciate its bite, oregano is a staple of raita and Greek salads and is a good complement to tomatoes and any vegetable that has a distinctive flavour, such as broccoli, beans and eggplant.

Greek Salad

Made with tomatoes and cucumbers still warm from the sun and freshly chopped oregano, this salad is as healthful as it is delicious and has only about 160 calories per one-cup serving.

3	large ripe tomatoes, chopped	3
2	cucumbers, peeled & chopped	2
1	small red onion, chopped OR	1
2	green onions, chopped	2
¼ cup	extra-virgin olive oil	50 mL
4 tsp.	freshly squeezed lemon juice	20 mL
3 tsp.	minced fresh oregano Salt & pepper	15 mL
1 cup	crumbled feta cheese Greek olives, sliced	250 mL

Mix together the tomatoes, cucumbers and onions in a bowl. Alternatively, slice and arrange them on a serving platter. Whisk oil and lemon juice with the oregano and salt and pepper until emulsified. Pour over vegetables. Sprinkle the feta and olives over top.

Makes 4 large servings.

Rosemary
Rosmarinus officinalis

Next to parsley, rosemary is the most frequently used herb in my kitchen. Lamb and pork demand

it, of course, but it is also wonderful in every sort of dressing and marinade. Reputed to stimulate the memory (it is one of the ingredients mentioned in Roger Bacon's *Recipe for the Cure of Old Age and the Preservation of Youth*), rosemary is also the herb traditionally worn by a bride on her wedding day and strewn on the marriage bed as a symbol of devotion and loyalty.

Once, when I was between gardens, I broke a branch off a rosemary tree that belonged to a friend in British Columbia. His shrub was like a little Christmas tree, with a trunk several inches in diameter. The twig lasted me all winter. In that blessed climate—not unlike its native Provence— rosemary can be left outside year-round. Gardeners in the rest of Canada are not so fortunate and must take their tender rosemary bush indoors when heavy frosts threaten. But the effort is worth it, if for no other reason than the pleasure of rubbing your hand over the needles as you walk through the kitchen, releasing essence of rosemary into the air. It is an antidote to weariness with the world.

The name rosemary comes from the Latin *ros marinus*, "dew from the sea." This describes perfectly its favoured conditions—the dry Mediterranean coast, where it is watered only with dew. Remember that when growing rosemary; it likes full sun and well-drained soil to keep it slightly arid. This herb does well in a terra-cotta container, which can readily be moved indoors if cold weather suddenly hits, and it can withstand occasional drought.

There are many cultivars of rosemary developed particularly for their growth habits, which vary from an upright bush to a herb that trails languidly along the edge of the herb bed, and for the flowers, which range from dark blue to pink. Fairies, it is said, use the flowers for cradles, but you won't be depriving their progeny if you pluck a few to eat.

Buy a rosemary plant, or take a cutting from an established bush, snipping off a few 4-inch branch tips in mid-March. Strip the lower leaves, dip the stems in rooting hormone, then stick them in a 4-inch plastic pot filled with potting mix. Put four to six cuttings in a pot, water them well, then tie the pot in a plastic bag punctured with a few tiny holes to keep the cuttings moist but ventilated. Put the pot in a northeast window where it will get light but not too much heat. Open the plastic bag daily to give the plants fresh air.

After a couple of weeks, test for root formation by tugging on the plants very gently. After six to eight weeks, they should resist. Transplant them into individual pots, keeping only the best cuttings. Set the plants in an east-facing window for a week

or so, then harden them off before planting them in the herb bed 10 inches apart. Rosemary is supposed to repel the carrot root fly, so you could perhaps plant one of the sprigs in the carrot patch.

Although you may transplant two or three into the bed, you probably want only one as a longtime friend. In the fall, give the others away, dig up the healthiest plant, and set it in a pot. Take it indoors, being careful not to wait until the last moment, since rosemary is very sensitive to cold weather. Mist it lightly throughout the winter.

The next year, you will be tempted to leave the plant in the pot instead of transplanting it in the garden. This seems easier but actually takes more care, because the plant has better access to water and nutrients if it is placed directly in the soil. Before setting it outside, prune it, shortening the winter growth by half. In the fall, when you bring it indoors again, trim the rootball and the top growth by a third to produce a nicely rounded shape. Keep the mature bush at about 20 inches. If it becomes too lanky, take some cuttings and start over.

Turid always makes sure there is a rosemary bush in her greenhouse so that she can brush it as she walks by. "The scent that is released makes me say, 'Ah, that is summer,'" she says.

Around January, the rosemary bush is covered with pale, powdery blue, mintlike flowers. It rarely suffers from pests, but if it is bothered by aphids, simply cut the bush back to get rid of the infestation.

Rosemary dries extremely well, losing little of its flavour. When the plant is small, refrain from excessive harvesting. As it grows larger, clip the herb fresh from the indoor herb garden, or break off a branch and hang it in the kitchen to dry, stripping off a few needles as you need them.

Rosemary looks like pine needles, and its fragrance and taste are a little resinous but sweetly so. It is especially good with green vegetables such as peas and with roots such as potatoes and carrots. Rosemary vinegar and rosemary oil are staples of Mediterranean cuisine. The flowers are edible too. In the 16th century, Gerard described sugared rosemary flowers as a delicacy that "comforteth the heart and maketh it merie, quickeneth the spirits and maketh them more lively."

HARDY PERENNIALS

Lemon Balm
Melissa officinalis

This hardy herb returns to Turid's garden reliably year after year, although exactly where is always a surprise. Lemon balm travels like its relative mint, poking through the soil farther down the row or among the lavender or hyssop. The lemony tang of its leaves is delicious in fresh green salads, a good substitute for lemon thyme, which is much less hardy. Its Latin name derives from the Greek word for honeybee, which frequents the herb, collecting nectar from the tiny white flowers.

When grown in fertile soil and partial shade, lemon balm grows over 2 feet tall, becoming a sturdy, deep green shrub with leaves like little serrated arrows that emerge from the square stem typical of mint. As the plant matures, the leaves become hairy and coarse like those of borage. Rubbing the leaves releases the most refreshing lemon fragrance, a characteristic that made it a popular strewing herb in Shakespeare's time.

Start seeds indoors early in March, or sow directly in the herb bed in May, pressing them lightly into soil that is never allowed to dry out. Better yet, buy a plant or get a root division from a friend. One or two clumps is plenty for a family's salad needs. Harvest leaves as soon as the plant is growing well, and cut developing flower stalks to prolong a healthy harvest of leaves. In late spring and again in early autumn, shear the whole plant back about 6 inches to produce a new crop of milder leaves.

Use young leaves whole in salads. Chiffonade older leaves, and use them sparingly. Lemon balm complements cucumber and tomato salads and is best used fresh. The dried leaves turn brown and lose much of their flavour, although they still make good tea.

Lovage
Levisticum officinale

Lovage has fallen out of fashion, but among gardeners who grow it, particularly German gardeners, it is considered an essential culinary herb. Called *Maggikraut* in Germany, it has lent its name and its characteristic taste to Maggi, the herbal extract used in soups, stews and sauces. Because it doesn't become bland with cooking, lovage is often added to stock, its robust flavour replacing those of meat and bones. Traditionally, lovage is thought to stimulate the digestive system, which makes it well suited to salads.

A vigorous, voluptuous plant, lovage does best in an exclusive place in the garden. It easily grows 5 feet tall and 5 feet in diameter, producing dark green leaves that resemble gargantuan celery and taste like a blend of sharp celery and parsley.

Lovage likes full sun and slightly damp soil,

deeply dug to give the roots lots of room. It starts easily from seed or from root divisions (see page 63.) When sowing lovage from seed, stratify the seeds to break the dormancy cycle (see page 143). In the first year, the plant will not amount to much, but it returns every spring, and as it becomes established, it provides a harvest from April to October and a wealth of leaves to freeze. Turid planted hers from seed seven years ago. After three years, it grew to full midsummer height; she now has two giant bushes and regularly gives shoots to her friends.

As a salad herb, lovage is at its best in the early spring. The sprouts resemble small, red-stemmed celeries, but do not use too much. Unlike most herbs, which intensify with age, lovage is at its most pungent when it first pokes through the soil; the leaves sweeten as they mature. When the leaves become too tough for salads, use them to flavour the water in which vegetables are blanched.

Late in the spring, the plant sends up flower stalks topped with umbels of greenish yellow flowers. Although edible, lovage flowers are never allowed to bloom in Turid's garden, because wasps love them and she is allergic to stings. Around mid-June, when the first buds form, cut out the flower stalks; then around the end of July, cut the whole plant back to about a foot. It quickly resprouts, producing a second harvest of young greens, not quite as good as the first but far superior to the mature leaves.

While it is a perennial, lovage is very sensitive to frost: it is one of the first plants to collapse in the fall. In spring, little cones of curled leaves thrust from the base of the plants. If the lovage has become too monstrous, dig up the whole plant, replenish the soil, break off a small chunk of root, and replant it.

Harvest the small centre leaves for salads, using them whole when they are young and cutting large leaves in chiffonade. When dried, they retain their flavour for only a short while; instead, preserve lovage by freezing. Lovage combines well with basil, dill and mint and is particularly good in bean and potato salads. For an early herb vinaigrette, combine a teaspoon (5 mL) of mixed herbs—garlic chives, lovage and salad burnet—with a clove of crushed garlic and two tablespoons (30 mL) each of rice-wine vinegar and extra-virgin olive oil.

Mint
Mentha spp

Like so many herbs, mint has a passionate, violent history. The nymph Minthe, while cavorting with Pluto, was discovered by his wife Persephone, who threw her down and trampled on her. According to Ovid, the nymph lives on in the herb, releasing her sweet, sad fragrance every time the leaves are crushed.

A mediaeval abbot with the unfortunate name of Geoffrey the Cross-Eyed wrote that if you want to enumerate the types of mint, you should first be able to count all the fish in the Red Sea. The mint family, Labiatae, comprises over 180 genera and 3,500 species. True mint, of the genus *Mentha*, embraces only a couple of dozen species, which still leaves abundant choice. The flavour of the mints comes from the volatile oils carried in resinous spots on the stems and leaves. The oil contains menthol, a topical anaesthetic that gives mint its cool effect on the tongue. Wrote Pliny: ''The smell of mint stirs up the mind and appetite to a greedy desire for food'' —a fine reason to toss a few leaves into a salad.

Common mint (*Mentha canadensis*), native to northeastern North America, has erect square stems, long pointed leaves and mauve flowers. Although it smells like peppermint (*M. piperita*), the flowers of common mint have circles of blooms around the stem, while peppermint flowers bloom in sessile whorls on long spikes. Spearmint (*M. spicata*) is even more branched and erect, with spikes of flowers. These are the most common and most pungent mints, but there are many milder varieties that are better suited to the salad bowl. English mint is the traditional herb for minted peas and carrots. Grapefruit mint, lime mint and orange mint all have citrus overtones; apple mint and pineapple mint are fruity. The only way to choose is to crush a leaf and sniff. When you find one you like, buy it or ask for a small root division, since mint cannot be propagated dependably from seed.

Mint likes deep, rich soil with lots of moisture and grows in either full sun or dappled shade. Don't put it in the herb bed, though. Plant it where it can have its head. Turid's grows in the shade of an apple tree, where it snakes through the grass. Mint also does well confined to a container: wooden barrels are better than clay pots because they don't dry out as quickly. Each spring, clean out the barrel—all but a dozen or so shoots—replenish the soil, and add fertilizer. The mint quickly fills it again. If you insist on having this invasive plant in the herb bed, plant it in a deep, bottomless tin bucket to contain the roots. Like horseradish and Jerusalem artichoke, once you plant mint, you have a companion for life.

When mint is 6 to 8 inches high, or before it flowers, cut it back by two-thirds, water well and give it a liquid fertilizer to stimulate a second crop of foliage. Turid keeps her mint in check by running over it periodically with the lawn mower. It continues to thrive. Not only is mint care-free, it is bug-free. In fact, the dried leaves are often used to repel insects.

Perhaps because mint dries exceedingly well, it is, according to food historian Waverley Root, the most widely used of all aromatic herbs. Personally, I cannot imagine tabouleh without it, or Greek salad, or peas. Use a few leaves fresh in a salad for a burst of flavour, or mince it to spice a dressing, particularly one with lemon or fruit juice to complement the oil. Mint quickly and powerfully flavours both vinegars and oils.

Raspberry-Mint Vinaigrette

As beautiful as it is flavourful, this dressing should not be obscured by a complicated salad. Serve it on mixed greens, especially a spring mesclun. Any berry can be used—currants, blackberries, loganberries—but it is delicious made with strawberries and served with spring lamb and the first mescluns.

⅓ cup	raspberries	75 mL
2 Tbsp.	finely chopped mint	30 mL
3 tsp.	brown sugar	15 mL
3 tsp.	boiling water	15 mL
½ cup	grape-seed oil	125 mL
2 tsp.	crushed pink peppercorns	10 mL
2 Tbsp.	raspberry vinegar	30 mL

Place a sieve over a bowl, and with a wooden spoon, press the berries through it until only seeds remain. Stir the mint and sugar into the berries, then add the boiling water, pouring it through the sieve to extract as much berry essence as possible. Stir until the sugar dissolves, then add the oil. Add crushed peppercorns and vinegar to the dressing, beating until evenly blended.

Makes enough for a large green salad for 6.

Salad Burnet
Sanguisorba minor

In Germany, salad burnet is known as *Wiesenknop*, or meadow button, because of the little red pompoms that bloom at the tips of the stiff, upright stems. In North America, this delicate perennial of the rose family is scarcely known at all, yet it adds a unique flavour and distinctive visual touch to the northern herb garden. Salad burnet grows in feathery, open, low rosettes to about 2 feet tall, spreading

1 ½ feet, with silvery green, deeply serrated leaves almost as delicate as a maidenhair fern. The young leaves taste faintly of cucumber, with an after-bite that grows increasingly bland until the leaves have about as much flavour as late-summer grass.

Salad burnet plants are available at nurseries and markets in the spring, but they also grow easily from seed. Around the first week of April, soak seeds for an hour, then plant in individual peat pots, a few per pot. At 70 degrees F, they sprout in 6 to 14 days. Like beets, there is more than one burnet sprout per seed. Thin to the healthiest. Around mid-May, harden off the plants, and at the end of the month, transplant them to the herb garden.

In early July, plants mature, sending up slender stalks topped with pom-poms consisting of minute male and female flowers. If you cut back the flower stems, the plants bush out, making decorative borders around herb gardens and flowerbeds.

In autumn, let the salad burnet die back naturally. Like most herbs with tough stems, it is quite frost-hardy. A light winter mulch helps ensure its comeback, and if a few flower stalks are allowed to mature, the burnet will likely reseed itself. In the spring, salad burnet is one of the earliest greens to show up in the garden.

In Germany, salad burnet is an important ingredient in green sauce. The leaves are also good in cucumber salad, especially for those who find dill too overpowering. And when the leaves are young and mild, throw them by the handful into mixed green salads. Freeze some for winter use, since flavour is lost in drying.

Frankfurt Green Sauce

For generations, Germans have bought the makings for green sauce at local markets: sheaves of fresh greens laid out on paper and wrapped up like a cigar. Goethe even made it in his kitchen. Developed in the city of Frankfurt, green sauce traditionally includes seven herbs, a lucky number. The varieties change with the season, so the contents of the paper cigar are always a surprise. With a herb garden at home, you can choose your favourites.

2 cups	fresh seasonal herbs (equal parts salad burnet, parsley, borage, chervil, dill, chives & tarragon)	500 mL
2	shallots, peeled	2
1 cup	plain, low-fat yogurt	250 mL
½ cup	cottage cheese	125 mL

Mince the herbs together in a food processor or blender. Add the remaining ingredients and process until smooth. Use as a dip for fresh baby garden vegetables, or add to bean or potato salads.

Savory, Winter
Satureja spp

Winter savory trades subtlety for loyalty. Its flavour is less delicate than that of summer savory, but it returns to the herb bed year after year, a commendable trait.

There are two perennial savories: *Satureja montana*, which grows to a 10-inch bush of dark green, hot-flavoured leaves; and creeping savory (*S. repandra*), a dwarf herb that sprawls along a border or down a wall, creating a mat of blooms resembling heather. Both stay green into late October and survive the winter, even in northern gardens.

Plant perennial savories in full sun and well-drained soil; don't let them sit in damp or shaded places. You can start them from seed, but seedlings are preferable. Buy one at a nursery, or propagate your own from cuttings (see rosemary, page 61), slips or root divisions. Simply ease away some shoots from the outside of an established clump. If the clump is large enough, take a wedge of the crown with established roots, cutting into it with a sharp knife or trowel. You can also layer winter savory by holding a branch to the ground with a piece of bent wire and waiting until root hairs form before cutting it off and transplanting.

Harvest and use winter savory exactly as you would its summer counterpart, which, we admit, is our favourite.

Sorrel, French
Rumex scutatus

Of the 10 or more species of sorrel, only one is worthy of the salad bowl. Common sorrel (*Rumex acetosella*) is also called sheep sorrel: it is bitter and is edible raw only when it is very young. Its large, thick leaves are often gathered from the wild for very early spring salads. Garden sorrel (*R. acetosa*) is also very acidic and used mainly for soups, but French sorrel (*R. scutatus*) is mild, the acidic bitterness downgraded to a delightfully sharp lemon tang. The slight bitterness of sorrel comes from a relatively high concentration of oxalic acid, which, as with parsley, binds iron and calcium so that the digestive system cannot absorb it.

Sorrel is a hardy perennial, a profusely leafy green with reddish stems and lance-shaped leaves

Common thyme is a hardy perennial that can winter in the garden.

waving at the end of long petioles. Some gardeners grow it as a hardy annual, broadcasting the seed and harvesting it as a cut-and-come-again plant. If grown as a perennial, it reaches a mature height of about 2 feet.

Although you can start sorrel from seed, it is preferable to use a root division. Sorrel expands rapidly, so you need only one plant. Transplant it into the herb bed, giving it about 12 inches of elbowroom. It grows best in warm, well-drained soil with high fertility and a good supply of lime, where it will mature in about 60 days. Prolong the spring harvest by planting a second root in a shady spot.

Once sorrel is established, it takes care of itself, weathering the winter and sprouting again very early in the spring. It is at its best during the moist, cool days at the beginning and end of the growing season; the quality degrades somewhat during high summer. When the flowering stem appears—it looks like rhubarb—cut it off so that the plant doesn't go to seed, and trim the wilted outside leaves to promote new growth at the centre.

Early in the season, toss whole leaves into green salads. As the flavour intensifies, chop leaves finely and add to dressings. Sorrel combines particularly well with lovage chopped in a yogurt mayonnaise, and we like it with snow peas and white onion rings in a white-wine vinaigrette flavoured with a little sesame oil. The first leaves are ready at the same time as wintered-over Jerusalem artichokes, and the two complement each other well.

Tarragon, French
Artemisia dracunculus sativa

John Evelyn so cherished this relative of wormwood (*Artemisia absinthium*) that he said a salad should never be without it. " 'Tis highly cordial and friendly to the head, heart and liver.''

Tarragon is a native of Siberia—hence its hardiness—and has been well known in Europe since the Middle Ages, when a botanist named it *tarktun* (little dragon), translated into French as *estragon* and thence into English, tarragon. Herbal folk-lorists do not seem to have an explanation for the mediaeval name: Are the leaves like dragon's teeth, or are the creeping, spreading roots as invasive as that mythical beast? Tarragon's reliability, its delicate flavour and the elegance of the mature bush suggest that dragons were more beloved than feared by the gardeners who christened the herb.

Tarragon is one of the few herbs grown dependably as a perennial in northern gardens. In its early stages, the slender, light green leaves may be mistaken for those of summer savory. At maturity, however, it is a feathery, branching bush that resembles an evergreen.

There are two varieties of tarragon, French and Russian. The Russian is bland and coarse. Choose only French tarragon when buying a seedling or digging up a root division. (You cannot start it from seed, because true French tarragon is usually sterile.) The plant may be expensive, but it is worth it. Four years ago, Turid bought her plant as a twig in a pot, and now it stands 3 feet wide and 3 feet high.

If you can, dig a piece from a friend's garden

in either early spring or late autumn. Cut into the soil with a spade, and remove a corner of a mature plant. Pot the division, and keep it outdoors until the herb bed is ready to receive it. If you buy one from a nursery, harden it off before you plant it. In the herb bed, tarragon grows in any light from full sun to deep shade, but it needs a generous supply of water and good, deeply dug soil enriched with a little lime and not too much nitrogen: soil that is too rich reduces the hardiness of the plant and the concentration of essential oils in the leaves. Once established, tarragon is virtually care-free, is almost never bothered by pests and rarely demands any special attention.

In spring, tarragon is among the earliest perennials to poke through the ground. By the last week of April, the little green spears already grace our salads. By July, however, tarragon starts to get out of hand, the leaves yellowing and wilting in the heat—a sure sign that the plant will soon flower. Before this happens, cut the tarragon bush back to about 5 inches. To stimulate new growth, dig some compost into the soil around the plant, or give it a deep soak of water followed by liquid fertilizer.

As summer fades, tarragon sends up a new crop of shoots that will actually thrive in the cool fall weather, even surviving the first few frosts. Before temperatures fall too low, gather a second harvest for winter. Some gardeners trim tarragon in the fall, but Turid waits until spring, cutting back the dry, dead branches and taking root divisions for friends. If it is a season in which there is not much snow cover, mulch so that the roots are not exposed to freeze-thaw cycles.

Although bouquets of tarragon branches are attractive hanging in the kitchen, the herb quickly turns brown and loses its flavour when dried. Instead, chop the leaves and freeze them, or savour tarragon's taste secondhand by preserving the leaves in vinegar. Dumas even says, ''There is no such thing as good vinegar without tarragon.''

Tarragon Vinegar

This is my standard winter vinegar. Mixed with extra-virgin olive oil, the vinaigrette needs no further flavouring for a perfect green salad.

1	bunch fresh tarragon	1
3	shallots, peeled	3
2	fresh bay leaves	2
5	black peppercorns	5
2	red nasturtium blossoms	2
	White-wine vinegar	

Place the herbs and spices in a wide-mouthed jar. Top with good-quality white-wine vinegar, and set in the sun for a week. Taste daily, and when the vinegar has reached perfection, strain off the liquid and bottle it, adding a sprig of tarragon for identification. For further information on making vinegars, see page 136.

Thyme
Thymus spp

Thyme first appeared in association with food in 2500 B.C., and over its long history, the herb has acquired an extensive mythology. Dionysius of Syracuse, famous for his parties, used to strew thyme throughout the palace so that guests would crush the herb underfoot, releasing its powerful aphrodisiac fragrance. When mediaeval knights set out on crusades, they wore scarves embroidered with sprigs of thyme to give them energy and courage. Long held to dispel demons, it was reputed to have been added to the straw in the manger of the infant Jesus.

Thyme, according to Pliny, was also a strong medicine. Boiled in vinegar, it could halt headaches. It was renowned as a cure for snakebite. And not only did it restore epileptics to health, but it countered colic, angina and nightmares. At the very least, it could dispel melancholy.

We grow it simply because it smells, tastes and looks so good. Thyme comes from the large family of aromatic herbs that includes mint. There are dozens of varieties of thyme, some, like mother-of-thyme (*Thymus serpyllum*), grown purely for their decorative, creeping qualities. The most popular cuisine variety is known as garden, or common, thyme (*T. vulgaris*). This robust plant has grey-green leaves and grows 8 to 12 inches tall. French, or summer, thyme, also *T. vulgaris*, has narrower leaves and is greyer and sweeter than the most popular variety, English thyme, also known as German thyme or winter thyme. English thyme, however, is more tender and needs mulching to overwinter.

Other thymes are known by their distinctive flavours: orange thyme, nutmeg thyme, caraway thyme, camphor thyme. Lemon thyme (*T. x citriodorus*) is excellent in vinaigrettes. It is a compact, bushy plant, more upright than trailing, with dark green leaves. Golden lemon thyme has variegated, yellow-edged leaves. This plant is not winter-hardy and is best eaten fresh; for drying or cooking, grow another variety.

Although English and French thyme are available as seed, most are sold only as plants. Buy a few, or ask friends for root divisions, sampling the

variety first to see if you like it. Set the plants about 6 inches apart in a sunny spot with well-limed but not too fertile soil. Allow trailing varieties to spill over a rock wall, the lip of a container or the edge of a raised bed. Generally, thymes spread so fast that they seem almost like weeds. Very delicate, slow-growing varieties like silver thyme can be extended by a process called layering. Press some shoots against the ground, holding them in place with hairpins or even stones. Toss a bit of soil over the contact point. When roots have formed, detach the new plant and transplant it.

Around mid-August, trim the plant back dramatically, leaving its woody skeleton. It will sprout a second harvest in the cool autumn weather. After September 1, however, don't cut the foliage, since the new growth robs the food reserves in the roots. Thyme is quite hardy, provided the soil isn't too fertile, which makes the plant grow too lush too fast. Thyme grown in masses is more likely to survive than single plants, since the mat of foliage and branches helps protect the roots against freeze-thaw cycles before there is a good snow cover. Late in the fall, dig some plants to bring indoors for a winter supply of the fresh herb, and give sensitive thymes some light winter protection.

Thyme is indispensable in the kitchen, a good complement to beans, asparagus, peas and beets. The herb dries well, but the flavour becomes very concentrated, sometimes slipping past aromatic into unpleasantly pungent. To preserve the flavour more delicately, push the fresh herb into a bottle and top with a high-quality white-wine vinegar.

Orange Thyme Dressing

Substitute any citrus juice for the orange, and the vinaigrette remains delicious, especially tossed with bitter fall greens such as second-growth sorrel, endive, chicory and radicchio.

1 tsp.	Dijon mustard	5 mL
¼ tsp.	salt	1 mL
½ tsp.	black pepper	2 mL
¼ cup	safflower oil	50 mL
2 tsp.	sesame oil	10 mL
2 Tbsp.	freshly squeezed orange juice	30 mL
2 tsp.	chopped fresh thyme	10 mL

Whisk together everything but the thyme until the mixture emulsifies. Just before using, stir in the thyme. Substitute tarragon, or add half of each when available.

Cool-Season Salads

Asparagus to Peas

Chapter Four

"I am tired of 'tossed green salads,' no matter what their subtleties of flavour," writes M.F.K. Fisher in *The Art of Eating*. "I want a salad of a dozen tiny vegetables: rosy potatoes in their tender skins, asparagus tips, pod-peas, beans two inches long and slender as thick hairs . . . . I want them cooked, each alone to fresh perfection. I want them dressed, all together, in a discreet veil of oil and condiments. Why not?"

Fisher recalls the *trattoria* of Venice, where waiters served trays of tender-crisp zucchini, cauliflower and "artichokes boiled in olive oil, as big as your thumb and much tenderer." She would choose the vegetables she wanted, then the waiter would scoop them into a bowl, splash them with oil and vinegar and hand her back "a salad as fresh and tonic to your several senses as La Primavera."

Too often when we think of salads, we think of greens. Yet there are dozens of vegetables that, when properly dressed, make delicious salads on their own—asparagus, beans, cabbage, carrots, peas. The solo salad performers divide neatly into the three types featured in the next three chapters: vegetables that produce their harvest in the cool weather of spring or fall; those that thrive in the heat of midsummer; and those like potatoes that mature in the dark. Among the most treasured, however, are the vegetables that appear in early spring—sometimes while snow is still on the ground—and yield their harvests again late into the fall past the first frosts, stretching the growing season in the northern salad garden to its delicious limits.

Artichoke
Cynara scolymus

The first person to eat an artichoke must have been very hungry indeed, for nothing about its appearance suggests the sweet, nutty pulp buried within. While technically a flower bud, an artichoke looks more like a plump, grey-green pinecone, with a chain-mail armour of "scales" overlapping a fuzzy, purplish orange core. Hardly appetizing in appearance, but inside those scales and underneath the

fuzz lies some of the most delectable, nutritious flesh in the vegetable kingdom. Chilean poet Pablo Neruda wrote an entire love poem to the artichoke and the ''halcyon paste'' at its heart. A favourite of California cuisine, artichokes can also be grown in northern gardens, although it takes the entire growing season to produce a harvest of buds that extends late into the fall. For patient gardeners, the artichoke is as exotic a salad as can be had.

Three different plants carry the name artichoke. Chinese artichokes (*Stachys affinis*) and Jerusalem artichokes (*Helianthus tuberosus*) are both grown for their tubers, but only the French, or globe, artichoke (*Cynara scolymus*) is grown for its huge, edible flower buds. The globe artichoke is a thistle-like perennial that tends to be invasive. Its name derives from two Middle English words, *hortus* and *chokt*, which literally translate as ''the garden strangler.'' (Northern gardeners need not worry: here it grows best as an annual.) Native to the Mediterranean and a relative of the thistle, the artichoke found its most famous champion in Catherine de Médicis, who so doted on them that she once fainted from overconsumption. Such behaviour was considered scandalous, not because it was shamefully gluttonous but because, in the 16th century, the vegetable was believed to be aphrodisiac.

Today, the fleshy little cones are reputedly good for the liver, and tests in the 1940s showed them to be so successful at lowering blood cholesterol that one of the vegetable's constituents, cynarin, was formulated into a drug for that purpose. Artichokes contain small but significant amounts of calcium, phosphorus, potassium and magnesium, are a good source of vitamin A and have appreciable levels of B and C. They contain about the same amount of iron as cauliflower or radishes and about as much protein as spinach or raisins, but their popularity in light Californian cuisine may be mainly because of their low calorie count—only 44 calories for an average artichoke, and the younger the flower bud, the lower the count. Artichokes are, however, high in sodium—80 milligrams in each medium-sized cooked bud.

In its native soil, the artichoke towers to 10 feet or more. Turid's artichokes grow only waist-high, but still, their grey-green foliage is so exquisite that they can be justified in the garden solely as ornamentals. 'Green Globe' (BL, NI) is the most common variety. More prized by gourmets, however, are the smaller purple artichokes such as 'Purple Sicilian' (BL). Common to the Mediterranean, they are so sweet and tender that small buds can be quartered and dressed, choke and all.

The artichoke is technically a flower bud.

In California, where there are fields of the feathery bushes stretching in every direction as far as the eye can see, artichokes are a spring delicacy, like asparagus; but in the north, they are a late-summer treat and one well worth the wait, especially for those who have never tasted an artichoke that has not travelled across a continent to get to the table. Gardeners are often surprised that we grow artichokes in Canada, but it is not difficult to get the plants to the budding stage provided you start them early enough indoors and give them a favourable environment. Artichokes have deep, branching roots, so they need a well-dug bed of fertile, moisture-retaining soil. They like all the sun and water they can get and thrive only in a warm, sheltered site: the cooler and more overcast the weather, the longer the flower buds take to mature.

Start artichoke seeds indoors in March or at least six weeks before the average last spring frost. Soak seeds overnight, and plant them a quarter-inch deep, three to each 3-inch peat pot. At 70 degrees F, the seeds sprout in about six days. Thin to the sturdiest plant in each pot.

By the time the frosty nights are over, the artichokes are healthy 6-inch plants. Slowly harden them off, then transplant them into a deeply prepared bed with plenty of manure and neutral pH, spacing them 2 to 3 feet apart in a row or planting as individual highlights throughout the garden. As soon as the plants are established, mulch well. Keep them continuously moist, always watering from

below: overhead watering may rot the hearts. If you don't mulch, give the plants a thorough soaking at least once a week.

Artichokes are very slow-growing. Turid transplants hers into the garden in early June, and the first flower stalk appears only in early August, rising from the middle of the plant. The stalk branches and sets up to a dozen or so flower buds; pinch off all but six so that these develop before the cold weather hits.

By the end of August, Turid is checking the plants daily, anxious to harvest the flower buds at their prime. The artichokes are ready for the table when the bud is still a compact mass of bracts, or scales, closely overlaid like a pinecone and about the size of a large lemon. As the flower bud matures, the bracts splay open like a rose to reveal a purple-centred, thistlelike flower. Like broccoli, however, it is edible only in the bud state at about two-thirds of its full size. Harvest the top one first by cutting it close to the head, encouraging the others to develop. A shot of manure tea or fertilizer strengthens the plant during the harvest, which can last until the beginning of October. (Artichokes withstand light frosts.)

Turid usually starts new plants each spring, but she has overwintered artichokes by cutting the plant close to the ground in the fall, hilling soil over the crown and burying it deeply in mulch. Pull back the mulch in the spring, and the plant resprouts, providing an earlier harvest than those grown from seed. When grown as a perennial, artichokes should be planted in the herb bed rather than in the main salad-garden bed.

Another alternative to starting seeds each spring is to cut small side suckers from a mature plant in the fall, leaving a bit of root attached. Transplant the suckers to 6-inch pots, cut them back, and set them in the winter greenhouse, where they resprout for transplanting outdoors in the spring. The problem with this approach is that artichokes attract aphids and other greenhouse pests, and once the plants are infested, the bugs are hard to find because the grey and cottony leaves provide camouflage. ''If you have any bugs at all,'' says Turid, ''they will find the artichokes. It's much easier just to start seeds each year.''

Outdoors, artichokes are not so attractive to bugs, although root aphids have occasionally been a problem in Turid's garden, and some gardeners report blackfly and greenfly on developing flower heads. In wet weather or heavy soil, slugs may infest young shoots. Artichokes are prone to diseases such as botrytis, a grey mould that attacks leaves and stalks. Short of fungicides, there is no cure; pull up and burn diseased plants.

As well as the flower buds, the stems of the artichoke can be eaten like cardoon (*Cynara cardunculus*), a closely related plant grown solely for its celerylike stalks. With both plants, the stems can be harvested and sliced for salads when a foot or two tall, but artichokes are best left to develop to the flower stage. When the bud harvest is over, bind the stalks together for blanching. Remove the outermost leaves, and wrap the stalks in burlap, newspaper or corrugated cardboard, tying loosely to avoid harming the flesh. Leave the top 4 inches exposed to catch the sun. Mound the soil around the base of the plant, and leave it for two or three weeks (longer, and the stem may rot). Remove the binding, and harvest by cutting the plant at the base, pulling away the leaves and eating the blanched midribs at the core. Before the first hard freeze in autumn, dig up any plants left in the garden. Lift gently from the bed, retaining a rootball. Set the artichoke or cardoon in a box, and cover with dry sand. Stored in a cool cellar, these plants—which look like Brobdingnagian celery—keep until Christmas.

Artichokes themselves last only two weeks in the refrigerator, sealed in a plastic bag to retain moisture; this might be necessary if you are trying to accumulate enough for company. Don't wash the artichoke first; just sprinkle a bit of water on the flower bud to forestall dehydration. They can be used as long as the heads are firm, solid and green; when the leaves are brownish, cracked or splayed open, artichokes are past their prime.

Although very small flower buds can be quartered and eaten raw, artichokes usually require some preparation before being eaten as a salad. Wash the artichoke by plunging it up and down in cold water, then cut off the stem so that it sits upright on a plate. Remove any small or coarse leaves from the bottom, and use a very sharp knife to trim about half an inch from the top. If any other leaves seem too sharp, trim off the pointed tips with scissors. Rub all cut edges with lemon to prevent discolouring, and if you are preparing a few at once, bathe the prepared artichokes in acidulated water until they are all ready to steam.

Some cooks prefer to take the choke out before steaming the vegetable so that none of its bitter flavour is imparted to the flesh. To do this, hold the trimmed artichoke under the tap until the leaves separate. Pull out the prickly leaves at the centre of the artichoke, and using a small teaspoon, scrape off the fuzz at the core. Sprinkle the exposed bottom with lemon juice, and press the cone closed.

To cook artichokes, arrange the prepared flower buds stem side down in a vegetable steamer, and place over boiling water. Reduce the heat, and simmer 25 to 50 minutes. The artichokes are done when a leaf near the centre pulls out with a light tug. Cool upside down on a rack or in a colander. For better flavour, add a bay leaf, a few peppercorns, a clove of garlic and the juice of a lemon (as well as a tablespoon (15 mL) of red-wine vinegar, if you like) to the steaming water. Chill, covered, in the refrigerator for several hours.

Serve steamed artichokes whole, with a dip of hollandaise, garlic or herb butter for the petals; or fill them with a creamy salad—seafood is especially good—which is dipped out with the spatulate bracts before the sauce-soaked bottom is eaten. You can also dismantle the artichokes in the kitchen and serve the parts separately. Pull off the outer leaves to expose the choke (if it was not removed) and the bottom. Remove the fuzzy thistle centre with a spoon. The bottom, with a few tender leaves attached, is known as the heart and is the gastronomic prize for dismantling the flower. The hearts are often marinated to create a salad in themselves or chopped to add to mixed salads.

Blanched artichoke or cardoon stalks can be cut into sticks, steamed and eaten like asparagus. Peel the stalks as you would rhubarb to remove any strings, and toss them into acidulated water to keep them white. Tie loosely in bundles, steam until tender, cool and serve with a piquant rémoulade sauce or a thick vinaigrette made with plenty of mustard.

Fresh young artichoke or cardoon stalks are one of the traditional vegetables, along with finochio, radishes, carrots, cauliflower and broccoli, served with *bagna caôda*, a hot garlic and anchovy dip popular in the Piedmont region of Italy. To make the dip, crush three garlic cloves using a mortar and pestle with half a teaspoon (2 mL) of coarse salt. Add a small can of anchovies and two slices of dry bread soaked in two tablespoons (30 mL) of milk for a few minutes and squeezed dry. (The milk-bread is traditional but often omitted in modern recipes.) Pound thoroughly or whir in a food processor, slowly adding a quart (1 L) of extra-virgin olive oil. Heat in a fondue pot until hot but not smoking, and swirl the raw vegetables in the hot, salty sauce. Serve with a basket of fresh bread and a bottle of good wine.

Artichoke Salsa

Artichokes are in season about the same time bell peppers redden and leeks ripen. Combining the three in a salsa, using the artichoke leaves as dippers, is every bit as tasty as hollandaise and is much lower in calories and cholesterol.

2	artichokes	2
1 tsp.	dark sesame oil	5 mL
1	small leek, chopped	1
¼ cup	finely chopped green pepper	50 mL
2	cloves garlic, minced	2
¼ cup	seeded, finely chopped tomato	50 mL
¼ cup	roasted chopped red pepper	50 mL
½ tsp.	freshly squeezed lemon juice	2 mL
¼ tsp.	salt	1 mL
	Hot-pepper sauce to taste	

Prepare, steam and dismantle the artichokes, chopping the bottoms finely. Heat the sesame oil, and sauté the leek, green pepper and garlic for about 3 minutes. Stir in the tomato, red pepper and lemon juice. Season with salt and hot-pepper sauce. Cook until thoroughly heated, then stir in the chopped artichoke bottoms. Cool the salsa, then serve it in a bowl, sprinkled with toasted sesame seeds and surrounded with a wreath of artichoke petals.

Asparagus
Asparagus officinalis

The first thing Turid planted on her property was asparagus. Even before she knew where the house or the garden would be, she dug a trench and buried a row of year-old crowns. It was an act of faith. With the first good harvest at least two years away, she knew that the sooner she got started, the sooner the salad would be on the table. A decade later, the row of crowns that she planted produces a glut of asparagus every spring and a feathery hedge that not only shades lettuces in high summer but remains a swath of beauty in the garden long after the foliage yellows and the berries turn cherry-red.

Like an orchard, asparagus demands a fair amount of work with few rewards in the early stages, but the benefits continue for a lifetime. In Kew Gardens in England, there is an asparagus bed that is still prolific after 118 years, a good thing to remember as you weed and mulch and water and nobly refrain from picking those first delicate spears.

A member of the lily family, asparagus has been grown and eaten for a long time, most often as a salad vegetable. Yet little is known about its past. The name derives from the Greek word *asparagos*, which means "as long as one's throat." Some people still refer to it as "sparrow grass," a 17th-century British corruption that is not inappropriate, since the vegetable thrusts through the soil at about the same time the birds return in the spring. Given its phallic shape, it is not surprising that asparagus has always been considered an aphrodisiac. "It manifestly provoketh Venus," wrote one coy Elizabethan. At that time, asparagus was just coming back to the table after an absence of several centuries. By the 18th century, asparagus was at its most popular: gardeners' guides of the time recommend planting two acres to feed a small family, a staggering quantity by today's standards.

Aside from its reputation for enhancing sexual vigour—in France, a bridegroom's prenuptial dinner traditionally included three courses of asparagus—it is also known as a stimulant for the urinary system. (In many people, a meal of asparagus produces a characteristic odour and green tint in the urine.) More important, it contains the three nutrients that biochemist Bruce Ames cites as most helpful in the body's defence against cancer: beta carotene, vitamin C and the mineral selenium. It has almost no fat or sodium but goodly amounts of cholesterol-fighting fibre. It is also wonderfully low in calories—a whole pound contains only 120 calories, although the butter and hollandaise sauce that traditionally dress asparagus add considerably more.

Modern transportation and chemical agriculture now bring asparagus to the stores in January, but for the gardener, the vegetable is truly a harbinger of spring. Not only is it early, it is one of the most delectable vegetables of the entire season. And what you grow is far superior to anything you can buy. One test showed that by the time asparagus travels from California to New York by refrigerated truck, it has lost two-thirds of its vitamin C.

Asparagus can be grown from seed, but this delays the harvest for yet another season. Most gardeners prefer to get a head start by buying one-year-old crowns from a reputable nursery or seed house. Two-year-old crowns are also available, but they are trickier to establish and therefore offer little saving in the long run. The same is true of transplanting old crowns: they are easily destroyed in the digging up.

When buying crowns, specify male plants only. Asparagus is dioecious, which means that male and female flowers are produced on separate plants. The males produce more spears; the females put some of their energy into setting inedible berries, which

A feathery asparagus hedge against a summer sky.

in turn produce shallow-rooted nuisance volunteers. Until now, the standard varieties, such as the widely available 'Mary Washington,' have been open-pollinated, but Rutgers University in New Jersey has developed male-only hybrids. Not only are the new hybrids, such as 'Jersey Giant' (TM, PA), more disease-resistant (and especially immune to fusarium wilt), but they are incredibly productive. In trials conducted by Cornell University in New York State, 'Jersey Giant' produced 5,334 pounds

to the acre compared with 1,396 per acre for 'Mary Washington.' With the all-male hybrids, count on a harvest of about half a pound per crown over the growing season.

Because asparagus is a perennial, choose a permanent place in the garden, taking into account that asparagus likes full sun and grows to a decorative 4-foot hedge, which acts as both shade and windbreak. Plant asparagus in its own bed or along the edge of the garden plot, as long as the cultivation of neighbouring vegetables will not disturb its roots. Planted in a north-south row, asparagus shades low-growing vegetables on its east side from the afternoon sun; planted in an east-west row, it provides day-long shade for plants to the north. Don't let the lawn or meadow rub up against the outer flank of the bed: invasive grasses quickly choke out the tender little shoots. The bed should also be far from meandering tree roots. For an average family of four—or two asparagus gourmands—make a bed about 3 feet wide and 30 feet long, enough to accommodate 20 crowns spaced 1 ½ feet apart in a single row. You can stagger asparagus throughout a wider bed, but cultivation is difficult. If planting more than one row, space the rows 6 feet apart: asparagus roots are far-ranging.

Prepare the soil in the fall, digging trenches 1 ½ feet deep and 1 ½ feet wide in the centre of the 3-foot bed. The soil does not have to be sandy, just free-draining. Asparagus likes deeply dug soil with a pH of 6.8 to 7. If the topdressing of soil is not loose enough, the spears will be deformed or fail to push through. Remove as many of the stones and weeds from the soil as possible. Fill the trench half-full of organic matter—old manure and rotted hay—and mix it in well. (If you don't have enough organic matter to fill a trench, dig individual holes and enrich the soil under each crown.) Asparagus also likes phosphorus, so add bone meal to the trench if soil levels are low.

In the spring, buy healthy young crowns with roots that are not dried out or damaged by mildew. Soak the crowns briefly in lukewarm water, then plant them 1 ½ feet apart in the trench, taking care to spread the roots horizontally in all directions to their full length. Cover with about 6 inches of soil.

After a few weeks, little spears will start poking through the soil. As they grow, gradually add more soil to the trench, leaving only the spear tip exposed. When the soil is level again, the bed is finished and the crowns will be buried under 8 inches of soil. In northern gardens, planting asparagus in a slightly deeper trench—at least 2 feet—protects the crowns from winter frost heave and the tender spears from late-spring frosts. The spears appear a little later, because they have farther to push and they are a little thicker, but they will be just as tender and welcome once they arrive at the surface. During the growing season, keep the bed watered and weeded, and add a little topdressing of manure in midseason. Turid always weeds by hand: roots and shoots are easily injured with a hoe.

In autumn, the foliage turns the colour of tamarack leaves, and the berries of female plants red-

den. It is good garden practice to remove the foliage then, but as Turid's hedge is rarely plagued by asparagus beetles, she leaves it for winter decoration, removing it early in the spring and saving the sprigs as shade covers for tender seedlings.

In the second spring, the spears are only a little heartier than the year before. Traditional wisdom advises that these delicate shoots be left alone, but research at Oklahoma State University suggests that harvesting may be a good idea. Early cutting apparently forces more shoots to develop. Harvest on a small scale, picking only the biggest and thickest shoots, not more than three from each plant. Allow the others to grow into ferns.

In the third year, cut all the spears over a period of about five weeks, then let the rest develop into a hedge. Each year, the harvest lengthens a little. Turid's rule of thumb is that after the third spring, she harvests as long as she sees the plant is in production, then she leaves about five stems to develop into the hedge. Typically, her harvest now lasts from the end of April until the first week of June.

Early in the season, Turid cuts two sharp edges along the bed to keep the weeds at bay. Once the harvest is over, mulch heavily around the base of maturing plants to discourage weeds, but remember to remove it in the spring: it keeps the bed cool and delays the emergence of spears. Late each fall or early in the spring, cut all the stems back to 2 inches; remove the debris, and fertilize the asparagus bed with manure tea, or dig in a couple of spoonfuls of granular organic general-purpose fertilizer around each plant.

Asparagus can also be started from seed, although it adds another season to the process. The advantage of seeds is that you have more control over the variety and the sex of the plants. Start seeds in early March, scarifying or soaking them for 48 hours before planting in individual peat pots. Set the pots on a propagation mat at 85 to 90 degrees F. The seedlings grow very slowly; around mid-May, transplant them to the garden. Let two full growing seasons pass before you start even the first tentative harvest.

Asparagus is prone to asparagus beetles, quarter-inch-long insects that emerge in the spring from the soil to lay shiny black eggs on the spears. Both the adults and their greenish grey, black-headed larvae feed on the spears and foliage. There can be up to five generations a year. Dust infested plants with rotenone, and avoid the problem by cleaning up the beds in the fall so that the beetles don't overwinter in the soil. Fusarium wilt can sometimes be a problem during hot, dry weather; choose resis-

tant varieties, and destroy infected plants. There are no chemical controls.

According to Alice B. Toklas, an asparagus spear "when it is picked should be no thicker than a darning needle." This is a little extreme. In fact, with asparagus, tenderness is strictly a matter of age: plump stalks are every bit as delectable as pencil-thin ones, provided they are young. When the spears are about 8 inches high, break or cut them off right at soil level. At their prime, spears are tightly budded and green at least two-thirds of the way down the stalk. Harvest all stalks that have reached the right height, even the needle-sized spears; letting them grow slows production of new spears.

Asparagus is best eaten immediately, but you can store spears in the refrigerator for up to five days. Keep asparagus like cut flowers: snap off the bottoms at the point where they break naturally, and set them upright in a jug of water. But remember, the longer they are stored, the lower the vitamin content will be.

Although you can eat asparagus raw, its flavour intensifies with cooking. It is a fragile vegetable, however, one that slips quickly from *al dente* to overdone. The Romans used an expression when they wanted something done in a hurry: "Do it in less time than it takes to cook asparagus." And that means pretty darn quick.

Ideally, cook asparagus upright, with the stems in boiling water and the tender tips steamed by the rising vapours. There are special pots sold for the job, but a recycled coffee percolator or a double boiler works well. Wash the spears in cold water, then tie in loose bundles, and stand upright in a deep pot. Add an inch (2.5 cm) of boiling water, and cover with the upside-down top of the double boiler. Cook until the bottoms of the stems are tender, 3 to 10 minutes depending on the thickness of the spears. Immediately run them under cold water until cool to the touch; drain well on absorbent paper towels or a clean tea towel. If the spears turn muddy green during cooking, leave the lid off: the acid released in cooking will dissipate into the air instead of denaturing the chlorophyll in the asparagus.

Serve blanched, freshened asparagus with watercress dip (page 44) or dressed in a simple vinaigrette made by mashing a clove of garlic with half a teaspoon (2 mL) of coarse salt, stirring in 1 ½ teaspoons (7 mL) of Dijon mustard, the juice of half a lemon and two teaspoons (10 mL) of red-wine vinegar. Whisk in half a cup (125 mL) of extra-virgin olive oil, and let the asparagus marinate in the refrigerator for a couple of hours until chilled.

For an Oriental flavour and an interesting textural variation, toss drained blanched asparagus with a vinaigrette of one tablespoon (15 mL) of sesame oil, a tablespoon (15 mL) of rice vinegar, two tablespoons (30 mL) of soy sauce, sugar to taste and half a cup (125 mL) of fresh chopped walnuts.

During asparagus season in Germany, restaurants serve this classic asparagus salad with a slice of ham and new potatoes. Save half a cup (125 mL) of broth from blanching two pounds (1 kg) of asparagus, and add to it a bunch of chopped chives, a few chopped lovage leaves and a white onion, sliced thinly. Shake well with two tablespoons (30 mL) each of light vinegar and extra-virgin olive oil. Season with salt and Tabasco sauce, then pour over blanched, freshened asparagus and allow to sit for several hours at room temperature. Garnish with pink chive flowers.

Asparagus in Mustard Cream

Lemon and mustard are ideally suited to bringing out the flavour of asparagus, and the yellow sauce perfectly complements the deep green of the spears.

2 lbs.	asparagus spears	1 kg
2	egg yolks at room temperature	2
2 Tbsp.	lemon juice	30 mL
¼ cup	Dijon mustard	50 mL
½ cup	extra-virgin olive oil	125 mL
	Salt & white pepper to taste	

Blanch, drain and chill the asparagus. Beat the egg yolks, lemon juice and mustard for 4 minutes with a whisk, an electric mixer or a food processor. On slow speed, beat in the olive oil in a thin stream until the sauce has the consistency of thin mayonnaise. Add salt and pepper, and chill thoroughly. To serve, spoon the sauce over asparagus and sprinkle with fresh parsley, or serve the spears separately with the sauce for dipping.

Because of the raw egg, do not leave the sauce at room temperature for more than 1 ½ hours, and do not keep leftovers.

THE BRASSICAS

In the steamy world of plants, a confusion of names is usually a sign of rampant interbreeding. In England, white cabbage is called winter broccoli, and in France, it is the flower stalk of the cabbage that is called broccoli.

It is true: brassicas crossbreed with shocking willingness and ease. All of the diverse members of this large, hardy family—cabbages, Brussels sprouts, cauliflower, broccoli, kale, kohlrabi—share a common ancestor, the colewort, or wild cabbage, called *bresic* by the Celts, who gave the family its name. So different are the various brassicas in flavour and form that it seems inconceivable they are related; yet these plants evolved not through hybridization or mutation but simply through the selection of specific elements all present in the original plant. Leaves curling inward were prodded to form heads; leaves with a tendency to crinkle became savoy; anthocyanin, a naturally occurring pigment that turns plants red or blue, was selected for until red cabbage appeared; the tendency to form little heads at the leaf axils produced Brussels sprouts; a swelling stalk brought us kohlrabi; concentration on the flower produced cauliflower, which has a centripetal inflorescence, and broccoli, with centrifugal florets. And the plant breeders are still busy interbreeding cousins, most recently producing Broccoflower and Floccoli.

Despite their differences, all the brassicas require similar growing conditions. Except for cauliflower, they are all quite hardy and, with the exception of Brussels sprouts, which need 100 days to mature, produce two crops a year, one sown indoors about six weeks before the last frost and the other seeded directly in the garden late in the spring.

Although seedlings are widely available in the spring, brassicas are easy to start from seed and a real bargain too—at least 200 plants from a package of seed. Furthermore, starting this family indoors ensures sturdier plants which are less susceptible to the insect attacks that have given brassicas such a bad name among gardeners. At least their infancy is free from worms and maggots.

For the spring crop, start brassicas around April 1, soaking the seeds overnight and planting them in six-packs, several to a pot, covered with a quarter-inch of soil. They all need light and heat to germinate. At 72 degrees F, there is usually 100 percent germination within a week. Move the six-packs to a bright windowsill or under grow lights, thin to the sturdiest per pot, and three weeks later, harden them off. Five to seven weeks after sowing, transplant the seedlings to the garden. Brassicas other than cauliflower will survive in the garden until two or three weeks before the last frost.

In the garden, brassicas like a sunny, sheltered spot with soil as fertile as you can make it, containing lots of phosphorus and potassium and having a pH close to neutral: 6.5 to 7.5. Add a little lime-

stone or wood ashes to make the soil more alkaline: brassicas do not do well in acidic soil. Prepare the bed in the fall, digging very deeply so that their roots will be able to reach water reserves deep underground. Brassicas prefer firm soil, so if possible, let the bed rest several months between digging and planting. But most important, rotate crops regularly: plant brassicas where beans and peas grew the year before, and follow them with leafy greens. Never grow brassicas in the same spot more than once every three years to avoid the worst of the soil pests and diseases that plague them.

At transplanting time, don't fork over the ground again; simply rake lightly, adding a little general-purpose fertilizer if necessary. If you didn't prepare the beds in the fall, dig individual holes about a foot deep and pack with rotted manure. Set the hardened-off transplants in staggered holes 18 inches apart, planting them an inch or so deeper than they were growing in the pots or flats and tamping down the soil firmly, creating a depression the size of a dinner plate where water can pool.

At transplanting time, forestall cutworms and root maggots, brassicas' worst enemies. To foil cutworms, set a collar around each stem so that it extends an inch into the soil and at least an inch above the ground. For double protection, sprinkle wood ashes around the collar. Then tuck 6 inches of well-rotted compost around each plant. The fly that produces root maggots can't get through the mulch to lay its eggs. Flea beetles, however, may still eat the leaves. Control these with rotenone or by covering the brassica bed with a floating row cover.

The sturdiest plants resist insect attack best, so keep the brassicas well watered, soaking them deeply through the mulch—not from above—at least once a week. While they are still young, treat them once to fish emulsion or manure tea. Do not overfeed with manure, however; it makes brassica foliage tender and susceptible to pests. Remove weeds by hand: hoeing can easily damage roots.

About 100 days before the first fall frost date, sow the second crop of brassicas directly in the garden. Brassicas don't mind growing in the cold, but they like heat to germinate. Before sowing, be sure the weather is settled and the nights warm. Plant soaked seeds two per inch in rows, or sow several seeds in groups 18 inches apart. Allowing several for flea beetles and cutworms, you need a generous seeding to get a few healthy plants. Cover the seed with a half-inch of soil and a thin layer of peat and keep it moist. When they sprout, thin to 18 inches apart or to the strongest in each group, and protect with collars. You can also sow the sum-

Autumn brassicas: kohlrabi, red cabbage, red Brussels sprouts, 'Romanesco' broccoli, purple cauliflower and flowering kale.

mer brassicas in a "nursery bed" or in six-packs kept close to the house. Move them to a permanent location when they are up to 5 inches tall.

Cabbage butterflies will likely invade the brassica patch: catch them one by one with a butterfly net. Some inevitably manage to lay eggs; larvae must be handpicked and destroyed. For a severe infestation, apply *Bacillus thuringiensis* (Bt), diatomaceous earth or rotenone. If slugs or earwigs get into the mulch, midnight forays with insecti-cidal soap should reduce their numbers. In Turid's garden, larger pests are also a problem. "Ground-hogs will walk through fresh grass and clover and settle in for dinner on the brassicas," she says. "The same with the deer later in the year. They only leave behind the tough, coloured leaves of flowering kale and the stems of Brussels sprouts."

Disease is a more serious threat. Clubroot occurs in all members of the cabbage family, causing plants to wilt during the day and older leaves to yellow and drop. Infected with the soilborne fungus, roots swell, stunting and sometimes killing the plant. There is no cure: prevent the disease with crop rotation and a soil pH over 7.2.

Diverse and colourful in the garden, brassicas are also a delight in the kitchen, where many are transformed by blanching: pale 'Romanesco' broccoli becomes intensely green, while purple Brussels sprouts metamorphose from deep purple to indigo-jade. The brassicas are well known for the

A vibrant Broccoflower: Brassica oleracea *(Botrytis Group).*

those who ate the most cruciferous vegetables had the lowest cancer risk. Major epidemiological studies around the world since then support the findings. Apparently, cabbage and its cousins work by stimulating the body's natural detoxification systems.

Oddly enough, brassicas have another toxicological association. All crucifers contain a natural toxin, thiocyanate, formed in the plant as a defence against insect predators. The toxin poses no problem to neighbouring plants during the growing season, but when broccoli, cabbage and the like are left in the soil, the toxin is released and overwinters, wreaking havoc on future crops, especially small-seeded vegetables such as lettuce and spinach. So after the harvest, clean up the cabbage patch, adding all the leaves to the compost, where heat rapidly breaks down thiocyanate. Don't worry about the effects of thiocyanate on humans. Researchers suggest that a diet would have to comprise more than 30 percent crucifers before thiocyanate would pose a danger—a lot of coleslaw.

Broccoli
Brassica oleracea (Botrytis Group)

"It's broccoli, dear," soothes the mother in an E.B. White *New Yorker* cartoon.

"I say it's spinach," replies the child behind his heaped plate of greens, "and I say the hell with it."

In the 1940s, broccoli was a garden novelty and alien to North American dinner tables. Today, the deep green florets are among the continent's favourite vegetables: in a poll in the United States, broccoli and cauliflower ranked first in a "Favourite Veggie" contest. But the change in popularity has not come overnight. Although glowingly described in John Randolph's 1775 *Treatise on Gardening* —"The stems will eat like asparagus and the heads like cauliflower"—it has taken 200 years for North Americans to learn to appreciate this brassica.

The broccoli Randolph described is *Brassica oleracea italica*, a vegetable with its origins in Italy. Its genesis is unclear, but food historian Waverley Root suggests that the Etruscans may have developed it from cabbage, although neither brassica thrives particularly well in the hot, dry Mediterranean climate. The Chinese adopted it from the West and perfected the rules for its preparation: always crisp and flavourful, never bitter and limp.

Broccoli is less pronounced in flavour than cabbage but not as mild as cauliflower. It has more vitamins than either. Each spear contains 4,500 units of vitamin A, 491 milligrams of potassium and 72 milligrams of calcium, all for only 40 calories.

strong odour that permeates the house during cooking. For salads, brassicas are only lightly steamed, if cooked at all, but the smell can be reduced and the vegetable enhanced by adding herbs such as dill or fennel to the blanching water.

Brassicas are gaining rapidly in popularity, perhaps partly because of the remarkable health benefits recently discovered in this family of cruciferous plants (so named because their four-petalled flowers look like a cross). In the past few decades,

scientists have come to believe that certain compounds in food may help prevent cancer or slow its development. The notion first gained credibility with the cabbage family, which contains substances called indoles that act as antidotes to cancer. In the mid-1970s, a study showed that 91 percent of the rats exposed to a carcinogen got breast cancer; when rats were given indoles, only 21 percent developed the disease. Another study of men with and without colon cancer found that

A cup of freshly picked, steamed broccoli florets has more than twice the recommended daily allowance of vitamin C. It is also relatively high in protein and a good source of dietary fibre, iron and niacin. Rich in beta carotene, broccoli tops the food lists of people who have low rates of cancer of the esophagus, stomach, colon, lung, larynx, prostate and pharynx. In tests done by the U.S. army in the 1950s, guinea pigs that ate broccoli did not succumb to otherwise lethal doses of radiation. In one study, women who ate broccoli were less prone to cancer of the cervix.

There are three main types of broccoli: purple-sprouting, white-sprouting and green-sprouting (Calabrese). To varying degrees, they all produce a second crop of side shoots once the main head is harvested. Purple-sprouting is the most popular home-garden broccoli in Britain. 'Early Purple Sprouting' (TM) is extremely hardy and forms very compact, prolific budding shoots that turn from purple to green when steamed. The rarer white-sprouting broccoli looks like cauliflower and is likewise very compact. Green-sprouting broccoli forms a huge, dome-shaped head. 'Italian Green Sprouting Calabrese' (NI) is particularly prolific, producing little heads deep into the warm summer. In Turid's opinion, the prettiest of the Calabrese broccolis is the widely available 'Romanesco,' whose cone-shaped florets grow in a spiral, like an enormous chartreuse conch nestled in deep green leaves. This unusual head is not only eye-catching in the garden but also beautiful served as individual spears, since each floret repeats the swirling conch pattern. Of the traditional Calabrese broccolis, we like 'Premium Crop' (DO) best.

Start early varieties of broccoli like all the brassicas, transplanting the hardened-off seedlings into the garden 18 inches apart in early May. For a second crop, sow broccoli seeds outdoors in the salad garden or a nursery bed 100 days before the average first autumn frost; Turid usually plants hers the first week of June.

Five to six weeks after transplanting or when the direct-sown plants are about 6 inches tall, fertilize with a liquid fish emulsion. To produce large broccoli heads, the soil has to be extra rich. Water well, especially in warm weather, soaking the soil deeply through the mulch. Do not sprinkle from above, however, since water sitting on the head encourages disease.

Buds start to set about two months after transplanting or when the nights cool in the fall. Harvest heads when the flower buds are tight and firm, cutting the stalk about 4 inches long. The word broccoli is actually a corruption of the Latin *bracchium*, meaning "branch" or "strong arm." The Romans used to refer to the vegetable as the five fingers of Jupiter, and with good cause. After the central flower head is harvested, sprouts continue to grow from the axils of the leaves, producing smaller florets that are equally delicious. (Actually, this is far more likely to take place in the fall than in the summer, because side shoots are most prolific when temperatures are below 70 degrees F.) Once the buds start to yellow, they are just a step from opening. If you miss the firm green stage, wait until they are open and sprinkle the edible flowers over the salad.

It is almost essential that broccoli be harvested at its prime; although it stores for a week in the refrigerator, nutritional content suffers. After 24 hours, refrigerated broccoli loses 19 percent of its vitamin C, and in two days, more than 30 percent. To store, place the stalks in a wide-mouthed jar of cold water, and cover the whole thing with a perforated plastic bag. If the flower heads get wet, they rot quickly, never a pleasant experience. Since I am never sure that I have plucked all the cabbage loopers, I usually soak broccoli heads in salted water for 20 minutes or so before storing: the worms die and float to the surface. Rinse and pat dry.

To prepare broccoli for salads, rinse well and cut off the woody part of the base. Peeling is rarely necessary with homegrown stalks, although it is often a requirement with tougher supermarket fare. Cut the head into bite-sized florets, and julienne the stalks or cut diagonally in quarter-inch slices. For salads, the less cooking, the better, although blanching for a minute or two helps reduce the gassiness for which raw broccoli is renowned. Steam it briefly, just until the colour brightens, then remove it immediately from the heat and freshen the florets under cold running water. Dry carefully, since the heads quickly become unpleasantly waterlogged.

Broccoli makes a lovely salad on its own, tossed in a tarragon vinaigrette. For colour and texture, I almost always add finely sliced white or red onion, strips of roasted red pepper, a sprinkling of almonds or edible flowers. Broccoli can also withstand a heavier sauce. For an Oriental salad, mix a quarter-cup (50 mL) of crunchy peanut butter, two teaspoons (10 mL) of sesame oil, three tablespoons (45 mL) of soy sauce, a teaspoon (5 mL) of sherry, half a teaspoon (2 mL) of lemon juice, two teaspoons (10 mL) of crushed garlic, one or two tablespoons (15 mL or 30 mL) of honey and half a cup (125 mL) of yogurt. Spice with a drop or two of chile oil, and toss with any blanched brassica, cold asparagus tips or fresh spinach, garnishing with toasted sesame seeds.

Flammifero

Adapted from Bert Greene's book *Greene on Greens*, this recipe uses broccoli stalks only. The name comes from the slicing technique, which reduces the stems to matches.

3 or 4	large broccoli stalks, peeled & julienned	3 or 4
2	small ripe tomatoes, peeled, seeded & chopped	2
1	clove garlic	1
¼ tsp.	coarse salt	1 mL
2 Tbsp.	extra-virgin olive oil	30 mL
1 tsp.	red-wine vinegar	5 mL
2 tsp.	lemon juice	10 mL
	Freshly ground black pepper to taste	

Mix the broccoli and tomatoes in a bowl. Mash the garlic with the salt, and whisk in the oil, vinegar and lemon juice. Pour over the broccoli. Add pepper, and toss well. Chill an hour before serving.

Cauliflower
Brassica oleracea (Botrytis Group)

"Cauliflower," wrote Mark Twain, "is nothing but cabbage with a college education." Much milder in flavour than its plebeian cousins, cauliflower—literally, cabbage flower—is also more difficult to grow. It needs rich soil, regular watering, assiduous pest control and, almost always, help in protecting its "curd," or flowering head, from the sun so that it blanches snow-white.

In the France of Louis XV, cauliflower was the vegetable of the rich. It has been grown commercially in North America only since the 1920s, and it did not become really popular until the past decade, during which consumption nearly doubled. Like broccoli (a relative so close, they share the same group), cauliflower has the cabbage family's cancer-preventing qualities, as well as large amounts of potassium and vitamin C (one cup supplies the recommended daily allowance) and good concentrations of protein and iron.

There are summer and fall varieties of cauliflower, the former more compact. Unless they are a self-blanching type, the leaves must be manually tied up to block the sun. 'White Sails' (ST) is reputedly self-blanching, but we tie it up anyway, and it reliably produces 10-inch snow-white heads. We also grow 'Sicilian Purple' (NI), a purple cauliflower that grows more slowly than the white but is easier to handle, since it need not be blanched. The florets sit on creamy green stems and appear to be spray-painted purple, although they turn green when steamed. Raw, it has a fresh, sweet flavour that becomes more strongly ''brassica'' the longer it is cooked. There are also the new chartreuse cauliflowers that are broccoli-cauliflower hybrids, sometimes called Broccoflower or Floccoli. 'Alverda' (JO) produces uniform medium-sized heads that look like a cross between 'Romanesco' broccoli and white cauliflower, although it tastes more like the former. It lacks the swirling conch design, but the rosettes form a pointed tip. Finally, there are miniature cauliflowers, which have much less foliage and require only a third as much space as other varieties. Gardeners with very short growing seasons may have more success with the miniatures and the hybrids.

Grow cauliflower in the same way as broccoli, remembering that it is the most temperamental of the brassicas: the seedlings are frost-hardy but do not thrive in the cold, so wait until after the last frost to move them into the garden. They need a deeply dug, fertile bed, a good supply of nourishment and water and a long, steady growing season. They do not head up well in hot weather, and a hot, dry spell can destroy a crop that has already set heads. Inadequate moisture causes stunted heads and brown spots, so mulching is very important. When you notice little heads forming, tie the leaves loosely together with binder twine or cotton cord, even on self-blanching varieties. Check first for cabbage butterfly larvae. (Cauliflower is subject to all the usual brassica bugs.)

Cauliflower gives the gardener a little more leeway at harvesttime than broccoli does, since the entire bed is less likely to mature at the same time. Pick the heads before the buds open, while the florets are still tight and bright white. Once it starts to separate into individual cream-coloured florets, the flavour is too strong. You can tell a good head by the smell: when overripe, cauliflower reeks of old cabbage. Unlike broccoli, cauliflower does not sprout little buds after the main head is harvested.

Cauliflower heads keep, unwashed, in the refrigerator for about a week. Wrap or bag them before refrigerating to keep humidity high, but leave four to six quarter-inch air holes to prevent carbon-dioxide buildup. To prepare cauliflower, remove the outer leaves, cut out the core and rinse, then break the head into bite-sized florets, dicing the stalks or slicing them thinly. Add raw to green salads, or serve as crudités with curried or horseradish mayonnaise (see page 128). Raw cauliflower can also be sliced finely and tossed with thinly sliced carrot, celery, radishes and green onion in a sauce made by blending two finely chopped hard-cooked eggs, half a cup (125 mL) of mayonnaise, half a teaspoon (2 mL) of salt, two tablespoons (30 mL) of lemon juice and five teaspoons (25 mL) of Dijon mustard.

For solo salads, steam the cauliflower whole or in florets. (Steaming it whole causes less damage to the florets, which are trimmed off the head after it is cooked.) A whole cauliflower takes 10 minutes or more, the florets only 2 minutes to the tender-crisp stage. Cooked longer, the heads become soggy and the taste stronger. Add a little lemon juice or white-wine vinegar to the cooking water to keep the cauliflower white. Never use an aluminum pot, as it darkens the florets. (Prolonged heat or the alkali in hard water will also tint cauliflower brownish yellow. Lemon juice or cream of tartar in the cooking water helps neutralize alkalinity.) A little milk in the cooking water will sweeten a cauliflower that is past its prime.

Auguste Escoffier, a world-renowned chef, recommended tossing steamed florets with an oil-and-vinegar dressing flavoured with chopped chervil. Caraway seed or minced dill are equally delicious. Or marinate in a nut oil and white-wine vinaigrette and garnish with sliced hazelnuts or pecans. A Lebanese favourite is steamed, cooled florets bathed in a dressing made by mashing a garlic clove with a pinch of coarse salt and stirring in three tablespoons (45 mL) of tahini (sesame paste), two tablespoons (30 mL) of cauliflower cooking liquid and one-third cup (75 mL) of lemon juice. Blend until smooth and white, and pour over the cauliflower. Do not toss lest the florets break apart.

Mustard Cauliflower Salad

This dressing contains no oil at all and is equally delicious on a mixed-brassica salad. For variety, add a little curry or cumin.

¾ cup	chicken stock	175 mL
1 tsp.	dill seed	5 mL
3	bay leaves	3
1	medium cauliflower, cut into bite-sized florets	1
2 tsp.	Dijon mustard	10 mL
1 tsp.	minced fresh dill	5 mL

Heat stock, dill seed and bay leaves in a stainless-steel pot. Add cauliflower florets, cover and simmer until tender-crisp, about 2 minutes. Uncover, cool, then chill the cauliflower in its stock for half an hour. Drain the florets, reserving the stock. Combine a quarter-cup (50 mL) stock with mustard, toss with cauliflower, and sprinkle with fresh dill.

Brussels Sprouts
Brassica oleracea (Gemmifera Group)

Unlike the rest of the brassicas, which produce two crops, Brussels sprouts are so slow-growing that they yield only a single harvest in the fall. From transplanting, they take the entire growing season, up to 120 days, to leaf out and develop the little cabbages along their stalks, so choose a permanent place in the salad garden for them. Luckily, Brussels sprouts are extremely decorative in the salad garden, resembling tropical palms, and they are well adapted to fluctuating seasons, being especially tolerant of cold. A little frost even sweetens the sprouts. A rare fresh vegetable that can be harvested well into November (and throughout the winter in warmer zones), Brussels sprouts elicit strong emotions from those who try them—people either love them or hate them. Yet they look as exotic on the plate as in the garden, and if harvested while young and sweet, we think they are indisputably delicious.

Brussels sprouts are also extraordinarily healthful, even for a crucifer. They are very high in vitamin C, richer in protein than most vegetables and very low in sodium and fat. But like all brassicas, they must be eaten as soon as they are picked: the vitamin C content of ''fresh'' Brussels sprouts should be as high as orange juice, but in one test, sprouts bought at a farmers' market contained too little vitamin C to measure. Along with broccoli and cabbage, they are the top brassicas on the food lists of people with low rates of cancer in general and stomach and colon cancer in particular. Animals fed Brussels sprouts and then the potent carcinogen benzopyrene developed fewer cancers than control animals and had greater liver-enzyme activity, which is known to forestall cancer formation. Of several vegetables tested, including cabbage, broccoli and cauliflower, Brussels sprouts were the most effective, providing twice as much protection as cabbage.

While nurseries often sell seedlings, Brussels sprouts are easy to start from seed, and you are more likely to produce compact, sturdy plants that survive transplanting well. Furthermore, purple varieties such as 'Rubine' (CG) are generally available only from seed. They mature more slowly than

'Sugarloaf' chicory, red cabbages, red Brussels sprouts and a hedge of asparagus combine colour and height in the garden.

green Brussels sprouts, but they are especially striking in the garden.

Brussels sprouts are grown like all the brassicas, although they need a little extra room. Start seeds early indoors, and transplant seedlings to the garden in mid-May. Set them about 2 feet apart in a sunny spot sheltered from wind, since they are top-heavy when mature. (You can also hill them to secure the base.) They like nitrogen-rich topdressing, so around mid-July, pack a layer of well-rotted compost around the base of the plant. Of all the brassicas, Brussels sprouts, particularly the purple variety, are least affected by cabbage butterflies. Turid's sprouts have never been bothered by aphids, usually a common hazard.

Brussels sprouts start to form heads about three months after transplanting, provided that night temperatures hover around 60 degrees F. The little cabbages mature first at the base, developing progressively up the stalk. When the bottom sprouts are half-size, about an inch long, break off the lower leaves of the plant to give the sprouts more air and room to grow. Repeat this as the later sprouts mature, but leave the top foliage intact to feed the sprouts. Eventually, the plant looks like a palm with a gnarled trunk and a tuft of leaves at the top. When frost threatens, pile dry mulch around the base of plants with undeveloped sprouts: they continue to grow even after the first snowfall.

Start picking the sprouts from the bottom of the

plants when they are about the size of a walnut and tightly closed. Cut them off with a knife, or snap them free with a sharp downward twist. Remove yellow leaves and any open "blown" sprouts as you harvest. When night temperatures regularly fall below 20 degrees F, pull up the whole plant and hang in a cool cellar, where you can continue to harvest sprouts for a couple of weeks.

Store sprouts, unwashed, in a plastic bag in the refrigerator for not more than three days. To prepare, wash thoroughly, removing any tough, withered or yellowed outer leaves. Although they can be shredded raw into salads, they are better steamed. Overcooked Brussels sprouts are the epitome of bad British cooking, but they need not be mushy or bitter. Marinating the little cabbages in dressing mitigates any strong brassica taste.

To steam Brussels sprouts, trim stem ends, cut the sprouts in quarters or eighths, and steam for 5 minutes. Or you can steam them whole for 15 minutes or so, cutting an X in the bottom of the sprout to ensure even cooking. Freshen with cold water, halve or quarter the steamed sprouts, then marinate immediately so that the dressing penetrates to the core. Brussels sprouts, green onions, pimentos and sliced Jerusalem artichokes tossed in a white-wine vinaigrette make a delicious late-fall salad.

Ruby Sprout Salad

Preparing purple sprouts is a vivid experience. The magenta cabbages fade as they steam, dyeing the cooking water bright teal-blue. Toss them in the marinade, and they turn the colour of rubies, worthy of their Latin name.

1 lb.	steamed Brussels sprouts	500 g
2 Tbsp.	rice-wine vinegar	30 mL
2 Tbsp.	safflower oil	30 mL
1 tsp.	sesame oil	5 mL
1 tsp.	honey	5 mL

Steam the sprouts briefly, freshen, and cut in quarters. Whisk the dressing ingredients until emulsified, and pour over sprouts immediately. Chill thoroughly. This salad keeps well for several days.

Cabbage
Brassica oleracea (Capitata Group)

Cabbages were among the first vegetables sown in North America: Jacques Cartier planted some when he landed in Canada in 1540. By the time the Americans declared their independence from Britain in

'Stonar': an autumn cabbage that stores well for winter salads.

1776, cabbages were common in native gardens.

Cabbage—the name is a corruption of an Old French word *caboche*, meaning "head"—is the true ancestor of all the brassicas. It was the Romans who developed many of the strains we enjoy today. An expensive vegetable, it was profitable for farmers and therefore worth the special attention that led to new breeds: head cabbage, red cabbage, Milan cabbage, savoy cabbage.

Given its cancer-preventing attributes, cabbage salad should be a regular on the family menu. Cabbage itself is remarkably low in calories: when shredded raw, only 15 calories per cup for the green varieties and 20 for the red types. It is very high in potassium (about 163 milligrams in an average serving), very low in sodium and fat and a good source of fibre and vitamin C, although less so than the brassicas mentioned thus far. In test-tube trials, cabbage destroyed bacteria and viruses and apparently boosted the immune functioning of animal cells. It also speeds up absorption of the drug acetaminophen. Cabbage appears to contain a natural antiulcer drug. No wonder this brassica was once known as "the doctor of the poor."

Cabbages divide into fast-growing types for early harvest and varieties suitable for storing, which require a long maturation time. Seed catalogues offer page after page of cabbage listings. Many of the varieties are bred for commercial cultivation and shipping over long distances. Look for disease resistance, if your garden is plagued by brassica bugs, and flavour. Spring cabbages generally have round or conical heads, smaller than cabbages for fall harvest. At the top of our list for early coleslaws is 'Salarite' (NI, CG), which takes less than two months to produce semisavoyed, very compact heads with juicy, deep green leaves. 'Express' (DA) is equally early, and we were especially taken with its unusual small, conical heads. Autumn cabbages are generally ball-headed. We like 'Stonar' (ST), which has a large, dense head that stores well. Savoy cabbages have crisp, puckered, dark green leaves that wrap around one another more loosely than the other heading cabbages. The tender leaves are milder and sweeter, never bitter but with good cabbage character. We grew, interplanted with ornamental flowering cabbage, 'Canada Savoy' (ST), which we harvested well into October after the frosts had sweetened their leaves. 'Langedijker Winterkeeper' and 'Savoy King' (DA) both store well. Red cabbages are very hardy and don't split as readily as the green do, but they do not store as well. We recommend 'Ruby Perfection' (ST), which stayed tight and tasty until January.

Spring cabbages mature the fastest of the brassicas. Start them indoors, growing them slowly in a cool place so that they develop short, thick main stems. Transplant them into the garden two or three weeks before the last spring frost, giving them shelter on cold nights. We start spring cabbages in mid-March, move them to the cold frame in mid-April and transplant at the end of the month. Plant autumn cabbages directly in the garden in late May or early June, staggering the sowing to prolong the harvest. Cabbages particularly dislike acidic soil, so if in doubt, dig some ground limestone into the bed.

Water cabbages regularly from below, and mulch heavily to help retain moisture. But too much water or a feast-or-famine regimen will cause the heads to split. To prevent this, some gardeners recommend grasping the cabbage head in both hands and giving the plant a quarter-turn twist to prune the roots, reducing the water uptake. As the heads mature, nourish the plants with liquid manure or

Lebanese cabbage salad made with a lemon-mint vinaigrette.

compost. Bordering the bed or interplanting with thyme, marigolds, fennel, leeks or onions may keep the usual brassica pests at bay. Kill slugs by sprinkling the plants with strong brine.

Harvest cabbage when the heads are firm and unyielding, cutting the ball out from the nest of leaves. There is no harm in taking a few heads early to extend the fresh coleslaw season. Instead of waiting until the head is huge, cut it off when it is the size of a grapefruit, pull up the plant, and seed fast-growing greens in the open spaces. Before the first frost, harvest all the cabbages; frost turns the outer leaves black and slimy. Cut off the roots and stems, remove outer leaves, and store the heads in straw-lined boxes in a cool, dry place. The leaves blanch white, and although they do not make superior salads, cold-cellar cabbages will get you through the winter.

In the kitchen, wrap cabbage heads in plastic and refrigerate. One of the hardier vegetables, cabbage lasts two or three weeks this way. To prepare cabbage for salad, wash and trim away tough outer

leaves. Cut the stem even with the bottom of the head. Cut the head in half or in quarters, turn each section flat side down on a cutting board, and slice it a quarter-inch thin with a long, sharp vegetable knife. Food processors do the job quickly, but the result is very fine: use the slicing rather than the shredding blade. A medium head yields seven or eight cups (1.7 L or 2 L) of shredded cabbage. Add a handful to green salads, or shred a whole head for slaw.

The classic preparation of raw cabbage is coleslaw, which simply means cabbage sliced. Cartoonist Gary Larson once penned a cartoon showing a group of elderly women carrying placards declaring "Bring Back Coleslaw." Associated in many minds with church suppers and fish-and-chip stands, coleslaw has an undeservedly tarnished reputation. It can be superbly crisp and delicious. There are thousands of recipes and usually a family favourite. In the interests of nudging your horizons, try slicing red and green cabbage together, adding shredded carrot, radish, celery, diced green and red pepper and handfuls of minced herbs such as parsley, chervil, fennel, mint and coriander. The Germans like caraway and dill; the Mennonites make it with cider vinegar and brown sugar. One of our favourites is "Cool Slaw"—three cups (750 mL) of shredded green and red cabbage mixed with a quarter-cup (50 mL) of chopped red onion and dressed with a half-cup (125 mL) of plain yogurt and chopped fresh parsley.

Lebanese Cabbage Salad

To bring coleslaw back to the family table, try this Middle Eastern variation. Typical of the region, it is very lemony, which helps curtail the vitamin C losses from the cut cabbage. If it is too sour for your taste, add a dash of sugar. The flavours combine wonderfully with grilled lamb.

2 cups	finely shredded green cabbage	500 mL
½ cup	thinly sliced green pepper	125 mL
1	small tomato, seeded & finely chopped	1
¼ cup	thinly sliced red or white onion or scallions	50 mL
2 Tbsp.	finely chopped parsley	30 mL
2 Tbsp.	finely chopped mint	30 mL
⅓ cup	extra-virgin olive oil	75 mL
¼ cup	freshly squeezed lemon juice, strained	50 mL
1	medium clove garlic, crushed	1
	Salt to taste	

Combine the vegetables and herbs in a salad bowl. Beat together the oil, lemon juice, garlic and salt until emulsified. Just before serving, toss the salad with the vinaigrette. Although this salad will keep, it is best served when the vegetables are still fresh and crisp.

Kohlrabi
Brassica oleracea (Gongylodes Group)

Kohlrabi—German for cabbage turnip—is as healthful as any cabbage and leads the family in vitamin C and potassium content. Unfamiliar to many North American gardeners, it is an enlarged aboveground stem that looks like an apple-green turnip with cabbage leaves sprouting from all sides.

There are two basic types of kohlrabi: the Viennas, with green, white or purple skin but always white flesh; and the new hybrids developed for greater heat tolerance, more sweetness and less woodiness. 'Early White Vienna' and 'Early Purple Vienna' (CG, ST) both mature in about 50 days, but the earliest for us was a hybrid, 'Grand Duke' (ST). All have white juicy flesh, although the green Viennas are best for spring and summer; the purple is preferred for late sowing and fall harvest.

For salads, kohlrabi should be harvested very young, so instead of planting indoors, seed this brassica directly in the garden during the first week of May and again in early June through mid-July for a fall harvest. For summer sowings, plant kohlrabi in the lee of taller plants, which will shade its exposed bulbs; too much sun causes kohlrabi to become stringy.

Grow kohlrabi like all the other brassicas, in rich soil with lots of moisture. Firm soil is not as vital as it is with the spindly-stemmed broccolis and cauliflowers. Sow the seeds half an inch apart, and when the plants start to widen at the base of the leaves, thin to an inch apart. You can add the thinnings to salads. Within six weeks of seeding, you can harvest baby kohlrabi to eat as crudités together with baby beets, spring onions and baby radishes. Nine weeks after sowing, they are at their peak salad size of about 2 inches across. To grow full-sized kohlrabi for storage or cooking, thin to about 4 inches apart.

Kohlrabi are quite hardy and keep better in the ground than in storage. To harvest, pull out the whole little plants, and once pulled, store the bulbs in the refrigerator for up to two weeks. Trim and discard all the leaves except the small tender ones near the centre. Add these to green salads as soon as possible, or use as a garnish for kohlrabi salads. Eat very young bulbs raw, but steam older ones, removing the skin after they are cooked to the tender-crisp stage, about 15 minutes. Use kohlrabi raw like carrots or cooked like potatoes: slice, dice or grate. Served raw, they are as crisp as radishes but consistently white and sweet, with no bite at all. Kohlrabi is often used in Schlemmer Salad (page 112) and Spa Salad (page 109). Toss it with celeriac, apple and walnuts in a nut oil/lemon juice vinaigrette.

Chinese Heading Cabbage
Brassica rapa (Pekinensis Group)

There are two types of Chinese cabbages: the tight, compact, heading Chinese cabbages known variously as pe tsai, celery cabbage, michihli and napa; and the looseleaf Chinese cabbages commonly called pak choi, mustard cabbage or Chinese mustard. The latter are best eaten very young as salad greens (see page 46), although the mature stalks can be sliced like celery for salads.

Heading Chinese cabbages are either short and barrel-shaped (napa type) or tall and cylindrical (michihli type). We grew 'Burpee's Two Seasons' (DO), a 10-inch-tall cylindrical head of crisp, pale yellow-green leaves. From a direct sowing in early May, we harvested heads in July, then seeded again in mid-July for a second crop harvested in September.

Chinese cabbages do not take well to transplanting, but for an extra-early crop, start seeds indoors in peat pots around the first week of April. In the first week of May, plant the seedlings outside, setting the tall varieties 12 to 18 inches apart. By June, you can pick the first outside leaves; by July, the plants are mature. Start the plants early enough to avoid the heat of summer, and water regularly. In hot weather, bolting is often a problem; autumn crops are easier to grow. Plant in the middle of July for a fall harvest, either seeding directly or sowing in pots close to the house for better control. Chinese cabbages are prone to all the usual brassica bugs but particularly the flea beetle. A floating row cover is the ideal and final solution, and it will prolong the fall harvest too.

To harvest, pull up the entire head and remove all wrapping leaves to expose the juicy, buttery core. (You don't have to rush. These cabbages tolerate light frosts.) Heading Chinese cabbages can also be tied up and stored in a cool cellar. In this case, leave the wrapper leaves on, and fasten with a rubber band. Remove the outside leaves only when preparing the cabbage for salads.

Chinese cabbage is as crisp and tender as lettuce, but it has a mild mustardy tang that makes it unique in a shredded salad. Remove tough outside leaves, and slice thinly crosswise through the head. For an unusual coleslaw, toss shredded napa with finely sliced ginger, soy sauce, sesame oil and rice-wine vinegar. The Chinese also add a little sugar. Include baby snow peas and shungiku blossoms for colour.

Napa Salad

Pale green Chinese cabbage makes an arresting late-fall salad when combined with dark green broccoli florets, a white daikon radish and a vinaigrette with an Oriental flavour. Made with almost no oil, the salad is extremely low in cholesterol and calories.

1	small Chinese cabbage	1
1	stalk broccoli florets	1

1	small daikon radish	1
1 cup	unsalted chicken stock	250 mL
2	thin slices fresh peeled ginger	2
½ tsp.	Szechuan peppercorns	2 mL
	Dash of sugar	
1 Tbsp.	Chinese black vinegar or balsamic vinegar	15 mL
½ Tbsp.	low-sodium soy sauce	7 mL
½ Tbsp.	safflower oil	7 mL
¼ tsp.	dark sesame oil	1 mL

Slice the cabbage crosswise into half-inch (1.25 cm) pieces, about a cup (250 mL). Steam the broccoli florets until tender-crisp, freshen under cold water, and drain. Slice the daikon into two-inch (5 cm) lengths, then peel each piece by slicing vertically along the perimeter five times, creating a pentangle. Then slice each piece very thinly, bathe the slices in ice water, and drain.

To make the dressing, heat the stock with the ginger, peppercorns and sugar, and cook until reduced to a quarter-cup (50 mL)—about 10 minutes. Remove the ginger slices. Let it cool, then whisk in the vinegar, soy sauce and oils.

Combine the steamed broccoli, sliced cabbage and daikon slices in a bowl. Drizzle the dressing over the vegetables. Toss and serve.

Chicory
Cichorium intybus

Napa salad with Chinese cabbage, broccoli and daikon radish.

Most people think of chicory as a coffee substitute or a blue-flowered roadside weed, but chicory is also a time-honoured salad plant. There are three types: heading chicory, which produces either tight romainelike heads or loose dandelion rosettes; root chicory, which is forced indoors (see page 121); and the dramatic red chicories, radicchio. A favourite of Italians, chicory may take some getting used to. North Americans tend to like their greens on the grassy side—mild and bland. Chicory, on the other hand, is assertive, with a bitterness that never quite loses its edge, even after blanching. If you don't like chicory at first bite, keep nibbling. It is an acquired taste and, given that chicory is hardy, vigorous and pest-free, one worth cultivating.

Chicory is a cool-weather crop, either started indoors very early in the spring or planted outdoors in the middle of the summer so that it matures during the cool days of autumn. In Italy, chicories are overwintered and the tender shoots enjoyed the following spring, but in most parts of Canada, the climate is too harsh. We grew the widely available 'Catalogna,' which in summer looked like a dandelion. In early April, this variety pushes up thick, leafy stems like asparagus, but we never saw them. The hay mulch was home to deer mice, and deer browsed on the sprouts before we got to them.

Chicories are not fussy about soil, although they do best in fertile ground and like open, sunny sites or dappled shade. They can be grown as cut-and-come-again mesclun plants—sow the seed thickly, and six weeks later, shear the bed with scissors to prompt a second growth—but to produce salad heads, be prepared to tend the plants for the duration of the season: they need a very long time to produce results. In northern gardens, they are best planted in summer for fall harvest, since in the spring, hot weather often arrives abruptly, prompting bolting and bitterness.

Heading chicory, often called by its varietal name 'Sugar Loaf,' looks like a Chinese cabbage or a somewhat undisciplined romaine. The tight upright leaves fold around one another, wrapping the inner leaves so that they blanch naturally. These greens are among the most decorative in the late-summer garden. We grew 'Pan di Zucchero' (SH) and 'Crystal Hat' (NI), which was a little lighter in colour and formed a slightly looser head. The plants are both heat- and frost-tolerant and seem to be totally bug-resistant. The rosette chicories grow close to the ground, somewhat like Boston lettuce. We grew 'Grumolo' (NI), the most common Italian rosette variety, which is also extremely cold-hardy.

For both the rosette and the heading chicories, start seeds in midsummer, sowing five seeds per inch directly in the garden in early July. Cover with a quarter-inch of soil, and water well. Shade them from the hot sun, especially when the seedlings first sprout, and keep them moist. Turid always plants a few near the house in peat pots so that she will have some in reserve if the direct seeding fails.

Transplant the peat pots a foot apart into the garden around the first of August, in beds shaded by taller plants. At the same time, thin the direct-sown plants, adding the thinnings to late-summer salads. Keep the chicories well hoed, and water regularly

The hardy chicory family provides delicious fall salads long after lettuces are no more.

so that the soil never dries out. When the plants are growing well, top-dress with compost and mulch.

The heads are ready to harvest in autumn. Moderately hardy, they last well into the snow season if covered with cloches or floating row covers before severe frosts. Harvest by cutting the stems at soil level. Discard the outer leaves, and use the creamy white centre.

Green rosette chicories can be overwintered under a blanket of mulch, resprouting as tender little heads in spring. 'Grumolo' was the only one we tried that proved totally winter-hardy. Sown in mid-summer, it was only 6 inches across by the time the snow fell. Under a mulch of hay, those leaves disintegrated, and the following March, deep green, foot-wide heads formed, resembling Boston lettuce. The plants quickly sent up flower stalks and by July formed a lofty 5-foot-tall hedge dotted with edible sky-blue daisies. Years of breeding may have produced tender first-year chicories, but in the second year, they are practically indistinguishable from their roadside cousin.

Radicchios are among the most prized greens in Italy, often named for the regions where they grow. Shepherd's, The Cook's Garden and Nichols all carry 'Rossa di Verona,' a very hardy cultivar, and 'Rossa di Treviso,' less hardy but one of the oldest strains, dating back four or five centuries. There are many different kinds of radicchio: red, green and variegated, loosely wrapped heads, tight romainelike ovals, open rosettes and the familiar round red ball of white-veined leaves.

Typically, radicchios are seeded directly in the garden around the middle of June for an autumn harvest, since they need cold to develop heads and the characteristic red colour. Sow the seeds a quarter-inch deep, about five per inch in the garden or in peat pots. They sprout in about a week; shade the seedlings as soon as they appear, especially during the Dog Days of summer. Transplant the indoor seedlings a foot apart in a spot shaded by tall plants such as Brussels sprouts; thin the direct-sown plants to about a foot apart.

All radicchios start off green, growing vigorously

through the summer, but as the growing season progresses, the rosette and romainelike varieties are treated differently. For rosette types, around the beginning of August, apply a little fertilizer and cut the coarse outer leaves away from the curled leaves at the centre. Pruned thus, all the energy goes to the heart of the plant. As the weather cools, the centre leaves curl more tightly in on each other and gradually turn a deep red. By mid-September, heads are 4 to 5 inches in diameter, solid balls of deep red leaves encircled with white ribs like fingers.

A recent cultivar is 'Guilio' (DO). Planted directly in the garden in spring, it forms a solid red head by the end of June. We started 'Guilio' indoors April 1, transplanted the seedlings to the garden in early May and harvested deep maroon heads by the end of June. Although the catalogue said this variety did not need trimming, removing the outer leaves seemed to improve head development.

The elongated romainelike strains of radicchio, such as 'Red Treviso' (NI), have long, slender, lancelike leaves that are green and very bitter in summer. The plant grows like sorrel, about a foot high and wide and very bushy. Five weeks before the first frost, shear the leaves to a 2-inch stubble. They quickly resprout and, with the onset of cool weather, turn deep red with a light green centre vein. To make the heart sweeter, blanch it by setting a box or flowerpot over top of it for a week or more. The leaves will be less bitter but also less colourful, fading in the dark from red to pink.

Not all the plants from a sowing turn red. With 'Red Treviso,' the percentage can be as low as a third. You can't tell which seedlings will change colour, so you may inadvertently thin out the red ones and keep the green.

Radicchios survive frosts well: after two heavy frosts, 'Red Treviso' was still healthy, even without mulch. Before the soil freezes solid, plant a few radicchios in pots and put them on a windowsill, where they will continue growing deep red, lance-shaped leaves. In September, we cut 'Castlefranco' (BL, CG) back to 2 inches and put it in the greenhouse. The variegated chicory produced beautiful rosettes of rounded, crumpled red, green and white leaves that added an unusual decorative touch to Christmas salads.

Chicory, unlike lettuce, keeps quite a long time in the refrigerator. Stored in an opaque plastic bag, heads stay fresh for up to a month. If the taste seems bitter, try soaking the leaves in lukewarm water. Use chicory sparingly in mixed green salads to add a bittersweet note. When using chicory alone in a salad, slice it thinly so that the dressing coats it more thoroughly, and dress it with a strong red-wine vinaigrette.

Italian Salad

This is similar to a composed mesclun, combining mild and bitter greens with flowers for a beautiful and tasty salad.

2	heads radicchio, thinly sliced	2
2 cups	corn salad, whole rosettes	500 mL
2	small heads Bibb lettuce, torn	2
2	handfuls arugula or cress	2
¾ cup	fresh minced basil leaves	175 mL
½ cup	calendula petals	125 mL
¼ cup	borage flowers	50 mL
2-3	fresh sorrel leaves, minced	2-3

Dressing:

1	small green onion, finely chopped	1
1 tsp.	Dijon mustard	5 mL
2-3 Tbsp.	lemon juice	30-45 mL
1 Tbsp.	dry white wine	15 mL
1	egg yolk	1
1 Tbsp.	minced parsley	15 mL
1 Tbsp.	minced chives	15 mL
½ cup	extra-virgin olive oil	125 mL
	Salt & pepper to taste	

Combine the greens and herbs in a salad bowl. Just before serving, whisk the dressing ingredients, drizzle lightly over the greens, and toss gently. Sprinkle flowers over the salad, and serve immediately. (Because of the raw egg, this dressing cannot be made ahead or stored.)

Endive
Cichorium endivia

Endive is native to Egypt, probably one of the bitter herbs Jewish people were enjoined to eat at Passover. Cultivated in Europe since the end of the 13th century, it has now made its way to North America, where it is not as rare in gardens and dining rooms as is its close relative chicory.

Like the chicories, endive is vigorous but slow-growing, a cool-season crop that is relatively immune to pests and diseases. Endive grows well in early spring and late fall and resprouts quickly when sheared, making it an excellent addition to early and late mesclun mixes. Grown to maturity, endive is not as bitter as chicory, although blanching sweetens it delectably for the salad bowl. Very high in vitamin A, it contains some potassium and iron and is very low in calories—only 10 per cup.

There are two types of endive: curly endive, or frisée, and the broadleafed type known as Batavian endive, or escarole. Curly endive, such as 'Frisan' or 'Salad King' (ST), is a very decorative plant, low to the ground, about 16 inches in diameter, with leaves that radiate flat on the ground like a huge dahlia-flowered chrysanthemum. The leaves are very pale apple-green, deeply indented with pointed scallops, ruffled on either side of the well-defined ribs like a fern. Escarole, such as 'Cornetto di Bordeaux' (RE), looks more like leaf lettuce, with rangy, fluffy leaves that have a heavy midrib. It, too, grows very slowly, eventually reaching18 inches across and lifting up more than the frisée types.

For a mesclun-style harvest, broadcast and harvest endive as you would cutting lettuce (see page 17). For mature heads, start curly endive and escarole in early to mid-July, sowing directly in the garden or, for more control, in individual peat pots, transplanting a month later to the garden. Because they spread horizontally, thin endive seedlings to at least a foot apart. Very prone to aphids, they may have to be sprayed with an organic insecticide.

A few weeks before maturity, blanch the plants, shutting out all light for a week to 10 days, until the hearts turn creamy and the flavour mild. Curly endive is so low-growing that upside-down seed flats work well. For escarole, gather up the leaves, tying them loosely into a bundle. Do this late in the day, when the leaves are dry. Blanch only a few heads at a time: you cannot eat the whole planting at once, and when you remove the cover, the plant turns green and bitter again. (Even after blanching, the leaves have a slightly bitter taste.)

In the kitchen, treat endive like chicory, washing frisée types carefully. Use in mixed green salads or alone, with a hearty vinaigrette to mitigate any bitterness. The Spanish make a ground-almond sauce called *Xato* that is delicious with bitter greens. *Salade Paysanne* is an Alsatian specialty made by tossing a large head of curly endive with *lardons* of uncured bacon, minced sautéed shallots, garlic croutons and a warm dressing of four tablespoons (60 mL) of white-wine vinegar, two tablespoons (30 mL) of dry white wine, half a teaspoon (2 mL) of salt and a pinch of sugar whisked with a little reserved bacon fat.

Pea
Pisum sativum

"Peas are, without contradiction, our finest vegetable," wrote Alexandre Dumas. Yet few vegetables are as persnickety as the pea. So delicate is this legume that it must be grown with a watchful eye, harvested at exactly the right moment, steamed immediately after picking and eaten as soon as possible. Meet the pea's exacting demands, and you will be rewarded with a salad that comes as close to earthly perfection as one could ever hope.

The name has evolved from the Latin *pisum*, through Old English to the British "pease" and finally to the shortened "pea" of modern times. The vegetable has a long, though unspecific, history. Known since biblical times in the Middle East, fresh peas were apparently first eaten by the Chinese. Columbus brought them to North America, planting them on Isabella Island in 1493. Native inhabitants adopted the pea and carried it south into Central America and north into Canada, where

Jacques Cartier reported the Hochelagan Indians raising peas at Montreal in 1535.

The pea, despite its humble name, is one of the most beautiful vegetables in the garden: pale green leaves, curling tendrils, orchidlike flowers as lovely as a sweet pea and sickle-shaped pods that are translucent in the morning sun, highlighting the row of pearly peas inside. Not only is it beautiful and tasty, but it is good for you too. Its only obvious drawback could be said to be its unfortunate lack of scent. Like all legumes, it is replete with cholesterol-reducing fibre. Only slightly less rich in vitamin C than citrus fruit and cabbage, peas contain vitamins A and B, thiamin, niacin, iron, riboflavin and considerable protein. Three-quarters of a cup (175 mL) of cooked green peas contains about the same amount of calories and protein as an egg but no cholesterol and hardly any fat.

There are four main types of peas: shelling peas, snow peas, edible-podded 'Sugar Snap' peas and asparagus peas. With shelling peas, you eat the seed and throw away the pod; with snow peas and asparagus peas, you eat the pod before the seeds mature; 'Sugar Snaps' are eaten, pod and all, when the seeds are fully developed.

Until recently, shelling peas have been the staple of North American gardens. There are two types, round and wrinkled, so called because of the relative texture of their respective skins when the peas are dried. Wrinkled varieties are larger, grow in more profusion, contain proportionately less starch and more sugar and taste better than smooth, round peas, which are hardier, quicker to mature and less fussy about soil conditions. Wrinkled varieties, long popular in Europe, are gradually gaining ground here, although seed houses rarely specify whether cultivars are round or wrinkled.

The very best shelling peas are the tiny petit pois peas like 'Frostiroy' (DA). These are not just immature peas but special varieties that produce tiny peas of exceptional sweetness. Of traditional shelling peas, 'Early Bird' (DO) was the earliest Turid grew, producing peas in just 50 days. Very dense, self-supporting and with lots of tendrils, it grew about 2 feet tall and produced white flowers and 3-inch-long pods, large for the size of the plant.

Particularly for gardeners with limited space, shelling peas seem wasteful: even a large harvest produces only a few cups of peas; most of the plant goes to compost. Snow peas (*Pisum sativum* var. *macrocarpon*) make much more sense: you eat the whole pod, and there is no tedious shelling. Aptly, the French call snow peas *mange-tout*, and they are sometimes listed in catalogues under ''Edible-Podded Peas.'' A staple in Oriental cuisine, they are also known as Chinese peas. More prolific and hardier than shelling peas, snow peas are our favourite for salads, although the season is limited to spring and fall. They don't mind cold or wet and can be seeded as early as six weeks before the last spring frost, but they will not tolerate the heat of midsummer. One of the most commonly available cultivars is 'Dwarf Grey Sugar,' a low-growing, bushy plant with short-lived but beautiful deep purple and mauve blossoms. Snow peas must be picked when slender, because the pods quickly become stringy. 'Dwarf Grey Sugar,' which grows only about a foot high, is perfect for container gardens. We've also had success with 'Oregon Sugar Pod.'

In the late 1970s, an Idaho plant breeder developed a dual-purpose pea called 'Sugar Snap' that is eaten pod and all when the peas are fully mature. We grew 'Rae' (PG), a late-season mildew-resistant variety with a heavy yield of slim pods. Most 'Sugar Snaps' have strings that must be removed before eating, but the widely available 'Sugar Pod' is stringless, very sweet and crisp. In general, 'Sugar Snaps' need warmer conditions to sprout successfully: plant later in the spring.

Asparagus, or winged, peas (*Lotus tetragonolobus*) are eaten like snow peas. Unlike other peas, asparagus peas are planted in early June like beans. They grow about 18 inches tall, stems radiating from the centre like a spiderweb. Brownish red flowers bloom in summer, followed by curious winged pods that must be harvested very young—they are fibrous and stringy when larger than an inch. Steamed, their flavour approaches that of artichoke crossed with asparagus, hence the name. If you harvest the pods regularly, the plant continues to produce for up to 10 weeks: from a single planting of 'Asparagus Pea' (TM) on June 1, Turid harvested pods from late July until after the first frosts in late September; it was the only pea to withstand such cold weather.

Shelling and snow peas are further classified by growth habit: bush varieties, which grow up to 2 feet, and tall vining types, which grow up to 5 feet. They all need some support, even those billed as self-supporting. Taller-growing peas need poles, strings or trellises to climb. For dwarf and bush peas, push twigs into the soil on either side of the plants to create a little hedgerow.

Peas are adamantly cool-season crops. They are the first seeds to go into the garden, planted as soon as the ground is workable. If you can't plant early enough or if hot, dry weather arrives suddenly, parching the pea plants in late May, try a warm-weather variety like the popular 'Wanda.' They aren't nearly as tasty and sweet, but they will produce peas despite the heat, when cool varieties simply stop developing. Maturation dates vary dramatically for peas, a characteristic that you will be able to use to your advantage. If you plant an early-maturing variety like 'Laxton's Progress' (55 days) and a late-maturing one like 'Tall Telephone' (70 days) at the same time, you will have successive crops from a single planting. Generally, peas planted in March and April are harvested in June and early July. Forget peas during high summer, then plant again in early August for a late-season harvest just before the frost.

Peas grow best in full sun in well-drained, rich soil with ample phosphorus and potassium but not too much nitrogen. They like sweet soil: add ground limestone if the soil is too acidic. When planting peas in a bed where Leguminosae have never grown, sprinkle inoculant on the soil or shake moistened pea seeds in a little plastic bag containing a teaspoon of the powder. Inoculant helps the pea plant develop root nodules that carry the symbiotic soil bacteria, *rhizobia*. The bacteria convert free nitrogen in the atmosphere to a form usable by the plants. This simple, natural additive increases the yield and improves the soil for the next crop.

If you care to try an experiment of your own, plant without inoculant and pull up a pea plant: if there are a lot of nodules on the roots, the bacteria are present and fixing nitrogen in the soil; if there are few nodules, it means you should add inoculant next time you plant.

Plant pea seeds in trenches so that you can push soil against the first few inches of stem and secure the seedlings, which are frail. The trench also acts as a water ditch, holding moisture close to the young roots. Dig trenches about 10 inches wide, 4 inches deep and 2 ½ feet apart. Between the pea rows, plant beets, carrots, romaine or some other salad vegetable that thrives on filtered light. Turid usually ends her rows with sweet peas, which like the same conditions and provide cut flowers throughout the summer. Before sowing, erect a trellis for climbing peas; bush and dwarf peas support themselves once they are growing.

Soak pea seeds overnight, then toss with inoculant or sprinkle inoculant in the trench. Drop seeds 2 inches apart, staggered within the trench. Cover with about 1 ½ inches of fine soil, and pat down with the back of a rake. Water the bed well.

The peas are up in about a week. Thin dwarf varieties to 3 inches apart, climbers to 4 and asparagus peas to 6. Water and fertilize as usual. When

Traditional shelling peas produce perfect June salads.

Snow peas can also be tossed briefly in a skillet with barely half an inch (1.25 cm) of water until the colour turns bright; then refresh in cold water, drain and set aside for slicing into salads or using with dips. Another delicious method is to stir-fry snow peas for a moment or two in sesame oil, then toss with soy sauce for a quick warm salad.

In the fall, when peppers and fall radishes ripen with the second-crop snow peas, we make this favourite Oriental salad. Blend three tablespoons (45 mL) of toasted sesame seeds, one-third cup (75 mL) of peanut oil, two tablespoons (30 mL) each of dark sesame oil and cider vinegar, one teaspoon (5 mL) of brown sugar, one tablespoon (15 mL) of freshly grated ginger, one minced clove of garlic and one tablespoon (15 mL) each of soy sauce and freshly squeezed lemon juice. Toss with a pound (500 g) of steamed snow peas, half a red pepper sliced thinly, half a cup (125 mL) of thinly sliced scallions and one-quarter cup (50 mL) of thinly sliced daikon radish.

Shelled peas are delicious added to mixed salads, but they also make interesting salads on their own. They look especially attractive with vegetables of contrasting colours—cucumber, 'Presto Pickle,' red pepper, carrots—and the flavour combines well with strong-flavoured nut and seed oils.

Minted Pea Salad

This is a minted variation of the classic petit pois salad, in which blanched peas are tossed with sliced scallions and yogurt, sour cream or mayonnaise. Mint is a refreshing addition and is at its peak just when the first peas are ready to harvest.

3 lbs.	shelled peas	1.5 kg
½ cup	mayonnaise	125 mL
¼ cup	low-fat yogurt	50 mL
1	small onion, thinly sliced	1
¼ cup	coarsely chopped mint	50 mL

Steam the peas until tender-crisp (about a minute). Freshen under cold water. Mix together the remaining ingredients, gently stir in the peas, and season to taste with salt and pepper. Chill thoroughly before serving.

As a variation, add a quarter-cup (50 mL) Dijon mustard to the mix, and substitute tarragon for the mint. The flavour of the peas is somewhat overwhelmed by the mustard, but the sauce is delicious and the contrasting crunch of the peas quite wonderful. This salad is especially good served with meat.

the plants are 6 inches high, mulch them with old manure, compost or clippings to keep the soil cool. In about a month, they will be a foot tall. At this stage, you should make the effort to support bushy, low-growing plants with twigs pushed into the bed between or on either side of the seedlings. They may need help grasping their supports, so twine their tendrils around the twig branches or tie them loosely to their strings.

Peas are prone to pea aphids, corn maggots, fusarium wilt and powdery mildew, a common problem at the end of the growing season. Choose resistant varieties, plant early, and compost the vines as soon as the harvest is over. Don't let them decompose on the garden bed.

Two months after our April sowing, we harvest our first petit pois and snow peas; by the first week of July, all varieties are producing. When harvesting peas, dispel all thoughts that "bigger is better." Check the vines daily. The more you pick, the more the plant produces. Sometimes it is difficult to spot pods in the dense foliage, but if you shake the plants a bit, the pods will swing and you can see them.

The shorter the time between picking and eating, the better. Like corn, peas contain natural sugar that turns to starch within hours of picking. This explains why the ones you grow yourself are so superior to those you buy—even at the farmers' market. If you have to store them in the refrigerator, three days is the maximum.

To prepare peas for salads, top and tail snow peas, 'Sugar Snaps' and asparagus peas; shell the pod peas. If they are young and tender, eat snow peas raw. Otherwise, they should all be cooked briefly. Even if you don't want to make the salad immediately, blanch the peas as soon as they are picked, adding the dressing just before serving. To blanch, drop the peas into boiling salted water for a scant minute (less if shelled peas are small), then plunge into cold water. Snow peas and 'Sugar Snaps' may take up to 5 minutes. Peas can also be steamed until they are tender-crisp, 8 to 12 minutes. The best method is to sample the peas often: the less cooking they are subjected to, the better.

High-Summer Salads

Beans to Tomatoes

Chapter Five

When the sun is too hot for greens, when peas and asparagus have had their day, when the low green hedge across the potato hills is nothing more than a fertile promise, the salad bowl need not lie empty. Summer may be short in the northern garden, but with a little help from indoor seeding, it is long enough to produce salad fruits and vegetables that are ordinarily more at home in the Tropics: tomatoes, peppers, eggplants, okra. Very sensitive to cold, the high-summer salad vegetables come into the garden only after the last spring frost is past and wilt at the first sign of frost in the fall. But for a few brief weeks in July and August, they offer a panoply of sun-ripened salads that are all the more precious for the shortness of their season.

THE BEAN FAMILY

"Bean" is a woefully nonspecific word: it refers to the plant, to the green pod and to the dry little red, white or black seeds inside. Gardeners and gastronomes are so casual with their use of the word "bean" that we no longer distinguish plants grown for different purposes. Within the vast family of beans (Leguminosae) are 600 genera, among them four that are grown as salad beans: *Phaseolus* spp, which includes common green beans, kidney beans, lima beans and runner beans; *Vicia faba*, broad beans; *Glycine max*, soybeans; and *Vigna sesquipedalis*, Chinese yard-long beans.

Within each genus, plants are grouped according to how they grow, from bush beans that reach only 15 to 20 inches tall to climbers that take up less garden space because they stretch vertically, sometimes as much as 8 feet. Often the same variety is bred to grow both ways—'Blue Lake' (ST), for instance. Common beans include both bush and pole types, but broad beans always grow on bushes, and almost all runner beans climb. In general, climbers mature later than bush types.

Beans are further differentiated by how they are used. With green, or snap, beans, the young pods containing immature beans are cooked and eaten. With green shell, or flageolet, types, the pods

Scarlet runner beans are ideal for the small garden and provide beautiful edible flowers.

mature until they are bulging, then the beans are removed from their shells and cooked fresh. The pods of most green shell beans can be left to dry on the vine, but beans bred specifically for that are listed as dry shell, or haricot, types.

The growing season for beans varies by as much as two months. 'Tendercrop' (PA), for example, is ready to harvest in 53 days, while 'Bush Kentucky Wonder' (PA) requires 125. (In northern areas, choose short-season varieties of dried beans so that the seeds mature before the fall rains rot the plants.) However long they take to mature, no beans like to be planted early. The soil temperature should be 60 to 65 degrees F and the weather stable. Broad beans tolerate somewhat cooler weather, while lima beans need soil at 75 degrees. Gambling with an early planting may pay off if the spring is warm, but often, the crop is lost or gets off to such a bad start that later plantings catch up and surpass it. We therefore recommend that gardeners delay the first bean plantings until two weeks after the last spring frost date.

All beans like full sun and well-drained soil rich in organic matter, a pH of 6 to 7.5 and an adequate supply of phosphorus and potassium; like peas, they provide their own nitrogen. Before planting, sprinkle inoculant on the seeds or the soil (see page 84). Seed spacing depends on the variety, but in general, sow them 1 ½ inches deep and 3 to 4 inches apart for bush beans, 5 to 10 seeds around each pole for climbers.

Keep the soil evenly moist, especially while seeds are germinating and until the flowers and pods have set. In sandy soil, side-dress with fertilizer in the middle of the growing season, or apply some wood ashes to add potassium.

Beans are heartrending to watch in the spring. Brown and spindly, they push through the soil and tremble, shivering, in the cool breezes. If they survive the weather, they still have cutworms to contend with. Rings of wood ashes or foil collars around the stems offer protection. Other common pests to watch for are aphids, cabbage loopers, corn earworms, cucumber beetles, European corn borers, leaf

miners and Mexican bean beetles, a ladybug relative only a quarter-inch long with 16 black spots on its back. Handpick the bugs, or apply rotenone, diatomaceous earth or Bt. Several bacterial blights affect beans, leaving dead, oozing spots on the leaves. They thrive in cool, wet weather, so wait for warm weather to plant, spacing the seeds so that the leaves will be well ventilated. Remember to stay out of the bean patch when the leaves are wet with rain or dew to avoid spreading fungal disease.

Harvest snap beans before the seeds fill out; regular picking stimulates higher yields. Harvest green shell beans when the seeds are full-sized, fresh and plump, while the pods are still green. Pick dry shell beans after the leaves drop off the plant, when the pods are papery. Pull out the whole plant, and if it is not quite dry, hang it for a few weeks in a moisture-free place. When pods are brittle, shell the beans and store them in airtight jars in the dark. (If they are not completely dry, place the shelled beans on cookie sheets in an oven on low heat.) Save some seeds for next year's crop: Leguminosae are self-pollinating and sprout reliably from collected seed.

Dry shell beans score extremely high on the nutrition scale. Protein content ranges from 6 to 11 percent, and they are rich sources of the B vitamins, including niacin and folacin. One serving of cooked dry beans can supply almost half the daily allowance of thiamin and B_6. Beans and peas supply more fibre than any food except bran. Several studies show that blood cholesterol goes down when cooked dry beans are added to the diet. Much of the fibre is soluble and good for the heart, but beans also have lots of insoluble fibre, which benefits the digestive tract. Beans and peas are low in fat but relatively high in starch and complex sugars. The starches have less effect on blood-sugar levels than other carbohydrate-rich foods, and they are digested slowly, which means you feel full longer and consume fewer calories. The complex sugars have a negative side effect, however—they are responsible for the flatulence that prompted the rhyme, "Beans, beans, the musical fruit . . ."

Green snap beans are far less rich in protein and carbohydrates. They are mostly fibre and water, are low in calories, are good sources of vitamin A, iron and potassium and contain some calcium and vitamin C.

Common Bean
Phaseolus vulgaris

This bean has a number of nicknames—snap bean, string bean, green bean, French bean. Since each has a slightly different meaning, we settled on "common bean," a direct translation of the Latin and an accurate description of its frequency in salad gardens. Raw, the common bean can be green, yellow or purple, but all turn green when cooked. There are flat-podded, pencil-podded, long-podded, short-podded and dwarf varieties. The pencil-podded types are usually stringless. Most common beans grow on compact, bushy plants, often referred to in catalogues as bush beans, although there are a few climbing varieties. Within this expansive category, there are green snap beans, flageolet beans for eating shelled fresh and haricot beans for drying.

Our favourite fresh green bean is the French filet bean, the classic, slender *haricot vert* from France, which is harvested when less than a quarter-inch in diameter and dressed whole. We grew the stringless 'Aramis' (DA). As a standard snap bean, 'Improved Tendergreen' (ST) is a crisp pencil-pod type of bush bean. 'Royalty' (DO) has tender, stringless indigo pencil-pods that turn deep green when blanched. The colour is especially appreciated at harvesttime: purple beans don't hide in the bushes as successfully as green beans do. Yellow wax beans tend to lose their crunch when blanched, but 'Dragon Tongue'(CG), a golden-podded variety with a violet stripe, proved the best of the lot. Of the pole snap beans, the widely available 'Blue Lake' and 'Kentucky Wonder' and 'Blauhilde' (DA), a purple variety, are reliable standbys with full flavour and overwhelming yields. For sliced beans, we like the climbing 'Romano' (N, BL, TM), a long, flat heirloom Italian bean. 'Vermont Cranberry' (RE) is an interesting red-mottled dry shell bean for beautiful winter salads.

One of our favourite salad beans is 'French Flageolet' (NI), the shell bean always served with lamb in classic French cuisine. We ate the 2-inch immature pods whole with the tops and tails trimmed; in midseason, we steamed and dressed the pods and the green shell beans together, like 'Sugar Snap' peas; and late in the fall, we pulled the plants and dried the last beans for winter salads. The most delicate of the dry shell beans, flageolets are small, vivid mint-green beans with a flavour reminiscent of lima beans (*Phaseolus limensis*), but they are much easier to grow in northern gardens. Most limas need soil temperatures of 75 degrees F to germinate and almost three months to develop. Flageolets can be planted two weeks sooner, their growing season is two to three weeks shorter, and the final harvest is more delicate for salads.

Plant bush-type common beans in a sunny spot out of the wind after the soil is warm and the weather settled. Turid doesn't recommend soaking the seeds overnight, because the outer skin often breaks and, if the soil is cool and damp, the seed rots. For a full bed of bush beans, stagger the seeds 6 inches apart. Drill individual holes with a stick or a pencil, add inoculant and two seeds, then fill in the hole and water. After they sprout, thin to the strongest seedling. Alternatively, plant in rows, sowing seeds 3 inches apart and thinning to 6 inches. Tuck soil or mulch against the stems to prop up the beans while they build a hedge.

Pole-type common beans need trellises, strings, tepees or individual poles. Put supports in place before planting. In the hill around each string or pole, plant five or more seeds about 1½ inches deep, sprinkling each hole first with inoculant. Once the seedlings are up, thin them to 6 inches apart, leaving three plants per pole. If planting along a trellis, drop seeds in a shallow trench 3 inches away from the support or stagger the seeds for bushier growth. Thin to 6 inches apart. When the plants have their second leaves, hill them up a little. Use a small stick to coax the free-waving young shoots to attach to the support; once they reach the pole or trellis, they climb eagerly. Keep the poles or trellis to a reasonable height so that you don't have to harvest from a ladder. Mulch the spindly ankles of these tall plants to keep them moist.

For both bush and pole beans, seeds take about two weeks to germinate and nine weeks to grow from seed to harvest. Succession-sow every two weeks until two months before the first fall frost date. While they are growing, water the plants well, soaking them at soil level; overhead sprinkling promotes disease. Mulch to keep the soil moist.

Common beans provide an extended harvest for up to six weeks. They have relatively insecure roots, so try to avoid pulling on the plant when picking the pods; hold the plant with one hand, pulling off the beans with the other. For snap beans, start picking when the pods snap in half but before the seeds bulge in the pods. Keep picking the young pods so that the plant stays in flower: the more you pick, the more the plant will produce. For flageolet or green shell beans, wait until the pods are rounded but not yellowed. For haricot or dry shell types, leave the pods on the plant until they turn papery brown.

In the refrigerator, snap beans stay fresh for up to a week, but don't store them longer. It is better to freeze the excess and continue picking fresh for daily salads. Use snap beans whole or cut into pieces; in either case, remove tops, tails and strings. Kitchen-supply stores sell "Frenchers," slicers that cut the bean into lengthwise slivers. Beans are almost always slightly cooked for salads. Steam until tender-crisp, about 7 minutes for whole beans, 5 for sliced. Freshen immediately in cold water so that they retain their colour, then drain and pat dry.

Winter and summer savory are favourite herbs for bean salad (see page 59), and dill is excellent too. Add two tablespoons (30 mL) of fresh snipped dill to a bowl of blanched snap beans and sliced onions, and toss with a red-wine vinaigrette spiked with Dijon mustard. For an Italian twist, toss Romano slices and chopped, seeded tomato with a lemon-juice vinaigrette flavoured with garlic and oregano.

The common bean originated in South America, where some of the tastiest dry shell bean salads are served. Wash pinto, black or kidney beans (all quite sweet), soak overnight, and drain. Add more water, bring to a boil, then reduce heat and simmer until barely tender. The first water is always drained to reduce flatulence. Instead of soaking overnight, however, you can bring to a boil, drain, then add fresh water and bring to a boil again. Drain, and while still warm, toss with a roasted-cumin vinaigrette: grind one tablespoon (15 mL) of roasted cumin seed, mix with a minced and seeded chile, a minced clove of garlic, one tablespoon (15 mL) each of lime juice, white-wine vinegar and coriander and half a cup (125 mL) of peanut oil. Add the pulp of the lime, if desired, and salt and pepper to taste.

French Bean Salad

Choose the thinnest whole French filet beans for this dish, or make it with French flageolets, either shelled fresh or dried.

1 lb.	fresh beans	500 g
3 Tbsp.	tarragon vinegar	45 mL
1 Tbsp.	hazelnut oil	15 mL
½ cup	extra-virgin olive oil	125 mL
2 tsp.	grated onion	10 mL
	Salt & pepper to taste	

Blanch fresh whole green beans in salted water for a few moments until tender-crisp. Freshen with cold water. Steam green shell flageolets until tender. Soak dry shell flageolets for 2 to 3 hours, change the water, and boil for an hour. Drain the cooked beans, and freshen in cold water. Beat together vinegar, oils, onion and salt and pepper. Pour over beans, and marinate for 1 hour.

To serve, line a platter with lettuce, arrange tomato slices around the edge, fill the centre with green beans, and sprinkle minced coriander over all. For a refreshing, low-calorie version, omit the olive oil and marinate in the vinegar and hazelnut vinaigrette.

Scarlet Runner Bean
Phaseolus coccineus

Runner beans have a fine, pronounced bean flavour, but they are larger, coarser and a little less hardy than climbing common beans and at maturity develop heavy strings. They are not, therefore, ideal for salads, except at a very young stage. But they are uniquely beautiful, especially in small gardens, growing vigorously up to 10 feet tall and creating foliage screens studded with edible flowers and vegetables.

Runner beans produce disappointing yields in acidic soil. In the fall, dig in manure, and two weeks before planting, add lime (if necessary) and general-purpose fertilizer. These beans need sturdy supports: a trellis, a pole tepee or a line of inwardly sloping poles laced together with horizontal ridge bars. Netting is too weak for such aggressive climbers.

One sowing of this prolific bean is enough. Plant the large seeds 1 ½ to 2 inches deep. This is the only bean that develops its first leaves underground, so the stem must lift the heavy sprout through the soil. To help them along, cover the seeds very lightly with potting soil, not garden earth. Train the plants toward their supports, and mulch to conserve moisture. Side-dress monthly with well-rotted compost. Remove the growing tips when the plants reach the top of the supports.

When in flower, runner beans attract butterflies and hummingbirds, which often kill the stigma when they thrust their beaks into the blossoms to extract nectar. This limits the harvest but not drastically. There are varieties that flower red (the most common) and white and another cultivar that is bicoloured red and white. Decorative and edible, the flowers make appropriate garnishes for bean salads.

Harvest runner beans when the pods are flat and less than 6 inches long, before the bean seeds start to swell. Picking every other day is essential to maintain production. If a few beans mature, the harvest stops short. Use the young pods whole or sliced in salads. If they overripen, the bean seeds can be used fresh like favas. Let the last beans mature on the vine, then use the dry shell beans for winter salads or next year's sowing. Store and use runner beans as you would common beans.

Fava Bean
Vicia faba

Also known as broad beans, these are the least fussy members of the family. They don't mind cool weather or poor soil, and they are sturdier on their feet. A member of the vetch family, fava beans have more protein than most other beans; they are sweeter than lima beans, and they are the earliest beans available for salads.

Favas are bush beans. They grow into stiff 3-foot shrubs, tall compared with other beans. There are two main types of favas: the long pods, which have 8 to 10 kidney-shaped seeds in each pod; and the slower-maturing Windsors, which have 4 to 7 round seeds in each short, broad pod. We grew the widely available 'Broad Windsor Long Pod.' 'Ipro' (JO) produces seeds half the size of Windsors but is heat- and disease-resistant. There are also dwarf broad beans that grow only 18 inches tall.

Sow favas a month before other beans. They don't mind cool soil, around 45 to 55 degrees F, as long as it is dry enough to crumble. The fava bed should be neutral or slightly acidic, well cultivated and situated in full sun. Soak seeds overnight,

then sow in holes 2 inches deep, staggered 5 inches apart. Inoculant is unnecessary. Cover the seeds with very fine potting soil instead of garden earth so that the cotyledons can push through to the surface without injury. The seeds take almost three weeks to germinate, but in Turid's garden, every one sprouted. When the seedlings are 4 inches tall, fertilize with fish-emulsion fertilizer or manure tea and mulch heavily. Push soil or mulch around the base of the plants, or stake them with twigs. When the plants are staggered, a hedge is established that allows the plants to hold one another up.

By mid-June, when other bean plants are only 6 inches tall, favas are 2 feet tall and flowering. As soon as the first beans form, pinch off the top 3 inches of stem so that the plant's energy goes into the beans. In late June, when the pods are 2 to 3 inches long, you can harvest them to eat whole like snap beans, but that deprives you of the treat ahead. Instead, allow them to swell until you can just barely see the profile of each seed in the pod. If you leave them too long, the scars on individual beans darken. At its peak, the bean is plump and the scar is white or green. Harvest the pods with scissors, leaving a little stem on the plant.

Fava beans are susceptible to black aphids. Pinch out and burn infested tops. If the plants are not too badly damaged, insecticidal soap helps. The problem may be avoided altogether by starting seeds indoors in individual peat pots in March. Transplanted outdoors in April, the beans mature a month before these pests are at their peak.

In early August, when the harvest is over, pull up all the plants. Shell the fresh green favas for salads. Hang overripe pods in the woodshed to finish drying, then shell them for winter salads or next year's planting.

Very young fava pods can be cooked whole like green snap beans. More mature pods should be shelled and the young beans steamed for about 4 minutes until tender-crisp. (Keep them in the shell until you use them; they will store up to a week in the refrigerator.) In texture if not taste, favas are a little like peas. With mature favas, peel off the parchmentlike outer coat and eat the deep bottle-green or white seeds inside. Dress with a mild lime-oil vinaigrette and finely chopped tarragon. For an Egyptian salad, toss tender-crisp favas in extra-virgin olive oil flavoured with chopped summer savory, minced dried chiles and ground cumin. Garnish with coriander.

Fava beans are up to 25 percent protein, high in vitamin A, B$_1$, B$_2$ and C and low in fat and contain only 19 calories per ounce. Some people have a severe allergy to the fresh beans, however, so sample your first salad carefully.

Fresh Shelled Salad

To improve the body's ability to absorb the iron in legumes, they should be eaten with foods rich in vitamin C, such as broccoli, tomatoes, green or red peppers and citrus juice. You can use any green shell bean in this recipe, or combine several types of beans: red cranberry, pale green fava, bright green lima and soybeans.

3 cups	various green shell beans	750 mL
1 cup	each thinly sliced red onion & green pepper	250 mL
½ cup	thinly sliced red pepper	125 mL
¾ cup	thinly sliced celery	175 mL
⅓ cup	fresh minced parsley	75 mL
½ cup	extra-virgin olive oil	125 mL
2 Tbsp.	white-wine vinegar	30 mL
2 Tbsp.	lemon juice	30 mL
1	large clove garlic, minced	1
1 Tbsp.	sugar	15 mL
1 tsp.	each fresh minced oregano, thyme & basil	5 mL
½ tsp.	each salt & pepper	2 mL

Blanch the beans separately until each type is tender-crisp. For extra flavour, add savory to the blanching water. Drain the beans, and toss with the onion, peppers, celery and parsley. Whisk the remaining ingredients together, and toss with beans. Chill several hours for best flavour. Serve very cold.

Soybean
Glycine max

During the last weeks of August, we often watched the chipmunks running across the yard, their cheeks bulging. We idly speculated on the nature of their harvest, since the poppy-seed capsules were already empty and the sunflower heads stripped bare. Turid discovered their secret one evening when she went to the salad garden, eagerly anticipating a fresh green shell soybean salad. She returned to the kitchen and her steaming bean pot empty-handed. Under every soybean bush lay a heap of empty pods, while rows of limas and French flageolets stood untouched just inches away.

The chipmunks apparently knew what they were doing. Soybeans are extremely high in protein

A colourful shelling bean: 'French Horticultural.'

—30 grams per cup, as much as half a breast of chicken—as well as in calcium, potassium and iron but low in sodium and fat. Soybean fibre lowers blood cholesterol, and there is also evidence that it regulates insulin levels, blood sugar and bowel function. It also seems to prevent stomach cancer and gallstones. My youngest son would never have survived without them. Highly allergic to most foods as a child, his first birthday cake was made from soybean milk, soybean flour, soybean oil and a little sugar.

For salads, we grew the green shell soybean 'Hakucho' (DA), an extra-early Japanese variety that matures in only 80 days. Soybeans are grown like most beans, except that the seeds are planted 4 inches apart. Pick the pods when the bean seeds are fully formed, before the foliage turns yellow—usually about 30 days before maturity. Each pod contains three flat beans that taste slightly nutty. Steamed fresh soybeans contain more vitamin A and C than dried. Nevertheless, you can allow some to ripen fully, picking them for winter dry shell soybeans when the plants and pods are brown.

Yard-Long Bean
Vigna sesquipedalis

Known in China as *dow gauk* and sometimes in seed catalogues as asparagus bean, the yard-long bean presents a challenge to northern gardeners and is ultimately more of a novelty than a necessity for

the salad gardener. The huge pod is devilishly difficult to produce during our short summer, and in the end, it is little more than a stretched snap bean.

If you want to try yard-long beans, start them indoors at the end of April in individual peat pots. Planted outside, they must be sown two weeks after bush beans, which does not allow them enough time to mature. Even under controlled conditions, germination is less than satisfactory. Transplant to the garden in the first week of June, providing 8-foot supports for the plants to climb. Space the seedlings 4 inches apart.

Don't overfertilize the garden soil, or you will get huge, lush 12-foot-high vines and no fruit. The plants are extremely sensitive to cold, but it never gets too hot for them, and they are tolerant of drought. The white and lavender flowers are large and pretty. Pick the beans when they are immature, pencil-thin and 6 to 8 inches long, instead of when they are a yard long and as tough as any old beans. Yard-longs are less juicy than other beans but have an unusual flavour. The plant is sometimes called a pea-bean, and its flavour is somewhere between the two.

Cucumber
Cucumis sativus

Cucumbers have always been high on the salad gardener's list. According to the Old Testament, Moses cursed himself for neglecting to pack a peck of cucumber seeds when he left Egypt. A member of

The ridged Armenian cucumber is almost seedless, does not require peeling and grows up to 3 feet long.

the gourd family Cucurbitaceae, related to pumpkins, melons and the like, the cucumber is a native of Pakistan, where the original bitter, brown-skinned vegetable still grows wild. Traces of cucumber spore have been found in Thai ''spirit caves'' carbon-dated at 7750 B.C., predating formal agriculture by thousands of years. Carried along with the spoils of war, cucumbers travelled from the Medes to the Persians to the Romans; in Rome, the vegetable was so popular that Emperor Tiberius was said to eat 10 a day year-round. In the 16th century, Spaniards took the cucumber to America, where it was so thoroughly adopted by indigenous people that later explorers thought it native.

There are two classes of cucumbers: English forcing cucumbers, the long, slender, seedless fruit grown in greenhouses and sold sheathed in plastic in the produce section; and common garden cucumbers, also called outdoor, or ''ridge,'' cucumbers, since they are often grown in long hills. Hardier than forcing cucumbers, the garden variety is still sensitive by northern standards—definitely a high-

summer salad crop. Garden cucumbers are smaller and have pricklier skins, but breeders are developing hybrids that are milder, more disease-resistant and increasingly similar to English cucumbers.

A recent development in garden cucumbers is gynoecious (all-female) cucumbers that produce yields two to three times larger and much earlier than standard varieties. The gynoecious seeds are sold with a few male seeds, stained a different colour, that must survive through sprouting and thinning in order to pollinate the females. But the newest cucumbers are also parthenocarpic, which means they set fruit without pollination, producing heavy yields of nearly seedless cucumbers. Parthenocarpic cucumbers continue to produce whether the fruit is picked or not, since production is not for the purpose of reproduction. Plants must be isolated from monoecious varieties (producing both male and female flowers) so that the parthenocarpic flowers are not cross-pollinated. Pollinated plants produce bitter fruits that look like half-inflated balloons.

Japanese ''Burpless'' are the smoothest-skinned of the outdoor cucumbers. They grow at least a foot long and more than an inch wide and are easy to digest. Any of the so-called Burpless hybrids, such as 'Japanese Long,' 'China' and 'Burpless 33' (DO), approach greenhouse cucumbers in quality.

'Serpent' (DO), the best slicing cucumber we've grown, is technically not a cucumber but a melon (*Cucumis melo* var. *flexuosus*). More commonly called Armenian cucumbers, they are pale green with a deeply ridged exterior and extremely mild, firm, almost seedless flesh. As thin as a Japanese cucumber, they sometimes grow up to 3 feet long and tend to curl. The plants are also called yard-long and snake cucumbers. Whatever name you give this unusual cucumber, the naturally scalloped slices are unsurpassed for salads.

Another salad option is the prolific apple variety —little, round, yellow cucumbers with outstanding flavour and juiciness. This New Zealand native stretches 6 feet in every direction, its branches hung with pale little lime-green balls that turn yellow, then mustard-orange when overripe. 'Lemon Cucumber' (NI) was not only one of the earliest bearers we grew, it also proved to be the zucchini of cucumbers: one plant is more than enough for a family of 14. On the other end of the scale, we do not recommend the dwarf bush cucumbers, because harvests are small and the plants take up more space than a trellised vine.

Cucumbers are tropical fruits, growing even in the Sahara, and they survive in a northern garden only if coddled through cool weather. To get a jump on the season, Turid always starts her cucumbers indoors, but no earlier than the first week of May, or the plants become too straggly to transplant well. Soak the seeds overnight. (Roman gardeners soaked them in honeyed wine in the hopes of producing sweeter fruit, but the theory remains unproven.) Plant the seeds half an inch deep, three to each 3-inch peat pot. At 70 to 75 degrees F, they germinate in about 10 days. About four weeks later, when all chance of frost is past, transplant the hardened-off seedlings into the garden.

Cucumbers like loose-textured, enriched soil that is not acidic. Give them a sunny, sheltered spot. I plant my cucumbers to climb the trellis fence that separates my yard from my neighbour's; Turid plants hers at the edge of the garden so that they ramble over the grass and down the hill, providing a prickly barrier to groundhogs and raccoons.

Prepare individual holes about a foot wide and a foot deep, 2 feet apart for ordinary varieties, 1 ½ feet for Japanese or Armenian trellised types and 6 feet for apple cucumbers. Half fill the holes with rotted manure, soak deeply with water, then set the plant in so that it rests an inch below soil level, firming the earth around it and leaving a plate-sized depression to hold water. Shade is especially important during transplanting because the succulent plants lose moisture quickly.

For a second crop, plant seeds directly in the garden after the last frost, at the same time as corn, when the soil is warm to the touch. Seeds won't germinate if temperatures fall below 50 degrees F. Prepare the holes as described above, planting five or six seeds a half-inch deep and eventually thinning to the best. Armenian types are slow to become established.

A steady supply of water is essential for a good crop of cucumbers. Soak the plants at least once a week. Mulch helps keep the soil cool and moist. For Japanese and Armenian varieties, supply a 5-foot-high trellis support: the plants are healthier and the fruits will be straighter and cleaner than if left to trail on the ground. Train the stems to the trellis, and pinch out the tips when they reach the top of the support. Remove the tips of other varieties after six true leaves appear, encouraging the plant to form fruit-bearing side shoots. Given long hot days and well-drained, humid soil, some plants produce 30 to 40 pounds of fruit in one season. However, a sudden drop in temperature or soil moisture or a sudden increase in sunshine or pruning causes the fruit to turn bitter.

Cucumbers are plagued by cucumber beetles, which eat the stamen and pistil, so the plant flowers but doesn't set fruit; squash vine borers; whiteflies; bacterial wilt (spread by cucumber beetles), which turns the sap of the plant sticky and white; mosaic virus; powdery mildew, particularly when the weather turns muggy; bacterial blight; and fusarium wilt. See page 150 for remedies.

Japanese cucumbers are at their best when small, green and firm. By the time they are fat, swollen and yellowish, the interior is bitter and contains more seed than flesh. Armenian cucumbers lag four to six weeks behind, but the plants are extremely heat-tolerant and prolific. The fruits do not become bitter or distended as they mature, although they do develop small seeds after they reach a foot long. The more you pick of both types, the more the plant produces. Use a sharp knife; don't tug the fruit off the plants. The first frost destroys all the cucumbers except the Armenians, which gamely carry on despite cool weather. In the refrigerator, a freshly picked cucumber lasts about a week, the Armenians a little longer.

It is hard to pick apple cucumbers early enough. They are spiny when young, but that is when they should be eaten—about 2 inches in diameter, no bigger than a golf ball. They never get bitter with age, but they become impossibly seedy. The young cucumbers, cut lengthwise, look like kiwi inside, fleshy and green. They store quite well. At the end of the season, we pulled the whole plant, storing some of the fruit in a cool, dark cellar at 45 to 50 degrees F, where it kept for weeks.

Since many people find cucumber skin difficult to digest, partial peeling is recommended for most types. Instead of removing all the skin, peel in alternate strips, or rake the vegetable lengthwise with the tines of a fork. Unfortunately, most of the little nutritive value a cucumber has disappears with the peel. Very young cucumbers can be sliced whole, but most should be seeded. (A salad made from seeded cucumbers lasts longer.) To seed a cucumber, cut it in half lengthwise, and scoop out the seeds with a sharp utensil, such as a grapefruit spoon, melon baller or butter curler. Cut very large cucumbers lengthwise in quarters, and slice off the triangle of seeds. Then dice or slice the seedless flesh for salads. Armenian cucumbers are the exception, since the skin is mild and too ridged to remove and the flesh is virtually seedless.

Some chefs insist that the secret to exquisite cucumber salad lies in the thinness of the slice. One should, the saying goes, be able to read the editorials of a newspaper through the gossamer circle of cucumber flesh. The French designed a tool called a *mandoline* for the task, a piece of wood inset with an adjustable razor blade; it is fast but dangerous until you master the knack. A sharp knife and patience work equally well.

Cucumbers are 95 percent water, with the result that many cucumber salads are unpleasantly soggy. The trick is to remove the water before adding the dressing. Put the slices in a colander with a dash of vinegar and a sprinkle each of salt and sugar (one teaspoon (5 mL) of vinegar, a half-teaspoon (2 mL) of salt and a quarter-teaspoon (1 mL) of sugar for two cucumbers). Set the colander in the sink for at least half an hour. The salt siphons out the water; the sugar and vinegar bring out the flavour. Drain, gently pressing out all the liquid with the back of a spoon. Pat dry with a towel before dressing. Alternatively, make use of cucumbers' wateriness by layering parboiled potatoes with cucumber slices and salt so that the cucumber juice moistens the potatoes.

A classic cucumber salad, the hands-down favourite in a test I conducted, is cucumbers in sour cream, a Russian dish. Layer the drained slices from two medium cucumbers with a mixture of two tablespoons (30 mL) of cider vinegar, one teaspoon (5 mL) of sugar, one cup (250 mL) of sour cream, a small minced shallot, one tablespoon (15 mL) of chopped chives, a quarter-cup (50 mL) minced dill and salt and pepper to taste.

Make *tzatziki*, the traditional Greek cucumber salad, by combining a minced, salted and drained cucumber with two cups (500 mL) of yogurt, drained overnight, and two or three minced garlic cloves. My own favourite cucumber salad is raita, a cool accompaniment served with spicy-hot Indian and Middle Eastern foods. To a peeled, seeded and diced cucumber add half a cup (125 mL) of low-fat yogurt, half a teaspoon (2 mL) of lemon juice, one teaspoon (5 mL) of fresh mint, a minced garlic clove and a dash of ground cumin. There are only 40 calories in the whole thing. For an Oriental touch, toss cucumbers with a quarter-cup (50 mL) each of julienned carrots, yellow squash and radish sprouts in a vinaigrette of two teaspoons (10 mL) of fresh grated ginger, two tablespoons (30 mL) of rice-wine vinegar, one tablespoon (15 mL) of peanut oil, half a teaspoon (2 mL) of dark sesame oil, a minced garlic clove and a dash of hot-pepper sauce. Borage flowers and Johnny-jump-ups add visual appeal. Perhaps, had Dr. Johnson been served a good raita, he would not have written, "A cucumber should be well sliced, dressed with pepper and vinegar, then thrown out as good for nothing."

Creamy Cucumber Dressing

This extra-mild, lumpy dressing is very good on salads made with sturdy greens such as romaine or radicchio, tossed with parboiled potatoes or mixed with cucumber chunks for a double hit of cucurbita.

1 cup	pared, seeded & minced cucumber	250 mL
2 Tbsp.	minced parsley	30 mL
1	medium clove garlic, minced	1
1 Tbsp.	minced scallions	15 mL
1 cup	low-fat mayonnaise	250 mL
1 cup	plain low-fat yogurt	250 mL
½ tsp.	salt	2 mL
	Freshly ground pepper	

Mix together the cucumber, parsley, garlic and scallions. Stir in the other ingredients and chill. For a smoother dressing, whir briefly in a food processor or blender, and for a nippier taste, add some Dijon mustard or chopped mustard buds.

Eggplant
Solanum melongena

The first Occidental to taste eggplant, so the story goes, went mad with the first bite. Travelling in China, he was so struck by this pendant vegetable, as delicate as a bird's egg, that he ate it raw and had a fit. Most eggplants no longer look much like eggs, and they certainly don't have psychological side effects, yet their infamous reputation has persisted through the centuries.

Cultivated in southeastern Asia for 4,000 years, eggplant is a relative newcomer to Europe, arriving in Spain with the Moors. The small pearly fruit grew larger as it moved west; when it reached the Mediterranean, it developed its characteristic amethyst hue. It was called *mala insana*—"bad egg," or "mad apple"—a sobriquet that survives in the Italian word for eggplant, *melanzana*. Linnaeus

Asian cucumber salad.

continued the insult, first calling the vegetable *Solanum insanum*, then recanting a little and renaming it *Solanum melongena*—"soothing mad fruit."

The suspicion with which early diners viewed eggplant was not entirely undeserved. The plant belongs to the nightshade family, Solanaceae, as does belladonna, but so do tomatoes, potatoes and peppers, all eminently edible. Far from causing epileptic fits and fevers, the eggplant is relatively healthful, high in fibre and rich in minerals and the amino acids that control essential proteins in the body. The flesh is well endowed with potassium, phosphorus, calcium and magnesium, yet a cup cubed, boiled and drained contains only 28 calories. There is some evidence that eggplant inhibits the rise in human blood cholesterol induced by fatty foods such as cheese. In the 1970s, an Austrian scientist found that animals fed eggplant with a high-cholesterol diet had much less atherosclerosis than animals denied the mad apple.

Eggplant, or aubergine, as it is also called, is one of the "fruit vegetables," a classification that includes tomatoes, peppers, avocados and breadfruit. The small, prickly shrub stands out in the salad garden: about 2 feet high, it has mauve flowers and large, powdery-grey leaves that drape protectively over polished purple, pear-shaped fruits. But there is more to eggplant than the familiar indigo pear. It can be white, green, orange, mauve or even striped, and its shape ranges from egg to teardrop to an Oriental type a foot long and only a couple

of inches wide. In general, these have smoother flesh, thinner skins and fewer seeds, but otherwise, most eggplants are similar in flavour and texture. The exceptions are Asian eggplants, which look like tomatoes and have bitter orange flesh, and a Thai variety, which grows in bunches like jade grapes and can be added whole and unpeeled to salads.

In choosing eggplants for salads, look for disease resistance, short growing time, firm flesh and shapes that produce nice slices with few seeds, like the long, thin heirloom 'Early Long Purple' (BL) and the French breed 'Prelane' (SH). Miniatures such as 'Baby Bell' (ST), when steamed whole, make a novel salad. The oval, glossy black 'Dusky' (ST) is an excellent short-season variety that matures to 5-inch fruit 60 days from transplanting. 'Italian Pink Bicolour' (ST) produces unusual cream and rose fruit in 75 days.

Eggplants like the same growing conditions and treatment as sweet peppers (see page 99). Start the seeds indoors around March 15, about a week before the tomatoes. Soak seeds overnight, then plant half an inch deep, three per 3-inch peat pot. Germinate at 75 degrees F, a little warmer than required by okra; they take up to three weeks to sprout.

Coming from the Tropics, eggplants love heat and wither in cool weather. Do not transplant them to the salad garden until two weeks past the last frost date. The soil should be at least 65 degrees F. Give the eggplant seedlings a sunny, sheltered spot in the garden. Turid plants hers in front of a south-facing stone wall, which traps solar heat and keeps the plants warm through the evening. To discourage verticillium wilt, a problem for all Solanaceae, rotate annually and do not plant where tomatoes, peppers or potatoes grew the year before.

Transplant the eggplant seedlings 1 ½ to 2 feet apart. Because the plants make such nice highlights, Turid usually spots them throughout the garden. Dig a hole bigger than the pot, fill it with manure, and water it down. Sink the pot somewhat deeper than the soil level to create a watering dish. Soak the plant well at least once a week, and mulch to keep the soil moist.

Four weeks after transplanting, trim three or four suckers from the bottom to encourage early fruiting, pinch out the tops of plants when they are about a foot high, and stake the stems. Even with an ideal location and diligent care, eggplants may fail if the summer is cool, damp and cloudy. They will not set fruit below 70 degrees F, although they don't mind hotter conditions. Once set, the fruit grows in a wider temperature range. For this reason, some gardeners keep their seedlings in greenhouses or cold frames until they set the first fruit.

One year, Turid's store-bought seedlings were eaten to the ground by moles. Now she surrounds the transplants with basil, and they are not bothered by many pests. Bugs that plague eggplants include aphids, red spider mites (indicated by pale mottling on the upper surface of the leaves), flea beetles, Colorado potato beetles and tomato hornworms. They are also prone to verticillium wilt and phomopsis blight.

Eggplants are ready to harvest from mid-August through September, earlier for miniatures. Count on approximately 20 weeks between sowing the seeds and picking the fruits, which ripen at different times. Harvest the biggest so that the rest develop. Do not pull eggplants off the stalk: cut them with scissors or secateurs.

Harvest fruit when the globes are well shaped and firm, with taut, glossy skin and uniform colour. Once they lose their shine, the flesh toughens and the seeds become bitter. Slack skin and a slightly puckered posterior are sure signs of an ageing eggplant. Press your thumb lightly on the flesh; if a blemish appears, the fruit was too long on the plant and will be discoloured under the skin. Ripe eggplant has a certain heft to it; overripe eggplant is lighter, indicating pulpy flesh. There is an inverse correlation between the size of the scar on the blossom end of the fruit and the seeds it contains: the bigger the scar, the fewer the seeds. Once it is picked, eggplant stores for a week or more at room temperature or in the refrigerator.

Because of its kinship with the nightshade family and no doubt because of its dark skin, eggplant has always had a dubious reputation. Some cultures put it in the same class as rattlesnake and blowfish: highly toxic in unskilled hands. Certainly, there are a few tricks to making eggplant delicious. The thick skin, seeds and juice are all bitter, so for a mild salad, peel the eggplant (except when very young) and slice it, sprinkling the cut sides with lemon juice to keep the flesh white and with coarse salt to suck out the fluid. Lay the slices in a colander to drain for 30 minutes or more. Rinse and pat dry to remove excess salt and moisture.

To eliminate any toxic solanine in the fruit, eggplant should always be cooked a little. Traditionally, slices are sautéed in olive oil, although this adds many calories to a dish. Salted slices absorb much less fat, and dusting them with flour first also helps. Lightly brushing with oil and broiling is more healthful, but the lowest-calorie way to cook eggplant is to prick it all over with a fork, then roast it over an open flame or broil it four inches from

Nightshade salad: Melitzanes salata.

the element for 25 minutes until the skin is black and crisp. When the eggplant is cool enough to handle, rub off the skin with a damp paper towel, then gently squeeze it to remove bitter juices. Cut it open, scoop out the seeds of older fruit, then chop, sprinkling with lemon juice to prevent darkening.

For great eggplant recipes, we turn to southern Italy and the Middle East, where the Turks claim to have a thousand ways of preparing it. Eggplant is the basis of *bab ghanoush*, a wonderful appetizer spread or dip made by broiling, peeling and mashing eggplant with tahini, lemon juice, garlic, onion and salt and pepper. And it is, of course, the crucial ingredient in ratatouille, also known as peasant caviar, a French vegetable stew that doubles as a savoury cooked salad.

One of the simplest ways to prepare eggplant, however, is to sauté salted and drained eggplant slices in olive oil until they are golden, then drain on paper towels. Sauté a thinly sliced onion and one or more cloves of garlic. While the eggplant is still hot, layer it and the onion, adding fresh lemon juice and salt and pepper between them. Allow to sit at room temperature for a couple of hours to blend the flavours, or chill overnight. For a change, add generous sprinklings of chiffonaded basil to each layer. Other herbs that enhance eggplant are coriander, thyme, rosemary and marjoram.

Melitzanes Salata

This traditional Greek salad is often served with *tzatziki* (see page 93).

2	medium eggplants	2
4 Tbsp.	lemon juice	60 mL
	Coarse salt	
1	large tomato, seeded & chopped	1
	OR	
1 cup	cherry tomatoes, halved	250 mL
1	large green pepper, diced	1
1	medium onion, finely sliced	1
1	large clove garlic, crushed	1
3 Tbsp.	red-wine vinegar	45 mL
3 Tbsp.	extra-virgin olive oil	45 mL
½ tsp.	salt	2 mL
	Freshly ground black pepper	

Dry-roast the eggplants. Peel, squeeze out the juice, scoop out the seeds, then cube or slice. Sprinkle immediately with lemon juice and salt. Let rest, then rinse and drain. Mix the eggplants with the tomato, green pepper, onion and garlic. In another bowl, whisk the vinegar, oil, salt and pepper, then drizzle over the vegetables and toss. Garnish with sliced black olives for an authentic Greek touch. For variety, add two tablespoons (30 mL) each of fresh, chopped basil and parsley.

Okra
Abelmoschus esculentus

For a time, Turid lived in the American Southwest, where okra thrives, and it became one of her favourite vegetables. Although northern yields are paltry by comparison, even here, the decorative, exotic plants produce enough dainty pods to grace high-summer salads.

Okra probably originated in Africa and was brought to North America by slaves, hence its common name in the American South, ''slave fruit.'' Technically not a vegetable at all, it is the edible pod of a hibiscus, a member of the family Malvaceae. The blossom that precedes okra's seedpod is as exquisitely beautiful as that of any hibiscus, a delicate unfolding of tissue-thin petals, yellow at sunrise, deepening in colour and opening wider as the day brightens, eventually disclosing a crimson heart just as the sun sets.

Arab physicians once called okra pods ''sun vessels'' and believed the ripening seeds contained therapeutic properties that lasted a lifetime. Indeed, okra has much to recommend it nutritionally. There are only three or four calories per pod, but the vegetable is full of minerals, especially potassium. Okra is also high in amino acids, is a good source of vitamin C and contains a fair amount of vitamin A, calcium, niacin and protein.

For the north, choose varieties that mature early. 'Annie Oakley' (JO) is ready for harvest in about 52 days. Turid also recommends 'Blondy' (DO), which has creamy lime-green pods, and 'Burgundy' (NI), which has deep red stems, branches and pods, beautiful both in the garden and tossed raw on green salads. Some types of okra, such as those from the southern United States, behave as short-day plants and do not flower well in the longer photoperiods of the northern summer. The University of Guelph, in Ontario, has experimented with cultivars from four countries and concluded that two Taiwanese cultivars, known simply as 'Taiwan 1' and 'Taiwan 2,' showed the most promise for southern Ontario. Not yet available from seed houses, they are cultivars to watch for. There is also an unrelated plant called Chinese okra, which is actually a luffa (*Luffa acutangula*) that produces fruit much larger than okra but with the same pronounced ridges. Although we have grown it only for sponges, the fruit, picked young and tender, is apparently delicious sliced and tossed on salads like cucumbers.

Treat okra like eggplant. It is tricky to grow, but gardeners who successfully produce peppers, tomatoes and cucumbers can also grow okra. Start seeds indoors the first week of April. Scarify and soak seeds overnight, then plant three seeds half an inch deep in each 3-inch peat pot. At 75 to 90 degrees F, seeds germinate in five days. Move them to a warm place with lots of light. The plants grow very slowly: after three weeks, they are still less than 4 inches high. The second leaves look pale and yellow, but the roots already penetrate the peat pot. Stick the whole pot into a 5-inch planter filled with soil, and water with a high-phosphorus fertilizer.

Once plants have settled, thin to the healthiest seedling, snipping off unwanted plants at soil level. After all danger of frost is past, transplant okra to the garden, spacing seedlings 18 inches apart.

In the garden, give okra the sunniest, warmest spot. The plants prefer deeply dug, well-fertilized soil with a pH of 6.5. Although they dislike wind, they should be well ventilated, since they are susceptible to downy mildew. The fuzzy little plants usually start off well, but by the time we put them outside, they inevitably look tortured. Therefore, at transplant time, we also plant scarified, soaked seeds directly in the garden, 18 inches apart and half an inch deep, three per hole. (Plant dwarf varieties a little closer together.) Later, thin to one per hole. Sometimes, the direct-seeded plants catch up and take over; other years, the ones started indoors survive best. We always start okra both ways. For very northern gardens or sites with unsettled weather, slitted row covers are a good way to keep young tomato, pepper, eggplant and okra seedlings warm: slits in the fabric provide ventilation, so the cover can be left in place even on hot days.

Water modestly, but don't fertilize too much as the okra grows, or you will get only leaves and no pods. When the first pods appear, thrusting upward from the leaf axils like little candles, side-dress with aged manure or compost, or water with manure tea. Although Turid seldom has pests, the plants are prey to stinkbugs, Japanese beetles, aphids, corn earworms and flea beetles. Handpick or dust with rotenone or diatomaceous earth. Verticillium wilt and fusarium wilt are also potential problems.

Harvesting begins in early August, about 60 days after planting. Pick unripe pods when they are bright green, no more than 2 or 3 inches long and as thin as a finger. (One of okra's other common names is lady's finger.) If allowed to ripen fully, pods become fibrous and indigestible. To harvest, cut the pods with scissors or a sharp knife, leaving about an inch of the stem. It is a good idea to wear gloves and long sleeves, because the leaves can sometimes cause a rash.

Okra pods ripen a few at a time. We collect them over several days and store them unwashed in the refrigerator, although they won't keep much longer. To prepare okra, wash first with a vegetable brush to remove the layer of fuzz on the skin. Raw okra tastes sharp and crisp but becomes gelatinous when cooked incorrectly. For salads, leave the pods whole, trimming the merest tip of the stem without piercing the pod. Blanch for less than a minute, then plunge immediately into cold water. (Do not use iron, copper or brass pots; these metals

Okra and cherry tomato salad.

turn okra grey. Red okra normally turns green when cooked.) Drain and pat dry, then slice lengthwise or crosswise before dressing.

Okra is unfamiliar to most North American menus, but it is widely eaten in other parts of the world, especially the American South. In India, it is often pickled with hot green peppers and garlic in a white-vinegar bath spiced with celery and mustard seed. North Africans eat the leaves as well as the fresh pods. To Arabs, it is such a delicacy that its Arabic name, *uëhka*, means gift. Try raw okra sliced crosswise, tossed with mixed greens. The thin discs look like wheels with seeds nestling between the spokes. Or toss tender-crisp whole okra with green beans and red peppers in a horseradish dressing (page 128). When you have enough pods to make a solo okra salad, toss them with cherry tomatoes (both halved) in a vinaigrette of one tablespoon (15 mL) each of red-wine vinegar, lemon juice and sour cream, four tablespoons (60 mL) of extra-virgin olive oil and a crushed garlic clove. Serve on radicchio, garnished with parsley.

Pepper
Capsicum annuum

Peppers are a classic case of mistaken identity, although not the only one in the field of botany. Christopher Columbus set out to find the Spice Islands, source of the king of spices—black pepper

A basket of peppers.

be spelled chilie, chilli or chili, we stick with the original Spanish chile.) They range from mildly hot to wildly burning, but even the tamest are best used as seasonings rather than in salads. The mildest are Anaheim, or long green, chiles and the blackish green, heart-shaped pasilla, or ancho, chiles. A touch hotter are the short, conical yellow wax chiles, the hot red cherry peppers and the hot yellow Hungarians. Among the three-alarm-fire chiles are the jalapeño and the serrano. There are also hybrids: 'Mexibell' (NI) looks like a bell pepper but tastes like a mild chile; 'Sigaretta' (RE) looks like a chile but tastes as sweet as any bell.

Keep a sharp eye on maturation times when choosing varieties. The new early hybrids reliably produce a harvest of green peppers 55 to 60 days after transplanting. Northern gardeners should avoid the thick-walled 'Bell Boy' types and look instead for thin-walled hybrids that survive lower temperatures and light levels. For salads, we recommend 'Italian Pepperoncini' (NI), a 4-inch-long, narrow, sweet green pepper that looks like a ram's horn. Another ram's-horn hybrid that we highly recommend is 'Super Sweet Banana' (ST), a giant yellow sweet Hungarian-type pepper that is extremely mild and prolific. 'Gypsy Hybrid' (DA) is a sweet golden bell pepper that turns orange in the fall. 'Pimento Sweet Pepper' (NI) is one of the most decorative in the garden, a 2-foot-high lush plant with huge dark leaves that droop down, concealing the stems and little red heart-shaped fruits. These are especially good for stuffing. 'Stokes Early Hybrid' is our standard green sweet pepper, producing fruit early enough that it turns red on the vine. For a novelty, try 'Chocolate Bell' (ST), which turns from green to a warm chocolate-brown with pink flesh, dark brown ribs and large yellowish seeds inside, or 'Purple Beauty' (DO), a thick-walled deep purple pepper that ripens red. One or two chile plants is more than enough. We always grow one jalapeño to spice dressings. Don't believe catalogues that claim to offer a mild jalapeño: we've tried several, and they were still too fiery for roasting or slicing into salads.

The piquancy of peppers comes from capsaicin, a volatile phenolic compound found in the placenta, the fibrous white ribs that secure the seeds. The seeds taste hot because they are in close contact with these veins. The pungency of chiles varies dramatically, but in general, the smaller the variety, the hotter it is.

Hot is not only pleasurable in the mouth; it works wonders in the body. Capsaicin is an expectorant, prompting the release of fluids that clear bronchial

(*Piper nigrum*). When he landed in the Caribbean, he thought he was in the Orient, and when they served him hot, piquant food, he assumed it was spiced with pepper. It was, of course, chile, of the genus *Capsicum*, but the name stuck, and these wonderful pendulous vegetables, red and green, hot and sweet, are now known collectively as peppers.

Peppers, like tomatoes, eggplants and potatoes, belong to the family Solanaceae. Native to Central America, peppers were used by indigenous Mexicans as early as 7000 B.C. Today, there are hundreds of pepper varieties grown around the world, ranging from sweet to searing. Among the sweet peppers (Grossum Group) are the bell peppers in green, red, yellow or chocolate-brown; the long, pointed Hungarian yellow wax peppers; the tapered red pimentos; and the slender, thin-walled Italian frying peppers. The hot peppers (Longum Group) are called chiles. (Note: chile pepper is a redundancy: "chile" means hot pepper. Although it may

'Cayenne' hot peppers ready in September.

passages and lungs of congestion. Hot peppers certainly clean out the sinuses and, some doctors believe, help prevent chronic respiratory problems. Hot pepper is also a local anaesthetic: capsaicin short-circuits the transmission of pain messages and is being used experimentally to treat chronic pain. Among people who eat a lot of chiles, like the Thais, thromboembolisms are relatively rare. Research now confirms that chiles increase the blood's ability to dissolve clots and also appear to lower blood cholesterol. Until recently, chiles were considered damaging to the digestive system, aggravating ulcers and haemorrhoids, but a 1988 study showed that hot peppers produce no ill effects.

South American natives have long eaten chiles to kill intestinal parasites. As an insecticide, chiles work well in the garden too. Put a hot pepper in the blender with some garlic and water, whir it smooth, then stir in some pure dishwashing soap (not a chemical detergent), and spray this directly on plants to kill aphids. It works wonderfully.

All peppers are rich in vitamin C, and red peppers contain nearly twice as much as green. Even so, a single pepper has more of the vitamin than a glass of orange juice. Red peppers are also a good source of vitamin A. All in all, peppers are considered one of the most nutrient-dense vegetables, high in amino acids, high in potassium and a good source of other minerals too.

Coming from the Tropics, peppers are not entirely happy in northern gardens. Plants produce peppers only if they are warm from seed to harvest. Start them indoors about two months before the last frost date. Soak the seeds overnight, and plant three to five seeds a quarter-inch deep in each individual peat pot. At 70 to 80 degrees F, germination takes about 10 days. Move to a warm, bright place, preferably under grow lights, and when the second leaves show, give them a diluted liquid fertilizer.

Harden off carefully. Transplant when the weather is completely settled and the soil temperature is above 65 degrees F. (Below 55 degrees causes blossom drop.) If the spring is cool, you may have to transplant the peppers to larger pots indoors while you wait for the weather to warm sufficiently for them to be moved into the salad garden. (Gardeners in the far north may have to keep capsicums in cold frames for the whole growing season.)

Like eggplants, peppers need a sunny, sheltered place in the garden. The bushy plants have fragile branches and a woody main stem that topples easily in high winds, so select a protected site. The soil should be well drained, with a pH of 6.5 and a good level of magnesium. Dig holes 1 to 3 feet apart, fill with well-rotted manure, water well, then set in the plant, creating a watering dish. Transplanting later in June may avoid the problem of cutworms, since their life cycle will be over, but to be sure, put a tinfoil or wood-ash collar around the stems to forestall the saw-toothed beasts.

Water regularly, keeping the soil uniformly moist. Soak deeply from below rather than sprinkling. At the first sign of yellow or pale green leaves, add nitrogen to the soil; dig in a tablespoon of magnesium sulphate dissolved in one gallon of water, or, preferably, dress with organic mulch. Without mulch, water every day during hot summer spells. A well-prepared, deeply dug, manured growing site makes fertilizer unnecessary while the plant grows, but when the fruits start to swell, give the plants a boost with manure tea.

Sweet peppers are susceptible to red spider mites and aphids, both of which succumb to insecticidal soap. They may also be plagued with Colorado potato beetles, corn earworms, pepper maggots, cucumber mosaic virus, fusarium wilt, verticillium wilt, bacterial leaf spot and blossom-end rot, most of which can be foiled by uniform watering, good ventilation, clean garden practices and crop rotation.

Each plant sets 6 to 12 fruits, unless temperatures below 55 or above 90 degrees F cause blossom drop. Start picking when the fruits are the size of tennis balls. This encourages production, and you can leave the later ones to turn red on the bush. (Northern gardeners should leave one plant untouched so that it concentrates its energy on ripening rather than on continued flowering.) The peppers seem to stay green on the plant for weeks, then suddenly, within a day or two, turn bright scarlet. The early hybrids are ready in mid-July, although harvest continues until late September. At the end of the summer, before the first frost warning, pull up the whole plant and hang it upside down in a dry place. Strip the leaves as they turn yellow; the peppers will ripen over the next several weeks.

Ripe peppers are glossy and firm, although, thankfully, they lack that unhealthy car-wax shine you see on supermarket peppers. Green peppers keep up to a week unwashed in the refrigerator, red peppers not quite that long, since they are riper. For sweet peppers, rinse, then remove stems by cutting vertically into the pepper tips and pulling them out, getting as much of the seed clusters as possible. Scrape out the interior ribs with your fingers or a spoon, then cut whole peppers into rings or thin lengthwise strips.

When handling chiles, wear rubber gloves. There is no other way to avoid injury: capsaicin-stained fingers inevitably go to your eyes. Wash your hands thoroughly after touching the veins, and do not leave any lying on the cutting board to contaminate other food. Capsaicin is extremely potent. Soaking fresh chiles in cold, salted water for an hour will quench some of their fire. Or you can use the heat to advantage by simmering several hot peppers in sesame oil to make your own Oriental hot-pepper oil.

Some peppers have tough skins, making them less than perfect for salads. And sometimes, even the flesh itself is too crisp. The best way to remove the skin and precook the flesh is by roasting. Place the whole pepper on a barbecue or in a 400-degree-F oven, and roast until the skin blisters and blackens, about 25 minutes. You can also broil on a rack lined with foil, but be careful to turn them often. Remove from the heat and put immediately in a bowl covered with plastic wrap; close tightly, and let the peppers sweat for half an hour. Hold the peppers under cold running water, and slip off the skins. Cut the peppers in half, and remove seeds and ribs. Use immediately, or store in the refrigerator for three days. If covered with olive oil, they keep for a couple of weeks. Roasted peppers also freeze well.

Hot peppers are as much a staple of Hunan and Szechuan cooking as of South American. Remove the veins and seeds and chop them finely, then add to an Oriental vinaigrette (see page 93), or sprinkle over salads of green shell beans, cauliflower, eggplant, celeriac and other bland, hearty vegetables. They also taste good in vinaigrettes served over bitter or strong-flavoured greens such as escarole and endive. Slivers of sweet red pepper add colour and flavour to almost any green salad. Use fresh, crisp sweet-pepper strips as crudités with yogurt fennel dip (page 113). Drizzle roasted sweet peppers with herbed olive oil, and add to an antipasto tray. Layer roasted yellow peppers with tomatoes, and serve with a red-wine vinaigrette flavoured with garlic and basil. For a Provencal touch, substitute tarragon vinegar and chervil for the basil, then scatter tiny Nicoise olives over the peppers and garnish with crisscrossed strips of anchovies. For contrasting colours and textures, toss roasted red-pepper strips with two cups (500 mL) of steamed broccoli spears in a lemon vinaigrette.

Roasted red peppers can also become a salad dressing. In a food processor or blender, combine two roasted red peppers, two cloves of garlic, one teaspoon (5 mL) of fresh rosemary, salt to taste and a pinch of cayenne. When smooth, add two tablespoons (30 mL) each of red-wine vinegar and extra-virgin olive oil. Toss the sauce with cooked new potatoes or green beans or serve with artichokes.

Marinated Roasted Peppers

This salad is lovely, the three peppers tossed together like tricoloured fettucine or marinated separately and arranged side by side on a plate. The peppers' texture is velvety and the flavour earthy.

6	peppers, 2 each of red, yellow & green	6
⅓ cup	almond oil	75 mL
3 tsp.	sherry vinegar	15 mL
1	clove garlic, crushed	1
1 tsp.	Dijon mustard	5 mL
3 tsp.	liquid honey	15 mL
½ tsp.	salt	2 mL
2 tsp.	each minced chives, parsley & marjoram	10 mL

Roast the peppers, peel, seed, and cut into thin strips. Mix remaining ingredients into a marinade. Pour over peppers and let sit for 2 hours or more, turning peppers occasionally. For a different flavour, substitute cold-pressed peanut oil and cider vinegar for the almond oil and sherry vinegar.

Squash
Cucurbita spp

Squash is a distinctly New World vegetable; together with beans and corn, it was the staple of North American Indian diets. Seeds have been found in Mexican caves dating back to 9000 B.C. The Iroquois called it *isquoutersquash*, a name the settlers shortened to "squash." Originally, it meant "something that is eaten raw," and although one rarely finds it served this way today, squashes do, indeed, make fine salads.

Only summer squash (*Cucurbita pepo*) and the butternuts (*C. maxima*) are appropriate for salads. Both winter and summer squashes come in bush and vine types. The bush varieties do not really form bushes but are more compact than traditional sprawling types. For all the cucurbitas, the slightest frost means a complete collapse of their lush leaves and pipelike hollow stems, although the fruits themselves don't mind the chill.

Summer and winter squashes are dissimilar in terms of nutrition. Summer squash is low in calories and sodium and high in vitamins C, A and niacin. Winter squash contains similar levels of vitamin C, but it has much more vitamin A and the anti-cancer carotenoids, including beta carotene. (Butternut has almost 20 times more vitamin A than zucchini.) The difference is colour. Deep orange squashes, along with carrots and sweet potatoes, belong to a triumvirate of vegetables that seem to protect against lung cancer. Butternut squash gives you more than a day's recommended allowance of vitamin C, fibre and carotene in a single serving. It is also a good source of riboflavin and iron, with very low levels of fat and sodium.

Despite their assorted shapes and names, summer squashes all taste pretty much the same: varieties are easily interchanged in recipes. Zucchinis—the name is derived from the Italian word for "sweetest"—are among the best salad squashes. Turid always grows Lebanese zucchini squashes, such as 'Clarimore' (DO), because they are so decorative in the garden, growing to a bush 3 feet high and 6 feet in diameter, with deeply indented, arrow-shaped leaves, dark green and splattered with silver blotches. The pale green fruits are very early, extremely prolific and taste slightly peppery. The widely available 'Gold Rush' is a deep yellow, very straight zucchini on compact plants. 'Sundrop' (DO) grows to a small, bushy plant yielding oval, clear yellow fruits, which are best harvested when the blossoms are still attached. 'Butterblossom' (CG) is grown mainly for its flowers: the male blooms are stuffed or strewn on salads, while the bulbous female flowers are left on the plant to grow dark green zucchinis.

'Golden Scallop' (BL) is the earliest scallop squash we tried. The little fruits, 3 inches across, are star-shaped when sliced crosswise. The widely available 'Peter Pan Hybrid' is a good green scallop squash. Spaghetti squash is in a class all its own. 'Orangetti' (NI) is a new variety with vivid orange, delicately flavoured flesh. Because it stores well, it is one of the best summer squashes for salads.

Winter squashes vary markedly in taste. They have a tough skin that keeps them moist through months of storage. Generally less watery and more nutritious, they also take a long time to mature. As a rule of thumb, the bigger they are, the longer they've been on the vine and the sweeter they'll be. Of the winter squashes, only the butternut is

'Orangetti' spaghetti squash with bell peppers, sweet chiles and vinaigrette.

really good for salads. 'Waltham Butternut' (DO) is one of our favourites. There are now space-saving bush butternuts, such as 'Burpee's Butterbush' (DO, DA), which matures up to three weeks earlier than conventional butternuts. The plants have no runners but bear about four 5-inch-diameter fruits.

Squashes have a reputation for not transplanting well. Many gardeners wait until early June, when the soil is around 70 degrees F, to sow directly in the salad garden. But around the same time, Turid moves her 10-inch seedlings into the salad garden and gains an advantage of several weeks on the harvest.

Start seeds in early May, soaking them overnight, then plant them edge-down, half an inch deep, three to each 3-inch peat pot. At 70 degrees F, the first seedlings are up within a week. Move them under lights or to a bright windowsill. They grow very quickly, the light green true leaves soon overshadowing the first succulent dark green leaves. Thin to the sturdiest one in each pot. Watch that the plants never dry out and that they don't get

too much sun on a windowsill with southern exposure. Fertilize once during their indoor growth.

Squashes like a sunny site and rich, sandy, well-drained loam with a pH around 6.5. After all danger of frost is past, transplant the seedlings, which may already need small sticks for support. Set bush plants 3 feet apart and trailing types 4 feet apart, with 6 feet between rows. Some gardeners let the squashes ramble through the corn patch, where their sandpapery leaves deter raccoons. Turid plants them on a slope at the edge of the garden, where they trail through the grass. To conserve space, you can train squash over a sturdy trellis, in which case 2 feet between plants is enough. (Support developing fruits with a net "hammock" secured to the trellis.)

Squashes are all heavy feeders. Dig deep holes, and add 12 inches of rotted manure. Soak the prepared holes before you transplant, then set the seedlings about 2 inches below the surface, leaving a depression to hold water. Water squash by laying the hose on the ground rather than by sprinkling from above.

During the summer, water frequently and mulch to retain the moisture. If the soil is fertile, don't side-dress during the growing season: it promotes leaves rather than fruit. When trailing varieties are 3 feet long, pinch out the shoots to encourage fruit-bearing side branches. Hybrids usually produce fruit somewhat earlier than open-pollinated types. During extended damp, overcast weather, help the reproductive process by picking male flowers and rubbing the anthers into the female flower (the one with the bulge under the blossom). In small gardens, cross-pollination within squash species always occurs, so don't collect seeds for next year.

Watch for cucumber beetles, fusarium wilt, mildew and blossom-end rot, a physiological disorder that is caused by fluctuating soil conditions or too much or too little moisture. The squash vine borer, a caterpillar hatched from eggs laid by a late-spring moth, pierces the hollow stems and causes the leaves to go limp and finally die, betraying its whereabouts with a pile of sawdust. Slit open the stem and ferret out the caterpillars. A plant

The staked indeterminate tomato can be underplanted with herbs and lettuces.

with side shoots easily recovers. We pick squash beetles and striped beetles by hand.

For salads, harvest summer squash when very small, cutting the little fruits carefully off the vine with a sharp knife, leaving an inch or two of stem attached. Think of them as you would gherkins: check the plants daily for new little fruits. Zucchini as big as elephants' ears do not make good salads; they should be plucked when they are as small as a big toe, what the French call *courgettes*. If you scrape one with a fingernail, the flesh is bright green rather than white. Pattypan squash, a little saucer-shaped squash with a scalloped edge, is best when smaller than a muffin. If you miss the tiny squashes, you can always harvest the gargantuan gourds and scoop them out as salad bowls, but use only baby squash for the salad itself. The exception is spaghetti squash: picked up to 9 inches long, the fruit is perfect, and the shell is usable as a serving dish. Spaghetti squash keeps at room temperature for about two months; store the others in the refrigerator for no more than a week.

Winter squashes take much longer than summer squashes to mature. They are grown the same as summer squashes, but toward the end of August, remove all the tips of new shoots and any surplus shoots so that only a couple of fruits ripen to full maturity on the vine. Squashes are best after a couple of light frosts, which help convert the starches to sugar. When you harvest, drum the shell. It should feel hard and sound hollow. Just before the first heavy frost, cut the fruits carefully off the vine, leaving about 3 inches of stem, and cure them in a dry location indoors. Stored in a cool, dry place (no cooler than 55 degrees F) with good air circulation, winter squashes keep almost until the next harvest.

Summer squashes require little kitchen preparation. If you harvest them small enough, they don't need peeling. Simply wash them with a damp cloth; don't soak them in water, or they become soggy. Slice older fruits as you would cucumbers, or sliver them like French beans. Picked in infancy, zucchini and pattypan squashes are delightful with dips on

a crudité tray. They are delicious tossed in a mixed high-summer salad, 8 or 10 to a salad bowl, either whole or sliced in half. Toss in a few squash blossoms too, rinsed, patted dry and sliced in half. Small courgettes, sliced thinly or julienned, are wonderful sprinkled with lemon juice, extra-virgin olive oil, chopped mint and salt and pepper, then served with a mustard cream sauce made by heating one tablespoon (15 mL) of Dijon mustard, two tablespoons (30 mL) of light cream and two-thirds of a cup (150 mL) of low-fat yogurt until just warm. For a true Italian salad, shred tender young zucchini and toss with lemon juice, extra-virgin olive oil and mashed garlic. Let it marinate overnight in the refrigerator, then toss with minced parsley and salt and pepper.

Spaghetti squash doesn't reveal its pastalike strands unless it is cooked in its shell. Bake a whole pierced squash uncovered in a 350-degree-F oven for up to 45 minutes, then turn and bake for another 45 minutes, or until the shell feels soft. Or boil young whole squash for an hour. Scoop out the seeds and clean them for toasting, then with a fork, gently pull the spaghettilike squash strands away from the wall, leaving a quarter-inch shell. (The shell of a freshly picked spaghetti squash won't collapse; in fact, it is possible to use it as a salad serving bowl.) Toss the ''spaghetti'' with pesto or a lime-basil vinaigrette. For a colourful salad, sauté a minced garlic clove, three slivered bell peppers and three sweet chiles like 'Sigaretta' in olive oil, and toss with the spaghetti squash in a safflower-oil and rice-vinegar vinaigrette spiced with sesame oil and a pinch of turmeric. Garnish with squash blossoms.

Winter squash should be baked, braised or boiled for salads. Cooking time varies depending on how big the pieces are and the density of the squash. Thin slices take about 10 minutes to simmer, the best way to cook butternut. Half a squash bakes in a medium oven in about 35 minutes.

Kaddu Raita

According to Varsha Dandekar in *Salads of India*, Kaddu Raita is always made for weddings, because it is easier and cheaper to make in large quantities than a raw vegetable salad.

1 Tbsp.	butter	15 mL
¼ tsp.	peeled, minced fresh ginger	1 mL
¼ tsp.	fresh green seeded, finely chopped chile	1 mL
½ tsp.	cumin seeds	2 mL

2 cups	peeled, seeded & coarsely grated butternut squash (about half a small squash)	500 mL
1/4 tsp.	salt	1 mL
1/8 tsp.	cumin powder	0.5 mL
1/8 tsp.	coriander powder	0.5 mL
1/8 tsp.	paprika	0.5 mL
1 cup	yogurt	250 mL
	Coriander leaves for garnish	

In a heavy-bottomed pan, heat the butter and add the ginger, chile and cumin seeds. Sauté 15 seconds, then add the squash and cook 5 minutes over medium heat, stirring constantly with a wooden spatula. Do not cook to a mush; the squash should remain firm. Remove from heat. Add the salt, cumin powder, coriander powder and paprika. Mix well, let cool to room temperature, and add the yogurt. Chill, garnish and serve cold. For a more textured salad, sauté two-thirds of the squash and add the remainder with the salt and spices.

Tomato
Lycopersicon esculentum

"I refuse to finish this," said our tomato taster archly, spitting a soggy red mash onto the plate. "It is not a tomato."

It *was* a tomato: 'Siberia,' a cold-hardy variety the catalogue described as "smooth, meaty, slightly tart and juicy . . . excellent for salads." But we had to agree with the taster. It was compact, and it ripened early, but its flavour could most kindly be called bland. Even the raccoons in Turid's garden left these tomatoes untouched.

Waverley Root devotes seven pages of his wonderful encyclopaedia *Food* to the tomato, tracing its development from its South American roots through the fruit-vegetable debate to its current popularity. "It did not come into its own until the early 1900s; it seems to be on its way out in the late 1900s," he writes. "We kept on improving the tomato until we had improved all the improvement out of it."

When the U.S. Department of Agriculture surveyed consumers in 1974, the greatest number of complaints were about the declining quality of the tomato. "Our tomatoes have become hard, grainy and tasteless because governmental researchers, serving agribusiness rather than the consumer, breed them for toughness rather than quality."

Indeed, we found no lack of quantity in tomato species but a distinct lack of quality. One catalogue offers over 300 varieties, ranging in size from marbles to softballs and in colour from white to indigo. The catalogues are effusive, the names of the cultivars promising: 'Crimson Cushion,' 'Mammoth Wonder,' 'Dinner Plate,' 'Summer Delight,' 'Bragger.'

Tomatoes have been developed for myriad uses, including meaty paste tomatoes, huge, gutless stuffing tomatoes, plump juice tomatoes, beefsteak slicing tomatoes. But salads make their own demands: the tomato should be sweet but not too starchy, medium to small in size, meaty, juicy and thin-skinned. Above all, a salad tomato must hold together when sliced or cut into wedges and not leave a puddle of pulp and seed in the bottom of the bowl.

Those who can choose their species carefully will get better tomatoes than cooks who shop at the local supermarket, but even discriminating gardeners sometimes have disappointing crops of mealy, tasteless, tough-skinned fruit. Tomatoes, we must admit, are a challenge. Like eggplants and peppers, the other members of the Solanaceae family grown in northern gardens, they are not particularly happy this far from the equator. They have to be coddled in their infancy, and the gardener has to get lucky; only a long, hot summer gives you tomatoes that live up to catalogue claims. Northern gardeners, therefore, should ignore the cultivars marked "late" and choose midseason varieties, which take 70 to 85 days from transplanting to harvest, and early types, which mature in as little as 45.

Although the array of tomatoes is mind-boggling, the multitudes can be divided into two classes, and your choice should begin here. Tomatoes are determinate or indeterminate. Check the small print; the class should be indicated on the seed packet or in the catalogue. If you buy seedlings, you may have to do a little research to find out which type of plant you have.

Determinate tomatoes are bush tomatoes, the ramblers. They flower and form fruits at the ends of their branches, which sprawl horizontally over the soil. They require a lot of space and need support under their branches or heavy mulch to lift the fruits off the ground. Mulch is a mixed blessing: it keeps roots moist but also serves as a cozy haven for tomato-stealing rodents. Instead, plant determinate tomatoes in cages, or train the plants over a low horizontal trellis. Turid simply raises heavily fruiting arms off the ground with forked branches. Determinate tomato plants bear more fruit because they aren't pruned as they develop. By midseason, when they have set some fruit, you can pinch out new sprouts, forcing the plant to put its energy into ripening existing tomatoes.

Within the determinate category, there are small determinate plants that form shorter bushes and hybrid semideterminate types.

Indeterminate tomatoes are staking tomatoes. They produce flower buds along the stem; the tips of their branches always produce leaves. The lead stem continues to grow, producing new flowers and fruit as long as the weather holds. This type of tomato plant is a real space saver: you can set them 18 inches apart. The fruits form high above the ground where air circulation is good, lessening disease. They ripen earlier, but the crop may be smaller.

The main stem of an indeterminate tomato is trained upward and tied to a single, very tall, very strong support. Most commercial stakes are totally inadequate. Instead, point one end of an eight-foot 1-by-2 and pound it a foot or two into the ground. Indeterminate tomatoes also grow well up a lattice fence. As the seedling grows, attach the stem to the stake or fence every eight inches or so. We add all the "ties" to the stakes when they go in the garden in the spring, so it only takes a minute to attach the new growth to its support (see page 148).

Staked tomatoes must be pruned regularly to confine the growth to a single stem. At every point where a leafstalk joins the main stem, a lateral shoot forms; pinch these out before they are 2 inches long. During the growing season, new shoots should be pinched every couple of days; the reward is an early, prolific crop of tomatoes. Once the plant reaches the top of the stake—about 6 feet—pinch off the growing tip, diverting the plant's energy into the fruit. Make sure that there is enough leaf cover to protect the tomatoes against sunscald. Staked plants are also prone to blossom-end rot, so see that they are evenly watered and have enough calcium.

Virtually every type of tomato is available as both a determinate and an indeterminate. Having decided how much space to devote to tomatoes, follow two rules of thumb when choosing cultivars: look for the shortest growing time so that tomatoes ripen fully on the vine; and select heirloom varieties, as they seem to have the most robust flavour. Remember that one well-cared-for tomato plant yields up to 30 pounds of tomatoes.

Our favourite salad tomato was the heirloom cultivar 'Principe Borghese' (BL), a wonderfully sweet, firm, early red determinate tomato used in Italy for making sun-dried tomatoes. This plum-shaped tomato didn't have too much pulp, cut beautifully into bite-sized quarters and had great flavour. The earliest determinate was the cherry-sized 'Whippersnapper' (PG), producing fruit in early July. The widely available 'Sweet 100' is a very early indeter-

Tomatoes, from the little 'Yellow Canary' to the giant orange 'Persimmon' that is perfect for stuffing.

minate cherry tomato that consistently wins the taste tests at a friend's annual "tomato trials." We also like the 2-inch indeterminate 'Yellow Pear' (NI). 'Currant' (NI) is a rare heritage tomato (indeterminate) that yields clusters of intensely flavoured, currant-sized tomatoes, usually red, but each seed packet may produce up to 10 percent yellow-fruiting plants. 'Caro Rich' (NI) is another old-time tomato, a midseason orange indeterminate that is intermediate in size, rich and full-flavoured, with a balance of acid and sugar. 'Persimmon' (BL), also an heirloom, is a very large indeterminate fruit, at least 6 inches in diameter. Bright orange, the flesh is slightly acidic with a sweet aftertaste. The popular indeterminate 'Better Boy' is our favourite slicing tomato, and for containers, we recommend 'Yellow Canary' (ST), a sweet determinate dwarf cherry tomato that grows less than a foot tall.

Tomatoes are low in fat and sodium, contain fibre and are high in potassium, phosphorus and vitamins C and A. (Tomatoes show up on the food lists of people with very low rates of stomach, lung and prostate cancer.) Orange fruits have the highest beta-carotene content, although red tomatoes contain another type of carotene called lycopene. One large raw tomato, unpeeled, contains about 40 calories.

To grow tomatoes, start seeds indoors six weeks before the last frost date. Sow half an inch deep, three seeds per individual peat pot. Germinated at 70 degrees F, they sprout in 7 to 10 days. Move under lights, and thin to the strongest. If the plants grow too high before the weather is warm enough to transplant, sink the whole peat pot into a bigger soil-filled pot and fertilize with fish emulsion or manure tea.

In the salad garden, plant tomatoes in full sun. Do not plant them where peppers, eggplants, tomatoes or potatoes grew the year before: they are susceptible to the same diseases and attract the same pests. A week before transplanting, prepare individual holes a foot in diameter, either staggered or in a row, 18 inches apart for staked tomatoes, 2 feet apart for cages and 3 to 4 feet apart for determinate types. Fill each hole with aged manure, and add a table-spoon of ground limestone if the soil is too acidic.

After the last frost date, remove the lower leaves of the hardened-off seedlings, and set a pot in each hole, a little deeper than it was growing, creating a watering dish. Protect for a week from sun and wind, then remove the sheltering boughs and mulch the soil but not too close to the stems—tomato roots like to be sun-warmed.

Even after the last frost, seedlings appreciate protection from chilly nights. Upending a plastic milk jug or paper bags over the seedlings at night helps preserve the day's warmth. Floating row covers are excellent, or consider the water-filled plant protectors now offered by many seed houses.

Water deeply at least once a week, more often if you don't mulch. Regularly pinch lateral shoots from indeterminate cultivars. When fruits are forming, side-dress with manure tea. Watch for aphids, Colorado potato beetles, flea beetles, cutworms, whiteflies and the tomato fruit worm. Blossom-end rot, blossom drop, sunscald, fusarium wilt, verticillium wilt, late blight and bacterial spot all attack tomato plants, but most fungi can be avoided by watering from below, feeding the plant well and keeping the garden clean. Some varieties, such as 'Beefsteak' and 'Big Boy,' are prone to tomato leaf roll, which is caused by the plant's being under stress from wet soil, drought or a heavy fruit load. Correct the condition, and the symptoms disappear.

Flavour in tomatoes results from the particular balance of sugars, acids and volatiles, chemical compounds that determine taste and aftertaste. A major factor in the development of tomato flavour is the amount of leaf area exposed to the sun. In general, tomatoes from small plants with lots of fruit will have less flavour than those from large, leafy plants with just a few fruits. The very early tomatoes such as 'Siberia' (DO) that set fruit when the plant is small, before the leaves have time to accumulate sugars, will likely be bland. The tomatoes we grew in the cool, wet summer of 1990 were mere shadows of the lip-smacking fruit we harvested in the long, hot summer of 1991. The leaves manufacture flavour and pass it on to the fruit, and although you cannot control the sun that falls on those leaves, you can make sure the plant has a good proportion of leaves. Therefore, when you prune, be judicious; heavy pruning may deprive the plants of the flavour factories in the leaves. And wait until the tomato is fully ripe before picking it: flavour compounds and vitamin C are concentrated in the gel around the seeds. The gel develops at temperatures above 60 degrees F as the tomato turns red.

Harvest red tomatoes as long as you can, but if frost threatens, pick all the green ones left on the vine. They ripen indoors on a windowsill. In northern Ontario, we rarely had red tomatoes in the garden. I wrapped each hard green ball carefully in newspaper, put them in a box in the cellar and opened juicy red treasures right up to Christmas. With cherry tomatoes, pick whole branches and hang them in a warm, sunny place.

Vine-ripened tomatoes need little more than a quick wash and coring to be ready for the table. Before chopping a tomato for salad, seed it by cutting it in half crosswise and squeezing gently, prying the gel and seeds out of the cavities. Occasionally, thick-skinned tomatoes need to be peeled. With a very sharp knife, cut a light X on the bottom of the fruit, and drop into simmering water for a few seconds, until the skin at the X curls. Plunge immediately into cold water. When cool, slip off the loosened skin. Tomatoes can also be roasted like peppers. Roast on a baking sheet at 400 degrees F for 20 minutes, or roast in a heavy cast-iron skillet over very high heat for 2 to 5 minutes. Allow to cool, peel,

squeeze out the seeds and chop. Mix with roasted peppers, onion, garlic and a lemon/oil vinaigrette spiced with coriander and cumin to create a Tunisian specialty known as *Salat Meschoui*.

For best flavour, store tomatoes at room temperature, unwashed, resting stem side down until they are slightly soft. Keep them out of the sun, or they will lose flavour. Refrigerate very ripe tomatoes unwrapped for about four days. For longer storage, try drying them. You can use a commercial dryer or the oven, but the high-summer sun works just as well. Slice tomatoes vertically, and lay them on an unpainted board (not treated with any chemicals). Salt well and cover with cheesecloth to keep insects off. Prop the board outdoors, perpendicular to the sun's rays and slanted so that juices run off. When the tomatoes are shrivelled, leathery and firm to the touch, they are sun-dried. Brush off the excess salt, and store in extra-virgin olive oil or dry sterile jars. These keep in the refrigerator for several weeks, but for longer storage, seal in a vinaigrette; the acid acts as a preservative.

Use sun-dried tomatoes, called *pumate* by the Italians, to make a wonderful dressing. Purée two cloves of garlic, half a cup (125 mL) of sun-dried tomatoes, a third of a cup (75 mL) each of roasted red peppers and pitted black olives, then add a third of a cup (75 mL) of red-wine vinegar, two tablespoons (30 mL) of balsamic vinegar and half a cup (125 mL) of extra-virgin olive oil. This dressing, similar to pesto, is superb on potatoes, green beans, eggplant or hearty greens.

Tomato salads are undoubtedly already a staple of the family kitchen. It is impossible to think of Italian, Greek, Spanish or Mexican cuisine without them. In China, they are served as dessert, the slices heaped high with white sugar. (In fact, a sprinkling of sugar does bring out the sweetness of tomatoes—but just a pinch.) In general, hearty vinegars such as red-wine, sherry and balsamic go well with tomatoes, as do the herbs basil, oregano, chervil and parsley.

Whole cherry tomatoes make great dippers, especially with fennel mayonnaise or yogurt cheese mixed with *fines herbes*. Tomato wedges mixed with scallions and tossed in a simple red-wine vinaigrette spiced with basil, oregano, coriander, chervil or parsley is sweet ambrosia. For a change, try tomatoes tossed in yogurt vinaigrette (see page 139). An unusual variation is to core, then slice medium-sized tomatoes in half lengthwise, set them flat on the cutting board and slice thinly. On each plate, lay a bed of soft lettuce, fan out the half-tomato slices and dress with a vinaigrette of sherry vin-

egar, garlic, extra-virgin olive oil and basil. Sprinkle julienned provolone cheese and prosciutto over the top. My personal treat is tomato slices topped with pesto, but I am also partial to slices sprinkled with parsley and chopped lemon zest and drizzled with cognac and extra-virgin olive oil.

Very large, seedy tomatoes are best stuffed. Slice off the stem end, and squeeze it gently to loosen the ball of seeds, then turn it upside down in a colander in the sink. Let it drain for 15 minutes or more, then scoop out the pulp. Fill with potato, zucchini or bean salad.

A final hint: never serve tomatoes cold. According to *Kitchen Science*, "cold hinders the conversion of the vegetable's linoleic acid to Z-3 hexenel, the compound that accounts for much of the desirable ripe-tomato scent and taste." And you can improve winter store-bought tomatoes by letting them ripen at room temperature for a couple of days. Nothing, of course, beats a tomato salad made with fruit still sun-warm from the garden.

Insalata Caprese

Choosing one tomato salad recipe out of thousands is a difficult task. Ultimately, we settled on tradition over test-kitchen experiments. This salad is a standard summer first course in sunny Italy.

	Whole basil leaves	
2	ripe tomatoes, sliced	2
½ lb.	fresh mozzarella cheese (Bocconcini), sliced thickly	250 g
¼ cup	extra-virgin olive oil	50 mL
2 Tbsp.	red-wine vinegar	30 mL
½ tsp.	balsamic vinegar	2 mL
1 Tbsp.	chiffonaded basil leaves	15 mL
	Freshly ground black pepper	

Arrange whole basil leaves on a platter. Fan tomato slices on the basil, alternating them with slices of mozzarella. Beat the olive oil, vinegars and chiffonaded basil until emulsified. Pour over the tomato slices, and top with a generous grinding of black pepper. For variation, omit the cheese, and sprinkle with two tablespoons (30 mL) of roasted pine nuts.

For a warm winter salad, omit the whole basil leaves, dress the tomato slices, then lay the cheese on top. Slide under the broiler until the cheese bubbles gently, then remove from oven, garnish with fresh parsley, and serve.

Buried Bounty

Beets to Radishes

Chapter Six

Gardening is partly a spectator sport. We dig and spray and pluck the weeds to ensure a good harvest, but the close contact also allows us to spy on the peas and tomatoes, hoping to catch that first promising bulge or blush of pink. One whole class of vegetables denies us this voyeuristic pleasure, however. Potatoes, radishes, leeks and fennel, to name a few, do their final ripening out of sight. What we see—the ferny carrot tops and yellow sunflowers of the Jerusalem artichoke—bears no resemblance to the vegetable buried under the earth. Harvesting these species is like shoving your hand into a box of Cracker Jack: you know roughly what the prize will be, yet retrieving it never fails to astonish and delight.

Another class of salad vegetables goes undercover only for the last few weeks of ripening. Leeks and finochio depend on darkness for their special tenderness but rely on the gardener to hill up soil so that the heart will blanch sweetly. Belgian endives yield their buried bounty only after harvest and storage, sprouting leaves for winter salads.

These are among the most expensive and exotic in the salad cook's repertoire, but like all vegetables that ripen in the dark, they are well worth the wait.

Beet
Beta vulgaris

"What's this?" asked the dinner guest, plucking a white half-moon from the salad. "I thought it was radish, but it's sweet."

"It's beet," said Turid.

"It can't be. It's white."

"It's beet."

"But it doesn't taste beety," insisted the guest.

"It's beet."

The conversation went back and forth, the guest incredulous, Turid adamant. His disbelief was so thorough that Turid left the table and returned holding a round white root triumphantly by its green top. By its leaves, he finally knew it. "It's beet," he admitted.

Our assumptions about food colours are deeply

ingrained. Beets are red; peas are green; potatoes are white. But plant breeders have devoted much research to adding colours to the garden palette. Now, peas are purple, potatoes are blue, beets are white. It reminds me of the line in Dylan Thomas's *A Child's Christmas in Wales*: "And still the dazzling sky-blue sheep are grazing in the red field under the rainbow-billed and pea-green birds."

The range in beet colour is not entirely new. Alexandre Dumas, in 1869, distinguished three shades of beetroot: red, yellow and white. Nor is the plant breeders' interest in colour entirely whimsical. The red dye in beets, for instance, bleeds profusely: whatever touches red beets—onions, potatoes, mayonnaise—turns bright pink.

Beets are biennials grown as semihardy annuals, the enlarged tuber harvested before the plant flowers in its second year. There are four types of beets: table beets, eaten mainly for the root; leaf beets, or chard, grown entirely for the greens (see page 39); sugar beets, developed in Napoleonic Europe to free the continent from its dependence on colonial sugarcane; and mangel-wurzels, coarse, yellow-orange beets grown as animal feed.

Beetroot is a good source of vitamin C and potassium and a fair source of vitamin A. It is sweet, yet contains only 55 calories per cup. The greens, which contain half the calories of and more vitamins than the root, can be harvested from young beets without harming root growth. In winter, leaves will sprout from stored roots, providing winter salads.

Although long storage was once the goal of beet breeders, they now select for colour, uniform shape, nonwoody centres, tall, glossy foliage and reduced "zoning," the tree-ring effect of a sliced beet. But it is shape that distinguishes the three categories of beetroot varieties: globe beets, tankard beets and tapered beets. Within each group, there are new hybrids and old heirloom varieties, which are generally bigger and more variable in size.

Globe beets, also known as turnip-rooted, round or ball beets, mature quickly and are good for fresh summer salads. Sown early, they may bolt if the weather turns hot and dry, so choose bolt-resistant types. The widely available red 'Detroit' beet is good for late-summer sowings and for storage. Globe beets also come in white—'Albina Vereduna' (CG)—and in yellow—'Golden' (SH, CG)—both of which have slightly higher sugar content than red beets. 'Crosby Egyptian' (BL) is an heirloom early beet, as is 'Chioggia' (JO, SH, BL), a very sweet ·Italian beet that shows concentric pink and white rings when sliced crosswise, a tie-dyed effect that is startling and beautiful in a salad. For variety, try

Spa Salad with fenugreek sprouts, grated carrots and a cider vinaigrette.

mixing several types of beet seeds together for each planting: white, red and striped beets mature together and combine for striking salads.

Tankard, or cylindrical, beets are excellent for winter storage, but they are also our salad favourites because the roots are long and sausage-shaped, easily sliced into uniform "coins." We recommend 'Formonova' (JO), a cylindrical beet about 4 inches long and 1 ½ inches wide that matures in two months to a salad beet with outstanding flavour. Because of their shape, these beets can be grown closer together in the garden, but they need hilling to cover the top, which thrusts up out of the soil like a mangel. Baby beets, such as the inch-round 'Little Ball' (SH), are tasty eaten whole, either pickled or raw with a dip.

Beets grow best in full sun, in well-drained, humus-rich soil with a pH between 6 and 7. They are sensitive to acidity, and good levels of phosphorus and potassium are essential. Plant them in a bed that is well dug and free of obstacles which might impede straight root development.

Beets are semihardy. Plant them directly in the garden as soon as the soil is workable, about two weeks before the last frost. Soak seeds overnight, then plant them half an inch deep and an inch apart, in single rows 8 inches apart. (Plant 'Golden' beets more thickly, since these seeds do not germinate well.) Press the soil against the seeds, then water well, keeping the bed moist until sprouts appear. Beet seeds are slow to start—germination takes 10 to 14 days—but once the seedlings push through the soil, they grow quickly. For a continuous supply, sow short rows at monthly intervals.

A beet "seed" is actually a cluster of several star-shaped kernels. Each seed produces a clump of tiny seedlings, so no matter how judiciously you plant, beets always need a lot of thinning. The only exception is the new "monogerm" globe beet that produces a single seedling from each seed.

Thin beet seedlings to 4 inches apart as soon as they are big enough to handle. Unlike most root vegetables, beets don't mind being transplanted. It slows them down, but this gives you another succession harvest. Lift the seedling carefully out of the soil, snip off the thready tip of the root, and replant in a trench or hole that has been watered until it is a slurry of mud. This keeps the transplant straight and encourages new feeder roots.

The tenderest beets are grown quickly with lots of moisture. Hot, dry weather results in a low yield of woody beets; drought followed by heavy watering splits the roots. Keep the bed weed-free, hoeing frequently but being careful not to touch the roots. Mulching keeps weeds down and preserves moisture. Because beets are heavy feeders, water deeply and side-dress the plants with a fertilizer such as manure tea when you thin and again in the middle of the season.

Beets prefer cool weather: in the heat of summer, red beets fade and toughen. A fall crop is often more successful, especially if summer arrives hot and fast. Plant a second beet crop at the end of July, moistening the furrows thoroughly before planting. Once they sprout, shelter seedlings from intense sun.

In our experience, beets are rarely bothered by pests. If leaf miners are a problem, cut and destroy infested leaves.

Harvest beets before they get too big and woody. Although they are semihardy and survive light frosts, they should be lifted when a hard frost threatens. Dig them up, shake off the soil, and twist off the leaves about 2 inches above the crown; leaving a stubble of stem prevents the root from bleeding. Discard damaged roots, or eat them immediately; store the rest like carrots, layering them in dry peat or sand.

Beetroots stay fresh in the refrigerator for up to two weeks. They can be eaten raw, but beets are usually cooked and sliced or diced before they are dressed. Always cook beets intact: never trim the topknot of greens or the tapering root. This reduces bleeding and retains maximum vitamins. Boil or steam for an hour (less if using a pressure cooker), until tender when pierced with a fork. To keep *all* the juices in, bake beets unpeeled in a covered casserole at 300 degrees F for about an hour. Cool the cooked beets a little, then hold them under cold running water and slide the skins off.

Cooked, peeled beets can be diced, sliced or julienned. The French and Italians in John Evelyn's time carved the slices into ''curious Figures to adorn their Sallets.'' Not a bad idea. American universities have named two beet dishes: Yale beets, dressed in orange sauce, and sweet-and-sour Harvard beets. According to Dumas, beets are best with ''glazed little white onions, slices of red-skinned potato, chunks of artichoke bottoms, steamed kidney beans, nasturtium flowers and cress.'' He also suggests serving them as an hors d'oeuvre, tossed with olives and sardines and dressed with tarragon vinegar, oil, shallots, salt and pepper and garnished with hard-cooked egg. One of the most common salads in 18th-century New France was boiled, sliced beets tossed simply with drained capers and olive oil.

Spa Salad

Conventional cooked beet salad is not a spur-of-the-moment dish. Using the vegetable raw, however, is not only quick but healthful. At German spas, raw grated beets are served as part of a composed salad of kohlrabi, carrots, celeriac, cucumber, finochio and radish, all flavoured with a simple marinade of lemon juice or vinegar with a pinch of sugar. In this variation, substitute any raw grated vegetable. Vary the flavour by adding fresh herbs such as dill, parsley or savory. Spiced with garlic or cumin, it adopts a Middle Eastern flavour.

½ cup	cider vinegar	125 mL
2 Tbsp.	water	30 mL
½ cup	canola oil	125 mL
	Pinch of brown sugar	
¼ tsp.	salt	1 mL
¼ tsp.	white or black pepper	1 mL
2 Tbsp.	finely chopped scallions	30 mL
6	large beets	6

Mix the marinade and add the scallions. Peel and grate the raw beets, adding them to the marinade. Let stand an hour or two before serving.

Red-beet salad keeps a day or two in the refrigerator; pink-beet salad, made from 'Chioggia' beets, should be eaten the same day. Serve white-beet salad within 2 hours, as white beets discolour rapidly, turning first grey, then rust-red. Make the marinade, and stir in the beets as you grate them. The fresh white colour lasts up to 3 hours.

Carrot
Daucus carota var. *sativa*

Carrots are such a humble staple of Canadian gardens that their history comes as a bit of a surprise. Native to Afghanistan, where one of the most unusual varieties, long purple tapers with yellow flesh, still grows, they were brought early to the Mediterranean. Generally, Romans preferred turnips to carrots, but they did concede to carrots a certain power over the loins. Caligula supposedly once fed Roman senators a banquet consisting entirely of carrot dishes in order to observe these gentlemen ''fornicating like beasts of the field.'' The success of his plan was not recorded.

Like finochio, celery and chervil, carrots are members of the family Umbelliferae. Seed catalogues list dozens of varieties beyond the standard uniform orange taper. Colours range from Halloween orange to pristine white. Some are on the table within 10 weeks; others take up to twice that long to mature.

Short-rooted carrots, the so-called ''earlies,'' are best for spring and fall sowings. They like full sun, developing quickly into round balls or finger-long stumps with a sweet, delicate flavour. 'Coreless Amsterdam' (ST) is an early stump-rooted carrot that matures in 55 days to about 8 inches long and an inch in diameter. Smooth-skinned and salmon-red, it is almost all flesh, with a scant quarter-inch core. The flavour is conventional, but the root is exceptionally firm and grates well. 'Touchon' (CG) is an heirloom early carrot of the Nantes type, which is generally longer, has broader shoulders and is sometimes grown as a main crop. Brightly coloured and practically coreless, 'Touchon' is a favourite in France. 'Paris Market' carrots, such as 'Parmex' (CG) and 'Orbit' (JO), are round globes, an inch or two in diameter, that develop quickly, some in as little as 50 days—a good choice for shallow beds and container gardens.

Intermediate carrots lie between short-rooted earlies and the long-tapered giants that store well but are not great for salads. Grown as a main crop through high summer, the carrots in this class may be stump-rooted, cylindrical or tapered. They tolerate partial shade and are larger, a little tougher and better for storing. For instance, 'White Belgian' (BL) is a tapered white carrot, almost a foot long, an inch through and over half core. It looks somewhat like a parsnip, is a little tough and crunchy but is very sweet and matures in 75 days. Oddly, the white varieties seem to have the strongest carrot flavour. Baby carrots, a distinct variety, achieve full colour and taste when very small. 'Baby Sweet Hybrid' (ST) was both the tiniest carrot we grew and the sweetest.

''Eat your carrots,'' my mother used to say, ''and you'll be able to see in the dark.'' I believed her, bolstered by my observations that rabbits, which ate carrots, played at night. Carrots *are* good for vision, but that may be the least of their therapeutic benefits. Carrots contain considerable potassium, calcium and phosphorus and more sugar than any vegetable except beets, but more important, they are replete with beta carotene, the most naturally usable form of vitamin A. One carrot can supply up to 8,000 units of vitamin A, more than

109

'Orbit' mini ball carrots, perfect for dipping, and the longer 'Touchon' for salads.

it gives them rough skin and encourages forking. The soil should be light, free-draining and deeply worked so that the roots grow straight. If your soil is stony, grow stump-rooted types. In spring, carrots like full sun, but because they enjoy partial shade in summer, it is a good idea to interplant them with tall-growing vegetables such as broccoli or Brussels sprouts.

Plant carrots directly in the garden when the soil is warm, then succession-plant through the summer. After years of planting early according to seed-packet directions, with disappointing results, we learned to wait to plant carrots until the soil is truly warm. Planted at the right time—when the soil is about 65 degrees F—there will be 100 percent germination within a week. The trade-off is that the sweetest carrots grow in cool weather. Therefore, if your climate heats up quickly, you may have better luck planting carrots as a fall crop, germinating the seed in the heat of summer and letting the carrots mature during cool autumn days.

Carrot seeds are very fine—20,000 to the ounce—which makes it difficult to sow them thinly enough. Try mixing the seeds with fine sand when you sow. Make a furrow three-quarters of an inch deep, soak with water, and sow as thinly as possible. Cover with half an inch of fine potting soil (carrots have a hard time pushing up through garden soil), leaving a slight indentation to hold water. Keep the bed evenly moist while the seeds are germinating; it should never dry out.

Within two weeks of sprouting, start thinning the carrots, spacing them 1 to 3 inches apart, depending on the type. They will pull out more quickly and easily if you water the trench before you thin. Most experts say carrots transplant poorly, but I have good luck relocating seedlings. Thin when the plants are tiny, and replant in a mud slurry, laying the hairlike root on your finger and guiding it straight into the mud. Protect the transplants from direct sun until they are established. The characteristic odour given off when carrot seedlings are pulled out attracts carrot rust flies, pests that lay their eggs against the carrots, which then provide food for the burrowing larvae. To minimize the risk of carrot-fly invasion, thin on still, damp evenings and dispose of the thinnings immediately. Some gardeners say that interplanting carrots with onions, garlic or pungent herbs such as sage also masks the odour the flies love so well.

You may notice a caterpillar crawling on the leaves: this is likely a swallowtail butterfly in the making. Don't mistake it for a pest. The real damage to carrots is done underground by rust-fly

the recommended daily dose. (Beta carotene is the yellow colouring agent in carrots, so the deeper the colour, the higher the concentration.) Convincing research suggests that foods high in beta carotene —carrots, broccoli, Brussels sprouts, spinach— reduce the risk of cancer. Furthermore, the fibre in carrots lowers cholesterol levels in the blood. In one study, 2½ medium carrots a day lowered blood cholesterol on average by 11 percent. Finally, since carrots absorb 20 to 30 times their weight in water, four times as much as bran, they are considered an effective ''bulking'' agent.

Their bright green, fernlike leaves make carrots one of the most decorative plants in the salad garden, so much so that they are welcome even in flower borders: if you leave a couple in the bed, the following spring, they will produce beautiful umbels of white flowers that closely resemble Queen Anne's lace, the true wild carrot.

Carrots like fertile soil but not fresh manure:

maggots and wireworms, which can be avoided by crop rotation and careful thinning.

Carrots are tricky to germinate and a pain to thin, but once started, they are easy to grow. After two weeks, fertilize with manure tea, and mulch so that they don't dry out.

For autumn carrots and a winter supply of storage carrots, sow again in July. Around the time you dig potatoes, lift the carrots out, soaking the soil first and using a garden fork rather than trying to pull them up by their foliage. Cut the tops to within half an inch of the crown, and store in layers between sand, ensuring that air is eliminated. Blemished roots keep in the refrigerator for a few weeks.

Carrots should be at least half an inch in diameter when harvested. Pulled too soon, they may have an objectionable piney flavour caused by terpene, a chemical that develops early in the roots and that is eventually balanced by sugars manufactured as the carrots mature. This vegetable keeps fairly well in the ground, although a couple of weeks after maturity, the roots become woody and tough and start to split. To prolong the harvest of fresh garden carrots in the fall, mulch heavily to prevent the soil and roots from freezing.

Don't peel young carrots; just scrub them well before serving. Mature carrots or those from storage should be peeled. Use young carrots raw and whole, but slice, julienne or grate mature roots. To make them soft enough for salads, steam older, larger carrots for about 2 minutes to the tender-crisp stage. (Do not boil: boiling leaches out a third of the potassium, whereas steaming preserves most of the minerals.) Ironically, cooking carrots increases the available carotenes. Cooked carrots—tender-crisp, not mushy—have two to five times more beta carotene than raw carrots.

One of the staple dishes in France is *assiette de crudités*, an assortment of little salads that invariably includes a fresh *salade de carottes rapées*, freshly grated carrots tossed with tiny currants and herbs and a simple lemon and olive oil vinaigrette. Herbs that combine well with carrots are chives, tarragon, dill, marjoram, nutmeg, cinnamon, basil, rosemary, chervil and perilla. Citrus juice and nut oils are also delicious: try a salad of blanched, julienned carrots tossed with sliced scallions and capers and a vinaigrette made with orange or lemon juice and walnut oil. Serve on nasturtium leaves. For variety, you might try substituting grated radish, chopped cucumber or young turnip for some of the carrot. In the Caucasus, where salads are eaten for dinner, lunch and even breakfast, grated carrot and diced cucumber are mixed with a lemon juice/olive oil vinaigrette and plain yogurt, herbed with dill, mint or chervil.

Moroccan Carrot Salad

This dish tastes strongly of cumin, a favourite spice in North African cooking.

1 lb.	carrots, julienned	500 g
⅓ cup	extra-virgin olive oil	75 mL
2 Tbsp.	fresh lemon juice	30 mL
2	large cloves garlic, peeled & pressed	2
1 tsp.	salt	5 mL
½ tsp.	each cumin, cinnamon & paprika	2 mL
⅛ tsp.	cayenne	0.5 mL
1 tsp.	sugar	5 mL
3 Tbsp.	minced parsley	45 mL
2 Tbsp.	minced coriander	30 mL
1 Tbsp.	minced mint leaves	15 mL

Blanch carrots a moment or two until tender-crisp and vivid in colour. Then freshen in cold water. Whisk together the remaining ingredients. Toss with carrots, and chill 4 hours to overnight. Bring to room temperature before serving. Garnish with lemon wedges, and serve on nasturtium leaves.

Celeriac
Apium graveolens var. *rapaceum*

Celery is a difficult vegetable for home gardeners to grow, since it requires a virtual bog. But the gardeners of the king of Persia were wise: 4,000 years ago, they bred two strains from wild celery—the traditional celery stalk (*Apium graveolens* var. *dulce*) and celeriac (*A. g.* var. *rapaceum*). All in all, traditional celery seems a lot of work for relatively poor returns. Even after great care and constant watering, the stalks are tough and slightly bitter, passable when cooked but not of salad quality and really appealing only to mice. As a result, we have abandoned celery and now grow celeriac for the crunchy flesh and use its young leaves for garnish. Richters offers leaf celery (*A. g.* var. *secalinum*), which we have not yet grown but intend to try: it purportedly adds celery flavour to salads in the form of a herb that looks much like Italian parsley.

Perhaps because of its unattractive appearance, celery root, or celeriac—also called knob celery and turnip-rooted celery—is almost unknown here, though popular in Europe. It looks utterly inedible, like a hairy, overripe turnip with warts, and it is somewhat difficult to prepare, but the texture is wonderfully crisp and the flavour surpasses even that of celery. Celeriac needs an even longer growing season than stalk celery, but it does not have to be blanched, only hilled up when the shoulders of the root push through the ground. And unlike stalk celery, it stores well and makes an excellent salad on its own.

High in phosphorus and sodium, a good source of potassium and low in calories (a scant 20 per cup), celeriac has an ulcer-healing agent also found in cabbage, a substance that stimulates the stomach lining to produce a mucous shield against acids.

Aboveground, celeriac looks like a slightly rangy celery, with hollow stalks that grow 20 inches tall. Young leaves and stalks can be used in salads, but the real point of this horticultural exercise is a swelling at the base of the stem that matures to a dense, knobby bulb usually 4 to 5 inches in diameter. 'Large Smooth Prague' (ST) was the smallest we've grown, just over 2 inches in diameter. It takes 110 days to mature, as does 'José' (JO), slightly larger with a very refined flesh inside. 'Dolvi' (NI) is in the ground a month longer but is the biggest, a 4-inch globe. All have a nutty, parsley-celery flavour and fibreless white flesh.

Celeriac likes fertile, water-retentive soil and a sunny spot. Like celery, it wants to be moist all the time, so if the soil is sandy, dig in some peat or compost to make it more spongelike. In most of Canada, the outdoor growing season isn't long enough to plant seeds directly in the garden, and it is extremely unlikely that you will find seedlings at a nursery. Celeriac is a plant you must start yourself.

In late March, soak seeds overnight, then sprinkle them on top of the soil in six-packs or flats; cover lightly with potting soil. Celeriac transplants easily, so peat pots are unnecessary. At 70 degrees F, seeds germinate in about two weeks. Move the plants to a cooler location but never lower than 55 degrees if you want a bulb. Within a month, thin the seedlings to one sturdy plant per pot or about 2 inches apart in a flat. Harden off the celeriac in a cold frame. By the end of May, transplant the seedlings into staggered holes 8 inches deep and a foot apart in the salad garden. When the plant is established, mulch to keep the soil moist.

Other than regular watering, celeriac is virtually care-free until mid-August, when you should cut into the ground with an eight-inch knife, tracing the bulb. This trims off the side roots and causes the plant to develop a nice heavy globe with only a tangle of roots below. Remove the lower leaves, and draw the soil over the swelling.

Leave celeriac to mature in the garden for most of the growing season, at least four months. Celeriac is quite cold-hardy, and a few light frosts prompt the starches in the root to convert to sugar. In some areas, celeriac overwinters but only with very heavy mulch. It is simpler to dig the roots up and store them like carrots. Much later than potatoes, just before the soil is in danger of freezing, lift the celeriac with a garden fork, and cut off all the remaining roots. To store, cut off the tops and cover with sand in a cool place (35 to 40 degrees F). Do not store with onions or other pungent vegetables, because celeriac readily absorbs flavours.

For gardeners who want to try celery, start the seeds exactly like celeriac, transplanting 12 inches apart into a well-dug bed laced with old manure. (Celery is susceptible to early blight, a fungus attacking dew-laden leaves, and late blight, a result of rainy weather. Severely infected plants die. A fungicide applied weekly helps; some gardeners forestall the fungus by soaking the celery seed in very hot water for half an hour before sowing.) Deeply soak the soil, then mulch heavily with straw. The plants need a constant water supply to produce crisp stalks. Once a month, pull back the hay and soak the plant with manure tea.

By mid-July, when the celery plants are about 16 inches tall, either hill them, or, if you don't want dirt in the stems, mulch heavily with straw to blanch the stems. (The drawback to using straw is rodents.) Some varieties are self-blanching, but even they need a little help. To harvest, remove the hay and cut off the celery at the base. It keeps unwashed in the refrigerator for up to two weeks.

Unwashed celeriac lasts in the refrigerator for only a week. To prepare the root, cut off the top and root ends and scrub it with a vegetable brush. Peel away the thick outer skin, and cut out the "eyes." Slice, dice, julienne, grate or peel into curls. Submerge the cut pieces immediately in acidulated water—three tablespoons (45 mL) of lemon juice or vinegar per quart (1 L) of water—to keep the flesh bright white. Although often used in soups and stews, celeriac makes an excellent salad vegetable because its flavour is actually better cold than hot. If it is too crunchy for your taste raw, parboil or steam it until tender-crisp, about 5 minutes for slices. Whole roots take much longer, but there is no risk of darkening.

In some parts of Germany, celeriac is eaten with other root vegetables as a traditional Christmas Eve dish called Schlemmer Salad (a salad for gorging). Carrots, potatoes, celeriac and albino beets are cooked together until tender, then drained, peeled and sliced, sprinkled with salt and pepper and dressed in a vinaigrette of vinegar, oil, onions and herbs. Made ahead of time, it is a simple prelude to the elaborate feasting of Christmas Day.

Celery Root Rémoulade

This is the classic celeriac dish served throughout Europe and wherever the vegetable has made inroads to North American tables. Traditionally, according to Escoffier, it is simply julienned celeriac tossed in a mustard cream: three tablespoons (45 mL) of prepared mustard mixed with a little salt, pepper and lemon juice and thinned with very fresh heavy cream. For a slightly less rich but equally delicious variation, toss celeriac with a lemon vinaigrette flavoured with a tablespoon (15 mL) of basil. But we like the following creamy version best.

4	large celeriac	4
1 cup	mayonnaise	250 mL
2 Tbsp.	sour cream or yogurt	30 mL
2 Tbsp.	heavy cream	30 mL
2 Tbsp.	grainy mustard	30 mL
2 Tbsp.	cider vinegar	30 mL
1 tsp.	salt	5 mL
1	large tart green apple, coarsely grated	1
¾ cup	toasted hazelnuts	175 mL

Trim and peel the celeriac. Julienne into 1-inch strips or peel into curls. Drop in acidulated water to prevent darkening. Whisk together all but the last two ingredients. Add drained celeriac, apple and a half-cup (125 mL) of nuts and toss. Chill 2 hours to blend flavours. Toss again, then mound into lettuce cups. Sprinkle with remaining quarter-cup (50 mL) of nuts.

Finochio
Foeniculum vulgare var. *dulce*

The name carries few associations for North Americans, but say "fennel" to the Italians or French, and their eyes will glaze over with fond recollection.

"You mean you grow it here? Real finochio?" asked an Italian singer-writer friend of mine. When I showed her the pale green bulbs rising from their mounds of earth in my front yard, she fairly swooned. We dug up a few, and she spent the rest of the afternoon happily munching on the sweet licorice stalks. In return, she taught me to pronounce my adopted favourite's name correctly— fin-knock-ee-o, with the emphasis on knock.

Europeans eat finochio like celery. Cool and crisp, the flat bulb is the vegetable equivalent of a tall glass of Pernod and has almost the same milky green colour. Indeed, the mild, licorice flavour makes it seem more like dessert material than the stuff of salads. Given such qualities, it is a wonder that fennel has not spread beyond ethnic gardens. As long ago as 1842, Thomas Jefferson's Italian correspondent recommended that the president cultivate finochio in his garden at Monticello. He did not follow the advice; we hope you will.

Finochio, also known as Florence fennel because of its Italian origins and sweet fennel because of its Latin name, belongs to the same family as the herb fennel (*Foeniculum vulgare*). The two species, though closely related, were developed with different emphasis—one for the head, so to speak, and one for the feet. Finochio is shorter in stature than its herbal cousin, but its feathery leaves are identical and equally tasty in salads. As it matures, finochio develops celerylike ribs that swell and overlap at the base to form a flattened bulb. When the bulb is the size of a golf ball, bury it under a hill of earth, where it enlarges and blanches to a unique vegetable with the crunch of celery and the sweet licorice ambrosia of its cousin herb. According to the French novelist Colette, female fennel plants, which have flatter bulbs, are even tastier than the male plants.

In its native Mediterranean region, finochio has long been used as a food, a flavouring and a medicinal herb. Fennel has the ancient reputation of being an all-round cure for everything from eye problems to obesity, flatulence and rheumatic pains. Socrates suggested that a stick of fennel and a glass of water were the only cure for gastronomic overindulgence. This may be because fennel is 94 percent water. But fennel is also extremely rich in vitamin A and is high in calcium and potassium as well.

There is confusion in many seed catalogues over the Latin names of herb and bulb fennel. Finochio is often referred to as *Foeniculum azoricum*, a variety grown for the essential oil in the flowers, and herb fennel is called *Foeniculum vulgare* var. *dulce*. Check to make sure that what you are buying is the bulb-type fennel—Florence fennel—and not the leafy herb. 'Zefa Fino' (JO) is a slow-bolting variety bred at the Swiss Federal Research Station. Sown in spring, it matures in 65 days. 'Romy' (SH) is an Italian heirloom variety noted for large, tender bulbs; the Swiss 'Fennel Fino' (SH) is somewhat smaller but also bolt-resistant.

Finochio is not difficult to grow, even in climates cooler than that of southern Italy. It needs richer soil than herb fennel—light and well drained but also well dressed with manure or compost. The pH should be neutral; if the soil is too acidic, add dolomitic lime. Plant the finochio in a sunny, sheltered location, where you can appreciate the beauty of its feathery foliage. Mine is located behind the nasturtiums and violets, right beside the path to the house, where I can pluck a stem or two to nibble every time I pass.

Finochio, like radicchio, does best in the shoulder seasons, sown indoors in early spring for an early-summer harvest or sown directly in the garden in late July for a fall harvest. The latter is easier, although you may get two harvests from a single early indoor sowing. Start the seeds in early March, sowing in peat pots, since disturbing the roots may cause bolting. Germinate at 70 degrees F, move under lights or to a bright windowsill, harden off, and transplant into the garden in mid-May, setting the plants 6 to 8 inches apart. (The seedlings can take some cool weather.)

For a fall harvest, sow finochio directly in the garden a quarter-inch deep in well-prepared, fertile soil, preferably in the vicinity of taller, shade-giving plants. (Because of its strong fragrance, finochio is considered incompatible with some plants, depressing growth in bush beans, tomatoes, kohlrabi and caraway.) Turid sows thickly because the seeds germinate inconsistently. When the seedlings are 2 inches high, thin them to 8 inches apart. Since they have a deep, central taproot, finochios don't transplant easily, although you can try moving them by the shovelful to another location, eventually thinning the group to the best plant. Press the soil around the base of transplanted seedlings so that they are not shaken loose by the wind.

Where summers are hot and early, finochio may bolt rather than form a bulb, especially if plants were started indoors and mature as the weather heats up. Finochio likes uniform, warm, moist conditions. Keep it well watered, since dryness and excessive heat prompt the plant to send up a flower stalk, diverting energy from the bulb. Fertilize once a month. As the bulb develops, harvest leaves occasionally for salads: they are a little tougher than herb fennel but delicious. Finochio is practically disease- and pest-free, although you may be fortunate enough to see some swallowtail butterflies: the larvae consider fennel a paradise.

Depending on the variety, finochio matures in two to three months. By mid-July, spring-sown plants are 2 feet tall; July-sown plants are at the same stage by mid-September. About three weeks before maturity, a swelling at the base of the stem signals that it is time to draw soil around the bottom of the plant, excluding light from the bulb as it forms. (This also protects fall fennel from early frosts.) Harvest the bulb when it is 3 to 4 inches in diameter, brushing away the soil and cutting off the bulb close to the ground with a sharp knife. When harvesting spring-sown plants, do not dig up the roots. Fertilized with compost or manure tea, the roots resprout within a couple of weeks, growing a ferny bouquet of leaves that are tasty and decorative in late-summer salads. If the summer is warm and long, you will harvest a second crop of smaller but equally delicious bulbs in early October. One warm fall, my finochio sprouted a third time, giving me bright green garnishes until December.

Finochio can stand fairly low temperatures, but when there is danger of a deep frost, harvest the bed or set a cold frame over it. If the finochio is well ventilated, harvest may continue into early winter, allowing you to observe the Italian tradition of serving finochio during the Christmas season.

All parts of Florence fennel are edible. To prepare, trim the stalks down to within an inch of the bulb, and cut off the base of the bulb, paring the hard parts away from the stem. Remove tough or discoloured outer branches. Reserve the leaves and flowers for garnishing, for tea, as a seasoning in court bouillon or for wrapping fish before grilling on the barbecue. Unwashed, the roots keep for a week in the refrigerator.

Serve young, succulent bulbs raw, cut vertically in quarters or wedges. In the Piedmont region of northern Italy, fennel is typically eaten raw as an appetizer, dipped in a *bagna caouda* (see page 69).

For the salad bowl, slice finochio crosswise in thin rounds. It is delicious tossed with apples, walnuts, raisins and yogurt in an ersatz Waldorf (only 50 calories per half-cup) or mixed with julienned carrots and zucchini in a lemon/walnut oil vinaigrette. Because of its sweetness, it is delicious with fruit vinegars. To bring out the fennel flavour, consider adding a dash of Pernod to the dressing.

Italians often include a little sliced fennel in rice and pasta salads, where it adds a refreshing zing. Fennel mayonnaise is also a treat. To two-thirds of a cup (150 mL) of mayonnaise (or half yogurt), add four teaspoons (20 mL) each of finely chopped fennel bulb and chopped fresh fennel leaves, two tablespoons (30 mL) of orange juice and one tea- spoon (5 mL) of sugar. This is delicious as a dip or as a dressing on cabbage salads.

Finochio à la Grecque

Escoffier dismisses finochio in a single sentence, saying it should be prepared like squash. What a travesty. The full licorice flavour is most obvious when stalks are eaten raw, but the bulb should be young and succulent. Older bulbs may be steamed lightly before being dressed with a vinaigrette, which mellows the taste a little.

¼ cup	extra-virgin olive oil	50 mL
¼ cup	lemon juice	50 mL
½ tsp.	salt	2 mL
2 Tbsp.	minced onion	30 mL
1/8 tsp.	dried thyme	0.5 mL
1 ½ cups	water	375 mL
1	small stalk celery, with leaves	1
3	sprigs parsley	3
10	peppercorns	10
10	whole coriander seeds	10
½	bay leaf	½
3	fennel bulbs, trimmed & cut lengthwise into quarters	3
1	sprig fennel leaves	1

Combine everything but the fennel in a saucepan. Bring to a boil, cover and simmer for 10 minutes. Add the fennel, and continue to simmer, covered, for 30 minutes or less, until the bulbs are tender-crisp. Remove the fennel from the pan. Strain the marinade, and return the liquid to the pan. Bring to a boil, and reduce to about half a cup (125 mL). Pour over the fennel, cover and chill until serving. For variety in texture, add a few stalks of fresh fennel to the marinade. The same bath is delicious with leeks or small artichokes.

Jerusalem Artichoke
Helianthus tuberosus

A woefully misnamed vegetable, the Jerusalem artichoke is neither an artichoke nor from Israel. Champlain, who first recorded the plant growing in what is now Cape Cod, remarked that its roots tasted like globe artichokes; the Jerusalem part is apparently a corruption of the Italian *girasole*, which means turning to the sun. Recently, breeders have rechristened Jerusalem artichokes "sun chokes" and "sun roots," the name we favour, since the plant is a sunflower grown for its roots.

Sun root is one of the few vegetables native to North America. As part of his booty, Champlain took the plant to Europe, where the roots became known as *patates de Canada*. The sun root was better received than the potato—although in early writings, the two are often confused—and was soon growing all over the continent. Back in its native land, however, it was not highly esteemed. In 1737, Mother de Sainte-Helène reported that famine had reduced the inhabitants of Quebec to eating Jerusalem artichokes "and other things not fit for human consumption."

The sun root is a hardy perennial sunflower that thrives even in northern zones. It has a root system that spreads far and wide from the main stalk, the young tubers producing new sprouts in spring. Each plant grows to about 6 feet in height, with coarse, hairy foliage and bright yellow flowers 2 to 3 inches across that bloom profusely in late summer. After the leaves fade in the fall, the tubers can be dug up like potatoes or left in the ground, mulched with dead foliage and lifted as needed during the winter. Turid often delays harvest until spring, when the frost has made the tubers sweet and the supply of root-cellar vegetables is exhausted.

The original 'French Mammoth White' (BL) produces large, knobby roots, but recent breeding has made sun roots sleeker and the plants less aggressive. The tubers of 'Fuseau' (BL) are extremely smooth and shaped like yams, about 4 inches long and an inch in diameter; there is a red 'Fuseau' type and a carrot type that is long, tapered and golden, about half the size of 'Fuseau.'

Tubers are available from seed houses, but they are very expensive. Get some from a friend if possible. Plant them like potatoes: cut them into "eyes," or plant them whole, dropping them in 6-inch-deep holes about a foot apart, creating a clump or hedge. (One or two plants is enough for most families.) Plant them away from the main garden, using the foliage to mask an unsightly corner of the yard. Sun roots grow in virtually any soil but prefer full sun or light shade. As the plants begin to grow, draw soil up around the stems, then leave them alone. They practically raise themselves.

Prolific producers, one sun root plant yields a two-gallon pail of tubers; one gardener reports harvesting a bushel from three plants. Use a garden fork to lift the nest of tubers out of the ground. Connected on long runner roots, the tubers range from the size of walnuts to that of apples. Dig them in the fall and store them in sand, or leave them in the soil to harvest in spring.

Finochio à la Grecque.

Wrapped in plastic, sun roots keep in the refrigerator for a week, but they are best used as soon as they are dug. A 3 ½ -ounce serving of freshly harvested raw sun root contains 7 calories; the same amount of stored root has 75. The sugar in sun root is inulin, which, unlike the sugar in potatoes, can be safely eaten by diabetics. Although sun root is nourishing—it is a good source of vitamin B, calcium, iron and magnesium—it also contains a starch that is hard for some people to digest. Eat it in moderation until you have developed some tolerance, and try preparing it with herbs, such as dill, that improve digestibility.

To prepare sun roots, scrub off the soil under running water, then peel, dropping them immediately into acidulated water to prevent darkening. If they are too gnarly to peel, put them in boiling water for 5 to 10 minutes to loosen the skins. (Do not use an aluminum pan: it blackens the flesh.)

Cooked sun roots resemble potatoes and, in fact,

can replace that vegetable in any of the recipes that appear on page 119. Or try serving sliced, steamed sun root with steamed asparagus, dressed in a lemon juice/walnut oil vinaigrette. Raw sun root is more like water chestnut, wonderfully crisp and succulent, with a slightly sweet, nutty taste. Shred raw sun root and dress it as a slaw, cut it into fingers for dipping, or slice it for pickles, marinating the white root in a good-quality vinegar for at least two days. Sun roots are especially good with tarragon and sorrel, herbs that coincide with spring harvest.

Sun Root Salad

This early-May salad uses sprouts from the windowsill, the last carrots from the root cellar, the earliest spring greens and freshly dug horseradish and sun root. Garnish it with edible spring flowers: violets, cowslips or apple blossoms.

½ cup	finely sliced raw sun root	125 mL
½ cup	grated carrot	125 mL
1 cup	fenugreek sprouts	250 mL
1 cup	young chicory or dandelion greens	250 mL
1 Tbsp.	freshly ground horseradish root	15 mL
2 Tbsp.	finely chopped tarragon & chives	30 mL
¼ tsp.	pressed garlic clove	1 mL
3 Tbsp.	extra-virgin olive oil	45 mL
2 Tbsp.	cider vinegar	30 mL
	Salt, pepper & sugar to taste	

Drop the sun root into acidulated water as it is sliced to prevent darkening. Drain and mix in a bowl with the carrot, sprouts and greens. Whisk together the remaining ingredients, adjust the seasoning, and whisk again until emulsified. Toss the vegetables with the dressing, and serve immediately.

Leek
Allium ampeloprasum (Porrum Group)

Leeks are the national emblem of Wales, but one of the more telling legends of their origin comes from Ireland. St. Patrick, it is said, was consoling a dying woman when she told him of a vision in which she had seen a herb floating in the air. Unless she ate that herb, she said, she would die. ''What was the herb?'' asked the saint. ''It looked like rushes,'' she replied. St. Patrick transformed rushes into

leeks, the woman ate them, and she was cured.

Leeks have a long and honourable history. They are mentioned in I Yin's guide to good eating written in 1500 B.C., and they were cultivated in the gardens of Ur-Nammu in 2100 B.C. Convinced that it improved his speaking voice, Nero chewed on a leek the way some men chew a cigar. Still a mainstay of the French kitchen, leeks are seldom grown in North America. Leeks may not live up to the claim that they cure everything from nosebleeds to grey hair, but the onionlike vegetable does carry a payload of nutrients. A handful of stems contains only 50 calories but 347 milligrams of potassium, 52 milligrams each of calcium and phosphorus and about 40 units of vitamin A per stalk. Leeks are also rich in dietary fibre.

''Onions are adored, and leeks are gods,'' wrote Juvenal, tongue in cheek. In fact, leeks are worthy of the accolade: they are among the more genteel alliums, hardier in the garden than onions and garlic but not as strong in the salad bowl, probably because they spend their last weeks in the dark. Only the brave would consider a salad made entirely of onions, and such an idea is out of the question for all but rabid garlic lovers, but leeks can be made into delicious salads. In taste and appearance, think of them as overgrown scallions, the flesh creamy, sweet and delicately infused with the flavour of onions.

Leeks are also among the most economical of salad vegetables. A nursery tray of leek seedlings contains hundreds of leeks, as thick as grass, yet each becomes a beautiful plant. If you can't find these bargain seedlings at a nursery, start your own from seed. There are cultivars developed exclusively for summer harvest, like 'French Summer'(BL); some, like 'Unique' (BL), that are very hardy; and others, like 'Winter Giant' (BL), that store extremely well. The widely available 'Elephant' leeks are very large and very winter-hardy. For salads, however, we recommend 'Carina' (SH), which have extra-long white shafts.

Sow leek seed indoors, like onions. Turid starts hers in February to get a head start on the season, since they can be planted outside as early as one month before the last frost. Sow thickly in flats. Germination is very slow. After they have sprouted, don't trim the tops as you do with onions. When seedlings are about 3 inches high, thin to 1 ½ inches apart. In early April, harden them off, and plant them 4 to 6 inches apart in a 3-inch-deep trench or in individual holes filled with well-aged manure. Overall, the plants need about a foot of blanching. As the leeks grow, hill up the soil gradually until the bottom 7 or 8 inches of each shaft is covered, or

mulch with hay, which is cleaner and helps cool the soil. Leeks are susceptible to heat, and if the soil is too warm, the buried bulb may rot. Side-dress with liquid fertilizer or manure tea once a month. Virtually immune to pests, leeks seem to guard other vegetables against certain insect plagues.

Leeks take three to four months to mature after transplanting. Watch them, though: there is no virtue in allowing them to become gargantuan. With this vegetable, small is beautiful, and anything over 2 inches in diameter is too stout for the salad bowl; save the larger ones for soup. Started at the end of February and transplanted in early May, our leeks were at their peak the first week of August— delicate bulbs an inch wide at the base, with 6 inches of creamy white stem blending into 2 feet of dark jade leaves that elegantly cascaded from the braided tops like fountains. You cannot buy such thin, tasty leeks: this treat is reserved for gardeners.

If temperatures never fall below 10 degrees F, leave the leeks in the garden all winter long. In colder climates, let them weather the first frosts of October, but before killing frosts, lift the remaining leeks with a garden fork, and store like carrots. You may want to leave a few in the garden under a blanket of mulch. The following summer, they flower like giant chives, sending up spectacular 6-inch-round lavender blooms on 4-foot stalks. When the leeks flower, little corms develop at the base of the plant. Gather the corms in the fall, then the next spring, plant them in fertile soil for a new crop of leeks. Gardeners who are organized and patient enough for the three-year cycle can have a steady supply without ever starting seeds or buying seedlings.

After digging the leeks, cut off and discard the root ends, and trim the tops to about 3 inches of green leaves. Don't discard the tops. Chop them coarsely, and place them in a bag in the freezer, adding them to winter soup stocks for a mild onion flavour.

Leeks can be refrigerated unwashed for up to a week. To prepare them for salads, strip off coarse outer leaves, then wash them—a notoriously difficult job, since the edible part has been hilled in soil that inevitably lodges in the overlapping flesh as it grows. Plunge the leeks up and down in a sinkful of warm water, then separate the braids slightly and hold them under the tap to remove the last of the dirt.

When no bigger than your finger, young leeks can be eaten raw like green onions, dipped in herb mayonnaise. Unlike other onions, they also make delectable solo salads and are often steamed first until tender, about 5 minutes. Overcooking makes leeks slimy and mushy, so test them frequently for doneness, and err on the side of crispness. Bathe the steamed leeks for a couple of hours in a marinade of a half-cup (125 mL) of finely chopped raw leek, the juice of half a lime, a half-cup (125 mL) of white vinegar, two tablespoons (30 mL) of extra-virgin olive oil, a half-cup (125 mL) of water, two tablespoons (30 mL) of parsley, a mashed clove of garlic, one teaspoon (5 mL) of sugar, and salt and pepper to taste. Serve on a bed of autumn corn salad, or cook them like finochio (see page 113).

Composed Savoy Salad

Prepared as a composed salad, this is a fresh, crisp accompaniment for Thanksgiving dinner.

	Leaves of variegated or red lettuce such as 'Speckles' or 'Red Sails'	
1	small savoy cabbage, shredded finely	1
4	small red apples, unpeeled, cored & sliced	4
4	small leeks, sliced thinly	4
½ cup	chopped parsley	125 mL
2 Tbsp.	slivered, toasted almonds	30 mL
6 Tbsp.	cider vinegar	90 mL
6 Tbsp.	extra-virgin olive oil	90 mL
2 Tbsp.	almond oil	30 mL
2 Tbsp.	finely chopped chervil	30 mL
1 tsp.	honey (optional) Salt & pepper to taste	5 mL

Toss the apple slices in acidulated water to keep them white. Drain and pat dry. Line a large bowl with the lettuce leaves, then compose the salad: cabbage on the bottom, drained apple slices overlapped around the outside, leek slices in the centre and a sprinkling of parsley and almonds over top. Whisk the remaining ingredients to an emulsion and pour over the salad. Toss at the table just before serving.

Potato
Solanum tuberosum

When the potato was introduced to Europe 400 years ago, it was cursed as evil. Scots wouldn't eat it because it was not mentioned in the Bible; Lord Byron accused the humble tuber of "unwholesome aphrodisiac effects"; and those who ate it lived in fear of contracting rickets, leprosy, consumption and, at the very least, warts. After all, its detractors pointed out, was it not a relative of the man-

Leek salad garnished with corn salad.

drake and the deadly nightshade? The potato's evil influence was insidious. "A diet which consists predominantly of potatoes," wrote Nietzsche, "leads to the use of liquor." Brillat-Savarin, the famous French gastronome and author of *The Physiology of Taste*, would have nothing to do with the tuber. "None for me," he said. "I appreciate the potato only as a protection against famine."

It was Frederick the Great who turned popular opinion around, launching a public relations campaign that included huge feasts where Prussian nobility was fed dishes devised by cooks from potatoes raised in the royal garden. Frederick dispatched soldiers to distribute seed potatoes among the peasants, adding as an incentive the promise that those who refused to grow and eat them would have their noses and ears cut off.

Typically, the French were more subtle. One enterprising gardener, claiming that potatoes saved his life in a German prison, convinced Louis XVI to allow him to grow the vegetable in a field protected by royal guards. The local villagers, believing the field contained something inordinately precious, raided the potatoes, and before long, *pommes de terre* were a staple of the French diet.

Spanish explorers took potatoes to Europe from South America, where they had been grown for 8,000 years. The vegetable wasn't introduced to North America, however, until the early 1700s, when Irish immigrants brought the tubers back across the Atlantic. The cultivation of potatoes rapidly increased

after waves of Irish fled the potato famine and emigrated to the United States and Canada. By 1900, North Americans were eating 200 pounds of potatoes per capita a year. But by 1950, that had changed. Potatoes were eschewed as fattening peasant food. Although consumption is again on the rise, thanks to fast-food outlets, potatoes are still among the first foods dropped from a dieter's menu.

Pity the poor spud: it has been unfairly maligned. Potatoes are rich in complex carbohydrates that lower fat levels in the blood. A single serving supplies a third of the recommended daily dose of vitamin C and significant levels of thiamin, niacin and riboflavin, as well as the essential trace minerals manganese, chromium, selenium and molybdenum. An average potato contains about 800 milligrams of potassium, more than a typical serving of any other common food. One study showed that men and women whose daily diet included as much potassium as is found in one medium-sized potato reduced their risk of a stroke by 40 percent. According to nutritionist Jean Carper, white potatoes, especially uncooked, have high concentrations of protease inhibitors, compounds that neutralize certain viruses and carcinogens. And the skins are rich in chlorogenic acid, which prevents cell mutations that may lead to cancer. However, potatoes raise blood-sugar levels quickly, so diabetics must be cautious.

The fat and sodium content of potatoes is near zero: a medium-sized potato contains only 100 calories compared with half a cup of cottage cheese, which contains 130. It is the mayonnaise in potato salads, not the potatoes, that is laden with calories and cholesterol. Dress potatoes differently, and you have a nutritious, delicious salad that deserves a place in every diet.

Potatoes have been around for so long that it is not surprising to find some 2,000 varieties worldwide: white, purple, red, yellow, smooth-skinned, rough-skinned, dimpled, fingers, balls and stout oblongs as big as bricks. The flesh may be flaky, floury, pasty or firm. But among these, only a few are perfect for salads. You will probably have to go to specialty potato-seed growers such as Becker's to find the varieties we recommend; they sell certified virus-free stock, which is more reliable than planting store-bought potatoes or simply reusing your own potatoes year after year. Order seed potatoes early, and store them in the cold cellar until planting.

The absolute supreme salad potato, bar none, is the European fingerling, also known as *jaune de Hollande*, ladyfinger and the banana potato. The narrow cucumber shape, 5 to 8 inches long and only ¾ to 1 ½ inches wide, ensures that the tuber cooks

Sun root salad: grated carrot, finely grated Jerusalem artichoke, dandelion greens, chives and horseradish.

uniformly. When sliced for salad, it produces small medallions of firm, yellow, buttery-smooth potato. The skins are a little papery but do not curl away from the flesh after cooking, so peeling is unnecessary. The flavour is very mild and slightly nutty. Fingerlings produce fairly large plants—ours stretch 4 feet tall—and mature later than many potato varieties, producing a heavy yield of virtually scab-free tubers. Sadly, this cultivar is not a good keeper.

One of the most unusual varieties is 'All-Blue,' an elongated tuber with a dark blue-black skin. It takes a little longer to cook than other potatoes, possibly because of its thick skin, and it should be peeled for salads. Inside, the flesh is slightly mealy and a light mauve-blue that is unique in the vegetable world. Unlike many vegetables bred for colour, blue potatoes have very good flavour. With potatoes, the genes that govern pigment also affect taste, so varieties with tinted flesh will almost certainly be tastier than snow-white types. Unfortunately,

'All-Blue' and 'Peruvian Blue' are not licensed for sale in Canada. Becker's, which once sold these varieties, has cleaned the tubers of viruses and hopes to be licensed to sell the novelty potatoes in the near future. In the meantime, your only hope is to cadge a few seed potatoes from a friend.

'Pink Pearl,' a gently ovoid potato with a deep pink skin, has the best flavour of any potato we've grown, and it stores quite well too. The texture is a little floury, so undercook it slightly for salad.

The best storage potato we've found is 'Bintje,' a Dutch potato developed in 1910 and now the most widely grown yellow-fleshed variety. Plants produce high yields of large, uniform tubers. The flesh remains fairly firm in cooking and is smooth and creamy, but it lacks a distinctive potato taste.

Store seed potatoes in the root cellar until mid-April or about a month before the last spring frost. Bring them into a light, room-temperature area, pinch off any sprouts, and spread them out to dry, turning cut pieces "eyes" up. Potatoes can be planted whole or cut in egg-sized pieces that contain at least two eyes. Fingerlings *must* be sown whole, and in general, we recommend the practice because uncut tubers are less susceptible to rot. Cut pieces, however, are more economical for large plantings. (To lessen the risk of bacterial and fungal attack, dust the cut pieces with powdered sulphur just before planting.) Leave the tubers exposed to indirect light for 10 to 14 days, spraying them with water now and again. The fingerling potatoes turn green and sprout short, stubby purple sprouts; all-blue potatoes become almost purple-brown.

While the potatoes are greening, prepare the garden bed. Potatoes like light, well-drained soil and plenty of sunshine. Don't bother planting them in the shade. To inhibit scab, soil should be acidic, with a pH of 5.6 to 6.5. Some gardeners dig a trench and bury their seed potatoes directly under rotting hay or organic matter. Humus does more than lower pH, however: it is one of the key factors in producing good potatoes. Potatoes are actually stem tubers, not roots, and they form from horizontal stems that grow out of the plant. Organic matter helps sandy soil hold water and lightens clay soil so that the stems can swell. It also aerates the soil, necessary for good potatoes since tubers require a generous supply of soilborne oxygen to form. High humus content reduces scab as well, which is also partially controlled through crop rotation. Potatoes should not follow tomatoes, eggplants, peppers or any of the other nightshades, because they share the same pests and diseases, but they profit when following such legumes as peas and beans.

A year's worth of potatoes uses up a lot of garden space for virtually the entire growing season, but even gardeners with tiny plots can enjoy freshly dug spuds by planting in a large container, such as a barrel or a garbage can, gradually adding soil through the season for a single tall hillful of potatoes. Or you can try one of the so-called first-early varieties that mature quickly for an early-summer harvest, freeing the soil for a second crop of lettuce or peas.

Potatoes are very susceptible to frost, yet they grow best in cool weather. Plant them early enough to catch the chilly spring days but late enough to avoid killing frosts. We plant them in early spring, two to four weeks before the last frost date. Dig 8-inch-deep trenches 1 ½ feet apart. Every foot or so, drop a seed potato into the trench, sprouts pointing upward, and cover with 4 inches of soil.

The first green shoots show about two weeks after planting; two weeks later, start hilling up the soil, the second secret to good potatoes. Hilling potato plants every two weeks through the growing season covers the stems, giving new tubers room to form. It also prevents the sun from turning the tubers green. Green tubers—and potato sprouts—contain solanine, a poisonous alkaloid that should never be eaten; it causes indigestion and sometimes serious gastrointestinal sickness.

Hilling up buries the tubers deeper in the soil where moisture levels are higher. Nevertheless, all potatoes, but especially the first-earlies, need copious watering. Water regularly, preferably by irrigation or by putting the hose at the base of the plant. If spraying is unavoidable, do it early in the day so that the leaves dry before nightfall. Wet foliage encourages fungal blight that wilts and discolours the leaves. If you subject your potatoes to a feast-and-famine watering regimen, they may develop "hollow heart." The potato is edible, but it has a gaping hole in the centre. Mulching helps hold in the moisture, but it may cause more problems than it solves for gardeners plagued with slugs or mice.

Colorado potato beetles are the biggest problem of the potato patch; most growers develop a deep loathing for this pest. The brown-and-white-striped beetles mate on the plants, and the females lay clusters of brilliant tangerine eggs under the uppermost leaves. The eggs hatch into bright orange, sausagelike larvae that nibble on the foliage. In small gardens, handpicking and stomping on the critters is a gruesome but satisfactory means of control. In larger gardens, powdered rotenone, dissolved in water and applied with a sprayer on a sunny day, effectively destroys the larvae.

Potatoes require from three to five months to mature. As soon as flowers appear on the plants, tuber formation begins in earnest and continues until the plants wilt or blacken with frost. In late July or early August, start poking in the earth for the first early potatoes. Scrape some soil from the mother plant and gently feel for egg-sized potatoes; don't harvest anything smaller. Replace the soil carefully.

The skin on these young potatoes is so thin, it rubs off under your thumb; when the skin is tough and no longer rubs away, it is a sign that the potatoes are mature and ready for harvest. On a dry, sunny day in late August or early September, when the foliage has withered, plunge a garden fork into the soil a foot away from the plant and jiggle the soil to loosen the potato nest. If you dig too close, you may spear some potatoes. Lift the tubers you can see, then feel around for stragglers. Spread the potatoes on top of the soil to dry for a couple of hours, turning them once. Each hill yields about a six-quart basket of potatoes. Before taking them to the house, rub off the loose soil and separate the damaged tubers for immediate use. Store the rest in a dark, dry, cool cupboard or cold cellar. We use cardboard boxes and cover them to exclude the light. Check stored potatoes once a month, and use up early sprouters first. Fingerlings sprout the fastest: by Christmas, there are already little roots emerging from the eyes. By breaking them off regularly, we prolong our enjoyment of fingerling salads until spring, although we make sure to conserve a few of the best as seed potatoes for the following season.

From a nutritional standpoint, the sooner you eat your harvested potatoes, the better. Vitamin C content deteriorates markedly with age—a six-month-old potato has only a third as much as a freshly dug tuber. And never store potatoes in the refrigerator. The cold encourages excessive starch conversion to sugar. To get the most food value out of your potatoes, eat them unpeeled, since most of the nutrients are in the flesh immediately under the skin. The same advice does not hold true for commercially grown potatoes. They are grown in soils heavily saturated with fungicides and insecticides, and most are sprayed with a sprout-inhibiting chemical that stays in the skin. All the more reason to find the space to grow your own.

Freshly dug potatoes are better for salads than stored tubers. They have more moisture and less starch and consequently absorb less cooking water and dressing. This also makes them less likely to break when being dressed and served.

Potatoes are always cooked for salads. Choose tubers of uniform size so that they cook consistently, and cook them whole, in their skins, so that the flesh does not become waterlogged. Scrub them well with a vegetable brush, then drop them into boiling water. Add a little cream of tartar or lemon juice to the water to keep them white: potatoes, like cauliflower and salsify, contain the pigment flavone, which turns brownish yellow when exposed to heat or the alkalis usually found in hard water. Cook the potatoes until barely tender—

underdone is preferable to mushy—drain and return briefly to low heat, shaking the pot lightly over the burner to dry them out.

If the skins are thin, leave them on: they contribute dietary fibre and most of the vitamins and minerals attributed to the potato. Older, stored potatoes will probably have to be peeled. As soon as the potato is cool enough to handle, hold it with a fork in one hand, and with the other, peel off the skin with a sharp knife. A fingerling slips out of its skin like a hand from a glove.

Chop or slice the potatoes, and dress while they are still warm, permitting the flavour of the sauce to permeate the vegetable. Toss the salad gently to avoid crumbling the pieces. Hands work better than utensils: separate the potato slices and dices delicately with your fingers so that each bit is coated with dressing.

Unless otherwise recommended, store the salad in the refrigerator for several hours until it is chilled and well marinated. Remove just before serving: potato salads made with eggs or mayonnaise should not sit out in warm weather for more than an hour or so because of the danger of salmonella. To mound a potato salad attractively, brush a round-bottomed bowl with a little safflower oil, press chervil and borage flowers onto the bottom and sides in a pattern, then press the potato salad into it. Invert the bowl onto a serving platter spread with lettuce or the leaves of ornamental cabbage.

Potato salad need not be fattening. Made with mayonnaise, a half-cup serving has 235 calories, but this can be reduced to 130 calories with a yogurt/sour cream dressing and to less than 100 calories if the dressing is made solely with yogurt. For a simple potato salad, toss the cooked vegetables with a yogurt vinaigrette (page 139), and add chopped parsley and shallots or scallions. Red Russian potato salad combines equal parts diced cooked potatoes and beets with a chopped onion and two tablespoons (30 mL) of capers, dressed with yogurt vinaigrette. For a salad milder in appearance and taste, toss sliced cucumbers and potatoes with Creamy Cucumber Dressing (page 94) and a tablespoon (15 mL) of dill. Layering salted cucumbers between the potatoes draws the juice from the cucumbers to moisten the potatoes and flavour them delicately. One of our favourite salads is fingerling slices tossed with pesto (page 53). For spur-of-the-moment dinners, make hot German potato salad, dicing freshly cooked potatoes and tossing while still warm with a warm cider vinaigrette (page 37). By far the most unusual cold potato dish is Blue Velvet Salad, which combines sliced blue potatoes, a sliced hard-cooked egg, chopped onion and cucumber with a dressing of one cup (250 mL) of yogurt, a tablespoon (15 mL) of lemon juice, a teaspoon (5 mL) each of garlic and Dijon mustard and parsley to taste.

Pearly Pink Potato Salad

This is a tangy, nippy dressing, not as heavy as that for a traditional creamy potato salad. The flavour of the red-wine vinegar soaks into the potatoes, so it is worthwhile using a top-quality vinegar. Even when pink potatoes are peeled, the flesh near the surface retains a pale rosy colour that is beautifully enhanced with red-wine vinegar.

4 cups	red-skinned potatoes, cooked, peeled & diced	1 L
2 Tbsp.	red-wine vinegar	30 mL
¼ cup	minced fresh parsley	50 mL
¼ cup	chopped green onions	50 mL
¼ cup	diced celery and/or diced sweet red pepper (optional)	50 mL
⅓ cup	low-fat mayonnaise	75 mL
⅓ cup	low-fat yogurt	75 mL
1 Tbsp.	Dijon mustard	15 mL
¼ tsp.	each salt, fresh-ground pepper & celery seed	1 mL
2 Tbsp.	capers	30 mL

Peel older potatoes, but leave the skins on new tubers. Place the cooked, diced potatoes in a salad bowl and sprinkle with vinegar, tossing to coat evenly. Add parsley and vegetables. In a small bowl, mix together remaining ingredients. Add to potatoes and mix gently but well. Taste and adjust seasonings. Garnish with parsley sprigs or celery leaves.

Serves 4 generously.

Radish
Raphanus sativus

A 65-pound radish? It sounds like material for a new round of jokes, but radishes as big as beach balls are not unusual in the Orient, the ancestral home of the radish and the place we must turn to for instruction in its delectable possibilities. In China and Japan, radish is more than garnish: it is a root to be taken seriously as a salad vegetable.

The radish has purportedly been under cultivation since Neolithic times—so long ago that its wild progenitor has disappeared from the scene altogether. The radish probably originated in the Far East, where it was first documented in 1100 B in an Egyptian inscription hono and radishes as the wonder foods that g workers strength to build the pyramids. Radishes were also held in high esteem in the Classical world: when vegetables were presented as sacrifices to the gods, turnips were offered on lead platters, beets on silver and radishes on gold. It was so much a part of the Roman diet that Cowper described a typical Roman meal as ''a radish and an egg.''

The radish is the fastest-maturing root vegetable in the garden and one of the most accommodating. Germination is very reliable, seeds sprout almost immediately, and edible roots are ready for harvest in three weeks. Because they are hardy, radishes can be planted both very early and very late. There are varieties that withstand the heat well too, although very high temperatures tend to make radishes hot. In the kitchen, the radish is equally versatile: it can be used as a piquant and colourful garnish in a green salad or go solo as a salad itself; it is among the first salad ingredients ready in the spring, yet with care, it can remain on the menu until winter.

Perhaps because they are so accommodating, radishes tend to be underrated and underused on this continent. Gardeners limit themselves to the traditional, ubiquitous 'Cherry Belle,' yet there are dozens of varieties, in shapes and sizes ranging from marbles to fist-sized cylinders to foot-long tapers and in colours from red to black. Choose your radish varieties first, however, according to season. In spring, we grow 'Easter Egg,' a widely available mix of mild purple, crunchy red and very hot white radishes that grow fast enough to complement our spring mescluns. 'Sparkler' (ST) is Turid's favourite, an inch-round radish, deep red on top and blushing white toward the base. Very fast-growing—only 30 days from seed to harvest—it has a tasty, bluish green leaf that looks like arugula.

For the summer season, we grow 'Minowase Spring Cross Hybrid' (DA), a white bolt-resistant radish with tapers 6 to 12 inches long, and the popular 'White Icicle,' a 5-inch-long, tapered, carrotlike radish with bright white skin and flesh. These large midseason roots were developed to withstand the heat. Typical ball radishes become too hot in the summer, but if you like the round shape and quick harvest, we suggest growing summer turnips (*Brassica rapa*, Rapifera Group), equally small, round and white, with a similar crunchy texture but very long-lasting mild taste. 'Presto Pickle' (DO, BL) is a little, fast-growing white turnip that is ready in 30 days. It grows well even in hot weather, never becoming radish-hot. Cultivated like a radish, it sits with its shoulders out of the ground like other turnips. Or try the pretty 'Purple Top White Globe' (DO), a heat-resistant, 3-to-4-inch white globe with lilac shoulders.

In Europe and North America, the little red spring radish holds sway, but in the Far East, winter radishes are more common. Slow-growing, monstrous roots, often black-skinned and sometimes rosy-fleshed, winter radishes are sown in late summer and need two or more months to mature. 'Long Black Spanish' (BL) grows to a 10-inch taper, with a black outer skin and crisp white flesh. 'Round Black Spanish' is a widely available heirloom radish, a 3-to-4-inch globe, with a similar rough, callused skin that resembles an overripe avocado. Several Chinese and Japanese (daikon) radish varieties are now available here. 'Green Skin, Red Flesh' (HU) is a 5-inch-long, 4-inch-thick root with green shoulders, white tip and purplish red flesh. It keeps well, the sweetness improving with storage. 'Miyashige' (JO) is a Japanese cultivar that stretches to more than a foot long and only 2 inches wide, while 'Mikado' (OS) grows up to 3 feet long. 'China White' (OS) is among the mildest, only 8 inches long but crisp, juicy and not too pungent. Finally, there are all-season Oriental radishes that can be grown from spring to fall. The 'All-Seasons Tokanashi' (BL) grows tender, mildly pungent white roots about a foot long.

Black-skinned winter radishes are very high in calcium, but otherwise, radishes are relatively low in nutrition. They contain some vitamin B, potassium, iron and sulphur, which accounts for the sharp peppery taste and for the fact that the root is not easy to digest and should be chewed thoroughly. But there are only 20 calories per cup.

Radishes prefer well-fertilized, well-drained soil free from obstacles. For the long daikon types, dig the soil very deeply, and add lots of compost to lighten the earth. Don't use fresh manure. Like brassicas, radishes prefer soil with a pH of about 5.5 to 7.

Because wireworms can be a problem, radishes should always be rotated. Don't grow them where other crucifers (cabbage, mustard) grew last year or even where the mesclun mix was a month before if it contained arugula, radishes or Japanese greens. Spring radishes like full sun, but radishes grown in the heat of the summer, especially the winter varieties, need a little shade. Sow these between taller vegetables.

Radishes are often sown with carrots to mark the rows of the slower-germinating seed, but in our experience, radishes are wasted this way. Instead, sow alternate rows of radishes and carrots so that the faster-growing radish plants shade the tiny car-

Winter-sprouting witloof, the leafy portion of Cichorium intybus.

rot seedlings. Radishes also act as natural cultivators. Mix radish seed with the mesclun greens: they will be among the first to sprout, the leaves are edible, and when you pull the little radishes out, they leave cavities behind that aerate the soil. Because they take up so little space, you can plant a few seeds every week, here and there about the garden, for a constant supply.

Radishes are truly a cool-weather crop, best sown in spring in weekly succession for early

harvests of summer radishes and again at the end of June for an autumn harvest of winter radishes. To sow a row of radishes, make a little trench a half-inch deep, water it well and drop in three seeds per inch. They sprout within a week. Thin them according to size—1 inch for 'Sparklers,' 6 inches for 'Round Black Spanish.'

Mild radishes are the result of steady, quick growth in cool weather. Any checks to their development—drought, heat, poor soil—produce peppery, tough, split roots; in hot weather, they bolt quickly. Water regularly, and keep the bed weeded and well hoed. Midway through the growing season, give winter radishes some liquid fertilizer, or dig in organic matter: they are heavy feeders. Radishes have the same problem with flea beetles that all brassicas have in early spring—use rotenone, diatomaceous earth or a floating row cover.

Harvest the spring and summer radishes as soon as they are plump and touching shoulders. Don't wait too long: an old radish will likely be hollow, certainly woody and definitely hot. For slicing, pull the daikons when they are 6 inches long. You can let them grow longer for grating or for winter storage. They are quite hardy, so you can leave them in the ground almost until Christmas, covered with some mulch to keep the ground from freezing. Lift them before the final hard freeze-up, and store just like carrots, in sand or peat to retain moisture. When harvesting spring and summer radishes, leave a few in the ground to flower; the blooms are decorative as well as edible, and we like the spicy green seedpods in salads.

In the kitchen, cut off the radish tops to within half an inch of the root. Refrigerate the roots this way for up to a week, two weeks for daikon. To prepare radishes, rinse well and cut off the roots and the tops. Leave spring and summer radishes whole, or slice, quarter or carve them into "roses." Daikons should be peeled, then sliced or shredded. In Oaxaca, Mexicans celebrate the Night of the Radishes on December 23 by carving giant radishes into three-dimensional sculptures of fantastic animals and people.

The simplest and one of the most elegant ways to serve radishes is to lay washed, untopped spring radishes on a plate with a little dish of coarse salt for dipping. Radishes and daikons can be sliced into green salads or shredded into coleslaws, adding a pleasant piquancy. They are also good diced and dressed with cucumber and carrot, adding a peppery taste and a welcome crunch. For a low-fat Chinese radish salad, slice radishes very thinly, add a finely slivered green pepper, and dress with two tablespoons (30 mL) of rice-wine vinegar, four teaspoons (20 mL) of low-sodium soy sauce and a tablespoon (15 mL) of sugar. For a creamy radish salad, grate a large radish in medium strips and toss with a quarter-cup (50 mL) of thinly sliced hazelnuts, four tablespoons (60 mL) of sour cream or yogurt, three tablespoons (45 mL) of walnut oil and a teaspoon (5 mL) of white-wine vinegar.

In German beer halls, radishes are as much a staple as accordions; in fact, they are cut into a simi-

lar form. It takes some practice but is worth a try. You need a long icicle radish like 'Munich Bier' (CG) or daikon, about 10 inches long and 3 inches wide. Do not peel. Cut the root along its length, not quite through to the bottom, in straight vertical slices a quarter-inch thick. Then turn the radish over and cut it on the diagonal, almost but not quite meeting the first cuts. The whole thing can be pulled out like an accordion and salt sprinkled in the folds. Put it back together and serve on a plate. Guests break off slices of radish to eat with pretzels and beer, a long-standing Oktoberfest tradition.

Namasu

This two-tone orange and white salad should be made in the morning for an evening dinner, but it also keeps for up to a week in an airtight container in the refrigerator, making it good for a party. Japanese cooking is too sweet for many tastes, but the sugar can easily be halved.

½ lb.	daikons, peeled & julienned	250 g
2	carrots, julienned	2
1 tsp.	salt	5 mL
⅓ cup	rice vinegar	75 mL
1 tsp.	soy sauce	5 mL
½ inch	piece of gingerroot, peeled & grated	1.25 cm
1 Tbsp.	sugar	15 mL

Cut both the daikons and carrots into matchsticks about 1 ½ inches (4 cm) long. Put them in a large mixing bowl and sprinkle with the salt. Leave for 30 minutes, then gently squeeze out as much water as possible. Whisk together the vinegar, soy sauce, ginger and sugar. Pour over the vegetables, mix well, then cover and refrigerate for at least 8 hours.

Witloof
Cichorium intybus

Witloof is the Houdini of vegetables. A member of the same family as chicory and radicchio, it grows vigorously all summer, but only after the roots are dug up and buried in a dark box do the small blanched shoots emerge, magically, in midwinter as chicons, a delectable salad vegetable.

Sometimes called root chicory, forcing chicory and Belgian or French endive, witloof is extraordinarily expensive to buy, and the quality is generally appalling, since what is offered in Canada is often flown here from Europe. Forcing chicons

at home is time-consuming, but the flavour of this delicacy is well worth the effort. One of the most common varieties is 'Toner' (JO). Like most witloof, it must be forced in soil, sand or peat, although cultivars have been developed, such as 'Witloof Zoom (F1)' (CG), for forcing without soil. There is also a cultivar, 'Witloof Robin' (CG), that produces pale pink chicons.

To start witloof, sow seeds directly in the garden in early June, planting five per inch in a moist trench and covering lightly with potting soil. The bed should be deeply dug, with well-drained soil so that the roots develop well. The seeds sprout within a week. Gradually thin to 6 inches apart. With mulch and a deep soaking now and then, the seedlings develop steadily into lush green plants. Treat them generally like the chicories (see page 81), but don't harvest any of the leaves: they are feeding the root. Remove flowering shoots if they form, and fertilize monthly with manure tea.

By mid-October, cut the leaves down to 2-inch stubs, and dig out the roots carefully with a garden fork. They should be 8 inches long and an inch wide at the top. Immediately lay the roots, not touching, in a planting tray filled with damp sand or peat; cover with peat, and put them in a cool place in the cellar.

After a month of dormancy, the roots can be forced to produce chicons. Set a few roots upright, 2 inches apart, in a deep, 12-inch flowerpot filled with soil. Cover with 4 inches of earth, water lightly, and upend a second pot over the first, giving the sprouts total darkness and room to grow. Move the pot into an area that is a little cooler than room temperature. In one month, the chicons are 3-to-5-inch buttery-yellow cones with a soft, lustrous sheen. Cut them off at soil level. Sometimes if you put the pot back, the roots resprout for a second harvest of a few leaves. After harvesting the chicons, keep the roots and replant them in the garden in the spring: they produce a lofty decorative hedge studded with edible blue daisies, exactly like the roadside chicory. The greens, unfortunately, are unpalatably bitter.

Store chicons in an opaque plastic bag in the refrigerator—exposure to light is what makes purchased witloof so bitter. To prepare, wash well, remove tough outer leaves and either quarter lengthwise or slice crosswise into thin rounds.

The rich bitter flavour of witloof chicory is excellent with citrus and capers or tossed with apples, walnuts and a walnut oil/lemon juice vinaigrette in a French version of the Waldorf. Or serve with the cress sauce on page 43.

Salad Seasonings

Chives to Vinaigrette

Chapter Seven

The frilly lettuce was picked less than an hour ago. Tucked among its curling May-green leaves are finely sliced 'Presto Pickles,' newborn zucchini no bigger than your thumb and burnt-orange ribbons of squash blossoms. This salad cannot be bought: it must be grown.

But a pile of vegetables in a bowl is not a salad. Technically, salad means salted. To turn this garden produce into a dish worthy of the name requires a dressing. The sauce has to be expertly blended from an appropriate choice of oils and vinegars, then subtly spiced with the herbs described in Chapter Three, with condiments such as horseradish and mustard and with spicy alliums—chives, garlic and onions. Decorated with edible flowers and served on garnish leaves, the salad is finally dressed and worthy of its name.

SPICY ALLIUMS

According to Turkish legend, when Satan was cast out of heaven, garlic sprouted where he first placed his left foot and onion sprang up under his right. Their sulphurous smell may mark them as the progeny of the devil, but spicy alliums lift salads into paradise. Without garlic, scallions, shallots and chives, salads would be quite mundane.

Turid has devoted yards of soil to growing alliums in an attempt to find varieties mild and tasty enough to be eaten raw in salads. And we have sorely tried our tongues in tasting them: one marathon afternoon left our palates raw, our stomachs queasy and our companions distant. We can report for certain: None of the onions grown in the north deserve such optimistic appellations as 'Sweet Sandwich' and 'Sweet Giant'; 'Wolverine' and 'Lucifer' are more aptly named.

Despite their bite, spicy alliums are indispensable. They are healthful, low in calories and high in potassium and phosphorus. They stimulate the tongue. Like hot peppers, onions contain an astringent oil that irritates the membranes lining the palate, prodding the taste buds into a state of alert. Given the biology of the spicy alliums, no salad gar-

den should be without them. Well chosen, they can even be, as Robert Louis Stevenson put it, "the poetic soul of a capacious salad bowl."

Spicy alliums fall into roughly seven categories. The bulb onions (*Allium cepa*) are arranged in three groups, created by botanists to gather together similar cultivars of one species. The Cepa Group is the familiar globe onion. Harvested young as a thumb-sized white bulb topped with thick, grassy shoots, it is called a green onion, or scallion, and cultivars are now available specifically for this early harvest. Multiplier onions are in the Aggregatum Group. They are also a variety of globe onion, but instead of one bulb, several develop, each one in turn producing several more when planted. Also in the Aggregatum Group are shallots, which grow like garlic and taste like mild, sweet onions. Egyptian, or tree, onions are perennials of the Proliferum Group; they produce their bulbs at the top of the shoots rather than underground. Welsh, or bunching, onions are a different species, *A. fistulosum*, and produce a perennial harvest of scallions. Chives (*A. schoenoprasum*) are the mildest, grassiest and most faithful of the spicy alliums, and garlic chives (*A. tuberosum*) may well be the most delicious. True garlic (*A. sativum*) is probably the most redolent of the family and the most indispensable in dressing a salad. Finally, there is the leek (*A. ampeloprasum*, Porrum Group), the only member of this family that makes a good salad on its own, which is why we included it in Chapter Five.

Chives
Allium schoenoprasum

The little spears of chives are among the first plants to poke through the soil in the spring. By the first week of April, our salads are already strewn with their grassy inch-long shoots. As the weather warms, the pink and lavender flowers not only attract butterflies to the garden but also festoon our mescluns. From April to September, we snip fresh chives, and in winter, a windowsill pot produces trimmings for salads, the flavour of the garnish supplemented by chive vinegar, pink-ened and mildly spiced by midsummer blooms.

Chives are ridiculously easy to grow, undemanding and totally pest-free. They grow from seed, but the plants are so ubiquitous that you probably know a gardener willing to share some. In autumn or spring, lift the mother clump with a garden fork, and carefully separate a group of the spindly bulbs to transplant into your prepared herb bed. If you cannot find a friend willing to share, buy a plant

at a nursery or start seeds indoors in pots very early in the spring, growing them like onions.

Transplanted to the garden, chives grow in virtually any site from full sun to dappled shade. Set the clumps of chives about 8 inches apart in a border, or disperse them through the herb bed. In early summer, after the chives flower, cut the plants back to stimulate a second harvest of fresh shoots. They do not need to be fertilized. The second-growth chives last until late in the autumn and overwinter without protection. Every second autumn, lift the plant out of the bed, improve the soil, then replant a small clump. Give the rest away, or plant new patches in the herb bed or in flower borders.

Turid grows two varieties of chives, one tall and one short (both given to her by friends, so their names remain a mystery). The compact plant grows only 6 inches tall but produces the most succulent chives; the tall one, which grows to a foot or so, produces the loveliest blooms. When begging or buying a plant, consider your own preferences in height, leaf and flower.

Snip a few sprigs of chives for every salad, swishing them under water before adding to the salad or chopping finely for dressings. Chives are particularly good in yogurt dressings combined with dill or chervil and parsley; allow the dressing to sit for an hour or two while the flavours assimilate. Chives can also be sprinkled on a dish at the last minute as a robust, dark green garnish.

Chives are one of the four essential ingredients of *fines herbes*. Make a fresh supply for summer dressings, but in winter, don't resort to dried chives. They lose their flavour quickly. Instead, chop chives finely and freeze. A small bag will last you through the chiveless months. You can also preserve the flavour by filling a jar with blossoms and topping with warm white-wine vinegar. Steep until the vinegar is sufficiently flavoured, strain into a bottle, and add a single chive blossom for identification.

Garlic Chives
Allium tuberosum

This distinctive allium is sometimes listed in seed catalogues as Oriental garlic chives, because it is popular in Chinese stir-fries. It grows much like traditional chives—easily, in clumps of succulent spears with umbel flowers—but its leaves are ribbon-flat and arch like narcissus, its flowers are large and white, and its flavour is distinctly garlicky. For those who find bulb garlic too strong or indigestible, garlic chives are the answer.

Garlic chives sprout very early in spring, growing

to about 18 inches. Position them in the middle of a bed—in front of nasturtiums, perhaps, which bloom at the same time. The flower buds, like the leaves, taste sweet and garlicky and are lovely chopped in a salad; the flowers are even more pungent than the buds. New varieties are available that bloom mauve and yellow.

Propagate garlic chives exactly as you do chives, by seed or root division. It prefers full sun and quickly goes to seed. We find the dried seed heads so beautiful that we leave them standing as everlastings in the winter snow.

Garlic
Allium sativum

An essential ingredient in the cuisine of southern Italy and southern France, garlic is best known for its effect on the breath. It has ever been thus. One historian reports that "the Moslems who encountered the first Crusaders were more terrified by their strong smell of garlic than by their armour." Some place garlic's origins on the Mediterranean coast, but in fact, it is found all over the world; a wild variety in the Americas, *Allium canadense*, was a favourite vegetable of pre-Columbian Indians.

"Eat leeks in March and wild garlic in May, and all the year after, physicians may play," goes an old Welsh rhyme. Not only does garlic have an impressive reputation in folk medicine, but mainstream doctors are now admitting that the odoriferous bulb may have genuine therapeutic benefits. Physicians from Hippocrates to Albert Schweitzer have prescribed garlic, and even as recently as World War II, garlic poultices were used successfully to stave off gangrene in battle wounds.

In 1944, garlic's smelly compound, allicin, was identified as an antibiotic: raw garlic, it seems, is more powerful than penicillin or tetracycline and fights some 72 infectious agents. Allicin is formed when garlic is crushed: if it doesn't smell, it won't work. In 1987, medical researchers confirmed that raw garlic boosts the immune system, the first line of defence against infectious disease. The bulb also does wonders for the heart, lowering blood cholesterol, thinning the blood and preventing embolisms. Unfortunately, garlic triggers allergic reactions in some people, but for those who can tolerate the allium, its health benefits are impressive, despite relatively low concentrations of vitamins and minerals. Garlic has such a well-established medical reputation that it is available in pill form, but you can reap its benefits and its wonderful flavour by eating it daily, raw, in salads.

Aside from regular garlic, there is Italian garlic (*Allium sativum ophioscordon*), which produces midsized underground bulbs and aboveground bulbils borne on stems that loop into beautiful dynamic interlacing. There is also elephant garlic (*A. scorodoprasum*), Turid's favourite, which comprises cloves as big as a conventional bulb. Cloves are easier to peel and have a flavour so sweet and mild that they can be sliced raw into salads. Some gardeners are not so enthusiastic, finding an unpleasant underbite in the flavour and limited success in the growing. This may be due to climate, so experiment with both before giving up. Plant cloves obtained from gardening friends or seed houses, not from the grocery store: the imported garlic may not be appropriate for your growing conditions.

If your season is long enough, you can plant garlic cloves early in the spring; elephant garlic requires 90 to 100 days to mature, common garlic slightly less. But it is easier to start the bulbs in the fall. Prepare a bed of well-drained soil rich in organic matter. Garlic likes full sun. By mid-November or before the ground freezes, sink individual cloves, point up, into the soil, 2 inches deep and 3 to 4 inches apart for regular garlic, 3 inches deep and 12 inches apart for the elephant type.

Mulch the bed with at least a foot of hay, straw or leaves. In mid-April, remove the mulch completely; little sprouts that look like blanched narcissus leaves will already be poking up. Some people eat the garlic shoots, but if you grow garlic chives, leave the shoots to feed the bulb. When the plants are established, pull the mulch back around them. Through the spring and summer, give them lots of moisture, and once they are a foot high, cultivate them well to eliminate competition from weeds. Once a month, side-dress with manure or compost. If flower buds develop, cut them off so that all the energy goes into the bulb.

At the end of July, when the garlic leaves turn yellow, don't bend them over like onions, but allow them to ripen, harvesting a few bulbs as needed for fresh salads. In late August, when the foliage is golden but not rotted, lift the bulbs out with a garden fork. (Don't leave them in the ground through the wet, cool fall, or they will split their husks and sometimes rot.) Spread the garlic bulbs out to dry, then braid them and hang them in a cool, dry, dark, well-ventilated place for the winter. This is the only effective way to store garlic, because the bulbs, like onions, continue to produce sulphur compounds even after storage, and unless neighbouring bulbs can breathe, they will rot in the garlicky respiration. Toward the end of winter, peel the remaining softening cloves and preserve in oil or vinegar, using both the cloves and the preserving liquid in salads.

Use garlic raw or cooked. Whole raw cloves are relatively mild; minced or chopped are stronger; mashed or pressed are the strongest. The more the flesh is bruised, the more allicin is produced. To peel a garlic clove, cut off the root end, crush it with the side of a heavy knife, then slip the skin away. Mince or squeeze through a garlic press.

Cooking turns garlic sweet and mellow, and roasting the cloves whole produces a soft, spreadable "butter" that is delicious served with toasted French bread and green salad. One of my favourite dressings (page 21) for spring greens uses a whole bulb, yet it is as mild as freshly picked violets.

Aioli Escoffier

The "butter of Provence," garlic mayonnaise makes a wonderful dip for midsummer vegetables. Although aioli can be made by hand, using a food processor is infinitely easier. The secret to preventing aioli from separating is to have all the ingredients and equipment at room temperature.

1 oz.	garlic cloves (about 5 medium)	30 g
1	large egg yolk, room temperature	1
¼ tsp.	salt	1 mL
1 cup	extra-virgin olive oil	250 mL
½ cup	olive oil	125 mL
1 Tbsp.	boiling water	15 mL
2-3 Tbsp.	lemon juice	30-45 mL

Chop the garlic cloves as finely as possible. Stir in the egg yolk and salt; trickle in the oil in a thread, blending continuously until the mixture thickens, then slowly whisk in the remaining oil, three tablespoons (45 mL) at a time, until smooth. Whisk in the hot water and lemon juice to prevent the aioli from separating.

If it does separate, start again with another egg yolk and a bit of lemon, then in a thin stream, as above, pour the failed aioli into the egg mixture. Refrigerate, tightly covered, until ready to use.

Makes 2 cups.

Onion
Allium cepa

My great-uncle Jim ate an onion a day, not marinated in a salad or braised in a stew but raw, like an apple. There must have been a genetic leap, because I cannot conceive of doing such a thing myself. On the afternoon that Turid and I undertook to sample the onion crop in all its pungent glory, I pushed myself away from the table long before she did. My mouth—and my digestion—have not managed to recover yet.

Within the family of bulb, or globe, onions, there are many individual types: cooking onions, storing onions, Spanish onions, yellow, white and red onions. Many, claim the seed catalogues, are bred specifically for mildness and bear such names as 'Sweet Sandwich,' 'Sweet Giant' and 'Sweet Winter.' Yet although we sampled the cultivars that sounded most promising, none of the globe onions we tested were what we would call sweet. The problem, we discovered, was day length. In its early stages, a globe onion puts its energy into roots and leaves. When days reach a certain length, the plant switches and puts its resources into the bulb. For each variety, bulb development is triggered by a different day length: there are long-day (15 hours of sun), short-day (12 hours) and intermediate onions. In the north, short-day onions never develop a big bulb or a mild taste. Canadian gardeners must buy the long-day variety to get large, sweet onions. Many seed catalogues do not indicate day length; Dominion, Blüm and Nichols are among the exceptions. We found 'Southport White Globe' (ST) and the widely available 'Carmen' the tastiest and the best for storing.

Scallion is a fancy name for green onions. Because onions are slow to develop, plant more than you need, and when the bulbs are about the size of your thumb, pull them up. These are milder than mature onions, and the flesh is very tender, which is why scallions have become such a staple of the salad bowl—so much so that cultivars have appeared which should be harvested only as scallions and not allowed to develop into true bulb onions. There are both white and red types, with no discernible difference in taste. The red colour is skin-deep and develops only in cold weather, a visual novelty at best. We recommend an all-season scallion such as 'Evergreen Long White' (BL) for summer salads until the fall crop of globe onions is ready.

Multiplier onions (*Allium cepa*, Aggregatum Group) are perennial globe onions that form clusters of three or four bulbs instead of a single growing centre. A large onion is planted the first year, producing a harvest of many small onions. These are replanted the second year, each growing to a large bulb, which divides in the third year into small onions. By planting both large and small multipliers each year, you can harvest large onions for the kitchen and small seed onions for the garden every fall, perpetuating the crop ad infinitum.

Shallots (*Allium cepa*, Aggregatum Group) are also multipliers, but they are not perennials. These are gourmet onions, the mildest and most delectable, with a flavour midway between garlic and onion. They are certainly the most expensive in the grocery store but well worth growing. French shallots have a pinkish cast and lean toward garlic in flavour; Dutch shallots taste more like onion. Shallots are compound, separated into cloves like garlic, and they are grown the same way. Buy sets and plant in the fall or in the spring as soon as the ground can be worked. Mulch and care for them exactly as you would garlic. By the time they are ready to harvest, the bunch of 6 to 10 shallots will practically sit on top of the soil, fanning out like an exploded garlic.

Egyptian onions (*Allium cepa*, Proliferum Group) are the most unusual of the globe onions, forming clusters of onion sets on long stalks 2 to 3 feet tall. The mild-flavoured little airborne onion sends up another sprout topped with flowers—a plant as exotic as it is tasty. Both the onions and the lush, hollow leaves and stems are delicious in salads. This is a truly perennial onion: you never have to replant it. When the clump gets out of hand, dig it up, replenish the soil, divide the mother plant, and replant a small piece, giving the extras away. The airborne seeds often propagate, falling to the ground, where they root and start new plants. Turid's clump of Egyptian onions is more than a dozen years old. The plant is virtually care-free: she doesn't fertilize it or water it but only harvests and keeps it from wandering into the tulip bed. You will have to acquire bulbs from a nursery or a friend, since this onion does not grow well from seed. "It is a nice perennial in the garden," Turid suggests, "but don't count on it to provide a lot of onion flavour for salads." The small onions have a sharp tang and are excellent for pickling.

Welsh, or bunching, onions (*Allium fistulosum*) are perennial scallions. They are not from Wales but moved west from Siberia. When they arrived in Germany, they were dubbed the *welsch*, or foreign, onion. Sown from seed in the spring, they should be left in the ground for the first season and not harvested until the second year, when there will be a clump of green onions where each seed was planted. Harvest all but a few from each clump. Mulch the clumps heavily to overwinter. The following spring, the clump replenishes itself, producing up to 20 scallions and sending up an impres-

sive 20-inch flower stalk at the end of June or early July. Break off the flower stalks to direct energy to the scallions. Harvest all but a few, let these overwinter, and the next year, they will provide a new supply. If you want to save seed, let a couple of the flower stalks bloom.

Most onions, with the exception of shallots and multipliers, are grown from seed, which requires a very early start. Two to three months before the last frost, around the end of February, start the seeds in the same long divided trays used to start lettuce. Soak the seeds overnight in lukewarm water, then sow them about two per inch, a quarter-inch deep. If they are exposed to light and kept at 70 degrees F, germination is close to 100 percent. When the seedlings sprout, set the trays in a cool, sunny location. As the onions grow, trim the tops regularly to a couple of inches in height. Controlled tests have not confirmed that this forces the energy to go into the root rather than the leaves, but it seems to make the seedlings sturdier at the base and easier to handle at transplanting time. Around mid-April, when the first hyacinths and daffodils bloom, harden off the onions in the cold frame, then transplant shortly before the last frost.

Plant the onion seedlings in a well-dug, weed-free garden bed in full sun. The soil, enriched with well-aged compost, should have a pH of 6.5 to 7.5. Dig individual holes or, better yet, a trench about 3 inches deep. With a long knife, remove a row of seedlings from the tray, and carefully pull them apart. If the roots seem potbound, trim them back by a third, and prune a third off the leaves too. Spread the roots, and plant the onion seedlings in the trench, 3 to 6 inches apart. It doesn't matter if they rub shoulders at maturity. Fill in the trench to just below garden level, creating a little depression to hold the moisture. During the growing season, water the onions often, and side-dress with fertilizer when the leaves are about 4 to 6 inches long. For large bulbs, keep the bed uniformly watered and free of weeds.

Up to this point, all onions are grown the same way. As they mature, however, scallions and bunching onions should be hilled to produce white stems, whereas the soil should be brushed away from the top half of globe onions so that they sit on top of the bed, the flesh exposed to the sun to form a dry skin. If an onion sends up a flower stalk, pull up the plant: it has gone into its reproductive mode, which means the weather has been too dry or the temperature has dipped to between 50 and 60 degrees F, a sensitive zone that makes this biennial skip the dormancy phase and plunge into

flowering. If autumn is cool, lift the onions and cure them, even if they haven't quite finished growing.

Onion seed can also be sown directly outdoors. In most of Canada, the season is not long enough to produce a bulb, because globe onions need 85 to 100 days to mature after transplanting. Scallions, however, can be successfully sown direct. We add leftover onion seed to mesclun mixes for a spicy touch. After the mesclun is finished, we pull out all the leafy greens and let the onions continue growing.

By the first week of August, onions are at their prime. Bend the stems over to halt growth and divert the plants' energy from the leaves to the bulbs. When the skin becomes papery, pull up the onions and drape them on the garden bed for a day or so to cure. If they are left any longer, the tops begin to rot. Rub off the soil, and spread them in a dry, sunny place for a week or so before braiding them. The Italians braid onions, garlic and red chiles together, a thoroughly practical idea. Hang the braids in a cool, dry, well-ventilated place. They prefer temperatures of between 32 and 50 degrees F and are most likely to sprout between 50 and 60 degrees—they will last longer at room temperature than in this lukewarm middle range. Eat the softest bulbs and those with wide necks first.

Cure shallots the same way, then hang in a net or a wire basket in a dry, dark, cool place. Shallots are very susceptible to mould and, at room temperature, have a shelf life of only about three weeks. If you want to keep them longer once they are brought into the kitchen from the storage room, wrap them loosely in a dry paper towel and store in the refrigerator.

Throughout the growing season, scallions can be harvested as needed. Wipe them well, and store in plastic bags with a moistened paper towel.

Stored onions may rot, but they rarely have problems with bacteria or fungi as a result of bruising. This is because when onion cells are damaged, they release an enzyme which converts the sulphur compounds in healthy cells to a natural antibiotic that fights germs while the plant recovers from the bruise. The same thing happens when an onion is cut. The antibiotic is called a lacrymatory compound—aptly named, since it produces the tears that stream down your face as you prepare onions; it also produces the characteristic sharp taste. Stronger-flavoured onions, which contain more of this lacrymatory compound, store better than mild-flavoured onions. This is not good news for salad lovers. However, cooking destroys some of the compound, and as the Mexicans have discovered, so does marinating the onions in an acid such as lemon or lime juice, which dissolves the pungency without softening the crisp, white flesh.

The sulphurous nature of onions is also the source of its many health benefits. Like garlic, onions have come highly recommended by doctors since the time of Hippocrates. Onions can be eaten in larger quantities, however, and have some health benefits entirely their own. All in all, those who eat onions seem to have healthier cardiovascular systems. Only half a raw onion a day is said to boost good HDL blood cholesterol by an average of 30 percent. Cooked onions act as an anticoagulant in the blood. Onions have been prescribed since ancient times for diabetes, and researchers have isolated the compound that lowers blood sugar. Like garlic, onion is a natural antibiotic, killing a long list of disease-causing bacteria, including *E. coli* and salmonella. It also works as an expectorant, releasing something akin to tears in the throat and lungs, thereby breaking up mucous congestion.

SPICING UP THE SALAD

Horseradish
Armoracia rusticana

Once called the rustic radish (*Raphanus rusticus*), horseradish is respected as a piquant condiment to add zip to meats and salad dressings, but its nutritional and health benefits are less well known. The gnarly root is a good source of calcium, potassium, iron and vitamin C, so much so that it was used to forestall scurvy. But it is also effective in treating pulmonary infections. Irwin Ziment, a professor of medicine at the University of California and the author of *Respiratory Pharmacology and Therapeutics*, recommends the folk remedy of a teaspoon of grated horseradish in a glass of warm, honeyed water to relieve sore throats and colds. Science substantiates this claim; like mustard, garlic and chiles, horseradish is an expectorant. Just as the nippy root makes your eyes water, so it turns on bronchial glands, causing them to secrete fluid that thins mucus and moves it out of the lungs.

A hardy perennial, horseradish belongs to the mustard family and likely originated in Germany, where it is still enjoyed today. Admirably tough and vigorously invasive, the plant has leaves as big as machetes, glossy, oval and sharply serrated along the edges. It is the only cultivated vegetable I know of that can stand up to twitch grass and win—it dotted Turid's overgrown northern Ontario pasture. Horseradish is so aggressive that many gardeners rely on these wild volunteers for sauce, but they

Beautiful in the garden, Egyptian onions are the most unusual of the globe onions.

are tough and stringy compared with the sweetly pungent roots and spring sprouts you can harvest from horseradish grown with a little tender care.

Allot horseradish its own private corner. Given half a chance, it happily takes over the garden. The root develops best in well-drained, deeply manured soil in a sunny location. To start a horseradish bed, use roots from a grocery store or a friend; it does not grow from seed. For each plant, you need a piece 6 to 8 inches long and a half-inch

wide in the middle. Cut the top off square, and trim the tip at a slant. (Two plants will be more than enough for a family of four.)

As soon as the ground can be worked in the spring, dig individual holes about 18 inches in diameter and fill with old manure. Water well, and press the root about 4 inches below the surface, the slanted tip pointing down. From a late-March planting, a little crown of leaves emerges in May. When the leaves are 3 to 4 inches tall, scrape away the soil

Potato salad dressed with a mustard-seed vinaigrette.

about a half-cup (125 mL) for two cups (500 mL) of grated root. Then stir in fresh cream to produce a sauce. (Some commercial sauces contain a little soybean oil as an emulsifier.) Seal immediately in small jars, and store them in the refrigerator or freezer. The horseradish sauce will keep its pungency for three or four months, but if you plan to keep it this long, omit the cream, adding it just before using. Add horseradish sauce to mayonnaise, sour cream or yogurt dips, or mix with regular mustard to give vinaigrettes more bite. For a delicious oil-free dressing that is especially tasty on cooked julienned beets, blend a quarter-cup (50 mL) of cider vinegar with two tablespoons (30 mL) of horseradish sauce, a quarter-teaspoon (1 mL) of caraway and sugar to taste. In recipes, use four teaspoons (20 mL) of prepared horseradish for each tablespoon (15 mL) of freshly grated.

Creamy Horseradish Dressing

Horseradish easily overwhelms delicate vegetables like peas or lettuce, but beans and okra measure up to the challenge. Use this dressing to give a bit of a kick to relatively bland salad roots like potatoes or Jerusalem artichokes.

¼ cup	horseradish sauce, drained OR	50 mL
2-3 Tbsp.	horseradish, freshly grated	30-45 mL
½ cup	low-fat yogurt or mayonnaise	125 mL
1 tsp.	lemon juice	5 mL
1 Tbsp.	chopped lemon thyme	15 mL
2 Tbsp.	chopped parsley	30 mL
½ tsp.	salt	2 mL
	Dash cayenne	
	Freshly ground black pepper	

Mix horseradish immediately with the yogurt and lemon juice so that it doesn't darken. Mix in the herbs and spices, and let rest for a couple of hours to blend the flavours. Toss with four cups (1 L) of steamed, trimmed green beans and half a cup (125 mL) of slivered red pepper. Or use a tablespoon (15 mL) each of tarragon and chervil for the thyme and parsley.

MUSTARD

After black pepper, mustard is the world's most popular condiment. Not only does the ground-up

from the top 4 inches of the root and trim the fine fibrous roots growing there. This produces a straight, compact horseradish. Draw the soil back around the plant, and add a heavy layer of mulch to discourage weeds. For the next four months, the plant needs only regular watering and occasional cultivation.

In October or November, after the first light frosts have sweetened the horseradish, lift the plant and strip off the roots, storing them, like carrots, in sand for use throughout the winter. Replenish the bed, digging manure deeply into the soil, and return a length of root to each hole. In the spring, trim the top of the new rootball as before.

The most pungent of the edible roots, horseradish is a reliable way to spice up a sauce. On one occasion, at a fine Chinese restaurant in Quebec, I tasted a cabbage and horseradish salad that brought sweat to my brow in seconds; yet in French restaurants, I have eaten the root sliced as an entrée, and it has been mild and palatable. The explanation lies in two substances, sinigrin and myrosin, normally distinct in the root tissues. The root can be cut with-

out disturbing the flesh much, but grating destroys the membranes that separate the sinigrin and myrosin. They combine to form the volatile oil allyl isothiocyanate, which brings tears to the eyes and pleasure to jaded taste buds.

Sliced or grated horseradish is good added to carrot, apple, celeriac, beetroot or potato salad. Grate it fresh into dressings for bitter greens, especially if strong-flavoured ingredients such as blue cheese or walnuts are added. Try up to two tablespoons (30 mL) of horseradish to a third-cup (75 mL) of dressing.

The most convenient way to use horseradish is as a sauce. Peel a large quantity of horseradish roots, storing them in a lemon bath to prevent darkening. Dice the roots, and grate finely in a blender or food processor, stepping back for a moment when you lift off the top to avoid inhaling the fumes. Proceed quickly so that the horseradish doesn't darken or lose its bite. Salt the grated root to taste, and mix in a good-quality white-wine vinegar until it has the consistency of a thick paste, seed tickle the taste buds, but it is strongly preservative, discouraging mould and bacterial growth. It also masks the rank taste of dishes that have gone a little "off." Not surprisingly, mustard achieved prominence in the Middle Ages: the Earl of Northumberland's household apparently went through 160 gallons of the yellow paste a year. But mustard is vital for another reason: it is an emulsifier, the essential ingredient that keeps the oil and vinegar blended in vinaigrette dressings.

Three distinct species of mustard are grown for seed to flavour dressings or to grind into prepared mustard. *Brassica nigra*, or black mustard, is used exclusively in Dijon mustard and was the most widely cultivated variety until the smaller Indian mustard, *B. juncea*, was adopted, being more suited to mechanical harvesting. *Brassica alba*, known in England as white mustard and in North America as yellow mustard, is the basis of the milder American-style hot dog mustard.

Grow mustard plants for seed as described for mustard greens (page 45), thinning to 8 inches apart and allowing the plants to mature. By the end of June, the plants are 3 feet high, with bright yellow flowers. By the end of July, they are 4 feet high, and their developing pods are making the tops heavy enough to need support. Throughout the flowering and early seed-developing season, check regularly for aphids. For a seed harvest, plants must be absolutely pest-free. One year, Turid waited too long to check and, at harvest, found a severe aphid infestation. Whole plants, their seedpods bulging, had to be thrown on the compost pile. If you find aphids, spray with rotenone.

In mid-August when the leaves turn brown, the stems become woody and the pods are lumpy with mature seeds, cut the top foot off the plants, wrap the bunches together with twine, and slip them into large paper bags. Tie securely, perforate with air holes, and hang upside down in a warm, dry place for several months, until the seedpods are as dry as parchment. Pull up the rest of the plants and compost them.

A grocery bag full of drying plants yields only a tablespoon of seed, which can be purchased for a few cents at a health-food store. Often, however, only the mild yellow seed is available, and while this produces a characteristic mustard flavour, *Brassica nigra* and *B. juncea* are the types that contribute pungency. Shelling and grinding your own seed may be the only way to obtain a sufficiently hot, grainy mustard—and although it is a labour-intensive job, it is not an unpleasant way to while away a winter afternoon.

To shell mustard seed, don clean cotton gloves, grasp the stems of the plants firmly, and pull them out of the bag, ripping off the pods, which fall into the bag. Then put both hands into the bag, and rub the pods vigorously between your palms. Check periodically to see whether there are still unopened pods, and continue rubbing until they have all burst. Then empty the bag into a large bowl of cold water, and swish the contents around. The seeds sink to the bottom, while the husks float. Skim off the bulk of the chaff, let the seeds settle, then drain and add fresh water to the bowl. Rinse several times, stirring the seeds vigorously each time to release the chaff. Drain the seeds in a very fine sieve or through cheesecloth or a coffee filter, and dry thoroughly. Any remaining chaff can be blown away after the seeds dry. Grind the clean, dry seeds to a powder with a mortar and pestle.

Mustard seed and mustard powder last a very long time in the cupboard. The pungency of prepared mustard comes from an essential oil that is formed only by the action of cold water on pulverized seed. Once it is mixed with water, however, it reaches full strength within about 10 minutes, then gradually loses its pungency, although it retains its flavour. Hot water and vinegar or wine also inhibit the enzyme action, producing a milder mustard. The enzymes of white mustard are the least easily damaged.

Use the ground seeds to make *moutarde à l'ancienne*, the grainy mustard that was standard until a way to remove the hulls was developed.

Grainy Mustard

The Dijonnais, famous for their mustard, have an expression for truly good mustard: *mont au nez*, meaning "coming up the nose." According to their rules, mustard should stimulate the appetite and aid digestion but never burn the throat or alter the taste of a dish—a subtle art, indeed.

Mix equal parts crushed seed and white wine, adding more wine, water or cream to produce a smoother texture. Add salt, turmeric and crushed black peppercorns, if desired. To make herb mustard, experiment with tarragon, rosemary, basil, oregano and sage, alone or in combination. For smoother texture and hotter mustard, mix equal parts crushed seed and mustard powder, then add liquids and flavourings.

For a cooked mustard, mix mustard powder and seeds to produce one-third of a cup (75 mL). Put in a saucepan with a tablespoon (15 mL) of brown sugar or honey and a pinch of salt. Beat two eggs with two-thirds of a cup (150 mL) of tarragon vinegar,

and stir into the saucepan in a thin continuous stream. Put the saucepan on moderate heat, and carefully warm the mustard, stirring continuously, until the mixture is thick and smooth. This makes about a cup (250 mL). Refrigerate and use within two weeks, or seal in small sterilized mustard pots.

SEEDS

"Gone to seed" has a dissolute ring, but to Turid and me, this final phase of a plant's life often holds gastronomic delights that merit a quick mention. The seed heads of many flowering plants are little nuggets of intense flavour, often the same flavour as the leaves or fruits but concentrated and refined. We eat the seeds when they are immature, chopping the green heads of dill, coriander, arugula, radish and mustard into a vinaigrette. The texture and colour they add is as desirable as the taste.

You can also save the fully ripened seeds, sprouting them in winter to add a bit of freshness to off-season salads. The flavour of the sprouts is a welcome reminder of summer: peanutty fenugreek, nippy mustard, pungent radish. Experiment with leftover garden seeds, provided they are not treated with chemicals.

SALAD TRIMMINGS

We have a friend who is a prodigious gardener. From April until November, his garden is a showcase as he tests the limits of his microclimate and of the plant breeders' imaginations. He is the first in his community with the new cucumber, tomatillo, okra or amaranth offered by the seed catalogues. But there is something missing: there are no flowers. "Why waste my time with flowers?" he shrugs. "I can't eat them."

He is wrong. Not only are flowers edible, but many are delicious and bring a piquancy to salads that is as gustatory as it is visual. Indigo violas, blue borages, scarlet nasturtiums, orange marigolds, yellow calendulas, white and pink carnations: the entire palette is available for our table. Although the eating of flowers is still somewhat suspect in our culture, Alexandre Dumas immortalized the practice when he included a recipe for chrysanthemum salad in his play *Francillon*.

Flowers have been used in the kitchen for centuries. Apicius mentions mallows, violets and roses with the list of herbs used in Roman cuisine. Early Egyptians, Persians, Chinese and Greeks also ate flowers. In the Middle Ages, flowers had medicinal value as well as magical associations, and adding them to foods was not strictly a matter of good taste. Flowers were pounded into sugars as flavourings, added to wine, preserved in jellies and strewn fresh on salads. Although rosewater and orange blossoms are still common ingredients in Middle Eastern cuisine and the French have retained the custom of strewing blossoms on salads, outside the Orient, it is unusual to find edible flowers for sale at any vegetable markets. In China, however, washed dark yellow chrysanthemums are offered by the bundle to local cooks. They believe that eating chrysanthemums and lilies prolongs life. "If you have two loaves," says a Chinese proverb, "sell one and buy a lily."

Mythology and taste notwithstanding, flowers are first and foremost a visual delight. A brilliant red nasturtium tucked like a boutonniere on the side of a cool green cucumber salad or a scattering of sky-blue borage stars over a creamy potato salad stimulates the eye and puts the other senses on alert. In France, flowers strewn on a bed of greens is called *fourniture de salade*—salad trimmings, like icing on a cake or lace on a collar.

When experimenting with flowers, consider colour, shape and taste, but also try including the flowers of some of the ingredients in the salad. Often, there are still blooms on the plant when the salad vegetable or herb is being picked—for instance, green bean salad sprinkled with scarlet runner flowers, chive blossoms for a yogurt-cucumber salad or zucchini blossoms on a courgette ratatouille. For unique harmony between eye and palate, make a centrepiece arrangement of the same flowers used in the salad.

Dot salads with the flowers of the vegetables you grow, or grow edible flowers solely to enhance the herb and salad gardens as well as the table. Clove pinks, Johnny-jump-ups and English daisies are border plants as beautiful as they are delicious. Some flowers, such as marigolds, help repel insects: interplant them with the cabbages. Some nasturtiums sprawl vigorously as decorative climbers.

Do not eat anything, however, without checking first that it is edible. We include a list of some common inedible flowers, but we strongly suggest you contact the local poison-control office or the botany department of a nearby university before sampling unknown blooms. Remember that some plants and their flowers can kill.

And don't eat just any daisy. For salads, only organically grown flowers will do. Bouquets from the florist have almost surely been sprayed with chemicals you should not ingest. Friends' flowers may contain pesticide and herbicide residues, and there is a good chance those picked along the roadside have been sprayed too. If you are going to eat flowers, grow your own. Not only will they be chemical-free, they will be the appropriate species.

If you haven't used insecticidal sprays, if the flowers are bug-free and if the garden is far from roads and protected from wind so that the blooms are dust-free, then you can eat them as is. In most cases, however, a quick wash is a good idea. Pick the flowers just after the dew dries, leaving a little stem where possible. Check them carefully for insects: earwigs are particularly adept at hiding in the crevices. Swish the flower heads gently in lukewarm water, pat dry or air-dry carefully, then put them in the refrigerator in a small vase, as you would a centrepiece bouquet. Float stemless flower heads in a bowl of water, or wrap them very gently in a moist paper towel. If you use the flowers whole—usually as a corsage at the side of a salad —freshen them by cutting the stem under cold running water just before serving. You can also separate the flowers from the stems or pull off individual petals to sprinkle over a dish. Because petals are even more delicate than the most delicate lettuce leaf, handle them gently and add them at the last moment, strewn over the salad so that they don't get lost in the toss.

Some flowers, like borage blossoms and anise-hyssop, give a heady burst of honey, but most other species have little flavour. The truly notable exception is nasturtium (*Tropaeolum majus*), in our opinion an essential plant in the salad garden and in the kitchen. Its leaves, flowers and fruit possess the same characteristic nip as watercress. The flowers have a delightful velvety texture and peppery taste—one flower that is as fine in the mouth as it is to the eye.

Of the many nasturtium cultivars developed specifically for flowers, our favourite overall is 'Scarlet Whirlybird' (DO), which produces brilliant Chinese-red flowers waving on long petioles above a lily-pad mat of green leaves, round and almost flat, with silvery spiderweb veins. It makes an excellent edging plant, each seed developing into a compact bush about a foot high and a foot wide. Other varieties may be too tall and aggressive for border plants. Canary creeper (*Tropaeolum peregrinum*) grows up to 8 feet tall and has bright yellow orchidlike flowers. Plant nasturtiums directly in the garden in full sun, and keep a sharp eye out for aphids, a persistent pest.

Nasturtium fruits can be pickled to simulate capers. True capers come from *Capparis spinosa*, a tough little plant native to the Sahara, but nasturtiums are an acceptable substitute. For capers, keep the soil nutrient-poor to ensure an abundance of flowers, then be sure to leave enough on the plant to produce seedpods, small tricornered knobs that look a little like cerebral lobes. Pick the seedpods when they are unripe and still green.

Given richer soil, nasturtiums produce few flowers and seeds but a wealth of leaves that are also eminently edible. Chop them into a salad like cress, use them as dippers for a mild salsa (see page 55), or overlap them around the salad bowl like a wreath.

The leaves of many plants can be used as edible plates for individual salads or as salad-bowl liners. Some plants, such as flowering kale, malva and amaranth, justify their place in the salad garden by the beauty of their leaves alone. Unabashedly cultivated for their looks, these plants should be positioned in the garden to the best aesthetic advantage: a brilliant purple amaranth silhouetted against the morning light or a deep green malva set behind pink opium poppies, where its luxuriant foliage transports you to imaginary, exotic places. And at the table, the unusual leafy underlay enhances both the beauty and the flavour of the salad being served.

Poisonous Flowers

The following is a partial list of some common poisonous plants. Do not eat any flower without first determining whether it is safe.

Castor Bean Plant (*Ricinus communis*)
Christmas Rose (*Helleborus niger*)
Common Oleander (*Nerium oleander*)
Crocus (*Colchicum* spp)
Deadly Nightshade (*Solanum dulcamara*)
Foxglove (*Digitalis purpurea*)
Golden Chain (*Laburnum anagyroides*)
Heliotrope (*Heliotropium europaeum*)
Lady's Slipper (*Cypripedium pubescens*)
Lily of the Valley (*Convallaria majalis*)
Lobelia (*Lobelia inflata*)
Mistletoe (*Phoradendron* spp)
Monkshood (*Aconitum napellus*)
Morning Glory (*Ipomoea purpurea*)
Pasque Flower (*Anemone pulsatilla*)
Periwinkle (*Catharanthus roseus*)
Poison Hemlock (*Conium maculatum*)
Rhubarb (*Rheum offinalis*)
Tansy (*Tanacetum vulgare*)

130

Edible flowers—borage, pansies, nasturtiums, garlic chives—adorn this broccoli salad.

In the past few years, ornamental cabbage and kale (*Brassica oleracea*) have become popular decorative garden plants and are frequently available at nurseries and markets. These brassicas do not actually flower, but their open rosettes of leaves are as beautiful as any bloom. The cabbage's leaves are rounded, while kale's are frilled like a crinoline.

Started around June 1, planted directly in the garden and grown like other brassicas, 'Miniature Ornamental Cabbages' (NI) turn shades of green, white and deep rose in the fall; the centres are often a creamy, buttery white. And they are survivors: after the marigolds blacken, after the carrots are pulled, after the radicchio is gone from the garden, the flowering cabbage and kale linger on, bright and crisp as carnations, even after the December snow starts to fall. With luck, you can garnish a Christmas salad with the leaves of these ornamentals, which grow leathery but never become bitter. If winter comes early to your garden, rescue one plant and pot it in a container deep enough to accommodate the root. It will last long into the winter in a cool room.

Malva (*Malva verticillata*) brings a glimpse of the Tropics to northern gardens. Grown much like okra, the plant produces leaves that are an intense jungle green and deeply frilled, as big as the palm of your hand. The flowers are not prominent—tiny white blooms tucked close to the stem, like those of the related hollyhock—but the leaves on

Continued on page 134

131

Edible Flowers

The chart below lists our favourite edible flowers, but there are others. Check the seed catalogues, and look for nontoxic varieties developed particularly for their flower heads. Follow the planting instructions on the seed packet, or consult a comprehensive flower-gardening book.

Name	Plant Cycle	Description	Flower	Season	Taste	Use
Anchusa *Anchusa azurea*	Perennial	3'; hairy, coarse leaves	Intense blue, like borage	Jun-Aug	Smoky	Lettuce, mixed greens
Anise-Hyssop *Agastache foeniculum*	Perennial	2' shrub; attracts bees	Blue, 2''-3'' terminal spikes	Jul-Aug	Spicy	Pull out tiny trumpets; scatter on cucumber salad
Arugula *Eruca versicaria*	Annual	2'; bushy	White, 4-petalled cross	Jun-Oct	Mild	Buds and flowers; mesclun
Bergamot *Monarda didyma*	Perennial	3'; attracts bees	Red-purple terminal head	Jul-Aug	Spicy	Pull individual 1'' blooms; green pepper salad
Borage *Borago officinalis*	Annual	1'-2'; bushy	Bright blue, 1'' stars	Jun-Sep	Sweet	Pull stars from sockets; mesclun, cucumber salad
Calendula *Calendula officinalis*	Annual	2'-3'; pot marigold	Golden yellow daisies	Jul-Sep	Spicy	Petals, saffron substitute; young leaves in mesclun
Chervil *Anthriscus cerefolium*	Annual	1'-2'; fernlike	Tiny white umbels	Jul-Aug	Anise	Sprinkle over carrots and beet salads
Chicory *Cichorium intybus*	Biennial	2'-6'; open, bushy	Sky-blue, daisylike	Jul-Aug	Spicy	Petals over courgettes
Chives *Allium schoenoprasum*	Perennial	1'; grassy spikes	Purple 1'' balls	May-Jun	Spicy	Individual bells in mesclun
Chives, Garlic *Allium tuberosum*	Perennial	1'-2'; lilylike	White, open globe	Aug-Sep	Spicy	Whole head or stars; best when just opened
Chrysanthemum, Garland *Chrysanthemum coronarium*	Annual	1'-2'; compact, bushy	Bright yellow daisies	Jul-Aug	Spicy	Petals; beans, potato salads
Clove-Pink *Dianthus carophyllus*	Annual & Perennial	½ '-1'; edging	Red and white carnations	Jun-Sep	Sweet	Garnish; broccoli, cauliflower salads
Coriander *Coriander sativum*	Annual	2'-3'; lofty	Compound umbels, white	Jun-Aug	Sweet	Whole or chopped; greens
Daisy, English *Bellis perennis*	Perennial	4''; ground-hugging	White-pink composite	Apr-Jun	Mild	Petals; mesclun

Name	Plant Cycle	Description	Flower	Season	Taste	Use
Dandelion *Taraxacum officinale*	Perennial	6''; rosette	Bright yellow daisies	Apr-Jun	Spicy	Petals; corn salad
Day Lily *Hemerocallis* spp	Perennial	4'; ribbonlike leaves	4''-6''orange trumpet	Jun-Jul	Mild	Garnish; tear petals in mesclun
Dill *Anethum graveolens*	Annual	3'-5'; feathery, grey	Large yellow umbels	Jul-Sep	Spicy	Separate small circles; leek, cabbage, cucumber
Fennel *Foeniculum vulgare*	Annual	3'-5'; dill-like	Large yellow umbels	Aug-Oct	Sweet	Whole or chopped over broccoli, finochio, leek
Geranium, Scented *Pelargonium* spp	Tender perennial	1'-3'; compact bush	White, red	Dec-Feb	Perfumy	Petals on mesclun
Johnny-jump-up *Viola tricolor*	Annual	8''; edging	Tricolour ¾'' pansies	May-Aug	Sweet	Whole blooms on all salads
Lovage *Levisticum officinale*	Perennial	5' shrub; large leaves	Yellow umbel	July	Spicy	Use sparingly, mild greens
Malva *Malva verticillata*	Annual	4'-6'; hollyhocklike	Tiny white flowers	Jul-Aug	Mild	Final touch on any salad
Marigold, Citrus *Tagetes tenuifolia*	Annual	6''-9''; hardy, bushy	Citrus-scented, yellow	Jun-Sep	Lemon	Chop in dressing
Mustard *Brassica* spp	Annual	4'-5'; shrubby hedge	Small yellow cruciferae	Jun-Jul	Spicy	Chop buds and blooms; mesclun
Nasturtium *Tropaeolum* spp	Annual	8'' low bush or 8' climber	Yellow and red 2'' flowers	Jul-Sep	Spicy	Individual petals; garnish
Primrose, English *Primula vulgaris*	Perennial	4''-6'' rosette	½'' flowers, many shades	Apr-May	Sweet	Spring mesclun; sun root salad
Rose *Rosa* spp	Perennial	2'-5' shrub	Many shades	Jul-Sep	Sweet	Individual petals
Squash *Cucurbita pepo*	Annual	Trailing bush or climber	Bright yellow trumpets	Jul-Sep	Mild	Whole flowers as garnish; tear petals on greens
Violet *Viola odorata*	Perennial	4'' low bush	Deep violet, white throat	Apr-May	Sweet	Early mesclun

Day lilies, geranium, nasturtium, anise-hyssop, dill: an edible bouquet.

ture to produce large, beautiful leaves. Be sure to taste them before encouraging your guests to sample their salad plates: at some point, amaranth leaves are reduced to a purely decorative role.

When harvesting garnish leaves, choose colours and textures to complement the salad they cradle. Having decided on variegated amaranth for the courgettes or emerald malva for the beets, select the most perfect leaves on the plant—palm-sized to hold an individual cucumber salad, a dozen small ones for a bowl of coleslaw or a sprawling green to line a serving platter for a six-person mesclun. Always pick more than you need in case some don't make the trip from garden to table successfully. Wash them gently, swishing curly leaves like malva and kale in warm water to loosen grit from the folds. Do not spin: the leaves are too large and may be damaged. Pat dry, and store in a plastic bag in the refrigerator. To serve, line the plates with the leaves and arrange the salad on it. Encourage your guests to eat both the salad and its edible plate.

Nasturtium Capers

It is difficult to grow enough nasturtiums to make a winter's supply of capers, but even one jar is a special delicacy. The spices in this recipe are optional: nasturtiums have a delightful flavour on their own.

1 ½ lbs.	nasturtium seeds	750 g
¼ cup	tiny pickling onions	50 mL
1 tsp.	powdered mace	5 mL
1 tsp.	whole cloves	5 mL
	Dried chiles (optional)	
1 pt.	white-wine vinegar	500 mL

Soak the nasturtium seeds in cold salted water for 4 days, changing the solution every day. Slice the onions crosswise. Boil the onions and spices in vinegar. Fill small, sterilized glass jars with seeds, then pour in heated spiced vinegar, filling to within half an inch (1.25 cm) of the top, and seal. Allow to cure for 3 months before using.

THE WELL-DRESSED SALAD

Having gone to the trouble of choosing the perfect cultivar, sprouting the seeds under lights, caring for the plants throughout the season, meticulously harvesting them and cleaning the choice ingredients for tonight's dinner, the gardener, in a momentary lapse of judgement, pours a glutinous glob of bottled dressing over her crisp, exotic vegetables. Using prepared dressings is convenient

Continued from page 131
this 5-foot-tall exotic make it worth growing. At maturity, the leaves of 'Curly Mallow' (NI) range from 5 to 9 inches in diameter, open and flat like large maple leaves with a ruffled fringe. They almost ask to be filled. Malva leaves are mild, slightly hairy and, when chewed, a little gelatinous, like okra. The friends at your table will not soon forget a mesclun strewn with the yellow blooms of the canary creeper and served on a crisp, curling malva.

Finally, Turid plants one or two amaranth (*Amaranthus tricolor*), also known as Chinese spinach, a vigorous, 5-foot-tall, bushy annual whose leaves emerge in a cascade of variegated red, green and gold. 'Joseph's Coat' (BL) is her favourite. At the best of times, amaranth is slightly bitter, like a meaty spinach infused with horseradish, and the bite intensifies as the plant matures. Some gardeners add very young leaves to salad, but they are always too tart for our taste. We prefer to let amaranth ma-

Ornamental kale.

and inexpensive, but what a travesty it is. A fine salad deserves a superior dressing, and like the vegetables it adorns, there is only one way to obtain it—by making it yourself. Whisking the perfect vinaigrette is no more difficult than growing a courgette, and the rewards are spectacular.

Dressings can be separated into creamy dressings, with a base of mayonnaise, yogurt or sour cream, and vinaigrettes, simple combinations of oil and vinegar or fruit juice and condiments or spices. Each has its place. I hate to dress greens in anything weighty, whereas chunks of cucumbers, potatoes or beans glory in a thick sauce. All dressings, however, contain some combination of oil and vinegar.

Oils carry a health burden because they are 100 percent fat. All oils contain about 45 calories per teaspoon, or about 14 grams of fat per tablespoon; "light" on the label refers only to taste. All oils that are liquid at room temperature are unsaturated. They contain no cholesterol and, in fact, lower the amount of cholesterol in the blood. Oils are classified according to the kind of fatty acids they contain—monounsaturated and polyunsaturated. Monounsaturated oils are most desirable, because they seem to increase the level of "good" cholesterol (HDL: high-density lipoprotein) while reducing the level of "bad" cholesterol (LDL: low-density lipoprotein), which clogs arteries and contributes to heart disease. Polyunsaturated oils reduce both kinds of cholesterol. Oils that contain high percentages of both polyunsaturated and monounsaturated oils are usually labelled simply "unsaturated."

All plants contain some oil, but seeds, beans, nuts and fruits are blessed with an abundance. Extracting oils from olives and nuts is not too difficult; they are simply crushed. Seeds are crushed too, but they are also heated to burst the walls of the oil cells. Seeds are pressed, then the last bit of oil is squeezed out chemically; the resulting seed cake is soaked in solvent, heated to evaporate the solvent, then refined through a complicated process that draws off impurities and often bleaches the finished product. Oils billed simply as "vegetable oils" are highly processed and virtually tasteless. The most natu-

ral oils, therefore, come from olives and nuts. If you enjoy having a wide array of oils from which to choose, buy them in small quantities.

Most oils remain liquid above 32 degrees F. The more unsaturated an oil is, the more likely it is to oxidize, which turns it rancid. Light and salt accelerate the process, which is why oils should always be stored in an airtight container in a cool, dark cupboard, preferably in a dark glass bottle. Some oils, like olive, sunflower and safflower, contain vitamin E, a natural antioxidant that allows them to keep longer.

Olive oil has such a long history that it has acquired a complex system of grading and a veritable dictionary of terms to describe variations in quality. "Extra-virgin" olive oil has the fullest flavour and aroma, with a maximum acidity of 1 percent. (Low acidity is the key to quality.) "Virgin" olive oil has an acidity as high as 3 percent, but it has not been exposed to heat during extraction, so most of the vitamins are intact. The olives are simply washed and centrifuged, and the oil is filtered. "Cold-pressed" means the olives are not submitted to anything as modern as a centrifuge but have simply been pressed, and the oil has been spun off one end. It is of higher quality than virgin olive oil. Oils that do not meet the virgin or extra-virgin standard are refined to remove impurities and reduce acidity. This makes the flavour very bland, so to restore the characteristic flavour, some unrefined virgin oil is added. This blended oil is labelled "100 percent pure olive oil," or simply "olive oil." The less virgin oil added, the blander or lighter the taste, resulting in oils labelled "light" or "extra-light."

Although olive oil was the first type commercially produced—the word "oil" actually derives from the ancient Greek word for olive—today, it represents only 5 percent of the world's oil production. But its use is increasing, which may be due in part to reported health benefits. It contains 74 percent monounsaturates and 8 percent polyunsaturates, the best ratio of any of the common vegetable oils. Aside from improving HDL-cholesterol ratios, olive oil appears to contain compounds that combat arterial buildups by blocking the blood's tendency to clot. A study of middle-aged Americans showed that olive oil in the diet lowered blood cholesterol by 13 percent. To prevent cardiovascular disease, some doctors now recommend substituting olive oil for all dietary fat. Olive oil seems to lower blood pressure, and it also works as a mild laxative.

Extra-virgin olive oil is the one to buy for the most health benefits and the best flavour in salad dressings: no other oil imparts its fresh, distinctly fruity flavour. It is the ideal oil for preserving herbs, because it is cold-pressed and is therefore free of chemicals and high in vitamin E. Most authentic Italian restaurants keep a row of green bottles filled with herb oils. To make your own, stuff half a cup (125 mL) of clean, dry herb leaves into a dark glass bottle. Top with about two cups (500 mL) of extra-virgin olive oil, and seal. Store in a cool, dark place for two weeks or so, then periodically sample the oil. When the flavour is fully developed, strain it and store in the refrigerator. For longer storage, mix three parts oil to one part vinegar as a preservative. Rosemary, basil, tarragon, chervil, coriander and sage all preserve well in oil. You can also flavour oil with peppercorns, anise, garlic, chiles or zest of lemon. I like to keep a bottle of peeled garlic cloves in oil: the garlic is milder, and a drop of the oil added to dressing is ambrosia.

Olive oil is the salad chef's staple, but there are other oils, more distinctive in flavour and less frequently used but still pleasant company in the kitchen. When using nut oils, check that none of your guests has an allergy to nuts. Even a drop can be lethal and can go unnoticed in a dressing until it is too late.

Walnut oil is a polyunsaturated oil (63 percent polyunsaturates and 23 percent monounsaturates), cold-pressed from dried, roasted nuts. If extracted by means of heat, it is inedible; if made from unroasted nuts, it is used by carpenters. The highest-quality edible walnut oil comes from the Dordogne region of France and is often an ingredient in the classic walnut-mâche salad of southern France. Light and air degrade walnut oil quickly, so store it in a cool, dark place. It turns cloudy in the refrigerator but clears again shortly after returning to room temperature. Because of the expense, cut it half-and-half with olive oil for a dressing.

Hazelnut oil tops the chart in monounsaturates —78 percent to 10 percent polyunsaturates—but it has been produced commercially for only a dozen years. It is even more expensive than walnut oil, but the flavour is more subtle. Because of the cost and because it goes rancid quickly, buy it in small quantities. To my taste, the nutty oils go particularly well with mild mescluns and bland vegetables.

Almond oil is 70 percent monounsaturates and 17 percent polyunsaturates. An even more recent entrant to the commercial market, this light, amber oil is made in France from Spanish nuts and is very expensive. Don't buy *amande douce* by mistake: it is often labelled "almond oil" but is used for cosmetics.

Peanut oil is not a nut oil. The peanut is a pulse,

like beans, and not a true nut. There is a startling range in peanut oil, from the virtually tasteless to an oil as potent as liquid peanut butter. Containing 46 percent monounsaturates and 32 percent polyunsaturates, this oil emulsifies easily and is ideal for salad dressings. If you want peanut flavour, avoid the refined oils that most grocery stores carry, and go to a specialty or health-food store to buy cold-pressed oil.

Sesame oil has a distinctly nutty taste. A staple in Asian cuisine, it contains 40 percent monounsaturates and 42 percent polyunsaturates and comes in two grades: a light yellow oil with a moderately sesame taste, and a dark brown variety made with roasted sesame seeds that would have made Aladdin weep with pleasure. Often, commercial sesame oil is a blend of sesame with other less flavourful oils. A few drops of the dark oil perfectly complement soy sauce and ginger. We use it more as a spice than as an oil.

Grapeseed oil is a bland, light-textured oil, first produced during World War I when other oils were in short supply. Because it contains 70 percent polyunsaturates and only 16 percent monounsaturates, use it sparingly. Its lightness is particularly welcome in yogurt dressings, but it tends to go rancid quickly, so buy it in small quantities.

Avocado oil, a recent favourite of Turid's, is produced without chemicals. It has a mild, unusual flavour, slightly anisette, that combines well with lime. Furthermore, it is akin to olive oil in its fatty-acid balance—79 percent monounsaturates and 16 percent polyunsaturates.

There is a group of vegetable oils on the market notable mainly for their blandness. Distinctly lacking in flavour, they allow the taste of vegetables and vinegars to shine through. Most, however, are high in polyunsaturates and low in monounsaturates. Safflower oil contains 12 percent monounsaturates and 75 percent polyunsaturates; sunflower oil, 20 percent monounsaturates and 66 percent polyunsaturates; and corn oil, the strongest-coloured but equally tasteless oil, 24 percent monounsaturates and 59 percent polyunsaturates. Most of the oils labelled simply "vegetable oil" are canola oil, touted as the best there is from a health point of view. In fact, it is a vast improvement over corn, safflower and sunflower oils, and it is true that it contains less saturated fat than most, but the composition of its unsaturated fats (56 percent monounsaturates and 33 percent polyunsaturates) is still inferior to olive oil for salad dressings.

The other primary component of salad dressings is vinegar. The word "vinegar" comes from

the French *vin aigre*, sour wine. Yes, it is sour, but the emphasis should be on the wine, since there are as many vintages in vinegar as in wine, and a good vinegar bears about as much resemblance to the cheap grocery-store variety as a Pouilly-Fuisée does to local plonk.

The vinegar and citrus juices in a dressing do more than add tang to a salad; the acid helps prevent a loss of vitamin C from cut vegetables. Vinegar is also a preservative, slowing the growth of harmful bacteria. Although vinegar also tastes good, the practice of adding it to a dressing stems from the belief that mild acid helps the body digest coarse, fibrous or stringy vegetables.

Vinegar has a long history: fruit has been fermenting to alcohol and bacteria have been converting that alcohol into acetic acid for millennia. Pasteur figured out what was actually going on in the bottles of old wine, but long before that, vinegar was a staple in Egyptian and Roman cultures as a drink, as a medicine and as a culinary accoutrement.

Only a "mother" can turn wine to vinegar. Vinegar mother is a mat of bacteria—*Mycoderma aceti*—that develops in fermented fruit juices. I have made it from cider and white and red wine. Simply leave the juice or wine for a few weeks at room temperature; the microorganisms develop at temperatures between 59 and 86 degrees F. Use a dark glass jar, leaving the top off and covering the mouth with muslin to keep the dust out. After a few weeks, the liquid becomes cloudy, then a jellyfishlike mat forms. The process can take weeks, even months, and sometimes the bacteria never invade the jar. If that is the case, just begin again. Cider works almost every time. Once the mother is visible, taste the vinegar every couple of weeks until it has enough bite for you. The flavour will be full and sour, rather than acidic. When the flavour is right, strain the vinegar into a clean bottle and add more juice to the mother. Don't let vinegar sit in the original jar indefinitely: when all the alcohol in the juice has been converted to acetic acid and there is nothing left for the mother to live on, it will die unless it is transferred to a bottle of fresh juice. Don't use metal utensils, because they will kill the mother. You can also divide the mother, starting several batches of different types of vinegar. One of my personal favourites is Chardonnay vinegar, which tastes like sun-ripened melons.

Homemade vinegar should not be used for preserving, since the acetic-acid content is not guaranteed, but it is wonderful in salads. If you are buying vinegar, you will get what you pay for. Cheap vinegar is acetic acid and water. Many vin-

Each ornamental cabbage leaf can be used as an edible plate.

egars are made by a speedy commercial process. A really fine vinegar has been aged, sometimes up to 50 years, in wooden casks.

Wine vinegar has an acetic-acid content of about 6 percent. As long ago as 1394, a professional vinegar makers' guild was formed in Orléans, and today, the best vinegars are still made using the Orléans process. The label will read "vinaigre à l'ancienne," "aged in wood" or "made by the Orléans process." Oak barrels are three-quarters filled with wine and laid on their sides with air holes drilled in the top. The temperature is kept at a steady 70 degrees F. A mother forms and turns the wine gradually to vinegar, which sinks to the bottom of the cask. As the vinegar is drawn off the bottom, more wine is added in the top. There are faster ways of making wine vinegar, but only the Orléans method comes close to achieving the full aroma of homemade vinegar. When making your own, the better the wine, the better the vinegar. Don't mix your vintages, but start a new batch if you have a heel of good wine that you don't know what to do

with. Occasionally, I admit, I combine wines for a blended vinegar; but never, never mix white and red.

Balsamic vinegar is the *ne plus ultra*, the champagne of vinegars. For centuries, it has been made in the Italian province of Modena: in 1046, a barrel of balsamic vinegar was among the coronation gifts to the Holy Roman Emperor Henry III. As dark as a good brandy and as aromatic, it is worth every penny of the price. Balsamic vinegar is made from grapes with a high sugar content. The juice is boiled down, transferred to a barrel and exposed to air. The fermentation of the wine turns some of the sugar into alcohol, but because of the high sugar content, some of the sugar remains, creating a unique sweet-sour vinegar. Balsamic vinegar is aged for years, sometimes generations; the oldest is more than 200 years old. The very best is never for sale: it is passed on as an heirloom or presented as a dowry. When Modena was bombed during World War II, families saved their barrels of balsamic vinegar above all else. What we buy, of course, is less precious, although Italian law requires

that it be aged at least three years in a wooden cask made of juniper, oak, chestnut or mulberry. (There is no balsam involved: the name comes from the fact that at one time, the vinegar was thought to be medicinal, especially as a cure for scurvy.) I like dressings made entirely with balsamic vinegar, but it colours the vegetables and has a very distinctive taste. You may want to cut it with a good white-wine vinegar; a drop or two is enough to impart the flavour.

Sherry vinegar comes from the southwestern region of Spain. It has full-bodied flavour, somewhat akin to that of balsamic vinegar. It is often aged 20 to 30 years before bottling and is therefore expensive, but it is excellent in salad dressings, particularly slightly sweet or fruity ones. To stretch sherry vinegar, substitute two-thirds white-wine vinegar. The sherry still imparts a lovely rich flavour.

Champagne vinegar, unfortunately, is not made from champagne. It comes from dry white wine made from grapes grown in the Champagne district of France. You can make your own from any good-quality still white wine or from champagne.

It is a very light vinegar, golden in colour and subdued in flavour, excellent for tender spring greens.

Malt vinegar is to beer what balsamic vinegar is to wine. Originally, in deference to the etymology of vinegar, it was called alegar, but the name did not catch on. Malt vinegar is made by fermenting barley mash into a crude beer called "gyle," which is then dripped through a vat of shavings, filtered and matured into vinegar. Initially, malt vinegar is clear: it is coloured with caramel to give it the look of balsamic. Very dark brown, it has a robust flavour that is especially good for bitter greens or for strongly flavoured vegetables and dressings with hearty spices and herbs.

Cider vinegar is relatively mild in flavour, with an acetic-acid content of about 4 percent. It is the easiest to make: when your apple cider "turns," take it out of the refrigerator, put a cloth instead of the cap over the top, and let it sit in the kitchen cupboard for a month or two. There are those who claim that cider vinegar cures arthritis and promotes fertility in cows. A good commercial cider vinegar starts with whole apples, ground to pulp and cold-pressed for the cider, which is fermented naturally in wooden casks. The alcoholic cider is exposed to air, which turns it to acetic acid. Cheaper cider vinegars are made with apple cores and peelings, the fermented juice converted to vinegar by artificially infusing the liquid with oxygen, and then they are bottled without ageing. You can make a far superior product at home, although it will be cloudy. Commercial manufacturers use sophisticated filters to make the vinegar clear. Like malt vinegar, cider vinegar has a distinctive taste and is good in dressings and marinades spiked with hearty herbs and spices.

Rice vinegar is made from rice wine, as it has been for 3,000 years in China. Although it can be red, black or white, the white variety is most commonly available. The red is made from red rice; the black has a flavour similar to that of balsamic vinegar; the white is pale gold with a delicate flavour. Rice vinegar is generally an extremely mild, slightly sweet vinegar that is easily overpowered. In typical Oriental vinaigrettes, the vinegar does not play a dominant role but is subservient to the nuttiness of the sesame oil and the salty spiciness of the soy sauce. The Japanese also make a variety of rice-based vinegars: su, which is mild but tart; aji pon, flavoured with soy sauce and citrus juice; tosazu, flavoured with fish stock; and ume-su, made from plums. It is worth browsing through ethnic grocery stores and sampling the unusual vinegars.

Herb vinegars are not made from herbs but are simply white-wine vinegars infused with the fla-

The flavours of herbs can be captured in homemade oils and vinegars.

vour of herbs. This is much more subtle than putting herbs in a dressing, and it is an ideal way of preserving the wonderful summer taste of herbs that don't dry or freeze well. Herb vinegars are easy to make. Simply poke herbs into an attractive bottle, about 4 tablespoons (60 mL) for 15 ounces (450 mL) of vinegar. The herbs should be washed and thoroughly dried, either left whole (more attractive) or crushed slightly to release their oils. Pour the vinegar over the herbs. You can use room-

temperature vinegar, but heating it first will help bring out the flavour of the herbs. Cork the bottles: don't use metal, as it affects the flavour of the vinegar. Stand the vinegar on a windowsill for a couple of weeks. Taste periodically after the first week, and when the flavour is to your liking, pour off the vinegar, strain out the herbs and rebottle, adding a single sprig of herb for identification. Store in a cool, dark place. You can also leave the herbs in, but the flavour may intensify, and you must make sure the plant is covered with vinegar, or it may begin to spoil. Basil, thyme, tarragon, rosemary, bay, dill, chervil and lemon balm make tasty herb vinegars. Try adding peppercorns, chiles, garlic or zest of lemon. Provençal herb vinegar combines rosemary, thyme, marjoram and basil with a clove of garlic and a fresh chile. And don't forget about flowers. My most resounding success was chervil-nasturtium-peppercorn-garlic vinegar, a veritable salad in a jar. The possible combinations are endless.

The classic salad vinaigrette is basically an oil-and-water emulsion—vinegar, after all, is 90 percent water. An improperly made vinaigrette separates quickly, tastes oily and slides off the lettuce leaves to pool in the bottom of the salad bowl. Yet a perfect, homogeneous vinaigrette is not hard to make. Put the dressing ingredients in a small jar, and shake vigorously up and down. A few desultory swirls with a fork definitely won't work, but a whisk and a strong wrist will. If using a whisk and a round-bottomed bowl, add the oil slowly in a stream to improve the emulsion. Shake or whisk until the oil and vinegar become a single substance, thick and opaque. This means all the oil is broken down to little droplets that quickly become anxious to recombine. The vinaigrette will eventually separate, but the process is slowed by emulsifiers that coat the droplets and keep them suspended in the water. Onions, mustard and the acid in vinegar and lemon juice are all emulsifiers. Also, the lower the temperature, the more stable the emulsion. Prechill the vinaigrette ingredients, the salad ingredients and the salad bowl, and make the vinaigrette immediately before serving.

The traditional ratio of oil to vinegar is three to one; varying these proportions affects both taste and stability. A dressing that is two to one is more stable and reduces the fat in your diet, but the higher concentration of vinegar gives it a tarter flavour. Play with the oil-vinegar combination, using milder vinegars or a little sugar in the low-fat versions and increasing the proportion of oil when using balsamic vinegar or lemon juice. Just remember that the consistency of the vinaigrette has more to do with mixing technique and stabilizers than with the oil-vinegar ratio.

In my standard vinaigrette, I mix half a cup (125 mL) of oil, a quarter-cup (50 mL) of vinegar, one tablespoon (15 mL) of Dijon mustard, a squeeze of fresh lemon juice, a pinch of salt and a few grinds of pepper. But the variations after this are endless. Add a teaspoon or two (5-10 mL) of herbs, chosen to complement the flavours of the vegetables in the salad or the meal it accompanies: basil for toma-toes or Italian dishes, horseradish for beans or German dishes, tarragon for asparagus or French dishes. For a sharper dressing, add horseradish, hot pepper or chopped mustard buds. Crushed garlic is practically a staple; soy sauce gives the dressing more body. Instead of vinegar, substitute orange, grapefruit, lemon or lime juice or the strained juice from pickles. If you are adding herbs and spices, make the dressing a few hours ahead so that the flavours blend. Your dressings are limited only by your imagination. A cautionary note, however: if you happen across an outstanding blend, write it down. Many of my more triumphant gastronomic moments have been lost to history.

Having made the dressing, when to add it? There are two schools of thought. If the vegetables are to absorb the flavour of the dressing, it is a marinade. The salad vegetables should soak in it for at least an hour and sometimes as long as overnight. Green salads, however, should be dressed immediately before serving. Some people serve undressed greens and a boat of sauce so that each person can dress his or her own. Properly, however, the salad should be tossed to coat all the leaves, and this is almost impossible to do in individual bowls. I prefer to make dressing the salad something of a dramatic event at the end of the meal, bringing the undressed salad and the dressing to the table separately and tossing them in front of the guests. That allows time for the dinner to digest a little, for the conversation to turn to the delicacy of the vegetables that are next on the menu and for our senses to tingle at the sight of the salad before us.

Yogurt Vinaigrette

This vinaigrette is excellent on any salad where creaminess is a virtue. It is delicious poured over slices of tomato and onion arranged in overlapping circles on a serving platter and sprinkled with parsley. Or add a tablespoon (15 mL) of freshly chopped dill, and serve the vinaigrette over cucumber fingers decorated with Johnny-jump-ups. When mixed with grated carrots, it turns the colour of orange sherbet.

¼ tsp.	sea salt	1 mL
¼ tsp.	herb salt	1 mL
1 tsp.	raw sugar	5 mL
1 tsp.	dry mustard	5 mL
1 Tbsp.	fresh lemon juice	15 mL
5 Tbsp.	cold-pressed safflower oil	75 mL
5 Tbsp.	low-fat yogurt	75 mL
1 tsp.	minced garlic	5 mL

Combine all the ingredients in a pint screw-top jar. Close tightly. Shake well until the dressing emulsifies. Store in the refrigerator. Let sit for several hours before using. Ordinary table salt and white sugar can be substituted, though the flavour is less interesting.

Mayonnaise

Essentially, mayonnaise is an egg-oil emulsion, with each egg yolk capable of holding about three-quarters of a cup (175 mL) of oil in suspension. The only real trick to making it is a steady hand and room-temperature ingredients. Even the tools you work with must all be body-warm too. I had several failures one winter, until I realized the food processor was stored in a cupboard against an uninsulated wall. The machine was like ice—and my mayonnaise like water. You can also make mayonnaise in a blender, by hand or with a whisk.

2	egg yolks	2
2 tsp.	white-wine vinegar	10 mL
	Juice of half a lemon	
½ tsp.	salt	2 mL
	Pinch of white pepper	
½ tsp.	Dijon mustard	2 mL
1 cup	canola oil mixed with ½ cup (125 mL) olive oil (or any combination of olive & vegetable oil, to taste) Dash of hot-pepper sauce	250 mL
1 Tbsp.	boiling water	15 mL

Process the egg yolks until light-coloured. Keep the food processor on, and add vinegar, lemon juice, salt, pepper and mustard. Add the oil, a drop or two at a time, until half a cup (125 mL) has been incorporated, by which time the mayonnaise will be thick. Continue to beat in the oil, about two tablespoons (30 mL) at a time. Season with hot-pepper sauce and, depending on your taste, more salt or lemon juice. Thin with the boiling water, which stabilizes the mix.

Makes 2 cups (500 mL). Store in a mason jar in the refrigerator. It keeps about 5 to 6 days. Bring small amounts to room temperature as you need them. Do not use mayonnaise that has been at room temperature for more than 2 hours.

For variations, add herbs such as tarragon, chervil, parsley, chives, curry, horseradish or minced fennel. Mixed half-and-half with drained yogurt, this is a wonderful dip for a raw-vegetable tray.

Practical Matters

A Garden Primer

Chapter Eight

Success in the garden is rarely serendipitous. More often, it is the consequence of hours spent poring over seed catalogues, making garden sketches, starting seeds and creating and maintaining beds. We hope the advice that follows will help to make your garden more productive.

PREPARING THE SOIL

Double-dug raised beds are the basis of our salad gardens. You can use rototillers and acres of earth to grow vegetables, but raised beds work so well that they are the only method we recommend. It is relatively easy to prepare good soil, maintenance requires only minimal effort, yields are higher because sowing is more intensive, and the method is adaptable to gardens large and small. Raised beds are a boon to people with bad backs, since they demand less bending. Beds also provide a release from the tyranny of rows: the gardener is more inclined to broadcast the neatly defined beds, creating beautiful as well as functional designs.

We suggest beds about 3 feet wide and 5 feet long as a standard size, but don't limit yourself to rectangles. Use the shape of the beds to add visual interest to the garden, creating triangles, circles or long skinny beds in stripes or herringbones. The only caveat is that you must be able to reach the centre of the bed from the edges. When making beds wider than 4 feet, lay steppingstones down the middle, little islands from which you can sow, weed, water and harvest.

Walking is taboo in raised beds. Every footstep compacts the soil and squeezes out the oxygen so necessary to healthy growth. Instead, leave pathways wide enough to push a wheelbarrow along and to walk on comfortably. We make ours the width of a rake, about 18 inches. The beds themselves should be a foot high: the soil warms faster, it drains well, and the entire depth can be improved. Don't worry about erosion: unless your garden is subject to tropical downpours, the plants in the bed keep the sloped sides intact. Raised beds are easy to mulch, and the paths double as irrigation ditches:

during dry spells, we build earth dams at the ends and fill them with water that soaks in at root level.

Situate the garden where it gets the most hours of sunlight. If it must be partially shaded, afternoon shade is preferable, since many plants like protection from the hot midday sun anyway. Don't despair if all your available land lies in dappled shade. Experiment for a season with container plants. You may be surprised at how many varieties will thrive in partial shade: lettuces, greens and a number of herbs. Turid has unlimited land and can choose prime sites for each vegetable. I have a tiny, shaded lot with no southern exposure except for the front yard. I dug it up for the tomatoes, peppers, onions and heat-loving herbs—much to the enjoyment of the entire neighbourhood—and built narrow raised beds in front of a lattice fence on the north boundary of the lot. My garden grows up to get the sun and produces beautiful summer salads. But wherever you put it, the salad garden is most useful close to the kitchen.

To start a new salad garden, mark the outline of the entire area with rope, hose or boards, then with a spade dig around the perimeter. Cut the sod into foot-square blocks, dig it out, and stack it to one side. Lift out any rocks and debris, then dig down about a foot, loosening and turning the soil, walking backward off the bed to avoid stepping on the newly turned soil. (If the garden is very large, consider tilling at this stage only.) Pick out injurious insects like wireworms and cutworms, and pull out every last shred of root you see: this will save you hours of weeding later on. Shake any soil out of the sod, then throw the grass on the compost pile.

Once the whole area is turned, dig out the walkways, throwing the soil on top of adjacent beds. Improve each bed with compost or rotted manure, topping it up until it stands about a foot higher than the paths. Rake the bed level on top, and slope the sides slightly. Dig a shallow ditch around the outside perimeter of each bed, renewing it periodically during the growing season to keep the beds distinct from the lawn.

Whether this is a new garden bed or you are preparing the soil in the fall for next year's garden, now is the time to assess and improve your growing medium. Good soil is rich brown, smells sweet and has tilth—coarse and full of air, it feels soft and spongy and clings together a little when squeezed. If it feels fine and gritty, it has too much sand. If it sticks together like cold porridge, it contains too much clay.

To improve sandy soil, add all the organic matter you can find: moistened peat, compost or green manure—a cover crop of buckwheat, clover, spinach or legumes sown in the bed and dug before it flowers. (If you don't have a compost pile, start one immediately so that you will have vegetable matter with which to replenish the garden after the growing season.)

Clay soil is harder to correct. It is grey or yellow, sticky when wet and hardpan when dry. Mix it half-and-half (or one to two if it is heavy clay) with sand, compost or fresh manure, although this definitely needs to be overwintered before planting. If the clay is extremely dense and your garden is not too large, you might consider digging it up and importing new topsoil.

This is the time, too, to determine how sweet the soil is. Invest in a pH meter, or send a soil sample to the local agriculture extension service for an accurate reading. (Test it before adding any nutrients to be sure of choosing the necessary ones, and test it again after you have altered the pH level.) The pH scale ranges from 0 to 14, with a neutral point of 7. Normal soil falls between 4 and 8: soil below 7 is progressively acidic and above 7 is alkaline.

Neutralize acidic soil (below 6) by adding ground dolomitic lime or wood ashes at the rate of ½ to 1½ pounds per square yard. Ground limestone can be used with fertilizer and manure, but if you are sweetening with hydrated lime, add it a month before or after digging in manure or fertilizer. To soil that is too alkaline, add peat.

Before digging in additives, make your garden plan: some vegetables prefer soils with a pH on one side or the other of neutral. In general, root crops such as potatoes like slightly acidic soil, while brassicas like a little lime. Most vegetables prefer soil between 6.5 and 7, although they will grow in soils with a pH as low as 5.4. Aromatic herbs like slightly sweeter soil, closer to 7.

Although soil is prepared in the fall, it is not a good idea to dig in leaves. They contain natural plant acids called phenols, which retard germination. Instead, collect dry leaves, and mow or shred them. Layer them in a corner and wait until the next summer, when they will have become leaf mould, a valuable soil additive.

Finally, the soil must be fertile. Compost, green manure and animal manures are the best ways to restore nitrogen and minerals to the earth and to improve its structure. As well as feeding the soil, organic matter serves as a sponge to hold moisture long enough for the roots to absorb the nutrients dissolved in it. Add about a barrowful of well-rotted manure for every 10 square yards of soil. Well-balanced soil does not need other supplements, although individual plants may have special needs. For instance, tomatoes thrive with an extra dressing of bone meal.

If you already have a garden, lift the last of the vegetables late in the fall. With a fork, dig up the soil and turn it over. Pick out every last wireworm and cutworm you see. Then dig in compost and manure. The winter cold gives slightly hot manure a chance to age. The garden will be clean, fertile and ready for planting as soon as the weather warms in the spring. If you cannot get around to preparing the bed until spring, dig in only well-composted manure and cover the soil with black plastic for 10 days to burn off any weed seeds. This is essential for mesclun beds. (If you do not have enough organic matter to replenish the whole bed at once, enrich the soil in each planting hole before you lay in the seed or seedling.)

Don't limit your planting to raised beds. Fill containers with some of this well-prepared garden soil. You can use any container, providing it holds enough soil, doesn't contain lead and drainage holes can be punched in the bottom. (If you don't want to cut holes, lay a few inches of pebbles in the bottom before adding soil and refrain from overwatering.) Remember that clay pots dry out quickly. You can make your own wooden planter boxes for edible gardens, as long as they are at least a foot deep and the wood is untreated.

PLANNING THE GARDEN

This is the leisurely indoor part of gardening, best done during the winter after the soil is prepared but before the planting season begins. On the basis of family preferences, make a list of what you want to grow, including a few experimental cultivars. Pace yourself. It is all too easy to become inspired by the catalogues, order 200 seed envelopes and run out of space and energy before all the seeds are in the ground.

Although local garden centres sell some seeds, the selection is limited, and they may not be for sale in time for early indoor sowing. Instead, order catalogues (pages 152-53), which usually arrive shortly after Christmas, and order your seeds immediately, because seed houses sometimes run out. Most seed houses offer discounts, bonuses or reduced shipping costs for large orders, so it may pay to limit yourself to two or three sources.

When buying seeds, order essential gardening supplies: a propagation mat, 2- and 3-inch peat pots, trays in various sizes with inserts, inoculant for the peas and beans, transplant fertilizer, rooting hor-

Raised beds should be prepared in fall or early spring in time to transplant seedlings.

mone and floating row covers. Growing lights (see page 144) are usually available from hardware stores.

Having decided what you want to grow, you must fit the salad vegetables into the garden in succession. This is like designing a three-dimensional game of tic-tac-toe. If planting in rows, arrange them to run east-west to minimize shading. Put tall plants on the north or to the west of smaller plants that appreciate afternoon shade. Keep related species together, such as the nightshades and legumes, since they like the same soil and care. In early spring, plant cool-season crops of lettuce, spinach and peas in the same bed where hot-weather tomatoes, peppers and eggplants will spend the summer. Rotate plants from year to year to foil insects and to utilize both the deep and surface nutrients in the soil. Large vegetables like potatoes need their own garden, while sprawling ones like cucumbers can meander across the lawn or up a fence.

A simple three-year rotation works well. If you are just beginning a salad garden, work out the whole rotation in advance. You can fill in the holes later, but the staple vegetables will always be the same. One system is to plant peas and beans in year one, followed by brassicas and roots in year two, other vegetables like onions, tomatoes and lettuce in year three, then back to beans in year four. For a longer rotation, limit year three to greens, go back to peas and beans in year four, and plant tomatoes, peppers and eggplants in year five.

There is a tradition among northern gardeners

of "putting in the garden" on the May 24 weekend and leaving it at that. But even at higher latitudes, sowing can continue from March to August. Work successive crops into your garden plans. Some crops, such as radishes, are finished in a month. Don't plant radishes again in that bed, but follow them with lettuce. Plant small radishes or fast-developing, low-growing vegetables between large vegetables that need months to mature so that one is finished just as the other requires the extra room. Look at the length of time each plant needs to mature, and figure out what can be sown after each is finished. As a general rule, for autumn harvests, the bed should be empty and ready to replant by the first of July. In succession cropping, take compatibility into consideration. For instance, early peas improve the soil for brassicas, so in early summer, after the 'Sugar Snaps' have been harvested, plant broccoli in the bed.

Your garden design should be sympathetic to the peccadilloes of the plants. We set peppers, tomatoes and eggplants, all of which like the same conditions, together in a sheltered, sunny site. Parsley, celery and celeriac benefit from the shade of taller companions, preferring the cooler moist air of the understorey. (Temperatures in shade may be 10 Fahrenheit degrees lower than in full sun.) And think of your own preferences too. I plant parsley, chervil, tarragon and chives in a row so that I can gather *fines herbes* with a single sweep of my hand instead of wandering throughout the garden.

And we always plant fast-sprouting lettuces and radishes to mark and border the beds where slower vegetables will sprout.

Don't ignore colour and aesthetics in your salad-garden design. Plant lettuces in waves of red and green instead of in rows. Border beds with edible flowers such as Johnny-jump-ups and dwarf marigolds. Turid's salad beds suggest edible relief sculptures in shades of red and green. Forget rows, and think instead of filling these raised beds as an artist fills a canvas, using plants rather than paint.

As you make a garden plan, also make a rough garden schedule to remind yourself, month by month, of what needs to be done. When the seeds arrive, divide them into the early indoor starters, those to be sown before the last frost and those that need warm soil. Take note of the ones you want to succession-plant. Turid bundles her seeds with rubber bands and labels them by date—May 1, June 15, and so on—so that when March 15 arrives, she simply pulls out the packets and gets to work.

STARTING SEEDS INDOORS

It is essential to start seeds at the correct time, whether you sow them indoors or out. Calculating the starting time depends on one key date: that of the average last spring frost. Don't rely on your memory: contact the local office of the provincial department of agriculture, or look up the date in the Environment Canada book *Canadian Climate Normals*, Volume 6: *Frost*. This provides a reliable average date, but microclimate may make your garden an exception. Low-lying areas are susceptible to frost, while sites on the banks of rivers or lakes are frost-free sooner. To be truly site-specific, start keeping a frost log for your garden. A week or two makes little difference, but if you sow too early, the plants will be potbound and spindly by the time it is warm enough to transplant. If you plant too late, the vegetables may not have time to mature.

Not all seeds are created equal. They vary in size from slightly larger than dust molecules to small pebbles, but more important, they vary in how they sprout; some need special treatment before they go into the soil. To hasten germination of seeds such as onions, presoak them overnight to soften the seed coat. Very hard seeds such as okra should be scarified—the coat chipped or scraped with a nail file or sharp knife—to help the embryo break out.

A few seeds such as parsley need to be stratified, a process involving prechilling and exposure to moisture, which mimics natural dormancy in the outdoors. The fastest way to stratify seeds is to throw the packet in the freezer overnight. A more accurate method is to mix the seed with three times as much moistened peat and put it in a plastic bag in the refrigerator for three to five weeks. Turid's technique is a little more finicky but can be done at the last minute. Fill an ice-cube tray with cold water, then add about 30 seeds per compartment. Freeze overnight, then defrost, drain, and dry the seeds on a paper towel.

For starting seeds indoors, you can use your own soil, but seedlings need a very light, porous mix that is sterile and completely free of weed seeds and pathogens. Homegrown soils are especially susceptible to fungi. If you want to experiment with garden soil, mix it with one part peat moss and one part sand, perlite or vermiculite, but we strongly recommend buying sterilized soil to give seedlings a healthy start.

Start seeds in any container 2 or 3 inches deep, provided it has drainage holes in the bottom. To kill fungi, soak recycled nursery pots in very hot water (160 degrees F), and dry them in bright sunlight. Plants that do not transplant easily should be started in peat pots that are set directly into the soil without disturbing the roots. Some seed houses sell "soil blockers" that make blocks for starting seeds, eliminating both kinds of pots. Set the containers in a shallow tray to catch drips.

Make the soil blocks according to instructions. Fill conventional pots to about three-quarters of an inch from the top with dry potting mix. Tap the soil down lightly. Set the containers in the tray, and pour very hot water into it, letting the pots soak from below until the soil is damp to the touch but not soggy. Let it cool. Plant the seeds according to the packet directions. In general, seeds are buried at a depth two to three times their diameter, but we plant seeds indoors a little shallower than outdoors because the soil doesn't dry out as quickly. If seeds are not deep enough, they may get too much light, and if they are too deep, the seed may run out of stored energy before the shoots break through the surface.

With peat pots, sow three to five seeds per pot, clustering them near the middle. To bury large seeds, poke holes with a pencil. Avoid using your hands, since you may inadvertently spread disease. Instead, use tweezers to drop in the seeds. Close the little holes with a fork, pressing the soil down very lightly. With tiny seeds, carefully spread them on the soil surface, sprinkle with a fine layer of soil, and press down lightly.

Seeds such as onions and lettuce are best sown in plastic trays with inserts that look like heat

Starting seeds indoors.

registers. Fill the insert loosely with sterile planting mix. With the thin edge of a ruler, press a furrow in the middle of each strip of soil, then fill the tray underneath with water and let it soak overnight. Label each strip before sowing. To reduce waste, Turid pours the fine seeds onto a sheet of white paper and uses tweezers to place them individually in the depression at a rate of three per inch. Then she uses a fork to brush a little soil over the seeds. Even if the envelope suggests that the seeds need light to germinate, Turid sprinkles a fine layer of peat over them to hold the moisture. (Peat must be kept uniformly moist, or it dries to a hard barrier impossible for seedlings to poke through.) For lettuce, fill the whole insert with soil, but plant every other slot. The soil won't dry out so easily, and the lettuces have room to spread. With leeks and onions, plant every section.

As well as planting in pots and inserts, you can seed indoors in flats. Turid's are wooden boxes 12 inches by 16 inches by 4 inches deep. Bigger boxes, once filled with soil and water, are too heavy to move easily. Put a sheet of newspaper on the bottom of the flat to hold in the water and soil. Fill with potting medium, and set in a bathtub of water to soak the soil. Set the flat on a disposable roasting pan to catch the drips. Either plant seeds spaced as directed on the package, or mix a cup of dry planting medium with some seed and broadcast it over the soil in the flat, pressing it down lightly, then sprinkling a quarter-inch of soil over the seeds.

This works well for an indoor mesclun or a meadow of coriander or looseleaf cutting lettuce.

Some seeds need light to germinate; leave these on the surface of the soil with only a light covering of soil or peat. Seeds that need darkness should be buried to the appropriate depth; for absolute darkness, cover containers with black plastic, cardboard or newspapers to shut out all the light.

When all the seeds are planted, mist the soil lightly. Keep the soil moist during germination by misting the containers with room-temperature water. (Watering from below seems to encourage surface mould.) Do not direct the mist at the soil, but aim it across the tops of the containers so that the tiny water droplets drift gently to the soil. Spray-mist daily to prevent the surface from drying out. For plants that need very humid conditions to germinate, cover the pot or flat with clear plastic or glass to create a mini-greenhouse. Every day, remove the covering (clear or opaque), dry it off, and replace it over the seeds.

Most seeds need warmth to germinate, and although the temperature varies with the species, 70 degrees F is usually adequate. Seed houses and nurseries sell special propagation mats that supply controlled bottom heat to pots and flats. But there are alternatives: a heating pad turned to the lowest setting, the heating coils used to thaw frozen pipes, the top of the refrigerator, a light bulb in a box, a cold oven with the light turned on, a small room converted to a nursery with a portable heater. Give them adequate, continuous warmth, but be careful not to cook the seeds: temperatures over 90 degrees quickly dry out the soil.

Most seedlings sprout within a week, although the seeds of some plants germinate erratically, sprouts appearing one after the other for over a month. Once the seeds have sprouted, most need cooler conditions. Too much warmth encourages fast, spindly growth. As soon as the leaves poke through the soil, move the plants to an area that is room temperature or a little cooler. Anything over 50 degrees F is usually fine.

All seedlings need light. Natural light is best: a greenhouse or greenhouse window, preferably, since overhead light produces straighter, stronger plants than light beaming from one side, as it does through a traditional south-facing window. (Windowsill seedlings must be turned regularly to compensate for the one-sided light.) Special propagation units are available commercially, but gardeners can start their salad plants at relatively little cost simply by installing fluorescent tubes. Plants need light in the blue spectrum to develop dense

144

foliage and stocky stems and in the red spectrum to grow healthy roots and stems. A two-bulb fixture with a warm (red) tube and a cool (blue) tube provides the full spectrum plants require. Bulbs marketed as "grow lights" provide the full colour range but are much more expensive.

Suspend the lights on chains over a table so that the height can be adjusted as the plants grow. Start at an inch for seedlings, which like strong light, and gradually increase the distance between the lights and plants to 6 to 8 inches, reducing the intensity as the seedlings grow. A two-bulb fixture lights about 4 square feet of growing surface; for increased efficiency, enclose the growing area with white cardboard that reflects light back on the plants. Keep the light source on 14 to 16 hours a day to simulate daylight. An automatic timer is a good investment.

Water regularly, preferably every morning, so that the seedlings have moisture during the warm day but dry out slightly by nighttime, when fungus is more likely to form. When the plants are tiny, misting is enough. As they grow larger, water from below or from above with a seedling watering can.

When seedlings have their true leaves (second set), it is time to fertilize. Cotyledons, the first seedling leaves, depend on the food stored in the seed, and they are often quite different from the second leaves, which use the nutrients in the soil. If you use a commercial sterilized potting mix, fertilize as soon as these second leaves develop. Use any concentrated water-soluble organic fertilizer with a slightly higher phosphorus level (the second number in the analysis listed on the package, often 10-52-10). Mix it with water as recommended, and apply it every week. We use fish emulsion, but manure tea, liquid seaweed and chemical products such as Plant Prod™ also work well as a foliar feed spray for seedlings.

Once the seedlings look sturdy and have strong stems, thin to the healthiest plant or to the correct spacing. Although it is heartbreaking to dispatch the little plants, thinning is essential. Crowded plants grow poorly and are more disease-prone. The improved air circulation goes a long way toward avoiding fungus problems. Some plants are so vigorous that you can immediately identify the strongest. With others, it takes longer for a clear winner to emerge. In this case, thin to two or three before deciding which one to keep. Thin by pinching the seedling off at its base; pulling it out may disturb the delicate new roots of its neighbours. Press the soil lightly around the remaining stems.

An alternative to thinning is transplanting, known at this stage as pricking out. The plants are

Seedlings started in small pots can later be transplanted into the garden.

separated carefully with the point of a knife and removed to individual containers filled with soil at least 3 inches deep. In pricking out seedlings, remove as much soil as possible to avoid disturbing the roots. Using a small paring knife, dig down beside each seedling and pry it up gently, holding onto the leaves rather than the stem of the plant. Supporting the roots with the blade of the knife, lift the seedling out, and insert it into a depression made in the soil. (You can also tip all the seedlings out

of the container and gently pry them apart so that each retains as much of its rootball as possible.) Quickly transplant them into prepared containers, and add damp soil to firm the roots. Position the seedlings at the same soil level as before. Press soil lightly around the stems, water well, and place the seedlings in a shady place to settle for a day before moving them back under the lights.

As the seedlings grow, watch for damping off. If the soil is sterilized and plants are thinned and handled as little as possible, this shouldn't happen. If it does, remove infected plants and make sure light, air and temperature conditions are close to ideal for the remaining seedlings. Pests are seldom a problem, but if your houseplants are infested with whiteflies or aphids, they will move to the seedlings. Watch the plants closely, and handpick any bugs; remove infested plants before the problem spreads.

Some seedlings, especially tomatoes, peppers and eggplants, grow indoors for almost two months, while others, such as cucumbers and squash, are inside for less than four weeks. Move frost-hardy salad vegetables outside as soon as the soil can be worked, usually mid-April in our gardens. Half-hardy plants, which in fact are so delicate that they cannot withstand any frost at all, must wait until after the last spring frost date.

Before seedlings go into the prepared garden beds, they need time to adjust to the outdoors. Through a process called hardening off, the fragile, coddled young plants gradually acclimatize to direct sun, fresh breezes and wind-driven rain on their leaves. You can harden off your seedlings by moving them outdoors to a porch or deck—any protected, warm place—during the day for increasing periods of time until they adapt. On the first day, put them outside in the shade for no more than an hour, the next day a couple of hours, then half a day. By the end of the first week, move them out of the shade and gradually give them a little sun. By the middle of the second week, leave them outdoors around the clock, exposed to as much sun as they will get in the garden. Bring them indoors only when frost threatens.

If you have started several dozen lettuces, cucumbers, tomatoes and peppers, this manual hardening off is quite a chore. It is much easier to put the seedlings in a cold frame, a movable outdoor mini-greenhouse. You can make one easily and inexpensively by building a wooden frame 3 by 4 feet, 16 inches high at the back and a foot high at the front. This holds six 11-by-21-inch growing flats; two basement windows rest comfortably on top. Set the cold frame in the garden, oriented to the south with the glass sloping toward the sun, and put the plants inside. Close the glass top at night to keep in the warmth, and open it during the day so that the temperature inside does not build to uncomfortable levels. The cold frame has to be checked often to ensure the seedlings are not too hot or too cold, but this is still less work than moving a hundred little pots in and out of the house.

Keep a trellis and a tarp beside the cold frame, the trellis for covering the open cold frame during

In midsummer, lattices provide shade for tender seedlings.

the day to protect the plants from exposure to direct sun and the tarp for covering the closed cold frame when frost threatens. And watch for thunderclouds —the seedlings are too delicate to sit exposed to the rain, at least during the first week. (If spring is late, the plants may outgrow the cold frame and require hardening off in the traditional way.) Don't take any chances. After two months of babying your seedlings, don't risk losing them because of an oversight.

TRANSPLANTING SEEDLINGS

The best gardeners keep one eye on the sky. When outdoor conditions are right and the seedlings look strong, it is time to transplant. Turid waits for an overcast day and transplants late in the afternoon, allowing the seedlings to settle into their new surroundings during the cool nighttime hours. She spends the early part of the afternoon gathering fresh fern sprigs, evergreen twigs or dead asparagus branches, piling them beside the garden beds to protect the seedlings from sun and wind as soon as they are in the ground. If you don't have branches, a lattice laid horizontally on upturned flowerpots works well too. Even though the day is overcast, shelter is essential: if you wait until a downpour starts or the sun beats down, you might lose a few seedlings before you notice they are in danger.

Transplant as quickly as possible. If you need to improve the soil, do it the day before. And don't plan to do a mammoth transplanting all at once:

stretch it over a couple of days. Assemble the tools and supplies: besides the shade branches, you need a hose and watering can, general-purpose organic fertilizer and water-soluble transplant fertilizer.

Dig the holes for all the transplants at once, spacing them as directed on the package or in the catalogue. Dig the holes deeper than the containers in which the seedlings grew. If the soil is poor, work a spoonful of organic fertilizer into the bottom of each hole and sprinkle with soil to prevent the plant roots from touching it directly. Water with the hose until the soil in each hole is soupy. The seedlings are usually set in the garden at the same depth they were in the pots. The exceptions are tomatoes and tall brassicas, which like to settle a little deeper in the salad-garden bed. After planting, pat down the soil around each plant to make a depression about half an inch below garden level, creating a saucer to hold the water close to the plant.

Remove seedlings from their containers so that the roots retain as much soil as possible and are exposed to the sun and air no longer than absolutely necessary. Plants grown in individual pots usually come out with a single tap, their rootball intact. Settle them into the mud slurry, backfilling dry earth to stabilize the plant. Where there is more than one plant to a pot or where plants were grown in flats, separate individual seedlings carefully and drop one in each watered hole. Firm the soil around each stem.

When transplanting peat pots, carefully remove about half an inch of the rim and set the plant in the slurry. Be sure the peat pot is thoroughly buried: if the pot is exposed, it acts as a wick, drawing water away from the plant's roots and into the air. For brassicas and other plants susceptible to insects, install a collar around the stem right away or sprinkle a ring of wood ashes or lime to discourage cutworms.

Immediately after planting, water seedlings again and give them a light solution of transplant fertilizer dissolved in water. Continue to water daily with plain water until the plant starts to put on new growth. Shelter the little plants from wind and sun with a canopy of boughs or a lattice, being careful not to weight them directly on the seedlings. Leave the shelter in place for a week to 10 days, or until the plants show new growth. If frost is expected, cover with newspapers or light tarpaulins. Floating row covers—15- or 30-foot sheets of translucent spun-bonded polypropylene fabric that is water- and air-permeable—are highly recommended for very early plantings. The material is light enough that the plants lift it as they grow, yet it keeps out flying insects such as flea beetles and maintains a temperature several degrees warmer than the air.

Despite all these precautions, the plants will probably sit in the salad garden looking sad for a few days. But eventually they adjust, and your diligence in hardening off and transplanting will speed the process.

DIRECT SEEDING OUTDOORS

Direct seeding in the garden starts as soon as the soil can be worked and continues throughout the growing season. Peas and mustard greens usually go into the garden first, followed by lettuce, exotic greens and cool-season vegetables that are planted throughout May. In very northern gardens, floating row covers protect plants from light frosts and raise the temperature, so gardeners do not have to depend on settled weather to get an early start. In June, warm-season vegetables like beans are planted, and from July on, the cool-loving autumn crops are sown.

The same rules apply whether you are planting seeds outdoors or indoors: bury the seeds to a depth of two to three times their diameter if they germinate in the dark; barely cover them with a sprinkling of fine potting soil if they need light to germinate. Keep them moist while they are germinating, spraying the bed daily with a gentle mist.

There are two approaches to outdoor seeding: the seeds can be placed individually in rows or patterns in the soil, or they can be broadcast randomly over the soil and left to grow in a bunch, like cut-and-come-again lettuces, or thinned to appropriate distances once they have sprouted, like carrots.

Such vegetables as carrots, beets, parsnips and peas are always seeded directly in the garden, but more demanding species are started in pots, even when the weather is warm. Turid germinates many salad vegetables in flats set close to the house in a protected, shady corner of the yard. In this nursery, she gives them the moisture and attention they need before making them fend for themselves in the exposed garden bed.

CARE AND CULTIVATION

Whether sown directly or transplanted, healthy plants are now growing in the garden. Although they have passed the critical points in their young lives, they still need the gardener's loving care.

If the beds were enriched and deeply dug before planting, the need for fertilizer is minimal. Deep feeders such as tomatoes and broccoli, however, still need a monthly boost during their growing season. If you do it on the same day each month, you are not likely to forget. Don't wait until the leaves start to yellow—that is the equivalent of a baby howling for food.

Water the soil well before fertilizing, then spread a little well-rotted manure or compost around the plant, which doubles as mulch, keeping the soil cool and moist. For plants with larger roots, scrape a tablespoon of general-purpose organic fertilizer into the soil, 4 inches away from the stem. Plants with more superficial roots, such as lettuces, prefer a liquid fertilizer like fish emulsion sprinkled over the foliage as well as soaked into the soil at the base of the plant.

Salad plants can survive without fertilizer, but they will never grow without adequate, regular water. Many salad vegetables contain high proportions of water, and without this essential element, they wilt and die. If you spread mulch between the plants, the garden will thrive with a weekly soaking. Without mulch, water at least every second day. (Organic mulch such as hay, straw or compost also reduces soil temperature by as much as five Fahrenheit degrees, a boon to cool-loving plants like spinach and peas.)

Very sandy soils may require daily watering. If you can avoid it, don't water from above with a hose or an automatic sprinkler system. Deep watering is more effective and conserves water. Set the hose on the ground and let the water soak gently into the soil, or dam the ends of the paths and fill them like moats. You can also try point watering:

sink an empty clay flowerpot in the soil close to large plants like tomatoes or broccoli, and keep filling the pot with water. Watering does more than prevent leaves from wilting: without adequate moisture, radishes get hot, tomatoes lack flavour, and lettuce becomes tough. As a general rule, the garden needs about an inch of water a week—you know it is time to give the plants a drink when the top inch of soil is dry.

Practise water conservation in the garden. Water early in the morning, never at noon, when evaporation losses are high and leaves may be burned. Night watering is unwise, since it encourages mould and fungi. Use soaker hoses or drip irrigation rather than sprinklers. Through evaporation, oscillating sprinklers lose as much as 50 percent of what they disperse. Soil with good tilth holds moisture better, so dig in lots of compost. In exposed gardens, plant a wind barrier: it cuts evaporation by 30 percent. And if your area curtails summer water consumption, don't panic. Collect water in cisterns or rain barrels for garden use.

Weeding is not the horrendous chore it is made out to be. Make it a practice with your morning coffee or afternoon tonic to cruise the garden, plucking weeds, checking the plants' progress, handpicking bugs and watching for disease. My routine is to water the garden as soon as I get up in the morning, while the coffee is dripping. I drink it outside in the company of my plants; then I meander through the beds for half an hour, pulling out weeds. The damp soil easily releases the entire root system, which cuts the weeding chore in half.

In fact, our gardens have very few weeds. They simply can't grow through the mulch, and the beds are usually planted so densely that weeds don't have a chance. Certain perennials such as tarragon and asparagus need closer inspection, especially early in the season. Among larger, well-spaced plants, use a hand cultivator to loosen weeds, and remove them from the garden, or they may reestablish themselves. Cultivation is a good idea in general, periodically loosening the soil around the plants. With close plantings in particular, cultivation keeps the soil ventilated and prevents fungi from taking hold.

Climbers such as cucumbers and scarlet runner beans, weak-stemmed plants such as peas, and heavy-fruiting salad vegetables such as tomatoes should be supported during their growing season. Gardeners with limited space may choose many climbing varieties—vertical gardening requires much less room—but even gardeners who select carefully to avoid climbers will have to do a little support work in their beds. Supports can be as simple as forked sticks or as extensive as permanent latticed fences. The important rule of thumb is to make it tall enough and strong enough to support the grown plant. Check the seed envelope for the plant's mature height, and add an extra foot for good measure.

In our experience, commercial cages and stakes are usually inadequate for fruiting vegetables. Instead, install 2-by-2 stakes for individual plants, driving them 2 feet into the soil or as far as possible. Triangulated structures, such as tepees and crossed-pole fences, are ideal, because they lean into each other, providing more support as the plant grows. Never shade the plant with the support—erect it on the north side of the plant. And consider the harvest: Can you reach the beans and tomatoes when they are ready to pick? If you grow climbers up a fence that divides two properties, install an angled barrier at the top so that runners and cucumbers double back into your own yard instead of draping into the neighbour's. Plants that need help attaching to the support should be tied very loosely: knot a piece of cloth to the support, then make a second knot around the stem just under a leaf axil. Make the loop large enough that young stems have room to grow.

Again, toward the end of the season, it is particularly important that you keep your eye on the sky. Clear fall nights, especially when the moon is full, often tend to bring frost. To prolong the season, you can drape blankets, plastic sheets or newspapers over the plants. Floating row covers and cold frames allow your plants to survive a few

Insects Common to the Salad Garden

Name	Plants Affected	Description	Control
Aphid	Beans, peas, tomatoes, cole crops, spinach	Tiny, soft-bodied, pale green, pink, black or yellow; clusters on tips of new growth and undersides of leaves	Reproduces rapidly; control while population still small; spray directly with insecticidal soap
Cabbage Looper	Brassicas, lettuce, peas, spinach, beets, celery, parsley, potatoes, tomatoes	Larva of a night-flying moth; caterpillar 1 ½ inches long, doubles up as it moves; 3 to 4 generations a year; chews holes in leaves, bores into vegetable heads	Spray leaf undersides with Bt when loopers are small; cover plants with netting
Cabbageworm	Brassicas	Larval stage of white butterfly with black spots on wings; damage similar to that of looper; eats leaves and bores into heads, leaving trails of dark green frass; several generations each year	Cover plants with netting, or catch butterflies in net during the day; spray with Bt when caterpillars are small, especially leaf undersides
Colorado Potato Beetle	Potatoes, tomatoes, eggplants, peppers	More common in east; 3/8-inch beetle with fat red larvae; adults overwinter in soil; lays egg clusters on undersides of leaves in spring; 1 to 3 generations a year; devours leaves	Thick organic mulch makes it difficult for beetles to reach leaves; handpick beetles; crush larvae and eggs; sprinkle wet plants with bran, causing beetles to swell and die
Cucumber Beetle	Cucurbits	Striped or spotted ¼-inch beetle with white, wormlike larvae; adults feed on leaves, larvae on roots; adults spread bacterial wilt and mosaic virus; adults overwinter on plant debris; lays eggs at stem base, 1 generation per year	Dust plants with organic insecticide when set out or when they emerge from soil; spray at stem base; cover young plants with netting; clean garden in fall
Cutworm	Brassicas, tomatoes, peppers, many other plants	Larva of a night-flying moth that lays its eggs in soil; larva feeds at night, burrows in soil during day; curls up tightly when disturbed; chews through stems at or below ground level, usually early in season	Install collars around stems; sprinkle a ring of wood ashes or diatomaceous earth to discourage adults; spray with Bt

light frosts without damage. Before frost arrives, bring inside plants that you plan to overwinter.

PESTS AND DISEASES

A clean, well-cultivated garden with deeply dug, fertile soil will likely be relatively free of pests. Good practices prevent both disease and bug infestations. Observe crop rotation rigorously. Choose seeds and seedlings carefully, selecting disease-resistant, bug-free plants. Prepare the ground properly so that it drains well. Feed and water correctly. Avoid overcrowding. Don't leave thinnings lying on the soil or the roots of harvested plants in the ground unless, like finochio, they resprout. Remove and destroy diseased plants immediately. Pay attention to insects' life cycles: if you catch cabbage butterflies with a butterfly net and pick adult Colorado potato beetles every morning while they are mating, these beasts will not lay eggs and hatch the swarms of larvae that quickly devour whole garden beds. Sometimes you can avoid a whole plague of insects simply by planting before or after they complete their life cycle. Some gardeners swear by companion planting, and although we have never seen clear evidence that it works, it is worth a try. Floating row covers are great for keeping flying insects like flea beetles off low-growing plants.

When pests appear, handpick them as soon as possible. Obtain a good basic reference book for garden insects and diseases, and learn to differentiate the good from the bad. You don't want to inadvertently kill a ladybug larva or praying mantid.

Name	Plants Affected	Description	Control
Earwig	Lettuce, celery, seedlings, blossoms	Reddish brown, lobsterlike inch-long night insect; feeds on decaying organic matter in damp, dark places	Trap by filling flowerpot with crumpled paper, inverting and propping with stick; insects hide in paper during the day; shake out and destroy
Flea Beetle	Tomatoes, eggplants, cabbages, potatoes, spinach, peppers	Tiny beetles feed on leaves, riddling them with holes; jump like fleas when disturbed; adults spread diseases; larvae feed on roots; adults overwinter in soil and garden debris	Control immediately; spray with garlic and hot-pepper sprays, diatomaceous earth; keep garden clean
Leaf Miner	Beets, peppers, spinach, lettuce, potatoes	Larva of a fly that lays eggs on leaf underside; maggots tunnel through leaf to feed, leaving winding trails, or "mines"	Pick and destroy infested leaves; maggots not affected by sprays
Slug	All plants	Mollusk, not insect; chews large, ragged holes in leaves, fruit, stems; feeds at night, leaving trail of slime	Set boards or cabbage leaves in paths as traps; collect slugs in morning; sprinkle wood ashes or lime around perimeter of bed; set out shallow pans of beer—slugs crawl in and drown
Wireworm	Potatoes, carrots, beets	Jointed, hard-shelled worm 1 ½ inches long, feeds on underground roots, stems, tubers, especially in new gardens; adult beetle is brown, ½ inch long, lays eggs in soil in spring	Bury potato pieces 2 to 4 inches deep in garden; remove after a week, and destroy potatoes and worms feeding inside

If a plant becomes hopelessly infested with leaf miners or aphids, break off that branch or pull out the whole plant and burn it.

Handpicking rids a garden of the most common pests. Lure slugs and earwigs to shallow tin cans baited with a little beer, the inside surface smeared with oil so that they can't climb out once they've fallen in. Dark-loving insects will also hide under a board laid along the edge of a garden bed. Lift it in the morning, and kill all the creatures lurking there. Plant collars are generally effective against cutworms. Digging around the base of the collars during the day usually unearths a frustrated cut-worm or two. There are also homemade sprays that sometimes work: tansy leaves steeped overnight in water, then boiled for 30 minutes, discourage aphids and flea beetles. Likewise, a spray made with ground hot peppers and garlic is often effective.

If such natural controls are insufficient, use insecticides, but choose safe, organic types. *Bacillus thuringiensis* (Bt), a bacterial insecticide that attacks a small variety of insects (including the larvae of cabbage butterflies and Colorado potato beetles), is considered relatively safe, except for those with weak immune systems. Rotenone and pyrethrum, botanical pesticides that are effective against aphids, beetles and larvae, also happen to be toxic to fish, frogs and toads as well as harmful, when fresh, to human beings. (As a consequence, it is very important that you do not use them within a week before harvest.) Diatomaceous earth, which is composed of the pulverized skeletons of tiny sea creatures, is actually so sharp that it lacerates soft-bodied insects such as cabbageworms. An insecticidal soap such as Safer's controls aphids, whiteflies and spider mites. Nontoxic to humans, all are nevertheless indiscriminate in their effects, killing beneficial insects such as ladybugs and praying mantids along with the undesirables. As much as possible,

Diseases Common to the Salad Garden

Name	Plants Affected	Description	Control
Blossom-End Rot	Tomatoes, peppers, cucurbits	Calcium imbalance in plant caused by moisture fluctuations, soil too wet, too dry or high in salts; water-soaked spot at blossom end turns brown and leathery, may rot; often happens if plants grow fast at first and set fruit in dry weather	Uniform watering; wet soil at least 6 inches deep; mulch to retain even moisture
Damping Off	All seedlings	Plants never emerge or sprouts die before an inch or two high; base of stem near soil is pinched and shrivelled; fungi common to all soils, especially when overly wet	Plant in well-drained soil; avoid overwatering; indoors, use pasteurized starting mix
Downy Mildew	Cucumbers, squash, brassicas	Irregular brown or yellow spots on upper leaf surface; lower surface shows hairy white or purple mould in humid weather; leaves die; fruit often small and bitter; moist weather spreads fungus	Choose resistant cultivars; avoid wetting tops when watering
Fusarium Wilt	Tomatoes, peppers, cucurbits, asparagus, peas	Soilborne fungus, common in hot, dry weather; lower leaves turn yellow, curl, wilt; when stem is cut, brown ring inside green outer layer; persists indefinitely in soil	Choose resistant cultivars; destroy diseased plants; no chemical control
Leaf Spot	Many plants	Various fungi and bacteria cause spots on leaves, which turn yellow and die; worse in warm, humid weather	Clean up garden debris; avoid overhead watering; water only in morning; do not work in wet garden
Nematodes	Tomatoes, celery, beans, spinach, many others	Various species of microscopic worms that feed on roots; infected plants are stunted, yellow, wilt in hot weather or die; roots may have small nodules; taproots develop small side roots; spread by infected soil, water, tools, plants	Choose resistant cultivars; keep soil's organic matter high to encourage nematode predators; plant marigolds as trap crop

be your own pest-control officer and do the dirty work by hand rather than with a spray.

END-OF-SEASON CLEANUP

By judiciously protecting salad plants during the first fall frosts, you can extend the growing season, but finally, the garden will succumb to the cold, the plants drooping like blackened rags against the soil. Pull up the plants as soon as they are hit by frost, shaking the earth off and adding them to the compost pile. Check for wireworms in the soil and rootballs, destroying them as you go.

When the plants are pulled, turn over the soil, digging in the mulch that covered it through the growing season and adding kitchen compost, manure and leaf mould. Sow a cover crop such as winter rye to be turned over as green manure, if desired. Rake the beds smooth, ready for planting after the winter's rest.

Most of the salad-garden perennials are in the herb bed. The tender perennials were brought indoors before the cold weather. Cut back the leafy herbs of the hardy perennials such as sorrel and lovage, but leave the woody perennials alone; allow them to die back naturally. Protect other tender plants with a foot of mulch such as hay or a mound of autumn leaves pinned down with chicken wire. Plant your garlic bulbs before the soil freezes, the last planting of the year.

When the perennials are protected and the salad-garden beds prepared for the spring, the tools are clean and the garden hoses drained, take an afternoon to think about next year's garden. If you have neglected to make a garden plan this year, do it now while the garden is still fresh in your mind. As the snow falls, you can rest assured that you have left a clean, healthy garden behind, ready to grow fresh new salads in the spring.

Name	Plants Affected	Description	Control
Powdery Mildew	Beans, cucurbits, lettuce, peas, many others	Powdery white growth on upper surface of leaves, which turn yellow and dry; older leaves infected first; fruits and pods may be covered with mildew; develops late in season on mature plants; thrives in cool, dry weather; spreads rapidly	Choose resistant cultivars; spray with fungicide
Verticillium Wilt	Eggplants, tomatoes, peppers, okra, many others	Soilborne fungus attacks lower leaves first, causing yellowing between veins and wilting; leaves die and drop off without wilting; plant usually lives but fruiting poor; brown ring inside lower stem	Choose resistant cultivars; destroy infected plants; 3-year rotation for susceptible crops
Viruses	Beans, celery, cucurbits, peas, peppers, tomatoes, potatoes	Many kinds with various symptoms, but often mottled, streaked, puckered, curled leaves, stunted plants, fruit with blotches and bumps; spread by sucking insects such as aphids	Control disease-spreading insects; destroy infected plants; choose resistant cultivars; buy virus-free seed potatoes
White Mould	Beans, lettuce, brassicas	Water-soaked spots on blossoms, stems, leaves and pods; enlarge quickly and become covered with cottony white mould; infected leaves wilt, yellow, die; infected pods rot; fungus overwinters in plant residues in soil	Destroy diseased plants immediately; avoid overhead watering; water in morning only; use 3- or 4-year crop rotations

Seed Sources

Alberta Nurseries and Seeds, Ltd.
Box 20
Bowden, Alberta T0M 0K0
Seeds for short-season areas. Catalogue
on request.

Becker's Seed Potatoes
RR 1
Trout Creek, Ontario P0H 2L0
Good-quality vigorous seed potatoes. Many
unusual varieties. Send SASE for catalogue.

The Cook's Garden
Box 535
Londonderry, Vermont 05148
Superior seed varieties of heirloom and
European vegetables; many lettuce varieties.
Also sells soil blockers. Catalogue on request.

William Dam Seeds
Box 8400
Dundas, Ontario L9H 6M1
Good varieties of untreated vegetable, herb
and flower seeds, including many hard-to-find
European types. Catalogue on request.

Dominion Seed House
111 Guelph Street
Georgetown, Ontario L7G 4A2
Vast selection of vegetable and flower seeds
with good growing instructions. Catalogue $2.

Golden Bough Tree Farm
Marlbank, Ontario K0K 2L0
Hardy fruits and nuts, including some Canadian
natives; noted for good asparagus. Catalogue $1.

J.L. Hudson, Seedsman
Box 1058
Redwood City, California 94064
Ethnobotanical catalogue of vegetables and
exotic plants. Catalogue $1 (U.S.).

Johnny's Selected Seeds
Foss Hill Road
Albion, Maine 04910
Vegetable and salad seeds, most untreated, for
northern gardens. Catalogue on request.

Lindenberg Seeds
803 Princess Avenue
Brandon, Manitoba R7A 0P5
Interesting vegetable varieties, especially for
western climates. Catalogue on request.

McFayden Seed Company
Box 1800
Brandon, Manitoba R7A 6N4
Good selection of vegetable seeds, onion sets
and seed potatoes. Catalogue $2.

Nichols Garden Nursery
1190 North Pacific Highway
Albany, Oregon 97321
Unusual Oriental and other ethnic vegetable
seeds. Catalogue on request.

Ontario Seed Growers
Box 144
Waterloo, Ontario N2J 3Z9
Catalogue on request.

Park Seed Company
Cokesbury Road
Greenwood, South Carolina 29647
Large selection of flower seeds and some
vegetables. Catalogue on request.

Prairie Grown Garden Seeds
Jim Ternier
Box 118
Cochin, Saskatchewan S0M 0L0
Small seed house but good varieties and lots of
excellent seeds in each packet; grown without
chemicals. Specializes in cultivars for dry
conditions. Catalogue on request.

Redwood City Seed Co.
Box 361
Redwood City, California 94064
Unusual vegetable, herb and flower seeds,
useful books and publications. Catalogue
$1 (U.S.).

Richters
Goodwood, Ontario L0C 1A0
Canada's herb specialist, also offers seeds for
some gourmet greens. Catalogue $2.50.

Seeds Blüm
Idaho City Stage
Boise, Idaho 83706
Heirloom and open-pollinated vegetable seeds.
Lots of good gardening hints, books and ideas.
Catalogue $3 (U.S.), free to previous customers.

Shepherd's Garden Seeds
7389 West Zayante Road
Felton, California 95018

Outstanding European varieties of herbs, edible flowers and vegetables, including unusual salad plants. Catalogue on request.

Stokes Seeds
Box 10
St. Catharines, Ontario L2R 6R6
Large collection of vegetable and flower seeds for the northern garden; helpful growing instructions. Catalogue on request.

Thompson & Morgan
Box 1308
Jackson, New Jersey 08527
An American branch of a British company with many hard-to-find varieties of flowers and some vegetables. Catalogue on request.

The Tomato Seed Co.
Box 323
Metuchen, New Jersey 08840
Over 250 varieties, including many old-fashioned types. Catalogue gives growing habit, size at maturity, resistance and whether there is a hybrid for each variety. Catalogue on request.

Whitehouse Perennials
RR 2
Almonte, Ontario K0A 1A0
A mail-order source for soil blockers.

Key to Seed Catalogues

BL	Seeds Blüm
CG	The Cook's Garden
DA	William Dam
DO	Dominion
HU	Hudson
JO	Johnny's
NI	Nichols
OS	Ontario Seed
PA	Park Seed
PG	Prairie Grown Garden Seeds
RE	Redwood City
SH	Shepherd's
ST	Stokes
TM	Thompson & Morgan
W	Widely (found in many seed catalogues)

Further Reading

The Bug Book
By the editors of *Organic Gardening*
Rodale Press, 1986
A complete reference for garden pests and
diseases and organic controls.

The Food-Lover's Garden
By Angelo Pellegrini
Alfred A. Knopf, 1970
Practical advice from a lifelong gardener on the
art and science of growing and enjoying
vegetables.

Grow Your Own Chinese Vegetables
By Geri Harrington
Collier Macmillan, 1978
Makes sense out of a confusing array of
Oriental plants. Includes preparation tips.

Unusual Vegetables
By the editors of *Organic Gardening
and Farming*
Rodale Press, 1984
Explicit information on vegetables no one else
talks about.

The Vegetable Garden
By Vilmorin-Andrieux
Ten Speed Press, 1981
Reprint of the original 1885 English edition;
thorough, fascinating and still useful.

Acetaria: A Discourse of Sallets
By John Evelyn
University Press of Virginia, 1983
Proof that there is little new under the
salad sun.

Food
By Waverley Root
Simon and Schuster, 1980
An indispensable encyclopaedia of the myths
and mysteries surrounding food.

The Food Pharmacy
By Jean Carper
Bantam Books, 1988
Food is your best medicine: a pharmacopoeia of
over 50 foods.

Good Food Book
By Jane Brody
W.W. Norton, 1985
Sound nutritional advice on basic foods.

Recipe Index